Corporate Governance in Asia

Corporate governance in Asia continues to attract global interest due to its critical importance to the world's fastest-growing region. The study of governance systems remains complicated by Asia's mix of legal traditions, market systems, and social history. This comprehensive textbook provides a comparative overview of the corporate governance framework, theory, and practice in major Asian countries. Readers at all levels will gain an understanding of corporate governance systems in Asia and how they compare with models attributed to the US, the UK, and Europe. Featuring six foundational chapters focusing on general theory and corporate governance systems and eight country-specific chapters, this book can be used as the basic textbook for a general course on comparative corporate governance or as an essential reference on corporate governance in Asia for a wide variety of professionals, including academics, jurists, students, practitioners, investors, creditors, policymakers, and analysts.

Bruce Aronson is an Affiliated Scholar in the US–Asia Law Institute at New York University School of Law, New York, United States.

Joongi Kim is Professor of Law at Yonsei University, Seoul, Korea.

CORPORATE GOVERNANCE IN ASIA

A COMPARATIVE APPROACH

Edited by

Bruce Aronson
New York University

Joongi Kim
Yonsei University

CAMBRIDGE
UNIVERSITY PRESS

CAMBRIDGE
UNIVERSITY PRESS

University Printing House, Cambridge CB2 8BS, United Kingdom

One Liberty Plaza, 20th Floor, New York, NY 10006, USA

477 Williamstown Road, Port Melbourne, VIC 3207, Australia

314–321, 3rd Floor, Plot 3, Splendor Forum, Jasola District Centre, New Delhi – 110025, India

79 Anson Road, #06–04/06, Singapore 079906

Cambridge University Press is part of the University of Cambridge.

It furthers the University's mission by disseminating knowledge in the pursuit of education, learning, and research at the highest international levels of excellence.

www.cambridge.org
Information on this title: www.cambridge.org/9781108420778
DOI: 10.1017/9781108355261

First published 2019

Printed and bound in Great Britain by Clays Ltd, Elcograf S.p.A.

A catalogue record for this publication is available from the British Library.

Library of Congress Cataloging-in-Publication Data
Names: Aronson, Bruce, editor. | Kim, Joongi, editor.
Title: Corporate governance in Asia : a comparative approach / edited by Bruce Aronson, Joongi Kim.
Description: New York : Cambridge University Press, 2018.
Identifiers: LCCN 2018014389| ISBN 9781108420778 (hardback) | ISBN 9781108430876 (paperback)
Subjects: LCSH: Corporate governance – Asia. | BISAC: LAW / Corporate.
Classification: LCC HD2741 .C77544 2018 | DDC 338.6095–dc23
LC record available at https://lccn.loc.gov/2018014389

ISBN 978-1-108-42077-8 Hardback
ISBN 978-1-108-43087-6 Paperback

For Daphne, Sasha, and Duncan

B. A.

For C. Y. K. and B. Y. K.

J. K.

CONTENTS

FIGURES

TABLES

CONTRIBUTORS

Bruce Aronson is an Affiliated Scholar at the US–Asia Law Institute, New York University School of Law, a research associate at the Japan Research Centre, School of Oriental and African Studies, University of London and a research associate at the Musashino Institute for Global Affairs, Musashino University, Tokyo. He was a professor of law at Hitotsubashi University's Graduate School of International Corporate Strategy, where he was co-director of the Global Business Law Program, where his research was undertaken. He received his undergraduate degree from Boston University and his JD from Harvard Law School. Professor Aronson was previously a corporate partner at law firm Hughes Hubbard & Reed LLP in New York, and a professor of law at Creighton University in the US. His main area of research is comparative corporate governance with a focus on Japan, and he has published in journals including *Cornell International Law Journal, NYU Journal of Law and Business*, and the leading law journals in Japan. He also serves as an outside director at Eisai Co., Ltd, a listed Japanese pharmaceutical company.

Christopher Chen is an associate professor of law at the Singapore Management University. He received a PhD from University College London. Dr. Chen's main research interests include financial regulation, derivatives, corporate governance, and transplantation of law in Asia in corporate, banking, insurance, and financial law, all of which he teaches. He has published articles and book chapters both in English and Mandarin Chinese in *Texas International Law Journal, Columbia Journal of Asian Law, Northwestern Journal of International Law and Business, Journal of Corporate Law Studies*.

Say H. Goo is Professor of Law at the University of Hong Kong (HKU), Deputy Director of Ronald Coase Centre for Property Rights Research, Director of Japan and Korea Programme, and former Director of Asian Institute of International Financial Law. He joined HKU in 1995 after over five years of teaching at University of East Anglia and the University of Exeter. A Fellow of the Institute of Chartered Secretaries

& Administrators in England and the Hong Kong Institute of Chartered Secretaries, he also sat on the Board of Directors of the Hong Kong Insurance Law Association and the Executive Committee of the Asia-Pacific Structured Finance Association. He is Visiting Professor at Columbia University, Distinguished Visiting Professor at the East China University of Political Science and Law, Honorary Visiting Professor at University of Exeter, Co-Principal Investigator of a major RGC research grant project on enhancing Hong Kong as an international financial center, member of the Hong Kong Government's Advisory Group on Corporate Insolvency Law Reform, member of the International Advisory Board of the Centre for Corporate Law and Securities Regulation at the University of Melbourne, editorial member of leading international journals, and reviewer for well-known publishers and journals. He was also a member of the Hong Kong Government's Standing Committee on Company Law Reform. He has published widely in corporate law, corporate governance, and land law, including *Corporate Governance: The Hong Kong Debate* (2003); *Hicks & Goo's Cases and Materials on Company Law* (1st–7th edns); *Minority Shareholders' Protection* (1994); plus many book chapters and journal articles. His work has been cited by the English Law Commission and the English and Hong Kong courts. He has visited many universities including Yale, Harvard, Oxford, and Cambridge and has spoken at UN, UNCITRAL, APEC, and INSOL conferences.

Jennifer G. Hill is Professor of Corporate Law at the University of Sydney Law School. She has held visiting teaching and research positions at various international law schools, including those at Cambridge University, Cornell University, Duke University, NYU Law School, University of Virginia, University of Texas, and Vanderbilt University. She is a Research Member of the European Corporate Governance Institute, where she sits on the Research Committee and chairs the Research Member Engagement Committee. She is a Fellow of the Australian Academy of Law and a member of the External Advisory Panel of the Australian Securities and Investments Commission. She is also a Research Fellow of the British Academy's recent Future of the Corporation Programme.

Joongi Kim is Professor of Law at Yonsei University, Korea. His research focuses on corporate governance, international arbitration, international trade, and good governance. A former attorney in private practice in Washington, DC and Scholar-in-Residence at WilmerHale in London, he served as the Founding Executive Director of the Hills Governance Center in Korea, which was established under the joint auspices of the World Bank, CSIS, and Yonsei University. He is an editor on the *Asian Journal of Comparative Law* and *International Investment Law and Arbitration* and served as an Academic Council Member for the Center for Strategic and International Studies' Hills Program on Governance. He sits on the Panel of Arbitrators of the World Bank's International Centre for Settlement of Investment

Disputes and the Korea–US and Korea–EU Free Trade Agreements. A former chair of the Executive Board of the Center for Good Corporate Governance in Korea, he was a visiting professor at Georgetown Law, University of Florida, National University of Singapore, and the University of Hong Kong. He holds degrees from Columbia, Yonsei, and Georgetown.

Yu-Hsin Lin is an assistant professor of law at City University of Hong Kong. Her research interests focus on empirical and economic analysis of corporate law and capital markets regulation. She has published in leading academic journals, including *International Review of Law and Economics*, *Columbia Business Law Review*, and *New York University Journal of Law & Business*. Dr. Lin holds a JSD degree from Stanford Law School, where she was appointed as the John M. Olin Fellow in Law and Economics. She had also been a visiting professor at Radzyner Law School, IDC Herzliya, Israel; and visiting scholar at Harvard Law School. Prior to joining City University of Hong Kong, she taught at National Chengchi University in Taiwan and has engaged in consulting projects for the Securities and Futures Investors Protection Center and Taiwan Stock Exchange. Before her academic career, she was a practicing lawyer specializing in international business and capital market transactions.

Dan Puchniak is the Director of the National University of Singapore (NUS) Centre for Asian Legal Studies (CALS), the editor-in-chief of the *Asian Journal of Comparative Law* and an associate professor at NUS Law. Dan has received numerous domestic and international awards for his academic research and teaching. He specializes in corporate law with an emphasis on comparative corporate law in Asia. He has published widely on comparative, Asian, Singapore, and Japanese corporate law and governance, and is regularly invited to present his scholarship and teach at leading law schools around the world. Over the past few years, Dan has been a visiting fellow in the Commercial Law Centre at Harris Manchester College (Oxford University), visiting professor and Global Challenge visiting scholar at Seoul National University School of Law, visiting associate professor at Vanderbilt Law School, and a visiting scholar of law at the University of Chicago Law School. In 2017, Dan was a visiting professor and taught intensive courses on comparative corporate law and governance with a focus on Asia at Chulalongkorn University and the University of Tokyo. He has been listed on the NUS Annual Teaching Excellence Award Honour Roll as recognition for receiving the university-wide NUS Annual Teaching Excellence Award three times. Prior to entering academia, Dan worked as a corporate commercial litigator at one of Canada's leading corporate law firms.

Umakanth Varottil is an associate professor of law at the National University of Singapore, where he specializes in corporate law and governance, M&A, and corporate finance. He holds an LLB (hons.) from the National Law School of India University, an LLM from New York University, and a PhD from the National University of Singapore. Previously he was a partner in a pre-eminent Indian law firm, and was ranked as a leading corporate/M&A lawyer in India. Professor Varottil has written widely on corporate governance issues pertaining to both India and Singapore, including *Comparative Takeover Regulations* (2017; co-edited with Wai Yee Wan) and chapters in books published by Cambridge University Press and articles in *American Journal of Comparative Law* and the *Berkeley Business Law Journal*.

Jiangyu Wang is a tenured associate professor at the Faculty of Law of the National University of Singapore. He is the co-executive editor of the *Asian Journal of Comparative Law* and deputy chief editor of the *Chinese Journal of Comparative Law*. His teaching and research interests include international economic law, international law and international relations, Chinese corporate and securities law, law and development, and the Chinese legal system. He practiced law in the Legal Department of the Bank of China and at Chinese and US law firms. He served as a member of the Chinese delegation at the annual conference of the UNCITRAL in 1999. He is a member of the Governing Council of the WTO Institute of the China Law Society, a senior fellow at the Law and Development Institute, and a fellow of the Asian Institute of International Financial Law. He has been an invited expert/speaker for the WTO, International Trade Centre, UNCITRAL, and UNESCAP. He has published extensively in Chinese and international journals on a variety of law- and politics-related topics, and is a regular contributor to leading newspapers and magazines in Singapore, Hong Kong, and mainland China. He has served as an external reviewer for dozens of international journals and publishers and research funds. He was seconded as an associate professor and director for the MPhil/PhD program at the Faculty of Law of the Chinese University of Hong Kong (2006–9), where he received the 2007 Young Researcher Award of the Chinese University of Hong Kong in recognition of his 2007–8 research.

PREFACE

The original impetus behind this book came from the lack of readily available classroom materials we each experienced while teaching a course on comparative corporate governance. After over a decade of piecemeal copying of materials from a variety of sources and different disciplines, accompanied by student complaints, we decided to create our own book that would also be suitable as a textbook for this course.

We were concerned about the lack of comprehensive materials on corporate governance in rising Asia. Much of the "Asian" comparative literature has focused narrowly on a comparison between one country in Asia and the United States or some other Western country. Little effort had been made to compare how various jurisdictions in Asia responded to broadly similar pressures to incorporate some aspects of "Western" corporate governance theory into local practice, for example the role of independent directors in Asian systems which typically had controlling shareholders. Students, academics, policymakers, legislators, judges, investors, analysts, employees, creditors, and other stakeholders deserved a single source from which they could learn both general theory and Western systems of corporate governance, together with an in-depth comparison of how the important jurisdictions in Asia are working to respond to pressures for reform.

Finally, we had the ambition to attempt to utilize Asian context and experience to make a contribution to the general theory of comparative corporate governance. In our minds this represents perhaps the ultimate test of the importance of comparative research that focuses on Asia.

Accomplishing these goals requires extensive knowledge of a number of Asian corporate governance systems and integrating best practices with general theory. This naturally led to an extensive effort to obtain close collaboration from a number of our colleagues in Asia who are working in the field of corporate governance. In assembling a team of leading corporate governance experts to contribute to this volume, we emphasized hands-on teaching experience and research expertise – we wanted the authority in each jurisdiction who actually taught the leading course on corporate governance, and we wanted them to create a book that each of them would be happy to use in the classroom and that could ideally be adapted for a wider audience at the same time. In countries which did not yet have such a course, we included leading scholars who taught overseas or who were willing to initiate such a course.

Our approach in this book is to begin with a traditional classification of corporate governance systems based on purpose, ownership structure, and monitoring. Such traditional classification usually contrasts the two models of a shareholder-oriented system (US/UK) and a stakeholder-oriented system (Japan/Germany); however, we have utilized Asian practice to add a new, third model of a "controlling shareholder system." Six out of fourteen chapters are foundational chapters focusing on general theory and widely known corporate governance systems in the US/UK and Germany, while the majority of chapters provide an in-depth analysis of individual countries in Asia. These eight country-specific chapters both follow a common template to provide a ready basis for comparison and highlight governance innovations and recent developments in each jurisdiction. The chapter authors generally emphasize the function of corporate governance systems rather than their form.

As corporate governance is a multidisciplinary field, this book is intended to be used as an introductory text in a number of fields, such as law, business, finance, and public policy. In the classroom it is intended as a full semester course. The book can be used as a textbook for a basic survey course on comparative corporate governance (the course we normally teach) through emphasis on the foundational chapters. In such case, teachers are free to rearrange the order of the chapters (for example, by moving up Chapter 13) and, depending on the allotted time for each class, devote more than one class to some early chapters (particularly Chapters 1, 2, and 4). They can also pick and choose which single-country chapters are of particular interest. Interest in specific Asian jurisdictions could be based on a number of perspectives, such as developed versus developing countries, model of development, political systems, legal system origin (UK or Germany), share ownership structure (state controlling shareholders, family-controlling shareholders, or no controlling shareholder), board structure and function, or enforcement.

The book can also be used to focus specifically on corporate governance in Asia. Although it is recommended that some foundational chapters be included (particularly Chapters 1–3), relative emphasis may be placed on country-specific chapters and comparisons among Asian jurisdictions. Priority among the Asian chapters could again be based on a number of perspectives as noted above, including geographic location.

This book is also designed to play an important role outside the classroom, as the first comprehensive textbook that makes it easy to compare and contrast corporate governance approaches in major Asian jurisdictions in light of both general corporate governance theory and local context and developments. As such, it is a useful reference book for investors, legal practitioners, businesspersons, policymakers, and researchers – anyone who wants both a general overview and specific introduction to corporate governance systems in the major jurisdictions in Asia.

ACKNOWLEDGEMENTS

The editors gratefully acknowledge the financial and administrative support of Hitotsubashi University, Graduate School of International Corporate Strategy and the National University of Singapore, Centre for Asian Legal Studies for this research project. Authors' workshops held in Tokyo and Singapore respectively were critical in defining the scope and approach of this book and in enabling a high degree of intellectual interaction and collaboration among the chapter authors.

The editors would also like to thank Miryung Yang and Hajar Mountassir for their research and editorial assistance.

We would also like to thank Cambridge University Press for its support and assistance in bringing this project to fruition.

PART

INTRODUCTION AND MODELS

1

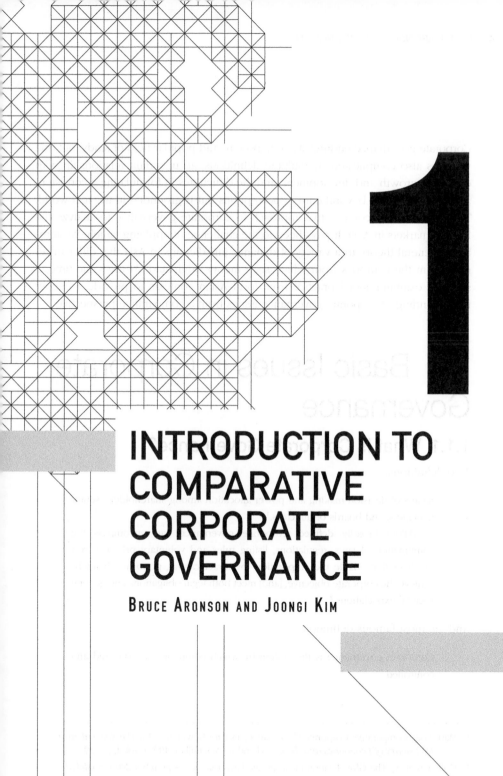

INTRODUCTION TO COMPARATIVE CORPORATE GOVERNANCE

Bruce Aronson and Joongi Kim

Corporate governance endures as an important and popular field of study, but one which is also complicated by multiple definitions, an uncertain relationship with economic growth and development, and the difficulties in formulating a consistent approach that goes beyond current perceptions but is grounded in the real world. This book takes a comparative approach to corporate governance to analyze the leading markets in Asia. It pays heed to the challenge of applying largely Western-based general theory to a variety of dynamic jurisdictions in Asia that differ materially from the countries from which such theory originated. At the same time, it seeks to examine actual practice from local Asian contexts to provide a deeper understanding of corporate governance issues from a comparative perspective.

1.1 Basic Issues in Corporate Governance

1.1.1 What Is Corporate Governance?

Two definitions:

> means of decision-making and power allocation among shareholders, senior managers, and boards of directors.[1]
>
> [M]ore broadly defined, corporate governance can encompass the combination of laws, regulations, listing rules and voluntary private sector practices that enable the corporation to: attract capital, perform efficiently, achieve the corporate objective, [and] meet both legal obligations and general societal expectations.[2]

And the most famous definition:

> Corporate governance is the system by which companies are directed and controlled.[3]

1 Mark Roe, 'Comparative Corporate Governance,' in Paul Newman (ed.), *The New Palgrave Dictionary of Economics and the Law* (London: Macmillan, 1998), vol. I, p. 339

2 Holly Gregory, 'The Globalization of Corporate Governance' (September 2000) 5 *Global Counsel* 52–65, at 55.

3 *Report of the Committee on the Financial Aspects of Corporate Governance* (1992) (the "Cadbury Report").

Notes and Questions

1. What is corporate governance? If there is more than one definition (e.g. narrow view versus broad view or shareholder-oriented system versus stakeholder-oriented system), does it matter which definition we use? Are there real-world consequences?
2. Corporate governance is a multidisciplinary field that includes not only a combination of law, finance, business, and economics, but may also include political science, international relations, history, and sociology, among others.

1.1.2 Comparative Corporate Governance

1.1.2.1 Overview

Arthur R. Pinto, 'Globalization and the Study of Comparative Corporate Governance' (2005) 23 *Wisconsin International Law Journal* 477–504, at 477–9, 484–5, 491–2

The particular comparative corporate governance scholarship that is part of the globalization debate involves two significant issues: first, whether the model of corporate governance should include a role for stakeholders other than shareholders (hereinafter 'the stakeholder model'); and second, how and why two particular ownership patterns for publicly traded corporations, that of either widely dispersed shareholders or concentrated shareholdings (hereinafter 'ownership models'), developed in certain countries and whether one ownership model will prevail … While the role of stakeholders and the ownership structure can be viewed as separate and distinct issues, there is a connection between them. Arguments for a stakeholder model of corporate governance seem more prevalent in countries where there is concentrated ownership. Thus, if dispersed ownership ultimately means shareholder primacy, then the extent to which it becomes the standard model could have an impact on the future role of stakeholders …

The publicly held corporation can be viewed in purely economic terms as a means by which capital is raised from a large number of public savers and used by businesses. Under that focus, corporate governance may concentrate on the suppliers of capital (creditors and shareholders) and the managers or those who control management. Since shareholders are owners, this view usually gives them primacy. Given the economic significance that many of these corporations have in different countries, however, a broader view has long been advocated by some because the governance of these large economic units has an impact on other interests who do not supply capital to the business. In some countries, these interests, including labor (which invests human capital) and other interests in the society where the business operates, have a role to play in corporate governance.

... Unlike traditional comparative law, financial economists have looked to see if a particular model is better or optimal. The financial economists' influence has both broadened and narrowed the study. It has broadened the study by showing corporate governance in the larger context of financing business and economic performance. It has narrowed the study by using the agency perspective to exclude non-finance issues such as the role of the corporation in society and other non-financial stakeholders. In addition, empirical research does not tell a complete story of a complex issue because it is difficult to consider non-economic factors, such as culture or societal norms, that may be significant for certain governance issues ...

Within comparative corporate governance scholarship, significant theoretical and empirical work has been designed to explain the outcome of dispersed and concentrated ownership. The widely dispersed ownership model usually relies more on market financing while the concentrated ownership model looks more to private financing. Because concentrated ownership seems connected with the stakeholder model, studies on concentrated ownership also relate to that model. A number of different stories have tried to explain the reasons for the different ownership patterns, and some have concluded that dispersed ownership has advantages over concentrated ownership ...

A traditional classification of corporate governance systems between shareholder-oriented and stakeholder-oriented systems is summarized in the first two columns of Table 1.1. The classification here is based on widely used factors of purpose, ownership structure, and monitoring, as well as the problem each corporate governance system is designed to ameliorate.

Corporate governance is often thought of as an approach to address and reduce potential problems of "agency costs." An agency relationship exists when a principal hires an agent to work for him and represent his interests. The agent may be obligated to work on behalf of the principal, but there is also an inherent conflict of interest: the agent controls the actual work and may develop an incentive to work in his own interest rather than on behalf of the principal, particularly when the principal has limited ability to effectively supervise the agent.

In the corporate context, the interests of those in effective control of the corporation (management) can differ from those who are external providers of capital (shareholders). Under a system with dispersed shareholders who have difficulty acting in concert, this conflict of interest is often described as an agency problem

Table 1.1 Simplified classification of corporate governance systems

Type of system	Shareholder system (US/UK)	Stakeholder system (Japan/ Germany)	Controlling shareholder system (family or government) (much of Asia)
Purpose	Maximization of shareholder wealth	Maximization of benefit for stakeholders and society	Maximization of benefit for controlling shareholder
Ownership structure	Widely dispersed	Relatively concentrated with block shareholder(s)	Highly concentrated
Monitoring	1950: shareholders generally today: independent directors/ institutional investors/market for corporate control	1950: replace corporate auditors with shareholders generally (Japan); supervisory board (Germany) Today: banks/ financial institutions Institutional investors Employees	Controlling shareholder? Government control: separate monitoring organization (e.g. Temasek); family control: "trusted" independent directors as facilitators
Main problem	Agency costs – management will act in own self-interest, not in best interests of shareholders	Oppression of minority shareholders – management will act on behalf of block shareholder(s) and against interests of minority shareholders	Oppression of minority shareholders – controlling shareholder will obtain private benefits of control
Solution to main problem	Reduce agency costs (protect shareholders generally from management) through legal rules and economic incentives	Protect minority shareholders from block shareholder(s) through legal rules and economic incentives	Protect minority shareholders from controlling shareholder through legal rules and economic incentives

between shareholders and management. Management is hired to work on behalf of shareholders, but may also have an incentive to act in its own interest by, for example, paying itself high compensation or reveling in the perks of privilege. In other systems with more concentrated shareholding, a large individual shareholder may be in a position to influence company management to act in a way that benefits that particular large shareholder. In such case, the conflict of interest may be characterized as being between such large shareholders and other smaller minority shareholders who are unable to influence company management.

Agency costs have been compared to friction in a gasoline-powered automobile engine. In an engine, friction is inevitable. Measures are taken, such as the use of lubricating oil, to reduce friction to a manageable level that does not interfere with the car's operation. Similarly, once you hire someone else to represent your interests, potentially your agent will not perform the same way that you would or in a way that you believe best represents your interests. While potential conflicts of interest cannot be eliminated, agency costs can be reduced to a manageable level through corporate governance. Laws, institutions, and procedures both inside and outside a corporation will seek to make certain actions illegal, require potential conflicts of interest to follow prescribed procedures and provide incentives that help to ensure that the agent's conduct will align with the interests of the principal.

1.1.2.2 The Role of the Board of Directors

In all modern corporate law statutes, the board of directors serves as the highest decision-making body of the corporation except for limited rights specifically provided to shareholders. The board of directors has two somewhat contradictory functions: advising management and monitoring management. Depending on the country, management is typically led by a chief executive officer (CEO) who may also be the president or managing director and other officers such as the chief financial officer (CFO), chief operating officer (COO), chief information officer (CIO), and other senior managers, including the executive vice president or treasurer.

Important differences exist in the role of the board in various corporate governance systems: should the board focus more on its management role and become involved in day-to-day decisions, or should it focus primarily on monitoring management and limit its decision-making to significant, strategic decisions? Although an oversimplification, shareholder-oriented systems are generally associated with a "monitoring board" that emphasizes the role of independent directors and acts to reduce agency costs by monitoring management on behalf of widely dispersed shareholders. In contrast, stakeholder systems typically involve a "management board" that emphasizes the role of experienced inside directors and focuses more on operational performance and benefits for a wider group of stakeholders. The relative strengths and weaknesses of an insider-oriented management board system and an outsider-oriented monitoring board system differ substantially.

1.1.2.3 What Is "Internal" versus "External" Corporate Governance?

"Internal" governance generally refers to the narrow definition of corporate governance discussed above. It focuses on relationships among the board of directors, management, and shareholders. "External" governance generally refers to outside forces, including legal and market mechanisms, that aid in the monitoring of management and enforcement of governance. These external forces would include both market forces such as product market competition and a market for corporate control, government regulation, gatekeepers, and the media. An example of legal and market-oriented monitoring mechanisms and an accompanying discussion are provided in Table 2.2.

Notes and Questions

1. Independent directors. The US and the UK rely on the use of independent directors within the board to monitor management on behalf of shareholders and thereby reduce the agency problem of management versus shareholders. How do you ensure that an "independent" director is truly independent? Legal definitions usually focus on a series of prohibitions: an independent director cannot have a substantial economic or financial relationship with the company, be a family member of the CEO, etc. This does not address the common situation where a new director could be influenced by social or personal ties with company management. The Organisation for Economic Co-operation and Development (OECD) has essentially given up on formulating an effective definition of independence and has merely stated that independent directors should be "independently minded." Legal definitions of independence vary considerably among countries.
2. Global spread of independent directors. Global institutional investors based primarily in the US and the UK have promoted the use of independent directors in all corporate governance systems, even though outside of the US and the UK the agency problem typically concerns controlling shareholders and minority shareholders. One question raised throughout the book is the role of independent directors in corporate governance in Asia, particularly where controlling shareholders prevail. Can their role be the same as in the US or UK? Can they work effectively? A few jurisdictions have attempted to create substitutes for independent directors in the monitoring of management (see the discussion of corporate auditors, or *kansayaku*, in Chapter 10 on Japan).

3. Enforcement. Enforcement of laws, regulations, and codes related to corporate governance is important, since actual corporate governance practices are more important than "law on the books." The US is known for active private enforcement through lawsuits by shareholders against corporate actors and public enforcement by regulators and prosecutors, while many countries remain hesitant about the economic and social costs of litigiousness. Several innovative countries in Asia have established a separate foundation or entity to pursue enforcement actions on behalf of shareholders. See discussions in Chapter 2 (US/UK), Chapter 5 (Australia), and Chapter 12 (Taiwan).
4. Gatekeepers. Monitoring and enforcement may also be aided by gatekeepers such as external auditors, credit agencies and analysts, who are professional service providers monitoring corporations as reputational agents. Substantial additional regulation of auditors in the US followed the passage of the Sarbanes–Oxley Act in 2002. Gatekeepers have generally not played a strong role in Asian jurisdictions. See Chapter 2.
5. Globalization. As globalization makes markets more accessible and integrated, including both product markets and financial markets, what effect will market competition and integration have on corporate governance? Will an efficient corporate governance system give some countries a competitive advantage? See the discussion in Chapter 4.

1.1.3 What Is the Purpose of Corporate Governance?

Presumably corporate governance is a means to achieve some broader goal, whether economic, social, or political and whether for the company or for society as a whole. General principles, like the OECD Principles, often refer simply to the "corporate objective" which is, however, defined by the corporation (and by law and society). But what is the goal that corporate governance is trying to achieve?

1.1.3.1 "Good" Corporate Governance

OECD, website (www.oecd.org/corporate/principles-corporate-governance.htm) and *G20/OECD Principles of Corporate Governance* (2015) at 9, 10, 18, 34

About the Principles

Good corporate governance is not an end in itself. It is a means to support economic efficiency, sustainable growth, and financial stability. It facilitates companies' access to capital for long-term investment and helps ensure that shareholders and other stakeholders who contribute to the success of the corporation are treated fairly.

... Corporate governance involves a set of relationships between a company's management, its board, its shareholders and other stakeholders. Corporate governance also provides the structure through which the objectives of the company are set, and the means of attaining those objectives and monitoring performance are determined ...

There is no single model of good corporate governance. However, some common elements underlie good corporate governance. The *Principles* build on these common elements and are formulated to embrace the different models that exist. For example, they do not advocate any particular board structure and the term "board" as used in the *Principles* is meant to embrace the different national models of board structures ...

Principle II. The corporate governance framework should protect and facilitate the exercise of shareholders' rights and ensure the equitable treatment of all shareholders, including minority and foreign shareholders. All shareholders should have the opportunity to obtain effective redress for violation of their rights ...

Principle IV. The corporate governance framework should recognize the rights of stakeholders established by law or through mutual agreements and encourage active co-operation between corporations and stakeholders in creating wealth, jobs, and the sustainability of financially sound enterprises ...

Notes and Questions

1. What is "good" corporate governance? Is there any recognized "best" system of corporate governance? The most influential international work on corporate governance is the OECD Principles (last revised in 2015), which often serve as the basis for evaluating "good" governance. Do they have a clear definition that, for example, favors one system of corporate governance over another (e.g. shareholder-oriented system versus stakeholder-oriented system)?
2. Some point to more fundamental values such as accountability, transparency, and integrity as being critical in achieving good corporate governance. Corporate governance reform measures are often touted, particularly following a significant corporate scandal, as necessary to "restore market confidence." What elements of "good" corporate governance are likely to relate to investor confidence? Should investor confidence play an important role in determining what is "good" corporate governance?

3. Shareholder primacy versus director primacy. Even if a corporate governance system has a clear orientation, such as maximization of shareholders' benefit, how will that be achieved? Who will be given the authority to pursue this goal? Will it be given to the directors to act "for" the shareholders (director primacy), or retained "by" the shareholders themselves (shareholder primacy)? Confusingly, the term "shareholder primacy" is also used to describe a shareholder-oriented system that seeks to maximize shareholder benefits as opposed to a stakeholder-oriented system.

1.1.3.2 Economic Performance

OECD, *G20/OECD Principles of Corporate Governance* (2015) at 10

The *Principles* are developed with an understanding that corporate governance policies have an important role to play in achieving broader economic objectives with respect to investor confidence, capital formation and allocation. The quality of corporate governance affects the cost for corporations to access capital for growth and the confidence with which those that provide capital – directly or indirectly – can participate and share in their value-creation on fair and equitable terms. Together, the body of corporate governance rules and practices therefore provides a framework that helps to bridge the gap between household savings and investment in the real economy. As a consequence, good corporate governance will reassure shareholders and other stakeholders that their rights are protected and make it possible for corporations to decrease the cost of capital and to facilitate their access to the capital market.

This is of significant importance in today's globalized capital markets. International flows of capital enable companies to access financing from a much larger pool of investors. If companies and countries are to reap the full benefits of the global capital market, and if they are to attract long-term "patient" capital, corporate governance arrangements must be credible, well understood across borders and adhere to internationally accepted principles. Even if corporations do not rely primarily on foreign sources of capital, a credible corporate governance framework, supported by effective supervision and enforcement mechanisms, will help improve the confidence of domestic investors, reduce the cost of capital, underpin the good functioning of financial markets, and, ultimately induce more stable sources of financing.

Sanjai Bhagat and Bernard Black, 'Non-Correlation Between Board Independence and Long-Term Firm Performance' (2002) 27 *Journal of Corporation Law* 231–74, at 231, 233–4

We study in this Article three related questions. First, does greater board independence produce better corporate performance, as conventional wisdom predicts? Second, and conversely, does board composition respond to firm performance? Third, does board size predict firm performance? Prior quantitative research on the first two questions has been inconclusive; for the third, two studies report that firms with large boards perform worse than firms with smaller boards. We report here evidence from the first large-scale, long-time-horizon study of the relationship among board independence, board size, and the long-term performance of large American firms. We study measures of financial performance and growth from 1985–1995 for 934 of the largest United States firms, using data on these firms' boards of directors in early 1991 and board data for a random subsample of 205 firms from early 1988.

Our principal findings: We find evidence that low-profitability firms respond to their business troubles by following conventional wisdom and increasing the proportion of independent directors on their boards. There is no evidence, however, that this strategy works. Firms with more independent boards (proxied by the fraction of independent directors minus the fraction of inside directors) do not achieve improved profitability, and there are hints in our data that they perform worse than other firms. This evidence suggests that the conventional wisdom on the importance of board independence lacks empirical support. Board size also shows no consistent correlation with firm performance, though we find hints of the negative correlation found in other studies ...

If our results are correct, the current focus on board independence as a core measure of board quality could detract from other, perhaps more effective strategies for addressing poor firm performance. At the least, corporate governance advisors and institutional investors should support efforts by firms to experiment with different board structures and be more tentative in their advice that other countries should adopt American-style monitoring boards.

We do not doubt that independent directors are important. No one else can effectively restrain insider self-dealing or fire the CEO when necessary. Indeed, one of us has stressed, in other recent work, the role of independent directors in controlling self-dealing. The policy question raised by our results is whether inside and affiliated directors also play valuable roles that may be lost in a single-minded drive for greater board independence.

Bernard Black, Hasung Jang, and Woochan Kim, 'Does Corporate Governance Predict Firms' Market Values? Evidence from Korea' (2006) 22 *Journal of Law, Economics, & Organization* 366–413, at 366

Corporate governance legal reforms and voluntary corporate governance codes are proliferating around the world. The overall effect of corporate governance on firm value or performance, however, remains unclear. This article employs an in-depth study of Korea to offer … evidence … consistent with overall governance causally predicting higher share prices.

Investor protection at the country level correlates with larger securities markets, less concentrated share ownership, and higher share prices (a higher value for minority shares) … A separate question, and the focus of this article, is whether the corporate governance practices of firms within a single country affects these firms' share prices. To what extent can a firm increase its market value by upgrading its corporate governance practices, and to what extent is it tied to its home country's rules and reputation? …

We construct and test a comprehensive corporate governance index (KCGI, 0~100) for a sample of 515 Korean companies, essentially the universe of publicly traded Korean firms … These results are consistent with causation running from good governance to higher market value.

Our results are economically important … The predictive power of our index comes from the overall effect of multiple governance elements, rather than the power of a few strong elements.

Second, we find a strong connection between board composition and share price … Our results suggest that outside directors may play an important role in emerging markets, where other controls on insider self-dealing are weaker.

We do not find strong evidence that better-governed firms are more profitable or pay higher dividends. Instead, investors appear to value the same earnings or the same current dividends more highly for better-governed firms. In effect, better-governed firms appear to enjoy a lower cost of capital.

Notes and Questions

1. Is "good" corporate governance related to good economic performance? This has often been assumed to be the case, but such a relationship has been difficult to prove objectively. When researchers try to find if there is a statistical correlation between good corporate governance and good economic performance, they must use a single number

as a proxy (variable) to represent good corporate governance. Do you agree that "good" corporate governance is represented accurately in the above research? Is it possible to accurately quantify "good" corporate governance?

2. Much of the empirical research on this question was conducted in the US in the 1990s and 2000s, at a time when many listed US corporations already had a majority of independent directors on their boards. If the number of independent directors is used to represent good corporate governance, such US research can only measure whether additional independent directors (i.e. a supermajority) will improve economic performance.
3. There are studies in Asian countries such as Japan and Korea that suggest that independent directors may, in fact, improve economic performance, although the number of such studies is far less than in the US. Black, Jang, and Kim find that in Korea independent directors do correlate with higher stock valuation, but not with firm performance. A Japanese researcher has reported that in his study the *first* independent director improves both firm performance and stock valuation. See Takuji Saito, 'Presence of Outside Directors, Board Effectiveness and Firm Performance: Evidence from Japan' (working paper, 2009).
4. Economic performance would seem to be easier to measure than "good" corporate governance. Does it matter if "economic performance" refers to firm performance or stock valuation? Is the economic purpose of corporate governance to improve firm performance, or to appeal to investors to lower the cost of capital and help strengthen financial markets?
5. If Bhagat and Black do not find any improvement in economic performance when the number of independent directors increased, does that mean that independent directors are valueless? Might independent directors serve some other useful purpose?
6. The relationship between corporate governance and economic performance, despite numerous studies, remains unclear with respect to causality. See e.g. Inessa Love, 'Corporate Governance and Performance around the World: What We Know and What We Don't' (2011) 26 *World Bank Research Observer* 42–70. What are the policy implications of this finding? Does it mean that corporate governance is not important?
7. Researchers investigate many questions involving corporate governance through statistical analysis to try to identify correlations whereby one factor is related to another factor. Even if a significant correlation is discovered, that does not imply causation and might be explained by a number of different hypotheses. Observations and statistics about matters in the real world generally do not permit the careful "double blind" studies that can be conducted in a laboratory where an experimental group and a control group are matched up in a drug experiment to make sure that the drug tested is the only significant difference between the two groups. In the "messy" real world, factors not included in the study may affect the results, and the direction of causality between two factors may also be unclear.
8. Some studies have found a relationship between a greater number of women executives in a corporation and better financial performance. Assuming such a statistical correlation exists and is significant, is that the same as causation? How many different hypotheses

can you devise in order to explain this relationship? Do any of your hypotheses contradict each other? How about a simple correlation that "if you hire Tom Cruise as the lead actor, your movie will be a commercial success." Does Tom Cruise make the movie successful? Is it possible that causation goes the other way?

9. If diversity is important to corporations, what should be done to promote it? Some European countries have legal requirements for gender diversity on the board of directors (see Chapter 3 on Germany and Europe and Chapter 7 on India). Would economic incentives be a better approach? Would social pressure be sufficient?

1.1.3.3 Corporate Social Responsibility

Thomas Donaldson, 'Defining the Value of Doing Good Business,' *Financial Times*, June 2, 2005

It is impossible for managers to sidestep corporate social responsibility (CSR). But while no manager can dismiss CSR, the broader and more pressing question is: "What does it mean?"

CSR is one of the rare business topics whose very existence is regularly called into question. Yet almost no one denies that issues arising under its banner are important: the environment (including sustainability), obligations to employees, sourcing from developing countries, host country government relations, relationships with local communities, and regulating gifts and sensitive payments.

Definitions of CSR range from broad ones that focus on large environmental and social problems, such as AIDS, poverty, health and pollution, particularly in developing economies, to more specific ones that focus on doing business with integrity and transparency.

The common denominator is that corporate activity should be motivated in part by a concern for the welfare of some non-owners, and by an underlying commitment to basic principles such as integrity, fairness and respect for persons.

The CSR debate

It seems strange that anyone would allege that CSR is a bad thing but some intelligent critics do exactly that. The economist Milton Friedman famously argued that the only social responsibility of business is to maximise profit. To do anything else, the logic went, is to slide dangerously towards socialism. The incomparable strength of a free market is its ability to allocate resources efficiently, and misguided managers who struggle nobly to enhance social welfare forget their proper function in the market: to compete and win.

Still worse, managers who pursue the dream of CSR are using other people's money. Investors give their hard-earned savings to managers in order to make more money. That is why they invest. So, managers who spend money to pursue CSR projects are "stealing" from their investors.

In response, CSR defenders note that business organisations do not live in a vacuum; they owe their very existence to the societies they inhabit. Corporations are allowed status as a single agent in the eyes of the law as a fictional person (persona ficta), and are usually granted limited liability and unlimited longevity. What is more, they are granted access to society's labour pool and its storehouse of natural resources, two goods in which every member of society has a stake.

Even Adam Smith, the father of capitalism, pointed out that the efficiency of the market rests partly on transparency, the absence of corruption and the avoidance of manipulation. At the same time, he did not believe that self-interested pursuit of profit was the right way to live. Benevolence, Smith argued, is the highest virtue.

In important ways, the battle over CSR is overblown. On closer inspection it turns out to be largely about whether to endorse a "fat" or "skinny" interpretation of responsibility. Even critics of CSR quietly state exceptions to their more aggressive denials and usually end up embracing a slimmed-down version ... The deeper issue, then, is not whether CSR exists, but how thinly or heavily it should be defined ...

Notes and Questions

1. How would you define corporate social responsibility? What, if any, should be the mechanisms to require or encourage corporations to follow it? At the international level, in 2011 the United Nations Human Rights Council adopted the United Nations Guiding Principles on Business and Human Rights, which is the first global standard relating to business responsibility to prevent and remedy human rights abuses (also known as the "Ruggie Principles" or "Ruggie Framework").
2. One popular argument to justify a variety of social endeavors by corporations such as greater diversity and corporate social responsibility is that they are "good for business." A company must satisfy its customers and other constituents to be successful in the long term so there is no real conflict between such "stakeholder" social goals and the shorter-term "shareholder" goal of maximization of profits. What do you think of this argument?
3. Concerns about climate change and sustainability were highlighted at the 2015 United Nations Climate Change Conference (COP 21) held in Paris. The resulting Paris Agreement calls for substantial long-term reductions in greenhouse gas emissions to limit global warming. How should individual countries and companies respond? Should their response be affected by the US announcement in June 2017 that it will withdraw from the Paris Agreement?

1.1.3.4 Other Purposes of Corporate Governance

Bruce Aronson, 'What Can We Learn from U.S. Corporate Governance? A Critical Analysis' (Spring 2005) 2 *University of Tokyo Journal of Law and Politics* 41–60, at 45–6

1. **Economic Performance [omitted]**
2. **Social and Political Values**
   Apart from the social role of corporations, some writers appear to emphasize political, particularly democratic, values. If a system of checks and balances produces good government over time then perhaps a similar system for corporations would also produce good governance. Even if there was no real evidence of economic benefits from corporate governance, there may be a value in utilizing "democratic" forms of governance in important organizations including both corporations and non-profit organizations. On a governmental level, there is also an argument by law and development scholars that with respect to developing countries the creation of a "good" governance system (which, for example, protects the rights of minority shareholders) would help create institutions and values which are more likely to support a democratic form of government.
3. **Corporate Governance as Risk Management**
   An alternative view holds that corporate governance is essentially a form of risk management. Under this view, a corporation with good corporate governance would effectively manage risks to lower the possibility of catastrophic losses or events and to respond effectively to perilous situations. It might thus be loosely analogized to a form of insurance, which does not eliminate risk but which limits it at some cost …
4. **Corporate Governance as Balancing Management Discretion and Management Monitoring**
   Corporate governance can also be viewed as an effort to achieve an appropriate balance between seemingly contradictory goals: providing management with authority and discretion to achieve good business performance and, at the same time, monitoring or checking management in order to ensure that management acts on behalf of stakeholders and does not abuse its decision-making authority. This balancing approach is fairly common in law generally, and an illustration in the business law area would be the business judgment rule. In deciding the individual liability of directors in shareholder derivative suits, this rule seeks both to allow directors to act boldly to improve corporate performance and at the same time to provide a liability-based incentive for directors to act in good faith in fulfilling their fiduciary duties to the corporation.

This view also implies the necessity of striking an appropriate balance between costs and benefits. "Good" corporate governance (perhaps like a "good" or clean environment) always involves some associated cost. In this case, the "cost" would include the time, effort and expense of maintaining internal and external mechanisms to monitor management and the possibility of slower and more risk-averse management decision-making.

Notes and Questions

1. If you think democracy is better than authoritarianism as a political system, how about as a management system? Would you prefer to invest in a "democratic" corporation which works as a team effort with a good system of checks and balances or with a brilliant authoritarian like Steve Jobs at Apple or the "Google guys." A substantial number of US corporations in the media and technology fields use "undemocratic" dual-class share systems so that the firm founders retain control of the corporation even after it goes public. Should investors avoid becoming shareholders in such corporations?
2. Family and state-controlled corporations are prevalent in Asia, and the ways in which corporate governance systems deal with such "controlled" corporations is a major theme of this book. For discussions which emphasize the corporate governance implications of both family and government-controlled corporations, see Chapter 8 on Singapore and Chapter 6 on Hong Kong.
3. Is it a sufficient purpose if corporate governance is a means to enhance risk management to minimize potentially catastrophic losses as a kind of insurance? Do corporations with potentially less volatility due to such insurance have greater value for shareholders and society? Might there be a correlation between "bad" corporate governance and riskier, more volatile performance?
4. Is the purpose of corporate governance to strike an appropriate balance between management discretion and management monitoring? Does such a purpose provide useful guidance with respect to the appropriate form of corporate governance systems?

1.2 The Rise of Asia and Corporate Governance Issues

1.2.1 The Rise of Asian Countries as Economic and Strategic Powers

The growing importance of Asia has become an increasingly popular topic, even though characterizations of the rise of Asia have shifted significantly over time. The postwar economic development of Japan led, in the 1980s, to the first discussion of a looming Asian challenge to the West. The rise of the "four Asian tigers" circa 1990 led to a new portrayal of an East Asian (rather than Japanese) economic "miracle." Rapid growth in China and India in the 2000s has cemented a popular view that we are living in the "Asian century."

Asian Development Bank, 'Asia 2050: Realizing the Asian Century: Executive Summary' (2011) at 3, 11. © Asian Development Bank. http://hdl.handle.net/11540/121. License: CC BY-NC-ND 3.0 IGO

Asia is in the middle of a historic transformation. If it continues to follow its recent trajectory, by 2050 its per capita income could rise sixfold in purchasing power parity (PPP) terms to reach Europe's levels today. It would make some 3 billion additional Asians affluent by current standards. By nearly doubling its share of global gross domestic product (GDP) to 52 percent by 2050, Asia would regain the dominant economic position it held some 300 years ago, before the industrial revolution (see Figure 1.1).

But Asia's rise is by no means preordained. Although this outcome, premised on Asia's major economies sustaining their present growth momentum, is promising, it does not mean that the path ahead is easy or requires just doing more of the same ...

The intangibles

Four overriding intangibles will determine Asia's long-term destiny. First is the ability of Asia's leaders to persevere during the inevitable ups and downs and to

Figure 1.1 Asia's share of global GDP (1700–2050)

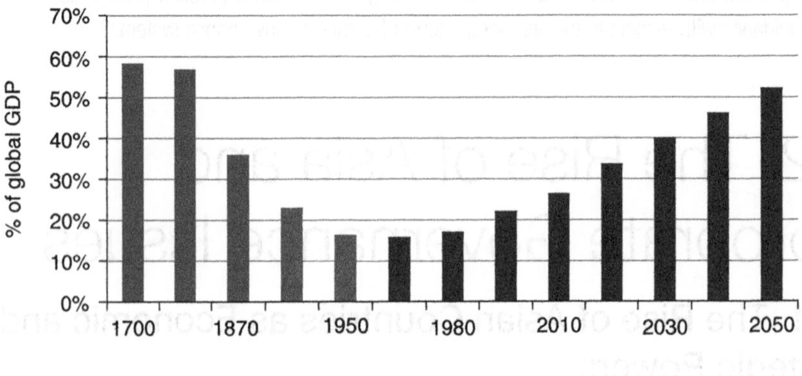

Sources: Maddison (1700–1950) (2007); Centennial Group International estimates (1951–2050) (2011). Data for 1750–1790 are PPP and data for 1991–2050 are in market prices

focus on the long term. The region's ability to maintain the current momentum for another 40 years will require continual adjustments in strategy and policies to respond to changing circumstances and shifting comparative advantages. This will place a tremendous premium on mature, far-sighted, and enlightened leadership. Second is the willingness and ability of Asia to emulate the success of East Asia to adopt a (so far) pragmatic rather than ideological approach to policy formulation and to keep a laser-like focus on results. Third is Asia's success in building much greater mutual trust and confidence among its major economies, which is vital for regional cooperation. And fourth is the commitment and ability of Asian leaders to modernize governance and retool institutions, while enhancing transparency and accountability.

Many of the required actions have long gestation periods that extend over many decades. Yet, their impact must be felt well before 2050 to allow Asia to continue on its path to prosperity. Asia's leaders must act with urgency if the promise of the Asian Century is to be realized.

Notes and Questions

1. Many economies in Asia have been growing rapidly and intraregional links are increasing. Since 2013, Asian corporations have dominated the Fortune Global 500 companies. In terms of capital markets, ten of the twenty largest stock exchanges in the world are in Asia (see Table 13.2) and Hong Kong has been the global leader in initial public offerings (IPOs) of stocks over the past several years, outpacing New York and London. As for trade, China has replaced the United States as the leading trade partner of most Asian countries. Furthermore, intraregional trade and investment continues to be strong despite ongoing territorial and other disputes and sometimes volatile diplomatic relations. Non-economic ties, such as academic exchange, tourism and pop culture also continue to deepen.
2. At the same time, a substantial group of skeptics exists with regard to the "Asian century." Some question assumptions that the high economic growth rates of Asian countries can be sustained for the long term in light of gradually maturing economies and societies. The above report by the Asian Development Bank (at p. 4), in addition to the optimistic "Asian Century" scenario, proposes an alternative "Middle Income trap" scenario. It suggests that middle-income countries may be unable to achieve high rates of growth to become high-income countries and will be competitively trapped between low-income countries with low costs of manufacturing and high-income countries with strong technology and innovation. Others refute the notion of a decline in the West, which may be implicitly included in discussions on the rise of Asia.

3. A more fundamental objection may arise with respect to the use of the term "Asia." Even if World Bank estimates turn out to be accurate that seven economies in Asia will play an increasingly large role in the global economy over the next few decades, some remain skeptical whether these countries are sufficiently united in terms of common goals and policy coordination. They question whether it is meaningful to speak of an "Asian dominance" with respect to global business, let alone international politics and security issues. See e.g. Clyde Prestowitz, 'What If It's Not an Asian Century After All?,' *Foreign Policy* (June 10, 2013).
4. Is it important that regional interaction in Asia to date has been dominated by private sector relationships, both economic and cultural, while formal state-to-state relations have lagged behind, as have institutions, laws and legal structures compared with regions such as the EU?
5. Asian Trade and Investment Agreements. Signed in 2018, the Comprehensive and Progressive Agreement for Trans-Pacific Partnership (CPTPP or TPP-11) is a trade agreement among eleven Pacific Rim countries that seeks to increase trade and investment through the further removal of trade barriers and harmonization of standards. The US formally withdrew from the TPP negotiations in January 2017 following the election of Donald Trump as President. China, which together with India was not included in the CPTPP, has instead been supporting the Regional Comprehensive Economic Partnership (RCEP) sponsored by the Association of Southeast Asian Nations (ASEAN) as an alternative. RCEP negotiations between 16 countries in Asia-Pacific continue without the US.

On the investment side, China took the initiative in forming the Asian Infrastructure Investment Bank (AIIB) in January 2016, partly as an alternative to the US and Japan-dominated Asian Development Bank. The fifty-two member states do not include the US and Japan. China is also pursuing its well-known "One Belt One Road" program to increase infrastructure and trade throughout Asia and Eurasia in a modern version of the ancient land and sea "silk road" trade routes. The leadership and direction of trade and investment relations in a rising Asia will remain an important issue for the foreseeable future.

1.2.2 A Problem with the Study of Corporate Governance in Asia: Are We Too Heavily Influenced by Perceptions of "Success" and "Asian Values?"

The field of comparative corporate governance was popularized in the early 1990s as US scholars sought to study the secrets of Japan's and Germany's success. Many were fascinated by the economic miracle of the 1960s through 1980s, during which Japan became the first non-Western country to modernize successfully. Experts attributed many exaggerated virtues to this economic success, including a well-conceived, consistent economic plan leading to the image of "Japan, Inc.": brilliant government bureaucrats who utilized administrative guidance to create a new government-led "variety of capitalism"; and, supposedly unique cultural traits, such as cooperation and consensus, that spurred success.

However, Japan's unique success was soon followed by an equally unique failure, brought about by the bursting of Japan's economic bubble in the early 1990s and two subsequent decades of low economic growth. Ironically, two of the factors previously cited as key to Japan's success – the ability of its government bureaucracy and its unique culture – were now seen as important causes of stagnation and failure.

Perceptions of a country's success, including the effectiveness of its corporate governance system, have continued to be influenced by its economic growth rate, despite the uncertain link between corporate governance and economic performance. During the 1990s the increasing importance of globalization and the perceived success of the US post-industrial model led to a new, overwhelmingly popular theme in the comparative corporate governance literature: a focus on the possibility that international competition among economic and legal systems would lead to global convergence, presumably toward a US-based "global" or "standard" model (see Chapter 4). The field of corporate governance, like many comparative disciplines that seek to include Asian countries, has struggled to define a neutral, useful, and consistent framework or standard for comparisons with Asia.

With the economic decline of Japan and rise of the four Asian tigers in the early 1990s, the cultural argument expanded into a broader discussion of "Asian values." This viewpoint, most closely associated with the former leader of Singapore, Lee Kuan Yew, emphasized Asian communitarianism in contrast to Western individualism. In addition to cultural questions, it was also premised on a more central role for government, as the Singapore system was sometimes described as one of soft authoritarianism.

Donald K. Emmerson, 'Singapore and the "Asian Values" Debate' (1995) 6(4) *Journal of Democracy* 95–105, at 95, 96, 100, 104

The "Asian values" debate is not a formally organized oral disputation between two sides advancing contrary answers to the same question. It is a large, diverse, and ongoing array of written and oral pronouncements and exchanges that share some relevance to a set of questions about "Asian values" – their existence, their contents, and the implications of the answers to these first two questions for policy and behavior.

Answers to these core questions have been offered since the time of the ancient Greeks, when the word "Asia" first entered the vocabulary of a people resident in "Europe" …

However ancient and dispersed the origins of disagreement over Asian values, the current phase of the debate may be described narrowly as a polemic of the 1990s conducted largely between Singaporeans and Americans …

Getting beyond polemics over Asian values means demolishing two straw men. The first of these we may call the Rudyard Kipling Fallacy: the obviously false notion that East is East, West is West, and never the twain shall overlap. It is absurd to affirm the existence of Asian values if by that we mean to ascribe a single set of beliefs to some 3.4 billion people – spread across dozens of countries, believing in different if not contradictory religions, speaking mutually unintelligible tongues – and to contrast that set with an altogether different list of Western values supposedly held by nearly a billion also diverse humans in Europe, the United States, and other places largely settled by Europeans.

Too often in the debate this straw man is knocked over with a flourish only to be replaced, by implication, with its polar opposite. With modest exaggeration we may call this equally romantic notion Rudyard Kipling's Other Fallacy: that there is one universal mode of moral conduct to which all 5.6 billion human beings adhere that entirely transcends all national or cultural differences.

These two straw men – one might also call them ultra-Orientalism and ultra-universalism – form the least plausible ends of a spectrum of possibilities. It follows that we ought to move at least partway toward the complex and ambiguous middle of this continuum. We should be willing, that is, to relinquish the purity of our positions for the sake of making them more accurate …

In 1977, Singapore's then-foreign minister confessed to having "very serious doubts as to whether such a thing as 'Asian values' really exists … It may exist as an image but it has no reality." Most Asians may well prefer certain values more – or less – than most Westerners do, but wholly or solely Asian values are indeed more imaginary than real. Widely held images can, however, affect reality by helping make some arrangements more legitimate than others. In this sense, the controversy over Asian values is not a debate at all. It is a struggle for the future.

Notes and Questions

1. Is there a sufficiently uniform Asian culture to support a thesis of "Asian values?" Do you think that culture played an important role in economic development and modernization in Asia?
2. The Asian values argument was also attacked by critics as an excuse to justify authoritarianism. In any event, the pendulum soon swung again, and the popularity of the Asian values argument declined significantly following the Asian financial crisis of 1997–8.

3. The rapid return of China beginning in the early 2000s made that country the new battleground over the role of government in economic and other development and also over cultural stereotypes. The corresponding stereotypes of Japan and China have been succinctly summarized thusly: "decisions about law in Japan are guided by norms of harmony" and "Confucian China will/will not respect the rule of law." See Nicholas Howson and Mark West, 'Law, Norms, and Legal Change: Global and Local in China and Japan' (2005) 27 *Michigan Journal of International Law* 687–93, at 692.
4. Even if the Asian values argument seems overly broad, a more local, national culture could play a significant role in influencing the evolution of corporate governance systems. See Amir Licht, 'The Mother of All Path Dependencies: Toward a Cross-Cultural Theory of Corporate Governance Systems' (2001) 26 *Delaware Journal of Corporate Law* 147–205.

1.2.3 Corporate Governance Issues in Local Asian Contexts: the Role of the Controlling Shareholder

Stijn Claessens, Simeon Djankov, and Larry Lang, 'The Separation of Ownership and Control in East Asian Corporations' (2000) 58 *Journal of Financial Economics* 81–112, at 82–3, 103

Much of the literature on the role and functioning of the modern firm is based on the assumption of the prevalence of widely dispersed ownership … We investigate the separation of ownership and control in 2,980 publicly traded companies in nine East Asian countries (Hong Kong, Indonesia, Japan, Korea (South), Malaysia, the Philippines, Singapore, Taiwan and Thailand).

In all East Asian countries, control is enhanced through dual-class shares, pyramid structures, and cross-holdings among firms. Voting rights consequently exceed formal cash-flow rights, especially in Indonesia, Japan, and Singapore. We find that more than two-thirds of firms are controlled by a single shareholder. Separation of management from ownership control is rare, and that top-management of about 60% of firms which are not widely-held is related to the family of the controlling shareholder. These findings have important implications for the ability and incentives of controlling shareholders to expropriate minority shareholders, as shown in a companion paper.

We find large family control in more than half of East Asian corporations. Significant cross-country differences exist, however. Corporations in Japan, for example, are generally widely-held, while corporations in Indonesia and Thailand are mainly family-controlled. And state-control is significant in Indonesia, Korea,

Malaysia, Singapore, and Thailand ... The concentration of control generally diminishes with the level of a country's economic development.

The evidence also suggests that in some countries much of the corporate assets rests in the hands of a small number of families. At the extreme, 16.6% and 17.1% of the total value of listed corporate assets in Indonesia and the Philippines, respectively can be traced to the ultimate control of a single family. The largest ten families in Indonesia, the Philippines, and Thailand control half of the corporate assets in our sample, while the largest ten families in Hong Kong and Korea control about a third of the corporate sector. The exception is Japan where family control is insignificant ...

OECD, *Corporate Governance Factbook* (2015), p. 11

1.1 The ownership structure of listed companies

The share of global market capitalisation held by countries with dispersed ownership is no longer dominant. The market share of countries with concentrated ownership structures has increased from 22% to 41%, since the adoption of the OECD Principles of Corporate Governance in 1999.

Ownership structures at company level can be characterised in various ways ... Considering the existence of multi-layer ownership structures and interconnections among shareholders through the use of control-enhancing mechanisms, a simple dichotomy between "concentrated" and "dispersed" ownership might be too simplified to allow a deeper understanding of the diversity of ownership structures. Nevertheless, the degree of ownership concentration remains one of the essential elements for consideration in framing corporate governance standards.

Three countries (**Australia**, the **United Kingdom** and the **United States**) are generally characterised as having a predominantly "**dispersed**" ownership structure. Figure 1.2 shows that the aggregate share of these countries in total market capitalisation decreased from 57% in the period of 1998–2002 to 41% in the period of 2008–2012. Five countries (**Canada, Germany, Japan**, the **Netherlands** and **Switzerland**) do not fall into either dispersed or concentrated ownership structure, but can be characterised as having a "**mixed**" ownership structure.

In other OECD and non-member countries, a majority of listed companies have a controlling shareholder. Figure 1.2 shows that the aggregate share of countries with "**concentrated**" ownership structure in total market capitalisation increased from 22% (1998–2002) to 41% (2008–2012). The increasing share of countries with concentrated ownership structures mainly results from the rapid development of capital markets in non-OECD G20 countries, whose share tripled from 9% to 27% in the same period.

Figure 1.2 Share of market capitalization of country groups with different ownership structures

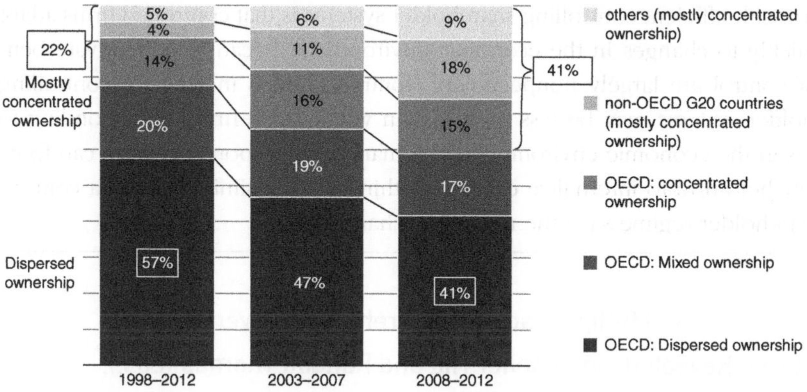

Source: OECD calculation based on World Bank data

Regardless of the country-level classification, there is a wide diversity in ownership structures of individual companies in each country, and the ownership characteristics in each country have also changed over time.

Ronald J. Gilson, 'Controlling Shareholders and Corporate Governance: Complicating the Comparative Taxonomy' (2006) 119 *Harvard Law Review* 1641–79, at 1642–4, 1673–4, 1678

As the issues surrounding hostile takeovers have clarified, attention has begun to shift from debating a phenomenon – observed largely in the United States and the United Kingdom, because only in those two jurisdictions is control of most public companies in the public float – to understanding the kind of control structure that dominates public corporations everywhere other than the United States and the United Kingdom. Put simply, public companies in the rest of the world typically have a single shareholder or group of shareholders with effective voting control, often but not invariably without corresponding equity holdings. Debate is now turning to the merits of these "controlling shareholder" systems …

[A] good deal can be learned by looking at the usual taxonomy of controlling shareholders through the framework of the controlling shareholder tradeoff: focused monitoring in return for some private benefits of control and at a cost in speed of adaptation. In particular, the framework highlights the value of distinguishing between efficient and inefficient controlling shareholder systems, and between pecuniary and nonpecuniary private benefits of control …

One straightforward implication of a more complicated taxonomy is the need to eliminate inefficient controlling shareholder systems ... The most serious policy concern with efficient controlling shareholder systems is that controlled firms adapt less quickly to changes in the economic environment. Because their private benefits of control are largely nonpecuniary, controlled firms in efficient controlling shareholder systems may be less nimble than widely held firms in responding to changes in the economic environment. The market for corporate control can force a widely held firm to internalize change; nothing plays a similar role in a controlling shareholder regime save the market mechanism ...

Dan W. Puchniak, 'Multiple Faces of Shareholder Power in Asia: Complexity Revealed,' in Jennifer Hill and Randall Thomas (eds.), *Research Handbook on Shareholder Power* (Cheltenham, UK and Northampton, MA: Edward Elgar, 2015), pp. 513–15

How has Asia produced world-leading companies, world-leading financial markets, and world-leading economies without American-style shareholder power? ... Indeed, the power that ... block shareholders [in Asia] wield directly over corporate governance often appears greater than the power that shareholders in America wield indirectly through hostile takeovers, independent directors, shareholder litigation, proxy battles, or any other means ... the realization that powerful block shareholders dominate corporate governance in Asia's miracle economies provides at least three other valuable insights.

First, it helps explain why many American-style mechanisms for shareholder power have gained little traction in Asia. Put simply, Asia's block shareholders inherently have power over corporate governance through their direct voting rights. They do not require American mechanisms, which are designed primarily to overcome the collective action problems of dispersed shareholders, as they do not have such problems to begin with. Obviously, hostile takeovers and proxy battles fade in importance in an environment where companies are dominated by large block shareholders who have de facto corporate control.

Second, it helps explain why some American mechanisms for shareholder power tend to produce unexpected results when transplanted into Asia. For example, in Asia's controlling shareholder environment independent directors are often transformed from being watchdogs for dispersed shareholders into a mechanism for amplifying the block shareholder's controlling power or a signaling device for "good" corporate governance with no real bite.

Third, as Gilson has observed, in a controlling block shareholder environment the focus of corporate governance shifts from minimizing managerial agency costs to minimizing private benefits of control. This valuable insight, combined with the realization that Asia's miracle economies are dominated by powerful block shareholders, suggests that analyzing the role of private benefits of control in Asia – an area which has too often been overlooked – is critical for understanding shareholder power in Asia's miracle economies …

Notes and Questions

1. Controlling shareholders prevail in many jurisdictions in Asia. This results in: (1) a different corporate governance problem that is based on conflicts of interest between controlling shareholders and minority shareholders; and (2) different functions for the same institutions such as independent directors. Although independent directors have been demanded by global institutional investors and are now utilized, what is their role in an Asian jurisdiction with controlling shareholders? Can they be effective?
2. Note that OECD data on the growth of countries with concentrated ownership structures largely reflects the rise of Asian economies and market capitalization. Issues in Asian corporate governance are in the process of becoming global issues.
3. Can controlling shareholders be easily divided into "efficient" and "inefficient" as suggested by Gilson? What is the basis for such distinction? Do you agree? What should we expect of controlling shareholders in the corporate governance context, and what makes a "good" or "efficient" controlling shareholder? How should they be evaluated?
4. The globalization of share ownership structure means that the percentage of foreign ownership has risen in markets throughout the world. To the extent that foreign shareholders are institutional investors, will this create pressure for corporate governance reform, particularly for the large companies that receive the bulk of foreign investment? What kind of reform will they seek?
5. Puchniak raises the problem of attempting to apply an essentially "Anglo-American" standard of corporate governance to Asian jurisdictions. How should we judge whether various Asian countries have "good" corporate governance?

1.2.4 Trying to Measure Good Corporate Governance and Rank Corporate Governance Systems

Phyllis Plitch, 'S&P Quits Rating Corporate Governance in US,' *Wall Street Journal* (September 13, 2005)

S&P, a unit of McGraw-Hill Co.'s, perceived an opportunity after a parade of financial meltdowns culminated in the Sarbanes–Oxley corporate-governance law of 2002, which introduced tough standards for the way companies and corporate officers ensure the soundness of their businesses. But this country's intense regulatory climate may have actually worked against S&P, as companies already spending a lot of time and money to comply with Sarbanes–Oxley weren't keen to shell out more money for an S&P rating …

S&P also drew some criticism for the governance-ranking operation's potential conflicts of interest: S&P scored only companies willing to pay for the checkup, after which it was up to the client whether to publicize its report card …

[An S&P manager] stressed that the service would continue in emerging markets like Russia – "marketplaces where a lot of international investors have reason to be concerned by virtue of where they're domiciled." …

Bottom-line benefit: Just because ranking governance isn't the business S&P had hoped, it's no reason for companies to slack off, another governance ranker suggests. Companies with poor governance over time tend to more often restate earnings or be caught up in accounting stumbles, according to GovernanceMetrics International, a New York firm.

Though academic studies have been inconclusive, GMI's research is the latest to yield a link between governance and performance. GMI's new round of ratings looks at more than 3,000 companies, measuring over 600 attributes such as whether firms have annual board elections (a positive) or unequal voting rights for different shareholders (a negative) …

Robert M. Daines, Ian D. Gow, and David F. Larcker, 'Rating the Ratings: How Good Are Commercial Governance Ratings?' (2010) 98 *Journal of Financial Economics* 439–61, at 440–1

[T]he predictive ability of the leading commercial governance ratings (CGQ, TCL, and GMI) is well below the threshold necessary to support the bold claims made for them.

The weak (and mixed) predictive results … have several interpretations. It is possible that corporate governance is an endogenous choice by firms that optimally adjust the costs and benefits of these governance choices …

Another interpretation of our weak and mixed results is that the commercial ratings contain a large amount of measurement error … It is instructive to note that there is very little correlation among the ratings …

The implications of this interpretation extend beyond the merits of these particular ratings. First, our results provide additional, if indirect, evidence regarding the merits of academic indices of corporate governance. If large commercial organizations with substantial expertise and extensive databases cannot devise reliable measures of corporate governance, it seems unlikely that the check-and-sum measures used by academic researchers have significantly better validity. Second, our results suggest a more fundamental issue with regard to the notion of "corporate governance" in general. The fact that experts cannot agree on the measurement of the quality of corporate governance structures highlights the need for future research on developing reliable and valid measures of the construct "corporate governance." Finally, these results suggest that boards of directors should not implement governance changes solely for the purpose of increasing their ranking.

Figure 1.3 CG Watch market sources (2010–16)

(%)	2010	2012	2014	2016	Change 2014 vs. 2016 (ppt)	Direction of CG reform
Australia	–	–	–	78	–	
1. Singapore	67	69	64	67	(+3)	Mostly sunny, but storms ahead?
2. Hong Kong	65	66	65	65	–	Action, reaction: the cycle of Hong Kong life
3. Japan	57	55	60	63	(+3)	Cultural change occurring, but rules still weak
4. Taiwan	55	53	56	60	(+4)	The form is in, now need the substance
5. Thailand	55	58	58	58	–	Could be on the verge of something great, if …
6. Malaysia	52	55	58	56	(–2)	Regulation improving, public governance failing
7. India	49	51	54	55	(+1)	Forward movement impeded by vested interests
8. Korea	45	49	49	52	(+3)	Forward movement impeded by vested interests
9. China	49	45	45	43	(–2)	Falling further behind, but enforcement better
10. Philippines	37	41	40	38	(–2)	New policy initiatives, but regulatory ennui
11. Indonesia	40	37	39	36	(–3)	Losing momentum after progress of recent years

Source: Asian Corporate Governance Association

Figure 1.4 Market category scores (CG Watch 2016)

(%)	Total	CG rules & practices	Enforcement	Political & regulatory	Accounting & auditing	CG culture
Australia	78	80	68	78	90	74
1. Singapore	67	63	63	67	87	55
2. Hong Kong	65	63	69	69	70	53
3. Japan	63	51	63	69	75	58
4. Taiwan	60	54	54	64	77	50
5. Thailand	58	64	51	45	77	50
6. Malaysia	56	54	54	48	82	42
7. India	55	59	51	56	58	49
8. Korea	52	48	50	53	70	41
9. China	43	38	40	36	67	34
10. Philippines	38	35	19	41	65	33
11. Indonesia	36	35	21	33	58	32

Source: Asian Corporate Governance Association

CLSA–ACGA, CG Watch 2016 (September 2016), pp. 3, 12, 15

If there is a single message from ACGA's survey, it's that the corporate governance ecosystems in a market are the differentiating factor between long-term system success and failure. Hong Kong and Singapore do not consistently top their survey by accident, they have the best institutions. This survey's inclusion of regional leader Australia brought that into sharper focus.

Notes and Questions

1. How useful are ratings generally in closing the information gap between companies and investors/the public? Have you used university rankings to help you make decisions on which university to attend? How reliable are such rankings? Do you take into account that ranked entities may try to game the system to improve their rankings?
2. Note that methodologies used in ratings vary widely and may be as simple as aggregating pre-existing data from a variety of sources. Note also that the ratings are often oversimplified to produce a single number or rank that will attract attention. The proliferation of ratings clearly indicates that there is some perceived benefit to the organization that produces these rankings. Such organizations may often have conflicts of interest: a policy interest in emphasizing the "problem" so that they can provide their preferred solution, commercial or business interests. How should the potential for bias resulting from such conflicts of interest be addressed?

3. Ratings in corporate governance are affected by the difficulty of defining good corporate governance and the lack of agreed ways to measure it. Does that make such ratings less useful, or is it still important to spur corporate governance reform by the use of such ratings?
4. Corporate governance ratings by GMI consistently rate Western countries higher than Asian countries. Is there some bias involved? What if the results depend to a large extent on heavily weighing a factor that is historically well accepted in the West, such as the number or percentage of independent directors? For example, GMI's 2011 rating of Japan, which moved slowly to require independent directors, was 33rd out of thirty-eight countries. Would such a result actually mean that Asian countries have poor corporate governance? For a persuasive argument that corporate governance measures to protect outside investors must be evaluated with separate metrics for companies without a controlling shareholder and companies with a controlling shareholder, see Lucian Bebchuk and Assaf Hamdani, 'The Elusive Quest for Global Governance Standards' (2008–9) 157 *University of Pennsylvania Law Review* 1263–1317.
5. The Asian Corporate Governance Association is an organization composed of institutional investors, listed companies, accounting firms, and other institutions who value governance systems that encourage and facilitate foreign investment. Could there be some connection between the relatively high rankings of Singapore and Hong Kong and the fact that these two countries are most consciously trying to become regional financial centers?

1.3 The Study of Corporate Governance in Asia from a Comparative Perspective

1.3.1 Approaches to the Comparative Study of Corporate Governance: Problems and Proposed Solutions

Given that economic development is the largest factor in the increasing attention paid to Asia, one might expect that corporate law and corporate governance, which are highly significant components of the legal infrastructure that supports such economic growth, would be important subjects of study. Many Asian countries face pressure to reform their corporate governance by incorporating some aspects of "Western" or "Anglo-American" systems, such as the use of independent directors to monitor management. The pressures for reform comes from a variety of sources, including corporate finance, international institutional investors, and the demands of globalizing markets.

In reality, however, the literature on comparative corporate law and corporate governance in Asia is surprisingly undeveloped with respect to in-depth comparisons among Asian countries. A substantial comparative law literature exists that narrowly focuses on the legal and corporate governance systems of one country in Asia in comparison with the US or some other Western country. On the other hand, a separate law and development literature looks at the role of law in economic development, and considers Asian countries on a limited basis in an attempt to prove a more general thesis concerning the relationship between law and development.

The weakness of the literature on Asian law falls in the potentially most valuable "middle ground," i.e. utilizing country expertise in a broader comparative context in Asia, particularly some portion of the region with relative uniformity in legal systems such as East Asia. The important potential benefits of such middle ground comparisons include providing both greater understanding of corporate law and corporate governance in each country and suggesting alternative approaches to dealing with common problems. This is no easy task due to the need to integrate in-depth knowledge of a number of Asian legal systems. This book addresses this need through collaborative research efforts among country experts by pooling resources and understanding.

Although the traditional classification of corporate governance systems (see Table 1.1) remains too crude to account for the local context in many Asian jurisdictions that is necessary to understand the functioning of corporate governance systems, we nevertheless utilise it as a useful starting point. This analytical classification results in a number of issues.

First, this framework tends to emphasise differences among corporate governance systems, whereas it would be possible to take a different approach that focuses on similarities – i.e. a typical range of responses to common corporate governance-related problems (see Reinier Kraakman et al., *The Anatomy of Corporate Law: A Comparative and Functional Approach* (Oxford: Oxford University Press, 3rd edn, 2017).

Second, this analysis focuses primarily on a comparison of the corporate governance of large listed companies, while unlisted businesses play a significant role in the economies of all countries and often have a different set of corporate governance issues.

Third, this framework, being somewhat stereotypical and rigid, encounters difficulty in evaluating the significance of corporate governance reform. Without a complete transformation of a system, for example, from a stakeholder-oriented system to a shareholder-oriented system, reform might not be reflected clearly within this framework's analysis. For a different analytical framework that places emphasis on a corporate governance system's ability to adapt to changing conditions, see Curtis J. Milhaupt and Katharina Pistor, *Law and Capitalism: What Corporate Crises Reveal about Legal Systems and Economic Development around the World* (Oxford: Oxford University Press, 2008).

1.3.2 The Book's Approach to the Study of Corporate Governance in Asia

Although any method of analysis has its limitations, we believe this traditional classification is still the most useful approach. We try to compensate for its shortcomings in a number of ways. The traditional classification of corporate governance systems is expanded to include controlling shareholder systems that are common in Asia (see the far-right column of Table 1.1). We take the view that all corporate governance systems are constantly evolving. The country-specific chapters both follow a common template to provide a common basis for comparison and highlight governance innovations and recent developments in each jurisdiction. Individual chapters convey important contextual information for each jurisdiction and are sensitive to the challenges involved in the application of concepts, such as the role of independent directors which are important in shareholder-oriented jurisdictions like the US and the UK, to controlling shareholder jurisdictions in Asia. The chapter authors generally emphasize the function of corporate governance systems rather than their form.

Although the approaches taken by the various chapter authors vary to some extent, the template used in each chapter can be summarized as follows:

1. introduction/overview;
2. purpose: shareholder versus stakeholder; social role; other related topics;
3. board function (internal governance): managing board versus monitoring board; independent directors; other related topics;
4. ownership structure: disperse versus concentrated ownership; problem of controlling shareholders; other related topics;
5. law and enforcement (external governance): public and private enforcement; hard law and soft law; role of markets; other related topics;
6. recent developments.

International Sources for Comparative Corporate Governance

Asian Corporate Governance Association
Asian Development Bank – publications
European Corporate Governance Institute
European Union – Comparative Study of Corporate Governance Codes
G20/OECD Principles of Corporate Governance
Institutional Shareholder Services
International Corporate Governance Network
International Monetary Fund – good governance page
International Organization of Securities Commissions (IOSCO)
OECD – corporate governance page
United Nations Conference on Trade and Development (UNCTAD) – Investment and Enterprise Division
World Bank – corporate governance page

2

US AND UK MODELS

Bruce Aronson and Joongi Kim

2.1 Introduction

The United States and United Kingdom are commonly classified together as "shareholder-oriented" systems based on their emphasis of shareholder interests over stakeholder interests, widely dispersed ownership structure, and enforcement that is generally robust and includes an important role for "external" market mechanisms. Even when the US was generally held out as the "global standard" for corporate governance (the late 1990s until the 2008 financial crisis), many commentators nevertheless referred to an "Anglo-Saxon" model. This model emphasized the possibility that such shareholder-oriented practices were not limited to the US, but were shared values that potentially had more general, or even universal, applicability.

However, this very broad view may overly de-emphasize the substantial differences in approach between the US and UK systems, even if they share some general characteristics. This chapter will discuss both the similarities and differences between the US and the UK.

The differences, which often are not systematically discussed, are summarized in Table 2.1.

Table 2.1 Significant differences between the US and UK corporate governance systems

Issue	US approach	UK approach
1. Corporate purpose	Narrow shareholder orientation	"Enlightened shareholder value" (broader approach)
2. Type of law	Primarily hard law (mandatory legal obligations)	Focus on soft law (voluntary compliance with best practice codes)
3. Board – independent directors	Supermajority of independent directors	Balance between independent directors and inside directors (including former company insiders who are non-executive directors)
4. Board – CEO and chair	No required separation between CEO and Chair of the Board	Separation of CEO and Chair of the Board
5. Institutional investors – tradition	Collaboration discouraged until early 1990s	Insurance companies and other "clubby" institutions in the "City" wielded substantial informal power

Table 2.1 (cont.)

Issue	US approach	UK approach
6. Institutional investors – recent trends	Increased role leads to "agency capitalism" and support for aggressive hedge fund activism	Internationalization of shareholders leads to Stewardship Code to help regulate behavior
7. Authority to protect shareholder interests	Director primacy (director's fiduciary duties and judicial enforcement)	Shareholder primacy (greater shareholder rights exercised by shareholder votes)
8. Hostile M&A	Directors can adopt defenses (court review)	Shareholder vote (no defenses by directors)

Notes and Questions

1. For an overview of the concept of an Anglo-American model of corporate governance, see Dennis Mueller, 'The Anglo-Saxon Approach to Corporate Governance and Its Applicability to Emerging Markets' (July 2006) 14 *Corporate Governance* 207–19 at 207. The author focuses on broad issues such as the problem of agency costs and the theory that common law systems in Anglo-Saxon countries and British colonies provide better legal protections for minority shareholders than civil law systems in other countries (see the discussion on convergence theory in Chapter 4).
2. For a counterexample that emphasizes the significant differences between the US and the UK, see John Armour, Brian Cheffins, and David Skeel, Jr., 'Corporate Ownership Structure and the Evolution of Bankruptcy Law: Lessons from the United Kingdom' (2002) 55 *Vanderbilt Law Review* 1699–1785, at 1701, who note the following:

   Given the similarities between the two countries, a logical way to test the various theories offered to account for the configuration of America's system of ownership and control is to see whether they have explanatory power in a British context. When this sort of analysis has been done, however, events occurring in the UK have tended to cast doubt upon each hypothesis. This has been the outcome, for instance, with theories concerning financial services regulation, political ideology, and minority shareholder protection.

2.2 Purpose

See Chapter 1 at Table 1.1 and pp. 6–14.

2.3 Board Function

Robert Hamilton, 'Corporate Governance in America 1950–2000: Major Changes But Uncertain Benefits' (2000) 25 *Journal of Corporation Law* 349–73, at 349–53, 360–3

I have chosen the year 1950 as a starting point because it has two characteristics: (1) it was a time when management enjoyed a very favorable reputation within the United States, based on the performance and contribution made by American industry during World War II; and (2) by 1950, management in most corporations had shifted from the initial founders of major corporations to professional managers who held their offices not because of their stock holdings, but because of their competence.

Writing in 1932, Adolf Berle and Gardiner Means developed a model of publicly held corporations that largely dominated theoretical analysis of the corporation for several decades, and was reasonably descriptive of boards of directors as late as 1950. Berle and Means assumed that typical shareholders in publicly held corporations were individuals who were widely scattered, often not well informed about corporate affairs, and relatively disorganized … In modem terminology, this structure of shareholdings creates a major "free riding" problem: no individual shareholders were willing to invest the necessary time and effort to monitor management because their interest was small and, if they did so, other shareholders would "free ride" on their efforts.

As a result, according to Berle and Means, shareholders who were unhappy with management exercised the "Wall Street Rule" and simply sold their shares into the market. In turn, this process of self-selection meant that shareholders of a corporation at any one time tended either to have a favorable view of management's performance or at least an acquiescent attitude toward management – a pro-management bias. With this composition of the body of shareholders, management was assured that shareholders would routinely approve management proposals, and that as a practical matter, the power of shareholders to select directors was purely theoretical …

In addition, the CEO largely dominated the decisional process within the board of directors …

In 1950, the board of directors was not viewed as an essential part of the governance process … Former Supreme Court Justice Arthur Goldberg in 1972 resigned all of his directorships with a public statement saying that boards of directors are "relegated to an advisory and legitimizing function that is substantially different from the role of policy maker and guardian of shareholder and public interest contemplated by the law of corporations."

Directors were usually compensated by cash payments, dependent on the number of meetings attended. This compensation was often viewed as the principal incentive to become a director …

This description of the roles of management and boards of directors in the governance of corporations as of 1950 is of historical interest, a measuring point to compare what was then with what is now …

IV. CORPORATE GOVERNANCE IN 2000

This Part describes generally favored, modem corporate governance practices …

Boards of directors are smaller today than they were nearly fifty years ago. Rather than fifteen to twenty directors or more, most boards today have between five and fifteen members, with many boards having fewer than ten members.

The number of "inside" directors has declined dramatically … An increasing number of boards, however, are "supermajority independent" boards. In these corporations the number of inside directors has declined to zero, and the board consists solely of the CEO and independent, outside directors …

Important functions that in 1950 were performed by the CEO (usually with only minimal board involvement) are now performed by committees of the board that often consist entirely or predominantly of independent directors. There are two "mandatory" committees staffed primarily by independent directors that deal with sensitive management issues: "nominating" and "compensation" …

In addition to these various committees, independent directors have exclusive power to make decisions in certain sensitive areas, including decisions to approve self-dealing transactions between the corporation and members of management, to recommend the dismissal of derivative lawsuits, to review incentive compensation arrangements to assure the deductibility of the compensation under the Internal Revenue Code, and to eliminate or continue poison pills and other defensive tactics …

Perhaps the best indication of the changed relationship between boards of directors and the CEO occurred during the recessionary period of the late 1980s and early 1990s. During this period, an unprecedented number of CEOs of well-known corporations were requested to resign by their boards of directors, sometimes at the suggestion of institutional investors that had significant holdings of the company's stock. These decisions reflected clearly both the modem roles of majority independent boards of directors as the supervisors of the CEO and the independent influence of institutional investors. CEOs today are increasingly being viewed as simply another employee – albeit an important one – of the corporation …

Jeffrey Gordon, 'The Rise of Independent Directors in the United States, 1950–2005: Of Shareholder Value and Stock Market Prices' (2006–7) 59 *Stanford Law Review* 1465–1568, at 1468–70

"Independent directors" – that is the answer, but what is the question?

The now-conventional understanding of boards of directors in the diffusely held firm is that they reduce the agency costs associated with the separation of ownership and control. Elected by shareholders, directors are supposed to "monitor" the managers in view of shareholder interests …

The move to independent directors, which began as a "good governance" exhortation, has become in some respects a mandatory element of corporate law … But why has the move to independent directors been so pronounced? …

The claim of this Article is that the rise of independent directors in the diffusely held public firm is not driven only by the need to address the managerial agency problem at any particular firm. "Independent directors" is the answer to a different question: how do we govern firms so as to increase social welfare (as proxied by maximization of shareholder value across the general market)? This maximization of shareholder value may produce institutions that are suboptimal for particular firms but optimal for an economy of such firms. Independent directors as developed in the U.S. context solve three different problems: First, they enhance the fidelity of managers to shareholder objectives, as opposed to managerial interests or stakeholder interests. Second, they enhance the reliability of the firm's public disclosure, which makes stock market prices a more reliable signal for capital allocation and for the monitoring of managers at *other* firms as well as their own. Third, and more controversially, they provide a mechanism that binds the responsiveness of firms to stock market signals but in a bounded way. The turn to independent directors serves a view that stock market signals are the most reliable measure of firm performance and the best guide to allocation of capital in the economy, but that a "visible hand," namely, the independent board, is needed to balance the tendency of markets to overshoot.

This Article develops this general theme through an account of the changing function of the board over the past fifty years, from the post-World War II era to the present. During this period, the board's principal role shifted from the "advising board" to the "monitoring board," and director independence became correspondingly critical. Although other factors are at work, there were two main drivers of the monitoring model and genuine director independence. First, the corporate purpose evolved from stakeholder concerns that were an important element of 1950s managerialism to unalloyed shareholder wealth maximization in the 1990s and 2000s. Inside directors or affiliated outside directors were seen as conflicted in their capacity to insist on the primacy of shareholder interests; the expectations of director independence became increasingly stringent.

Second, fundamental changes in the information environment reworked the ratio of the firm's reliance on private information to its reliance on information impounded in prevailing stock market prices ... The belief that markets "knew" more than the managers of any particular firm became increasingly credible as regulators and quasi-public standard setters required increasingly deep disclosure and this information was impounded in increasingly informative stock prices ... The richer public information environment changed the role of directors. Special access to private information became less important. Independent directors could use increasingly informative market prices to advise the CEO on strategy and evaluate its execution, as well as take advantage of the increasingly well-informed opinions of securities analysts. Independents had positional advantages over inside directors, who were more likely to overvalue the firm's planning and capital allocation capabilities. In the trade-off between advising and monitoring, the monitoring of managers in light of market signals became more valuable. The reliability of the firm's public disclosures became more important. Indeed, by the end of the period, boards came to have a particular role in assuring that the firm provided accurate information to the market.

Thus, fidelity to shareholder value and to the utility of stock market signals found unity in the reliance on stock price maximization as the measure of managerial success. From a social point of view, maximizing shareholder value may be desirable if fidelity to the shareholder residual (as opposed to balancing among multiple claimants) leads to maximization of the social surplus. This is the shareholder primacy argument. Independently, maximizing shareholder value may be socially desirable if stock prices are so informative that following their signals leads to the best resource allocation. This is the market efficiency argument.

Walter Fiederowicz, 'Corporate Governance Reforms and the Role of Boards of Directors' (Dec. 2003) 27 *Directors Monthly* 12, at 3

The approach preferred in the United Kingdom is to create a counterweight to the power of the CEO and senior management by instituting a strong chairman's role, granting additional powers to the independent, non-executive directors and effectively mandating term limits for independent directors. This could be seen as a kind of system of checks and balances designed to prevent the abuse of corporate power, similar to the political system envisioned in the U.S. Constitution to prevent the abuse of political power in this country.

... In many respects, the principles of good governance contained in the Combined Code [now Corporate Governance Code] are similar to those operative in the United States, with two exceptions.

First, the Combined Code clearly advocates splitting the roles of chairman of the board and CEO. It states:

> "There are two key tasks at the top of every public company – the running of the board and the executive responsibility for the running of the company's business. There should be a clear division of responsibilities at the head of the company which will ensure a balance of power and authority, such that no one individual has unfettered powers of decision."

The result: More than 90 percent of listed companies in the United Kingdom separate the roles of chairman and CEO. In the United States, recent surveys indicate CEOs and former CEOs hold more than 90 percent of chairman's posts in U.S. publicly traded companies.

The second difference is that the Combined Code has long advocated a "balance" between executive and non-executive directors "such that no individual or small group of individuals can dominate the board's decision taking" … "Balance" is not in the lexicon of good governance advocates in the United States, nor was it part of the debate leading to Sarbanes–Oxley.

Notes and Questions

1. How would you describe the evolution of corporate governance in the US? Has the purpose or problem sought to be addressed by corporate governance (see Table 1.1) changed over time? Is corporate governance now "better" than it was in 1950? How would we try to measure any such change? What "benefits" should we be looking for?
2. What caused the changes in US corporate governance over time? In another section of his article, Hamilton cites four factors in order of importance: (1) the growth of institutional investors; (2) the development (and subsequent decline) of takeover bids; (3) political scandals in the 1970s such as Watergate; and (4) proposals for improved corporate governance. Gordon focuses on the new role of independent directors to mediate between management and external markets, particularly the stock market. What do you think of these explanations? Can you think of other factors?
3. As the independence and importance of the board of directors has increased, would it now be possible to say that the board "manages" the corporation in the US? Can or should the board undertake such a role?
4. Compared to the US, the UK approach has placed somewhat less of an emphasis on the role of independent directors, both by placing a greater value on the contributions of non-independent directors to the corporation and by assigning greater importance to the role of an independent chair of the board to monitor, and prevent an overconcentration of power in, management. Does this make more sense than the US approach?

2.4 Ownership Structure

The US and the UK are generally classified as corporate governance systems with widely dispersed shareholders. However, share ownership evolves over time. How would such changes affect corporate governance in these systems?

Ronald Gilson and Jeffrey Gordon, 'The Agency Costs of Agency Capitalism' (2013) 113 *Columbia Law Review* 863–927, at 864–7

But as we shall see, the Berle–Means premise of dispersed share ownership is now wrong. In 2011, for example, institutional investors owned over 70% of the outstanding stock of the thousand largest U.S. public corporations.

In this Article, we address the impact on corporate governance of the ownership reconcentration of U.S. public corporations. Beneficial owners now typically hold their equity interests through a set of intermediary institutions like pension funds and mutual funds, which are the actual record owners and hold equity as fiduciaries for their beneficiaries. This shift from the Berle–Means archetype of widely distributed ownership to concentrated institutional ownership gives rise to what we call "agency capitalism," an ownership structure in which agents hold shares for beneficial owners. The consequence is a double set of agency relationships: between shareholders and managers and between beneficial owners and record holders.

The familiar Berle–Means agency problem arises because of the divergence between the interests of managers and shareholders. In an agency capitalism world, there is added a new agency problem that results from the gap between the interests of institutional record owners and beneficial owners. As developed below, a significant percentage of these institutional fiduciaries have business models that limit their incentives and capacity to monitor the business choices of their portfolio companies except through assessing stock market performance. The combination of limited institutional investor incentives and limited capacity establishes strong reasons to sell the stock of underperformers rather than to undertake a governance intervention. Record owners prefer exit to the exercise of governance rights even when a governance approach is more valuable to the beneficial owners. This devaluing of governance rights means that the reconcentrated (record) owners will have limited interest in or capacity to reduce the Berle–Means agency problem ...

In this analysis, the activist shareholders are governance intermediaries: They function to monitor company performance and then to present to companies and institutional shareholders concrete proposals for business strategy through mechanisms less drastic than takeovers. These activists gain their power not because of their equity stakes, which are not controlling, but because of their capacity to present convincing plans to institutional shareholders, who ultimately will decide whether the activists' proposed plan should be followed. As this Article develops, institutional shareholders are not "rationally apathetic" as were the dispersed owners on whose behalf the institutions now hold shares, but instead are "rationally reticent": Intermediary institutional holders will respond to proposals but are unlikely themselves to create them. The role for activist shareholders is to potentiate institutional voice; specialists in monitoring combine through the capital markets with specialists in low-cost diversification to provide a form of market-based stewardship.

Office for National Statistics, 'Ownership of UK quoted shares: 2016' *Statistical Bulletin* (November 29, 2017)

The proportion of UK domiciled companies' quoted shares (in terms of value) owned by investors outside of the UK has increased substantially since 1963. By 1998, holdings had increased to 30.7%. This proportion has continued to increase and stood at 53.9% by the end of 2016, a slight increase from 2014 levels. The large increases since 1994 reflect the increasing internationalisation of the UK stock market and the increasing ease with which overseas residents can invest in UK-quoted shares (for example, electronic trading).

As a result, a large part of the ownership of rest of the world investors represents international investors owning international companies ...

The proportion of shares held by individuals has declined since 1963, when individuals owned approximately 54% of UK quoted shares in terms of total value. In 2014, this same sector's holding in comparison stood at 12.4%. In 2016, individual ownership remained steady at 12.3% of all shares in quoted UK domiciled companies. This long-term reduction in the proportion of shares owned by individuals in part reflects the increasing internationalisation of the London Stock Exchange over the period (individual overseas investors being classified to the "rest of the world" sector).

The proportion of shares held by insurance companies grew from 10.0% in 1963 to a high of 23.6% in 1997. Since then insurance companies' holdings have fallen, reaching 4.9% in 2016, reducing 1.0 percentage point from 2014. This is the lowest recorded percentage of holdings by insurance companies on record. The fall could reflect insurance companies switching from UK equities to alternative investments.

Notes and Questions

1. Historically speaking, the US and the UK are the two main countries that are thought to have evolved from a concentrated shareholder structure to a diverse shareholder structure (although recall that the OECD *Factbook* in Chapter 1 lists Australia as a third such country and also lists five major countries with mixed ownership systems). However, as noted in Chapter 1, our examination of corporate governance focuses on large, listed companies that tend to have more diverse shareholders than smaller companies. In addition, ownership and governance structures are always evolving. In the US there has been a "reconcentration" of ownership as a result of the rise of institutional investors. What is the importance of a division between the "nominal" or "record" owners (large financial institutions who manage the shares) and the interests of the "real" beneficial owners who supply the capital?
2. Evolution in the UK has included a large increase in foreign shareholders. Although such a trend has also occurred elsewhere, including Asia, the UK made a particular effort to welcome foreign investors in order to retain its importance as a global financial center. This increase in foreign ownership is an important reason why the UK promulgated a Stewardship Code to establish and spread corporate governance best practices for institutional investors with respect to their relationships with their portfolio companies.

2.5 Law and Enforcement

2.5.1 Law: Hard Law versus Soft Law

Corporate governance systems generally include a combination of "hard" law, i.e. mandatory legal duties and "soft" law, i.e. encouragement of voluntary compliances with best practices. Nevertheless, the US is often cited as a "hard law" or "rules-based" jurisdiction, while the UK is widely known as a "soft law" or "principles-based" system. In 1992, the UK became the originator of a corporate governance code to encourage the spread of best practices.

Anand, Anita Indira, 'An Analysis of Enabling vs. Mandatory Corporate Governance Structures Post-Sarbanes–Oxley' (2006) 31 *Delaware Journal of Corporate Law* 229–52, at 229–30, 234

In the United States, certain aspects of corporate governance have become the subject of mandatory regulation under the Sarbanes–Oxley Act. Other major common law jurisdictions, such as the United Kingdom, Australia, and Canada, have rejected mandatory corporate governance legislation of this nature. These countries have opted for an enabling, or partially enabling, regime under which firms can choose governance practices they will adopt from a list of best practices, but they must disclose their choices and the resulting governance structure of the firm …

Proponents of the free market system dismiss the notion of a mandatory corporate governance regime, arguing that if enhanced corporate governance practices were beneficial and desired by investors, firms competing for scarce capital would implement them voluntarily. On the other hand, investor advocates argue that an enabling regime is insufficient, since there is no guarantee that all firms will implement the reforms necessary to provide investors with adequate checks on agency problems. On this view, mandatory corporate governance – like rules prohibiting insider trading – is necessary to protect investors …

I do not seek to slot entire governance regimes into either the mandatory or the enabling category: most regimes exhibit characteristics of both. State corporate law in the United States in particular is largely enabling at the state level, providing default rules to which corporations must adhere if they do not choose an alternative arrangement that will govern them. Despite the enabling character of state corporate law, most would agree that Sarbanes–Oxley cannot be characterized as enabling legislation …

The term "mandatory," as used here, means legally mandated, with penalties applying to those who fail to comply with the legal rule in question. The terms "voluntary" or "enabling" (here used interchangeably) denote a firm's choice to adopt corporate governance practices or standards in the absence of a mandatory legal requirement to do so. Such practices can, but need not be, set forth in guidelines or best practice regulatory instruments, typically issued by securities regulators or stock exchanges. The enabling code does not necessarily replace, but can be in addition to, a corporate governance regime already in place under statute, for example.

The Committee on the Financial Aspects of Corporate Governance and Gee and Co. Ltd, *The Financial Aspects of Corporate Governance* (1992) [the "Cadbury Report"], at 1–2

1.1 The country's economy depends on the drive and efficiency of its companies. Thus the effectiveness with which their boards discharge their responsibilities determines Britain's competitive position. They must be free to drive their companies forward, but exercise that freedom within a framework of effective accountability. This is the essence of any system of good corporate governance …

1.3 At the heart of the Committee's recommendations is a Code of Best Practice designed to achieve the necessary high standards of corporate behaviour. The

London Stock Exchange intend to require all listed companies registered in the UK, as a continuing obligation of listing, to state whether they are complying with the Code and to give reasons for any areas of non-compliance. This requirement will enable shareholders to know where the companies in which they have invested stand in relation to the Code. The obligation will be enforced in the same way as all other listing obligations. This may include, in appropriate cases, the publication of a formal statement of censure …

1.5 By adhering to the Code, listed companies will strengthen both their control over their businesses and their public accountability. In so doing, they will be striking the right balance between meeting the standards of corporate governance now expected of them and retaining the essential spirit of enterprise.

1.6 Bringing greater clarity to the respective responsibilities of directors, shareholders and auditors will also strengthen trust in the corporate system. Companies whose standards of corporate governance are high are the more likely to gain the confidence of investors and support for the development of their businesses.

1.7 The basic system of corporate governance in Britain is sound. The principles are well known and widely followed. Indeed the Code closely reflects existing best practice. This sets the standard which all listed companies need to match …

1.9 Had a Code such as ours been in existence in the past, we believe that a number of the recent examples of unexpected company failures and cases of fraud would have received attention earlier. It must, however, be recognised that no system of control can eliminate the risk of fraud without so shackling companies as to impede their ability to compete in the market place.

1.10 We believe that our approach, based on compliance with a voluntary code coupled with disclosure, will prove more effective than a statutory code. It is directed at establishing best practice, at encouraging pressure from shareholders to hasten its widespread adoption, and at allowing some flexibility in implementation. We recognise, however, that if companies do not back our recommendations, it is probable that legislation and external regulation will be sought to deal with some of the underlying problems which the report identifies. Statutory measures would impose a minimum standard and there would be a greater risk of boards complying with the letter, rather than with the spirit, of their requirements.

Financial Reporting Council, The UK Corporate Governance Code (2014), at 4

Comply or Explain

1. The "comply or explain" approach is the trademark of corporate governance in the UK. It has been in operation since the Code's beginnings and is the foundation of its flexibility. It is strongly supported by both companies and shareholders and has been widely admired and imitated internationally.

2. The Code is not a rigid set of rules. It consists of principles (main and supporting) and provisions. The Listing Rules require companies to apply the Main Principles and report to shareholders on how they have done so. The principles are the core of the Code and the way in which they are applied should be the central question for a board as it determines how it is to operate according to the Code.
3. It is recognised that an alternative to following a provision may be justified in particular circumstances if good governance can be achieved by other means. A condition of doing so is that the reasons for it should be explained clearly and carefully to shareholders, who may wish to discuss the position with the company and whose voting intentions may be influenced as a result. In providing an explanation, the company should aim to illustrate how its actual practices are consistent with the principle to which the particular provision relates, contribute to good governance and promote delivery of business objectives. It should set out the background, provide a clear rationale for the action it is taking, and describe any mitigating actions taken to address any additional risk and maintain conformity with the relevant principle. Where deviation from a particular provision is intended to be limited in time, the explanation should indicate when the company expects to conform with the provision.
4. In their responses to explanations, shareholders should pay due regard to companies' individual circumstances and bear in mind in particular the size and complexity of the company and the nature of the risks and challenges it faces. Whilst shareholders have every right to challenge companies' explanations if they are unconvincing, they should not be evaluated in a mechanistic way and departures from the Code should not be automatically treated as breaches …
5. Smaller listed companies, in particular those new to listing, may judge that some of the provisions are disproportionate or less relevant in their case. Some of the provisions do not apply to companies below the FTSE 350 …

Notes and Questions

1. Hard law versus soft law. Compare Sarbanes–Oxley in the US, which in 2002 created a mandatory requirement that the boards of all public companies have a majority of independent directors, with a similar provision added to the UK corporate governance code in 2003. Is it better to require individual companies to immediately comply with a mandatory provision as soon as it is enacted (the US approach) or to make such compliance voluntary

on the assumption that there will be gradual improvement over time for companies as a whole (the UK approach)? Which is likely to be more effective in promoting improvements in corporate governance? How soon? At what cost? Should we care whether such a change would "fit" the circumstances of individual companies?

2. Compliance with the code in the UK. Compliance with the corporate governance code in the UK has been strong, especially among the largest FTSE 350 companies. Over half of the FTSE 350 companies are reported to be in full compliance, while the rest typically fail to comply with only one or two provisions. As a group, such large companies comply with 97 percent of the code provisions. What happens when a company does not comply and chooses to "explain" instead? What if the explanation is not very informative and is essentially a 'boiler-plate" provision? How can it be ensured that explanations are truly informative? Should we not worry about such individual cases if corporate governance is generally improving at companies as a whole?
3. The UK approach of voluntary codes with comply-or-explain enforcement has proven quite popular. Over eighty countries now have some kind of corporate governance code. A list of all such codes can be found on the website of the European Corporate Governance Institute under codes and principles. Since the 2008 financial crisis, the view of US corporate governance as representing a clear "global standard" has been declining. There is vigorous and ongoing debate about what now constitutes "good" corporate governance standards. Is there a new "multi-polar" global standard? Should countries in Asia pay less attention to "Anglo-American" ideas about corporate governance and focus more on developing their own standards? What would those standards be?

2.5.2 Enforcement: What Mechanisms Are Important?

The US system of corporate governance is particularly known for strong enforcement mechanisms, both public and private. Opinions within the US are far from uniform, as the substantial costs of litigation, public disclosure and investor activism are often more visible and easier to measure than the presumed benefits. Outside the US and the UK, and particularly in Asia, countries are sometimes criticized for lax enforcement and this is noted as a corporate governance problem. If such countries may be reluctant to accept the economic and social costs of high levels of litigation and other features of the US system, the question may then become what alternative enforcement measures are available that can be effective and be a good "fit" for their corporate governance systems?

Some of the main enforcement mechanisms in the US system are discussed below. The legal and market-oriented monitoring mechanisms are summarized in Table 2.2.

Table 2.2 Monitoring of management: comparison of legal and market forces

Legal mechanisms	Market mechanisms
Fiduciary duty	Publicity and politics
Public disclosure	Market for products
Right to information (state inspection rights)	Stock market
Right to communicate (shareholder proposals)	Market for managers
Challenges to management control	Market for corporate control
Shareholder suits	
Appraisal rights	

Source: compiled from Robert Hamilton, 'Corporate Governance in America 1950–2000: Major Changes But Uncertain Benefits' (2000) 25 *Journal of Corporation Law* 349–73

Notes and Questions

1. With respect to Table 2.2, note that, in reality, there are strong links between "internal" and "external" mechanisms. For example, one may think of directors' fiduciary duties as primarily an "internal" device, but enforcement generally relies on "external" mechanisms such as public (government) enforcement and/or private enforcement (shareholder lawsuits). Similarly (external) media coverage of corporate issues can have a profound impact on various actors within a corporation and affect both management policies and the monitoring of management.
2. As a whole, which set of mechanisms – legal or economic – do you think is more effective in the monitoring of management? How should that result be reflected in laws, policies, and practices relating to corporate governance?

2.5.2.1 M&A: the Market for Change of Control

Henry Manne, 'Mergers and the Market for Corporate Control' (1965) 73 *Journal of Political Economy* 110–20, at 112–13

The Corporate-Control Market

The basic proposition advanced in this paper is that the control of corporations may constitute a valuable asset; that this asset exists independent of any interest in either economics of scale or monopoly profits; that an active market for corporate control exists; and that a great many mergers are probably the result of the successful workings of this special market.

... Perhaps the most important implications are those for the alleged separation of ownership and control in large corporations. So long as we are unable to discern any control relationship between small shareholders and corporate management, the thrust of Berle and Means's famous phrase remains strong. But, as will be explained below, the market for corporate control gives to these shareholders both power and protection commensurate with their interest in corporate affairs.

A fundamental premise underlying the market for corporate control is the existence of a high positive correlation between corporate managerial efficiency and the market price of shares of that company. As an existing company is poorly managed – in the sense of not making as great a return for the shareholders as could be accomplished under other feasible managements – the market price of the shares declines relative to the shares of other companies in the same industry or relative to the market as a whole. This phenomenon has a dual importance for the market for corporate control.

In the first place, a lower share price facilitates any effort to take over high-paying managerial positions ... It is far more likely that a second kind of reward provides the primary motivation for most take-over attempts. The market price of shares does more than measure the price at which the normal compensation of executives can be "sold" to new individuals. Share price, or that part reflecting managerial efficiency, also measures the potential capital gain inherent in the corporate stock. The lower stock price, relative to what it could be with more efficient management, the more attractive the take-over becomes to those who believe that they can manage the company more efficiently. And the potential return from the successful take-over and revitalization of a poorly run company can be enormous ...

But the greatest benefits of the takeover scheme probably inure to those least conscious of it. Apart from the stock market, we have no objective standard of managerial efficiency. Courts, as indicated by the so-called business-judgment rule, are loath to second-guess business decisions or remove directors from office. Only the take-over scheme provides some assurance of competitive efficiency among corporate managers and thereby affords strong protection to the interests of vast numbers of small, non-controlling shareholders. Compared to this mechanism, the efforts of the SEC and the courts to protect shareholders through the development of a fiduciary duty concept and the shareholder's derivative suit seem small indeed.

John Armour and David Skeel, Jr., 'Who Writes the Rules for Hostile Takeovers and Why? – The Peculiar Divergence of U.S. and U.K. Takeover Regulation' (2006–7) 95 *Georgetown Law Journal* 1727–94, at 1728–30

A key mechanism for rendering managers accountable to shareholders is the market for corporate control: namely, the threat that if the managers fail to maximize the share price, the company may become an acquisition target. Given that this mechanism is thought to be pivotal to making dispersed ownership viable, it is strange that so little attention has been paid to the significant differences in the way in which takeovers are regulated *between* the two systems that together comprise the "Anglo-American model." Both the *mode* and the *substance* of the regulation are startlingly different.

In the United Kingdom, takeovers are regulated by the City Code on Takeovers and Mergers (the "Takeover Code"), a body of rules that is written and administered by the Panel on Takeovers and Mergers (the "Takeover Panel"). Staffed by personnel on secondment from the professional community that it regulates, and untrammeled by the procedural and precedential niceties of the courtroom, the Panel responds in a flexible and well-informed fashion to disputes and governs their resolution in "real time." In contrast, most U.S. takeovers are governed by the courts of Delaware. As courts go, these are quick and flexible, but they nevertheless tend to lend an *ex post* flavor to dispute resolution.

The content of takeover regulation differs just as markedly on the two sides of the Atlantic. In the United Kingdom, the Takeover Code is strongly weighted toward protecting the interests of shareholders. The Code's equal treatment and mandatory bid requirements prevent acquirers from making coercive bids. Moreover, unless shareholders consent, the Code strictly prohibits management from employing any defensive tactics that would have the effect of frustrating an actual or anticipated bid. In contrast, management in the United States has a good deal more flexibility to engage in defensive tactics, provided that these can be justified in accordance with their fiduciary duties.

These differences raise a number of interesting questions. First, how are the divergences between these two superficially similar systems to be explained? At the level of substance, why is Delaware's jurisprudence so much friendlier to managers than the British Takeover Code? …

… we suggest that the *mode* of regulation has influenced – indeed, determined – its *substance*. By mode, we mean who the regulators are and the context in which the regulation takes place: informal guidance by the Takeover Panel in the United Kingdom, Delaware judges and the federal securities law in the United States. It is these differing modes of regulation that best explain why the substantive rules – which give almost complete authority to shareholders in the United

Kingdom, but provide significant managerial discretion in the United States – look so different in the two countries ...

Notes and Questions

1. There is a strong view in the United States, particularly among law and economics scholars, that the market for corporate control is the most important method of monitoring management and assuring their performance on behalf of the corporation and its shareholders. Henry Manne is generally considered to have provided the seminal article on this viewpoint. Manne's argument depends on a correlation. What is it?
2. What is corporate managerial efficiency? Is there any objective standard for corporate managerial efficiency? Is it an empirical question? Who decides or judges whether management is efficient? What are the results of such a process for corporate governance?
3. As noted briefly in the introduction to this chapter, hostile takeovers is the area that most strongly highlights a fundamental difference in approach between the US and the UK: the US approach of (1) creating directors' fiduciary duties on behalf of shareholders to act in the shareholders' best interests, (2) providing the directors with relatively broad discretion to adopt defensive measures against takeovers and (3) enforcing such directors' duties after-the-fact in court cases in Delaware, versus the UK approach of (1) creating shareholder rights to decide whether to accept acquisition bids, (2) permitting no discretion to the directors to adopt defensive measures and (3) enforcing takeover rules (the Takeover Code) in "real time" through an administrative Takeover Panel. Which approach is preferable in achieving a market for corporate control in countries where there presumably are widely dispersed shareholders? How about in other countries with more concentrated share ownership?
4. Rather than substantive shareholder rights, Armour and Skeel focus on "the striking differences as to who the regulators are in the two countries and the context in which takeovers are regulated." How and why would the identity of the regulator be so important?

2.5.2.2 The Role of Institutional Investors

Bernard Black, 'Shareholder Activism and Corporate Governance in the United States,' in Paul Newman (ed.), *The New Palgrave Dictionary of Economics and the Law* (London: Macmillan, 1998), vol. I, pp. 459–61, 464

Activism by large institutional shareholders has been part of the US landscape for over a decade, long enough to begin to assess whether it affects firm performance. The evidence to date suggests that activism, American style, has little effect on firm performance. The evidence on whether long-term "relational investing" by investors correlates with improved firm performance is also mixed. Particular institutional investors may have the skill to improve the performance of their portfolio companies, but this skill may be scarce among institutional investors as a whole …

One could hardly say that institutional investor activism is a bad thing. But the best reading of the currently available evidence is that institutional investor activism doesn't importantly affect firm performance. In particular it can't substitute for a vigorous corporate control market …

Shareholder activism in the US comes primarily from large financial institutions rather than individuals. It has generally involved two distinct approaches: (i) presenting (or threatening to present) a shareholder proposal on a corporate governance issue at a company's annual shareholder meeting; and (ii) jawboning of a particular firm's managers or board of directors to achieve a change in management or strategy …

Even the most activist institutions spend less than half a basis point (.005%) per year on their governance efforts. They concentrate on governance issues, and disclaim the specialized knowledge needed to decide company-specific issues such as whether a particular company is pursuing a sensible business strategy, or has the right CEO … The institutions' unwillingness to spend significant amounts on activism says something about the returns that they expect from this activity …

Institutional investors vote on thousands of issues a year, and devote only limited effort to deciding how to vote on a particular issue at a particular firm. In the vast majority of cases, an institution will either support management or follow a preexisting voting guideline. Activists, faced with semi-informed voters, usually present proposals already offered by other shareholders at other firms, rather than develop novel or company-specific proposals that might fail simply because they required detailed investigation by other shareholders …

Shareholder proposals submitted by institutional investors come mostly from state and local government pension funds. These "public" pension funds may be more willing to offer proposals because they face weaker conflicts of interest in challenging managers than other institutions. But state and local pension funds may sometimes have political, rather than profit maximization motives. More generally, the institutions face their own agency and information costs, which may reduce their effectiveness as monitors.

Only a small minority of institutional investors have *ever* submitted a shareholder proposal … once an institution targets a firm for a governance proposal, the institution will often informally approach the company, seeking quiet agreement on governance changes. Often the quiet approach succeeds, and no shareholder proposal is formally submitted …

An important factor is whether a proposal wins majority shareholder support is the recommendation of Institutional Shareholder Services [ISS], a private consulting firm that provides proxy voting advice and voting services to institutional investors ... As a result, shareholder proponents often tailor their proposals to meet ISS's guidelines on which proposals it will support, and devote significant effort to convincing ISS to support their proposals. Company managers, in turn, lobby ISS to oppose shareholder proposals and support management proposals on such matters as approval of stock option plans.

From a theoretical perspective, ISS is a specialized informational intermediary, which prospers because its existence lowers the institutions' costs in deciding how to vote, and thus permits more informed, hence higher quality, voting. Its existence today, when no similar voting service existed a decade ago, is consistent with voting having more salience for institutional investors today than a decade ago ...

Coordinated shareholder activism by a number of institutions might be more effective than sole action by any one of them. Yet formal coordination is rare. Instead, each institution acts as a lone wolf, and the institutions stay out of each other's way – two institutions try not to target the same firm in the same year. This practice contrasts sharply with Great Britain, where coordinated institutional investors often approach a company jointly, to increase their influence ...

From a comparative perspective, the apparent failure of institutional activism to make much of a difference shouldn't be surprising. German banks have influence that American institutions can only dream about, yet have not distinguished themselves in using this influence to improve the companies they invest in, and have not infrequently failed to prevent gross mismanagement. Japanese banks are also monitors of uncertain effectiveness. British institutions are larger and face fewer legal restraints. They do more than their American counterparts, but not dramatically more. We ought to expect less of American institutional investors than of their British, German or Japanese counterparts. Perhaps what little we seem to get, we should have expected.

Notes and Questions

1. How would you describe "shareholder activism" by institutional investors? What measures do institutional investors use in their activism? Do they devote significant resources to acting as monitors, and do they have a strong economic incentive to do so?
2. Does shareholder activism appear to be effective? Is there a correlation between shareholder activism and firm performance? What are the presumed benefits of shareholder activism and how should we measure its impact on corporate governance?
3. Does typical investor activism by traditional institutional investors deal with company-specific business plans and business performance? Should it?
4. What could be done to make shareholder activism more effective?

2.5.2.3 Private Enforcement: Derivative Litigation

Roberta Romano, 'The Shareholder Suit: Litigation Without Foundation?' (1991) 7 *Journal of Law, Economics, & Organization* 55–87, at 55–6, 84–5

Shareholder litigation is accorded an important stopgap role in corporate law. Liability rules are thought to be called into play when the primary governance mechanisms – board of directors, executive compensation, and outside block ownership – fail in their monitoring efforts but the misconduct is not of sufficient magnitude to make a control change worthwhile. By imposing personal liability on corporate officers and directors for breach of the duties of care (negligence) and loyalty (conflict of interest), litigation is thought to align managers' incentives with shareholders' interests.

The efficacy of shareholder litigation as a governance mechanism is hampered by collective action problems because the cost of bringing a lawsuit, while less than the shareholders' aggregate gain, is typically greater than a shareholder-plaintiff's pro rata benefit. To mitigate this difficulty, successful plaintiffs are awarded counsel fees, providing a financial incentive to the plaintiff's attorney to police management. There is, however, a principal–agent problem with such an arrangement: the attorney's incentives need not coincide with the shareholders' interest. For instance, settlement recoveries in shareholder litigation may provide only for payment of attorneys' fees. Critics of the shareholder suit assert that most of the suits are frivolous and that the plaintiff's bar is the true beneficiary of the litigation …

The data support the conclusion that shareholder litigation is a weak, if not ineffective, instrument of corporate governance.

(1) Lawsuits are an infrequent occurrence for the public corporation and, while most suits settle, the settlements provide minimal compensation … The principal beneficiaries of the litigation therefore appear to be attorneys, who win fee awards in 90 percent of settled suits.

(2) There is little evidence of specific deterrence …

(3) A possible interpretation of the data is that managers are so deterred by the prospect of shareholder litigation that suits involve only trivial violations. This proposition cannot be tested against the alternative – that shareholder litigation is by and large an ineffective governance structure … the failure to find much in the way of specific deterrence undercuts this proposition, and suggests that general deterrence is weak …

(4) The evidence of indirect benefits from litigation serving as a backup monitor of management is mixed. There is scant evidence that lawsuits function as an alternative governance mechanism to the board …

(5) One potential social benefit from a shareholder suit that is ancillary to its role as a governance device has not been discussed: legal rules are public goods. All firms benefit from a judicial decision clarifying the scope of permissible conduct …

Edward Rock, 'Saints and Sinners: How Does Delaware Corporate Law Work?' (1997) 44 *UCLA Law Review* 1009–1107, at 1016–18, 1106–7

My claim here – which is a descriptive claim – is that the Delaware courts generate in the first instance the legal standards of conduct (which influence the development of the social norms of directors, officers, and lawyers) largely through what can best be thought of as "corporate law sermons." These richly detailed and judgmental factual recitations, combined with explicitly judgmental conclusions, sometimes impose legal sanctions but surprisingly often do not. Taken as a whole, the Delaware opinions can be understood as providing a set of parables – instructive tales – of good managers and bad managers, of good lawyers and bad lawyers, that, in combination, fill out the normative job description of these critical players. My intuition is that we come much closer to understanding the role of courts in corporate law if we think of judges more as preachers than as policemen.

… [T]he *process* … leads to reasonably precise standards ... through the elaboration of the concepts of independence, good faith, and due care through richly detailed narratives of good and bad behavior … [T]hese standards of conduct are communicated to managers by corporate counsel, and ... the judgments of the courts play an important role in the evolution of (nonlegal) norms of conduct.

An appreciation of how Delaware law works has implications, first, for how lawyers advise their clients. Second, it affects our view of the role of shareholder litigation in the Delaware courts, finding greater benefits than the current skepticism recognizes …

The fiduciary duty cases of the Delaware courts form an important part of U.S. corporate law. We know, or at least have good grounds to believe, that U.S. corporate law works reasonably well. But we know extremely little about how that system works, about the connections between corporate law and corporate managers …

Notes and Questions

1. Is shareholder derivative litigation against a company's directors worth it: i.e. do the benefits exceed the costs? What are the benefits and how would we measure them?
2. Who benefits from a plaintiff's victory in a derivative suit? Who has an incentive to bring such litigation?
3. In shareholder litigation Delaware courts often write very long and comprehensive opinions on defendants' motions (to dismiss plaintiffs' claims) even when they grant the motion and there is no finding of director liability. Such cases could be handled routinely with very short opinions. Why do Delaware courts do this? Whom do they expect to influence? How?

4. In addition to derivative suits that allege directors' violation of fiduciary duties, shareholder suits also include securities class actions that allege some "fraud" as broadly defined under securities laws. Many people think that such securities class actions have a greater impact on companies than shareholder derivative suits. Also, some countries in Asia that have adopted the system of derivative suits seem more reluctant to authorize a system of securities class actions. Why might securities class actions be considered more significant and why would Asian countries display a more cautious attitude toward them?

2.5.2.4 Outside Professionals as Gatekeepers

John Coffee, Jr., 'Gatekeeper Failure and Reform: The Challenge of Fashioning Relevant Reforms' (2004) 84 *Boston University Law Review* 301–64, at 302–6

Securities markets have long employed "gatekeepers" – independent professionals who pledge their reputational capital – to protect the interests of dispersed investors who cannot easily take collective action. The clearest examples of such reputational intermediaries are auditors and securities analysts, who verify or assess corporate disclosures in order to advise investors in different ways. But during the late 1990s, these protections seemingly failed, and a unique concentration of financial scandals followed, all involving the common denominator of accounting irregularities … To date, much commentary has broadly and loosely attributed these scandals to any or all of a number of circumstances: (1) a stock market bubble; (2) a decline in business morality; (3) weak boards of directors; or (4) an increase in "infectious greed." Without denying that any of these factors could have played some role, this article begins from the premise that explanations phrased in terms of greed and morality are unsatisfactory because they depend on subjective trends that cannot be reliably measured …

This article will focus on an alternative explanation for the wave of accounting and financial reporting irregularities that surfaced in 2001–2002: namely, that the gatekeepers failed. That is, the professionals who serve investors by preparing, verifying, or certifying corporate disclosures to the securities markets acquiesced in managerial fraud – not in all cases, to be sure, but at a markedly higher rate than during the immediately preceding period. While the concept of gatekeeper will be discussed and refined later, this term certainly includes the auditors, securities analysts, and securities attorneys who prepare, review, or analyze disclosure documents … The behavior of gatekeepers cannot be examined in isolation, but rather appears to have been significantly influenced by the incentives that drove corporate managers over the same period … the blunt truth is that both the recent accounting scandals and the broader phenomenon of earnings management were the by-products of a system of corporate governance that has indeed made corporate managers more accountable to the market. Sensitivity to the market, however, can be a mixed blessing – particularly when the market becomes euphoric and uncritical. As a result, a corporate governance system that was adequate for a world in which the agents' incentives to act opportunistically were weaker failed when these same agents – managers, gatekeepers, and financial intermediaries – responded to stronger incentives and rationally pursued their own self-interests to the detriment of shareholders.

… [T]he factor that most destabilized our contemporary corporate governance system was the sudden change in executive compensation during the 1990s. As executive compensation shifted to being equity-based, instead of cash-based, a greatly enhanced incentive arose for managers to manipulate earnings – and to induce their gatekeepers to let them. To this extent, blaming the board is a myopic theory of causation that leads nowhere because it does not explain the sudden surge in irregularities. In truth, in most cases, boards cannot detect earnings manipulation in the absence of warnings from their professional gatekeepers.

… the relative absence of accounting scandals in Europe over the 2000–2002 period, coupled with the limited use of equity compensation in Europe, tends to corroborate the basic hypothesis advanced … that changes in executive compensation destabilized American corporate governance …

Although gatekeepers need to face some legal threat if they are to remain faithful to shareholders, the optimal level of deterrence is much harder to estimate. Some recent commentators have proposed a strict liability regime for gatekeepers, arguing that only strict liability provides gatekeepers with optimal incentives to prevent client misconduct. Other commentators have disagreed, replying that strict liability may cause the market for gatekeepers to fail or may simply deny some law-abiding, but higher risk, issuers access to the capital markets. Although the magnitude of the litigation "threat" that is now facing gatekeepers can reasonably be debated and probably varies with the type of gatekeeper, the increasing risk of gatekeeper insolvency in at least the U.S. context suggests the need to consider alternative reforms that can modify gatekeeper behavior by means that do not directly threaten gatekeeper solvency …

Notes and Questions

1. What are "gatekeepers?" What role can they be expected to play in corporate governance? How important is their role?
2. The Sarbanes–Oxley Act in 2002 substantially increased US regulation of external auditors (who audit public companies). Such regulation is generally lighter in Europe and Asia. Is this an important area for corporate governance reform?

3. The financial crisis of 2008 and the Dodd–Frank Act of 2010 highlighted the role of another gatekeeper, credit rating agencies. Might they need tighter regulation? If so, how would that be accomplished?
4. Over the last decade or so the role of proxy advisory firms has also received increased attention. What issues might they raise for corporate governance systems?

2.6 Recent Developments: "Activist Hedge Funds 2.0"

The hottest topic in US corporate governance over the past few years beginning in 2013 has been the consequences of the rise of a new type of hedge fund activism. The number and size of hedge funds have generally increased dramatically during the 2000s following the tech stock market crash in 2000–2 and the resulting search for alternative investments. Within that group, activist hedge funds, which seek to directly influence a company's business strategy and management, have grown from some US$12 billion in assets in 2013 to $112 billion in assets in 2014 with estimates up to $200 billion in 2015. This ten-fold growth, which occurred primarily after the 2008 financial crisis, includes both "pure" activist hedge funds and multi-strategy hedge funds that increasingly resort to activist strategies.

Activist hedge funds have evolved significantly from the "corporate raiders" of a generation ago, who operated solely for their own self-interest. The new "activist hedge funds 2.0" are far more sophisticated, often producing expert policy analyses of a target company's business and management problems, and discussing specific measures to reform the company in light of best practices and to increase shareholder value. Critically, activist hedge funds now position themselves as defenders of shareholders generally and shareholder value. Activist campaigns against corporate targets are no longer a matter of the activist bluntly threatening a takeover in an attempt to squeeze concessions from management to benefit only or primarily the activist; such campaigns now involve public debates designed to win over shareholder support for the activist position.

To win a public debate, it has become critical for activist hedge funds to obtain the support of traditional "passive" institutional investors, such as pension funds and mutual funds, and activists have become increasingly successful in this effort. They have been aided by the growth of passive investing generally, and the concentration of such growth in a few dominant industry players such as Blackrock, State Street, and Vanguard. Their potential support means that activist hedge funds can now muster the firepower to target even the largest US companies. And unlike the traditional approach of a "corporate raider" acquiring a 5 percent or higher stake in the shares of a company (which requires a securities filing within ten days) and raising the threat of a possible hostile takeover, well-known activists can pressure companies with as little as a 1 percent stake or can form "wolf packs" of activists with each of them holding well below 5 percent.

Although traditional institutional investors generally support hedge fund activists quietly (for example, voting in favor of activist-led proposals without much fanfare), in a number of striking recent instances traditional institutional investors have partnered openly with activist hedge funds to conduct activist campaigns against targeted companies. The best-known cases include the California public pension fund CalSTRS partnering with the activist hedge fund Relational Investors against Timken in 2013 and a pharmaceutical company, Valeant, partnering with activist hedge fund Pershing Square (and openly supported by traditional institutional investors) to attempt a takeover of another pharmaceutical company, Allergan, in 2014.

The emergence of "activist hedge funds 2.0" has intensified the ongoing debate over whether activist hedge funds create or destroy long-term value for a targeted company and its shareholders. On one side, opponents of hedge fund activism argue that such activism merely pumps up the price of the target company's stock for the short term, which benefits the activists who quickly cash out, but harms the company and its shareholders over the long term. Supporters of activist hedge funds retort with empirical evidence finding that an activist intervention generally produces a short-term gain but no long-term detrimental impact on the target company or its shareholders, and accordingly there is no need to have special limits on a company's shareholders who are activist hedge funds.

Notes and Questions

1. What do you think of this recent trend in which traditional institutional investors support hedge fund activists in their campaigns against portfolio companies? Is this an appropriate role for traditional institutional investors to maximize their influence and effect change? Or is it a mistake to support aggressive activists who may be focusing primarily on their own short-term profit? Does it result in a "better" corporate governance system? Note that even with "activist hedge funds 2.0" the period of investment by such activists generally remains short, typically six–twelve months.
2. Beginning in the 2000s the number and role of hedge funds and other "aggressive" activists has increased. These shareholder activists tend to focus on companies' business plans and pressure them to improve performance (i.e. increase corporate value) for the benefit of shareholders. Is this more effective than the activism of traditional institutional investors who focused on more traditional "good" corporate governance issues? Is this an improvement?
3. Hedge fund activists are sometimes criticized for focusing on short-term performance and profits rather than improving a company's long-term results. Is that a valid criticism?

4. Battle of the correlations. Much of the debate on activist hedge funds centers on empirical studies that gather and interpret statistical evidence concerning whether activist interventions produce a long-term negative effect on corporate value. For the leading study that argues that there is no negative long-term impact, see Lucian Bebchuk, Alan Bray, and Wei Jang, 'The Long-Term Effects of Hedge Fund Activism' (2015) 115 *Columbia Law Review* 1085–1155. For arguments opposing this idea (and activist hedge funds), see Martin Lipton, 'A Personal Reflection on Corporate Governance: Is 2015, Like 1985, an Inflection Year?' (December 8, 2015) *Harvard Law School Forum on Corporate Governance and Financial Regulation* (and five studies cited therein).

List of Statutes and Regulators

US

Statutes and Rules

State Corporate Law (in particular Delaware General Corporate Law and Model Business Corporation Act)

Securities Act of 1933

Securities and Exchange Act of 1934 (includes Sarbanes–Oxley Act)

Stock Exchange Listing Rules (in particular New York Stock Exchange Listed Company Manual Section 303A)

Regulators

State Attorneys General (corporate law enforcement)

Securities and Exchange Commission (SEC)

Public Company Accounting Oversight Board (PCAOB) (within SEC)

Stock Exchanges (primarily New York Stock Exchange and Nasdaq Stock Market)

UK

Statutes

Companies Act 2006

Financial Services and Markets Act 2000

Regulators

Financial Conduct Authority (FCA) (securities regulation)

Financial Reporting Council (corporate governance)

London Stock Exchange

3

GERMAN AND EUROPEAN MODELS

Bruce Aronson and Joongi Kim

3.1 Introduction

In the comparative corporate governance landscape, Germany (together with Japan) traditionally stands as the counterpart to the US and UK. A host of contrasting characteristics between the models represented by these leading economies serve as the basis for a fundamental debate on the best way to achieve successful corporate governance in developed countries. First, as a civil law-based country, "Deutschland AG" embodies the classic stakeholder-oriented model that emphasizes long-term growth and stable employment rather than short-term gains. Second, companies of a certain size are required to have a two-tiered board structure consisting of a supervisory board and management board. Third, another bedrock of the German model is co-determination under which worker representatives participate in decision-making on the supervisory board and mandatory works councils. Fourth, block shareholders control large companies and banks, the so-called ***Hausbank***, play a key role in protecting insiders and providing capital.

Across continental Europe, Germany's stakeholder-oriented model remains prevalent. A dozen countries have regulations that stipulate a minimum number of employee representatives on the board. Austria, Hungary, Luxembourg, and Norway, for instance, require one-third of the board, whereas Denmark, Finland, France, and Sweden call for anywhere from one to three representatives. Most countries that require employee representatives also mandate or allow two-tiered boards. Concentrated ownership continues as the dominant norm.

Continental European companies therefore operate in an environment where stakeholder interests are given priority. Shielded from the short-term pressures of shareholders, boards can better manage risk and can make corporate decisions based upon longer time horizons in line with the preferences of large block shareholders. Labor strife is generally avoided. The European system is arguably less vulnerable to the volatile swings of US and UK companies that must operate under the whims of shareholder capitalism.

The chapter provides an overview of the corporate governance of continental Europe, primarily through the example of Germany with additional focus on France, Spain, Netherlands, Sweden, and Italy, the five countries with the largest stock market capitalization. The contrasts with the US and UK will be highlighted and serve as important bases for the classification of corporate governance systems and as indications of what countries in Asia can learn from a comparative perspective (see Table 1.1).

3.2 Purpose

European countries place far greater weight on the welfare of employees than the typical shareholder-oriented "Anglo-American" company. As the key stakeholders in a corporation, employees are given a host of preferences and powers that would be the envy of many US workers. Shareholder capitalism with its central focus on shareholder value is disfavored when compared with the broader interests of workers, customers, the community, and society at large. Europeans remain very uncomfortable with the high level of compensation received by Anglo-American CEOs. The purpose of European corporations is embodied in their corporate governance.

Kent Greenfield, 'September 11th and the End of History for Corporate Law' (2002) 76 *Tulane Law Review* 1409–30, at 1424–5, 1427–8

It is worth noting, however, when it is said that the worker involvement model is obsolete, that Germany provides for its workers much better than the United States does. Of all the great industrialized nations, Germany has the shortest working week and the highest wages. What's more, the gap between the best-paid and the lowest-paid workers is not as wide as in other countries. Germany is much more egalitarian than the United States or even France.

Essentially, what we know is that a shareholder-oriented model does a better job of protecting shareholders. A worker-oriented model does a better job of protecting workers. Which does a better job with the economy or with society as a whole? Note that it is very difficult to make cross-cultural comparisons on that ground …

In any event, it is worth emphasizing that Germany's version of power sharing at times gives it more flexibility in responding to economic crises. During the recession years of 1981 and 1982, employers and trade unions agreed to keep wages down, so as to maintain the viability of companies that would otherwise be in distress. In some cases, the workers even agreed to salary cuts. Because the cuts were negotiated rather than imposed, workers could continue to feel as if they were partners in their firms rather than merely hired hands …

Workers, however, have every incentive to make sure that the companies they work for survive and thrive. Employees are not diversified in their labor investment because they typically work for one or two employers at a time and may have invested much time and effort to develop firm-specific human capital. Workers are not risk neutral; as to their employment, they are risk averse. Rather than being indifferent as to the liquidation risk of the company they work for, they care deeply about their firm's financial health because they face harsh consequences from unemployment if their firm suffers. If their company fails, workers typically lose a great deal. They not only lose their jobs but also the value of any firm-specific skills and sometimes a good portion of retirement or pension benefits ... In contrast to shareholders, workers prefer that management not make decisions with a high variance, even when such decisions have a high expected return. Workers instead want decisions that value stability, even with a lower-expected total return.

Workers' interests may thus function as a better placeholder for the best interests of the firm. Because shareholders are largely indifferent as to the possibility of any single firm failing, managers who make decisions according to what is good for the shareholders will bring about the failure of their companies more often than managers who make decisions based on what is good for a broader mix of stakeholders. If one really cares what is better for a specific firm, it is not so clear that shareholders' desires should dominate, at least if we define "what is better for the firm" to include survival.

Finally, workers have continuing relationships with firms in ways most shareholders do not. Because of this relationship, taking account of workers' interests can inure to the firm's benefit in yet another way, by building "positive reciprocity." This is simply a fancy term for the notion that people largely respond to others in the way they are treated. There is almost no room for this effect to occur in the company's relationship with most shareholders, because the contribution of capital is usually an isolated act performed by someone who bought stock from the firm years previously. Workers, however, can "give back" to the firm when they are treated well. For example, when workers believe they are treated fairly by their employers, they are more productive and obey firm rules at a much higher rate than when they feel they are mistreated. The employment relation is not a zero-sum game.

One can show evidence of this effect even at a macroeconomic level. Although the rate of union membership is about three times higher in Germany than in the United States, the number of days lost to strikes in Germany is about 1/20 of the U.S. total. Indeed, Germany has the lowest level of strike activity in the Western world.

Notes and Questions

1. What is the employees' role in corporate governance? As Greenfield suggests, do they care more for the corporation than shareholders, to the benefit of the corporation and society? Are they better monitors of management? Can they be coopted? Does management trust employees with confidential information?
2. Does labor inhibit M&A activity to the benefit or detriment of the company and/or society?

3.3 Board Function

Many European countries allow or require companies to have two-tiered boards with employee representatives. Austria, Germany, and Poland, for instance, mandate two tiers whereas the Czech Republic, Denmark, Finland, France, Hungary, Netherlands, Norway, and Switzerland give companies an option between one or two tiers. Italy and Portugal also permit companies to adopt a traditional model as a third option under which a board of statutory auditors is established. Belgium, Greece, Spain, and Sweden, however, only allow one tier. Overall, the role, function, and composition of the supervisory board remains a central focus. There is constant debate over the extent to which the supervisory board should participate in managerial decision-making as opposed to merely monitoring the management board. The following article explores the efficacy of two boards and how corporate governance is affected by the presence of employee representatives on a board.

Klaus J. Hopt and Patrick C. Leyens, 'Board Models in Europe' Law Working Paper No. 18/2004 (January 2004), ECGI, at 5–10

2.1.1 The Role of the Supervisory Board

The central feature of internal corporate governance lies in the organisational and personal division of management and control by a two-tier structure that is mandatory for all public corporations, regardless of size or listing. While the clear responsibility of the management board is the running of the business, the role of the supervisory board is not easy to describe. Its legal functions are primarily the appointment, supervision, and removal of members of the management board. Recently its important "soft functions" were highlighted from a comparative perspective. Networking with stakeholders and business partners and the balancing of interests within the corporation have been rated as indispensably valuable, particularly for resolving desperate situations. The supervisory board controls the management (not the corporation), its compliance with the law and articles of the corporation, and its business strategies. The supervisory board cannot directly become involved in managing the company, but if articles so provide or the supervisory board so decides, specific types of transactions may become subject to its approval. Its control efficiency and the extent to which the supervisory board exercises its task to advise management is subject to considerable differences, mostly due to size and shareholder structure. In some public corporations the management board de facto picks the supervisory board. In contrast, in family-owned corporations or those owned by major shareholders, approval rights play an important role and are sometimes used to substantially extend the powers of the supervisory board. Committees are less common compared with the United Kingdom or the United States. However, a strongly growing tendency towards nomination, remuneration, and audit committees can be observed, and the majority of the larger listed companies has already installed them.

The supervisory board is responsible for bringing actions of the company against members of the management board.

2.1.2 Board Composition, Independence, and Labour Co-determination

Membership in the supervisory board is incompatible to simultaneous membership in the management board. Further, one person cannot take more than ten parallel supervisory board mandates. However, business relationships are inherent characteristics of the German supervisory board and can involve difficult questions of independence, objectivity, and conflicts of interests. Many companies make use of their former managers' business knowledge by offering them seats on the supervisory board when they retire. In particular, the chairman of the management board often changes over and takes the chair of the supervisory board. Further seats are offered to representatives of business partners, particularly in cases of cross shareholdings.

An illustrative example for inherent conflicts of interests is the common practice of mandating representatives of banks or of their investment branches. Because of the German universal banking system, the bank then takes on a double position as depository voting rights are to be exercised in the interest of shareholders, and conflicting interests can result from a creditor relationship between bank and company. The position is even tripled if the bank holds a participation in the company. The Deutsche Bank AG was the first to address this problem explicitly. Their Corporate Governance Principles of 2001 stated that members of the management board do not, in principle, assume the chairmanship of a supervisory board outside the group …

The German Corporate Governance Code does not provide a general definition of independence. The issue of former managers sitting on the supervisory board is taken up by the recommendation to limit their number to two seats and to not give the chair of the audit committee to a former member of the management board. Parallel mandates in management or supervisory boards of competitors or advisory functions for such competitors are seen as incompatible. The issue of business relationships – especially the German system of cross shareholdings – has encountered major criticism by foreign investors. The recommendation to disclose affiliations of supervisory board members in a report to the general meeting is welcome, but it does not explicitly name cross shareholdings. Further, disclosure is only recommended for the case of existing conflicts of interests, i.e., for affiliations that are classified as such by the supervisory board itself …

A German peculiarity is its strong labour co-determination. Companies with 2,000 workers or more must have half their supervisory board composed of labour representatives; in large enterprises, this amounts to ten of twenty board members (in coal and steel it is twenty-one). The casting vote of the chairman gives slightly more power to shareholders. Labour participation is at the heart of industrial democracy ... It is reinforced by the duty of management to take into account the coalition of interests between shareholders and stakeholders, including those of employees and even the public interest.

... The basic problems of size (up to 21 members) and the inability of the German system to impose adequate qualification standards are further consequences of codetermination ... In Germany, it is impossible to set a general standard above a certain level of financial literacy because the workforce and unions would not always be prepared to nominate adequate candidates, and a corresponding strict liability would seem unfair ...

The few who name the problems correctly distinguish between the above-mentioned deficiencies of the German supervisory board and the difficulties of German codetermined companies regarding competition and the raising of capital on international capital markets. Foreign investors will be (understandably) reluctant to choose a German co-determined company if global markets offer alternative investments not subject to co-determination. If the workforce takes its tasks seriously, it will seldom be prepared to support cross-border restructurings, which in most cases usher in the danger that jobs will be lost to entities outside the country. It is striking – and will hardly be understood by an international observer – that the German reform agenda excludes co-determination almost as a matter of political principle.

2.1.3 Internal Controls and Auditing

Recent proposals on improving internal control plead for an increase of approval rights of the supervisory board. The success of both stronger involvement in management decisions and the strengthening of control efficiency as a whole depends foremost on the level of information. The functioning of information systems as they exist under the law or as recommended by the German Corporate Governance Code is strongly determined by the two-tier structure. The exclusion of the supervisory board from management and its limited rights to obtain information directly from executives can make it difficult for its members to develop an objective picture of the company's performance.

The interplay of the supervisory board and external auditing is a central point of the corporate governance debate. Under the two-tier system, internal control is an instrument of the management board and confidence must not be undermined by the supervisory board or its committees. Further, the law does not allow audit committees to take over resolution power in matters reserved for plenary decisions of the supervisory board, as is the case with the approval of the annual accounts ...

The external auditor is elected by the general meeting, and thus primarily serves as a control device of shareholders. However, the role of the auditor as a "partner" of the supervisory board has also been strengthened several times. As a consequence of the KonTraG reform in 1998, the supervisory board concludes the auditing contract and confers the auditing mandate, which should cover all matters relevant to the work of the supervisory board. Information flow was triggered by the KonTraG because the auditing report is directly handed over to the supervisory board, and the auditor has the duty of taking part in the meeting on approval of the annual accounts. Further, the auditing mandate was extended; in addition to the checking of the accounts, it now includes the control of the risk management systems ... Any further extension of the auditing mandate to business matters was rejected by the Regierungskommission due to the fear that this could lead to a disadvantageous discharge of the supervisory board or even push it away from the exercise of its control duties.

Notes and Questions

1. How would you describe the function and effectiveness of the two-tier board? What are the greatest strengths and weaknesses of supervisory boards? What about co-determination? Is it a net positive for corporate governance?
2. Given the apparent success that Germany has had with its model for boards, can we say that it is possible to achieve both management efficiency and good monitoring? In Germany, one person can sit on up to ten supervisory boards and one 2010 study found that more than one hundred persons sat on more than five other supervisory boards. Is this too much? Furthermore, many of the supervisory boards consist of, and are led by, former management board members. Management board members must wait for two years to be elected unless the shareholders permit this.
3. Is the two-tiered board structure sustainable or will it ultimately change due to international pressures and incentives? What kind of reforms, if any, would you suggest?
4. For the management board, almost every major European country requires the establishment of an audit committee. Furthermore, Denmark, Greece, the Netherlands, Norway, Portugal, and Spain, among others, require that half or more of the members of the audit committee be independent, and Hungary and Italy require that they all be independent. For nomination and compensation committees, most countries recommend them through

codes or principles, with Spain being the only major country that follows the US and Indian approach and legally requires both of them. Switzerland only requires compensation committees. How would you account for this varied treatment of board committees? What ramifications does this have?

5. In terms of independent directors, Italy and Spain require that listed companies have two independent directors (for Italy, one, if the board is fewer than eight directors). The Netherlands recommends the entire board except one be independent, Switzerland recommends that more than one-half be independent, and France recommends either one-half (for listed companies with no controlling shareholder) or one-third (for listed companies that are controlled) be independent. Do European companies need more independent directors?
6. In France, for companies with a controlling shareholder, at least one-third of the directors must be independent. Similarly, Italian companies in groups that are controlled by a listed company must have a majority of independent directors. Should other European countries adopt similar requirements?
7. In Europe, like the US, France, Italy, and Spain require board approval of non-routine or material related party transactions but, like the UK, Germany, Netherlands, and Switzerland do not. Italy and Spain also require review by independent directors or the audit committee and, under certain conditions, shareholder approval.

3.4 Ownership Structure

One of the most significant differences with the US and UK is that European companies are generally marked by concentrated ownership structures where one or more shareholders hold substantial blocks of shares. As a result, the primary tension in European companies is a horizontal agency problem between the block shareholders and general shareholders. This contrasts with the vertical agency problem between managers and shareholders found in dispersed ownership companies. In Europe, as with most of the world, institutional investment and the portion of foreign ownership have increased considerably over the years. More specifically, Germany, the Netherlands, and Switzerland, among others, have even shown some signs of mixed ownership, with more dispersed ownership often found in larger listed companies. Yet, concentrated ownership remains common. And even though comparative corporate governance frameworks traditionally focus on "block" shareholders in the German system rather than on majority or controlling shareholders, controlling shareholders are also relatively common in a number of European countries. In Italy, for instance, two-thirds of all listed companies are controlled by a single shareholder and in Spain one-quarter of the listed companies are controlled by a majority-owning shareholder. The effect of dispersion on Europe's concentrated ownership structure is reviewed in the following article extracts.

Wolf-Georg Ringe, 'Changing Law and Ownership Patterns in Germany: Corporate Governance and the Erosion of Deutschland AG' (2015) 63 *American Journal of Comparative Law* 493–538, at 508–9, 516–26

1. Equity dispersion

[Table 1] displays the current ownership structure of the companies listed on the major stock index DAX30. The major German firms contained in this stock index show a diverse picture of ownership patterns, ranging from firms in majority control (Beiersdorf, with a 50% shareholder) to total dispersion (e.g., Deutsche Bank, BASF or Allianz). The average size of the largest blockholder in these firms is 16.50%, the median is only 9.92%. What matters, too, is relative control, as compared with the second largest shareholder. Again, no uniform picture is recognizable, but the difference between the first and the second blockholder amounts to roughly 43% on average. This seems to give large shareholders (where they are present) still a comfortable position on average.

Placing these figures into relation with earlier findings, we establish that the ownership concentration in large German firms is on the decline ... When controlling for relative control, it appears that the difference between the largest and the second largest shareholder has decreased: whereas it was 44.31% on average in the 2001 sample, this gap amounted to only 25.27% in 2014 (51.29% versus 37.83% in the full sample) ...

These studies all point in a similar direction: ownership stakes are falling, and the traditional network is eroding. The old presumption of Germany as a closed system of strong networks, dominated by blockholders and cross-participations, may thus no longer hold true. To be sure, the academic studies reviewed here are limited – with varying sample sizes – to listed firms, and it appears that the strongest drop in concentration applies to the DAX 30 companies ...

1. Globalization and market pressure

Among the most frequently quoted reasons for equity diffusion is the growing globalization with the increased international competition for banks it entails. The traditional role of banks in Germany had very much been to be part of the bank-centered system of corporate finance (as opposed to capital market-based finance). By the 1980s, however, as globalization gained ground, German banks were increasingly tempted by the profitability of investment banking and the mergers and acquisitions (M&A) market instead of their traditional lending role ...

Further, studies show that the profitability of holding large blocks of shares decreased over the 1980s and 1990s. This tendency is also attributed to globalization pressure: growing competition on product markets reduced managers' discretion, which in turn reduced the beneficial effect of monitoring activities formerly carried out by blockholders. Blockholders were not as easily able to extract rents and private benefits. With growing international competition, the costs of holding an undiversified block of shares in a company therefore began to exceed the blockholders' private benefits, and the economic case for blockholding thus disappeared.

Finally, researchers have observed that growing internationalization reduced the effectiveness of monitoring within the "Deutschland AG." Within the boundaries of a relatively small and controllable system like the German corporate sector of the 1980s, banks were able to oversee their portfolio companies' activities, monitor, and influence strategic decisions.

2. Dispersion due to regulation

[W]e can juxtapose against this narrative a number of regulatory interventions that provided even stronger incentives and accelerated this ongoing process. The most prominent of these interventions was the reform of taxation laws that took effect in 2001/02. New § 8b(2) of the Corporation Tax Code (*Körperschaftsteuergesetz*, KStG) abolished the former 40% taxation rate on the divestiture from domestic holding companies of equity stakes in domestic companies – and thus encouraged both industrial firms and banks to sell minority stakes they had previously held. In fact, the very reason for this taxation reform was – besides tax systematic reasons – to "give important impulses for the necessary modernization and restructuring of the German economy" ...

Apart from this front page-news taxation reform, other legislative measure may have been equally effective despite not equally present in the public limelight. For example, the adoption of the Restructuring Act in 1994 (*Umwandlungsgesetz*) in 1994 facilitated and streamlined restructurings of German firms in various ways (mergers, breakups, spin-offs, transfers of assets and changes in legal status). Further, KonTraG the groundbreaking 1998 reform of the *Aktiengesetz,* de facto abolished multiple voting rights, voting restrictions and other potential obstacles to a market for corporate control.

3. EU market integration

The final nail in the coffin for concentrated ownership may then well have been the increasingly strong powers exercised by the EU to push further market integration.

As is well known, there is a strong correlation between the advancement of market integration and the extent of equity dispersion ...

Many instances suggest that the development of an EU-wide market for equity ownership is also exhibiting a similar trend. Early measures include a comprehensive company law harmonization program, serving a twofold purpose: creating a level playing field for companies that wish to engage in business transactions in other EU Member States, and protecting investors and creditors who interact with a company from another jurisdiction. For example, the EU has pushed member states to privatize previous state-run monopolies such as telecommunication services, thus promoting retail investment in shares and the development of a stock market generally (for an example involving Deutsche Telekom). More recently, the EU has seen a massive wave of federal integration in capital and financial markets law: the Financial Services Action Plan from 1999 heralded a decade of market integration, while the tsunami of legislation following the 2007–2008 financial crisis seized the opportunity to integrate market supervision and to establish an institutional setup for a genuine European capital market.

Out of these efforts, two elements are worth emphasizing. One is the EU Shareholder Rights Directive, an instrument fostering and stimulating cross-border ownership of shares and streamlining information rights and other aspects to support shareholders. The other is increasingly self-confident case law on free movement of capital, banning all national obstacles to capital flows between EU member states, such as golden shares and other restrictions to cross-border share ownership …

B. Banks' retreat from equity ownership

The trend towards equity dispersion in general has had one particular field of application: equity ownership by banks. Many financial institutions have re-oriented their business model in recent years and have contributed to the erosion of the traditional network of cross-participations …

Banking competition increased due to privatization of previously state-owned banks (Postbank, for example), and in the form of "direct banks" – Internet-based banks which were able to offer traditional banking services at lower costs, without having to rely on the expensive maintenance of branches and offices …

In their hunt for profit, large German banks responded to this pressure by reducing their industry participations, which seemed low-return investments by comparison. These were sold, reduced, or simply transferred to a separate, new investment department within the same financial institution. The revenue from such divestments could be used to finance new, international acquisitions, which allowed them to be present on international capital markets. In 1995, Dresdner Bank acquired Kleinwort Benson, a leading private investment bank based in London, and became its international investment-banking arm. In a similar move,

Deutsche Bank purchased Bankers Trust, a New York-based investment bank and derivatives dealer, in 1999.

This entirely new re-orientation of the banking sector had enormous consequences for the dynamics of the German market as a whole, since the banks had been the glue that had kept Deutschland AG together. As a result of the complex reorientation of their business model, the large banks – especially Deutsche Bank, as the core of the system – left the cooperative, long-term oriented, safety-oriented model of Germany Inc. and took up competition with their global counterparts. As we have seen above, and accelerated by strong taxation incentives, this led, *inter alia,* to a sizeable reduction in their equity participations ... The receding equity investments went hand in hand with a slow reduction of the supervisory board seats held by banks ...

C. Growing internationalization of share ownership

We have seen that banks' ownership is declining, and concentration of shareholdings generally is on the decline. As a third trajectory, it is submitted that German ownership is increasingly becoming more international. Whilst this phenomenon is not unique to Germany – in fact, it is observed in many countries – its influence on the previously closely-knit network of German corporations and their cross-ownership patterns is remarkable. Data suggest that the international share of ownership for German listed firms has been steadily increasing over the past years ...

A study carried out by the German business newspaper *Handelsblatt* in 2011 found that almost half of the companies listed in the leading German stock index DAX have a majority of foreign shareholders, and that these foreign owners together hold a total of 55.8% of all shares contained in the DAX. The study found that the proportion of foreign ownership has increased by about 8% compared to the previous year. Especially large institutional investors, led by the global investment management firm BlackRock, have bought into German corporations. But also sovereign wealth funds, mostly from the Middle East, account for the increase in foreign ownership.

In 2013, the same newspaper published a more sophisticated story, documenting the rise in foreign ownership for DAX companies over the years 2001–2013, climbing from 36% to 55% ...

... But why are German shareholders not equally interested? The reason seems to be partially related to the structure of German share ownership. Domestic institutional investors are by comparison a relatively small player on international capital markets, mainly due to the fact that the German pension system is predominantly state-run and does not involve large pension funds that have to make investment decisions.

John Coffee, Jr., 'A Theory of Corporate Scandals: Why the United States and Europe Differ' (2005) 21 *Oxford Review of Economic Policy* 198–211, at 199

While Europe also had financial scandals over this same period (with the Parmalat scandal being the most notorious), most were characteristically different than the US style of earnings manipulation scandal (of which Enron and WorldCom were the iconic examples). Only European firms cross-listed in the United States seem to have encountered similar crises of earnings management. What explains this difference and the difference in frequency? This short essay will advance a simple, almost self-evident thesis: differences in the structure of share ownership account for differences in corporate scandals, both in terms of the nature of the fraud, the identity of the perpetrators, and the seeming disparity in the number of scandals at any given time. In dispersed ownership systems, corporate managers tend to be the rogues of the story, while in concentrated ownership systems; it is controlling shareholders who play the corresponding role. Although this point may seem obvious, its corollary is less so: the modus operandi of fraud is also characteristically different. Corporate managers tend to engage in earnings manipulation, while controlling shareholders tend to exploit the private benefits of control.

Wolf-Georg Ringe, 'Changing Law and Ownership Patterns in Germany: Corporate Governance and the Erosion of Deutschland AG' (2015) 63 *American Journal of Comparative Law* 493–538, at 502–5

D. *How Do Legal Rules Respond to These Facts?*

Legal rules are, or should be, a function of economic realities. Corporate law is no exception. The vast body of German corporate law is a response to the parameters of corporate ownership that have been described above. The main objective of German legal rules is to help reduce intra-shareholder agency costs, and they also attempt to curtail the role of banks to some extent … Since the economic realities in continental Europe have hitherto been different, and since blockholder-dominated corporations prevail there, the law has needed to provide a different toolbox to address the main policy concerns present in the corporate sector. Comparative scholars have demonstrated that Germany is indeed one of the countries where minority protection is most pronounced; they have found that Germany comes top among a number of jurisdictions when asking for shareholder protection, and that it even increased this protection between 1970 and 2005.

Yet how minority protection is regulated deviates in many ways from Anglo-American legal ideals. For example, the derivative suit, a main element of minority protection in the United States, remains extremely rare in German corporations. Other mechanisms of minority protection are mostly found in statutory rules. In what follows, I present a number of key German legal principles that characterize the gist of corporate law and governance, and I will explain how they map onto the economic realities presented above.

1. Equality of Shareholders

One of the key principles underlying German corporate law is the rule of shareholder equality, which has been enshrined in § 53a of the [AktG]. This section holds that, under identical conditions, the company is obliged to treat all shareholders equally. The addressee of this obligation is "the company," which can either mean the management or indeed a shareholder resolution. In both variants, § 53a AktG becomes a strong tool of minority protection, since it prohibits the majority or the management (appointed by the majority) from differentiating between different shareholders without a justificatory reason. For example, this can apply to voting rights, distribution of profits, preemptive rights, or participation in liquidation proceeds. Once the shareholder can show that she is treated unequally, the burden of proof is on the company to demonstrate that overriding reasons justify the unequal treatment. The courts usually apply strict limits to such justifications.

The principle of equal treatment is also represented in the Second EU Company Law Directive, an instrument harmonizing some aspects of legal capital, and across the EU …

2. Duties of Loyalty Between Shareholders

Although the statutory material is silent on this question, it has long been established in German corporate law – by way of judicial creativity, as reflected in the case law – that shareholders are bound by fiduciary duties both towards their fellow shareholders and towards the company. The common justification for this rule is that it counteracts the far-reaching influence that shareholders may have on the strategy of the company and on the interests of its members. This strong influential power arguably requires an intensive duty program as a corrective (in order to create a correlation between influence and responsibility) … For the most part, these loyalty duties apply to majority shareholders, thus making the principle an important tool of minority protection, and responding to the prevalence of blockholders in the German corporate landscape. There have, however, also been cases where the minority shareholder has been held to be subject to a duty of loyalty towards the majority.

Notes and Questions

1. Do you think that dispersion will continue for Germany's large listed companies? Will German banks continue their transition away from being the center of finance for "Deutschland AG" and will international ownership continue to increase? What factors would you cite in support of your conclusion?
2. How will the new ownership landscape reshape corporate governance in Germany? Does it matter if banks have fewer positions on supervisory boards? In what way?
3. Will these ownership patterns contribute to an eventual convergence of German corporate governance with that of widely dispersed shareholder systems like the US and the UK?
4. Does the nature of corporate governance scandals differ depending on ownership structure?
5. How do blockholder systems like Germany address their corporate governance issues? Given that the fundamental agency problem is different from dispersed shareholder systems, are the techniques to address the problem also different?
6. Shareholders generally remain passive in Europe. Some attribute this to the lack of independent institutional investors and the limited powers of shareholders. Compared with the US and UK, hedge funds and private-equity firms are not as active.
7. Other than Germany, Spain, and Switzerland, almost all of Europe's remaining countries are part of one of the four major international stock exchange groups (NASDAQ OMX, Euronext, London Stock Exchange Group, and the CEE Stock Exchange). What effect might this have on corporate governance?

3.5 Law and Enforcement

Jürgen Odenius, 'Germany's Corporate Governance Reforms: Has the System Become Flexible Enough?' (2008) IMF Working Paper, WP/08/179 (2008), at 13–14

V. External Control Mechanisms: the Market for Corporate Control

External control is an important, complementary mechanism to internal control. Grossman and Hart provide a theoretical basis for the takeover market's disciplining function in their groundbreaking 1980 article. A potential failure of internal control mechanisms would eventually cause a substantial deviation of a firm's market value from its potential, thereby inviting possible takeover bids. While the literature provides little empirical evidence that the market for corporate control effectively carries out this function, Goergen, Manjon, and Renneboog (2004) nevertheless conclude that the "existence of an active market for corporate control is material."

Germany's market for corporate control is considered small by international standards. The market was largely dormant prior to the hostile takeover of Mannesmann – a traditional German manufacturer turned into a mobile phone operator – by the British Vodafone in 2000. The dominance of large shareholders is widely seen as a major reason for the virtual absence of takeovers until this decade. In addition, Goergen, Manjon, and Renneboog (2004) attribute this outcome to the prevalence of pyramidal structures and extensive, albeit declining, cross-shareholdings. Schmid and Wahrenburg (2004, p. 278) also point to the two-board structure and codetermination as a further obstacle, stating: "To an unwelcome bidder, attaining control over the supervisory board might prove a challenging task. For one thing, shareholders have no power of removing labor representatives."

In response to the arrival of hostile takeovers, parliament adopted a legal framework earlier this decade. The 2001 takeover law (WpÜG) replaced the earlier voluntary takeover code and combines elements of legislation enacted in the U.K. and U.S.A. starting in the 1960s. Just like the U.K. framework, the German takeover law aims at protecting minority shareholders and stipulates a strict mandatory bid requirement. This requirement aims to provide minority shareholders with an acceptable exit option, as takeovers fundamentally change company policy. More precisely, in transactions that exceed 30 percent of voting rights, the law requires a mandatory offer by the acquiring party to all shareholders. The mandatory bid requirement tends to raise the costs of takeovers and, therefore, is also seen as benefiting management.

In contrast to U.K. law, German law allows for defensive measures to stave off takeovers bids – consistent with the EU framework. A further important feature of German takeover law is how it resolves the question whether management is granted the right to interfere with hostile takeover bids through defensive measures, or whether management is obliged to abstain from intervention and retain its so-called neutrality. German takeover legislation grants management the right to interfere with takeover attempts, allowing four different types of defensive measures, although not all are considered effective. While some of these measures require shareholder approval, the MB [Management Board] with the approval of the SB [Supervisory Board] may also use specified defensive measures without shareholder approval, including the purchase or sale of important assets. The 2001 law, however, is consistent with the EU Takeover Directive that came into force in 2004, after some 30 years of protracted negotiations.

Creating a level playing field in the market for corporate control requires restoring management neutrality. There is broad-based agreement in the literature that the takeover law falls short of creating a level playing field and, therefore, it does not leave markets as final arbitrators. Both the mandatory bid requirement and the appreciable scope granted to management to engage in defensive measures are seen as raising the costs of a takeover. Against this background, Baum (2006) concludes: "Together with Austria, the German takeover regime is probably the most intensely regulated takeover law worldwide." In the words of Baums and Scott (2005, p. 22) the decision to give the MB power to use defensive measures without SB approval "has entrusted the wrong people with the decision whether the market for corporate control should operate." Enhancing the effectiveness of the market for external control, and especially involuntary takeovers, could serve as a major step toward enhancing corporate governance, especially given the inherent weakness of internal control mechanisms.

Jean J. du Plessis and Niklas Cordes, 'Claiming Damages from Members of Management Boards in Germany: Time for a Radical Rethink and Possible Lessons from Down Under?' (2015) 36 *Company Lawyer* 335–53, at 335, 336–42, 349

Actions initiated by the supervisory board

The supervisory board is the independent monitoring, governing or supervisory body in the Aktiengesellschaft [AG], and under s. 111(1) [AktG] is required to control the lawfulness, expediency and efficiency of the management board's actions. This control task includes an obligation to determine possible claims for damages against management board members and to institute action against members of management who have breached their duties, when the breach has resulted in the company suffering damages. In accordance with s. 112(1) AktG, the supervisory board also has the right to represent the company in judicial and extra-judicial affairs and has the legal standing to pursue claims for damages to the benefit of the corporation.

Furthermore, under s. 93(4)(3) AktG, supervisory boards are obligated, if they have reason to suspect a breach of duties, to enforce claims of damages against the members of the management board, unless there are reasons for not doing so that are to the company's benefit. The best interests of the company will be the guiding principle for not instituting action: for example, the supervisory board may decide not to act if instituting action would severely damage the company's reputation or would be particularly disruptive to the ordinary day-to-day running of the company, including impairment of the working atmosphere. However, a discretionary power is not granted, with the result that a decision about whether or not to initiate a lawsuit is subject to judicial review. Furthermore, a breach of this duty to sue can lead to a liability risk for the supervisory board itself ...

Powers of the shareholders' meeting to compel the supervisory board to take action

In cases where the supervisory board fails to pursue a claim for damages or regards a requirement for enforcement as non-existent, under s. 147(1) AktG a resolution could be passed at a shareholders' meeting to direct the supervisory board to institute an action to claim the damages. The fact that shareholders have this power improves the capital position of the company, in the sense that there is more than one way to claim damages. Also, it is a form of indirect control over the management board by the shareholders, because members of the management board are personally liable under this regime. If such a resolution is passed, the supervisory board has to institute the action within six months. This period is to preclude any postponing of the action or arbitrary delaying of it. The risks and the costs of the following lawsuit are taken by the corporation alone, because the supervisory board, which had been forced by the shareholders' meeting to initiate the proceeding, is the organ that will be representing the company in court.

Along with the power of the general meeting to enforce a claim for damages by resolution, s. 93(4)(3) AktG states that prior to issuing waiving statements and settlement agreements, the consent of the general meeting must be obtained. This is intended to ensure that secret deals are not made between the members of the management board and the supervisory board. Such deals would be seen as collusive behaviour and would provide incentives for the supervisory board not to proceed with the claims.

It will be clear from the discussion above that actions against members of management boards will generally be instituted by the supervisory board, either because it has identified breaches of duties by members of management boards causing the company to suffer damages, or because a resolution of a shareholders' meeting directed it to do so. However, there may be circumstances where the supervisory board is unwilling to institute such action and the majority of shareholders also do not want to direct the supervisory board, through the resolution of a shareholders' meeting, to proceed with such actions …

The shareholders' lawsuit (statutory derivative action)

The shareholders' lawsuit or statutory derivative action was introduced in Germany as recently as 2005 by way of the Corporate Integrity and Rescission Law Modernisation Act (UMAG). The primary aim was to strengthen shareholders' rights (in particular minority shareholders) to institute actions on behalf of the company against members of management boards and improve the enforcement of claims for damages against members of the management board. The statutory derivative action is another way to claim damages from management board members in breach of their duties. This action is contained in s. 148 AktG. The intention of the legislature, according to the explanatory memorandum, was to develop a balance between making it easier for shareholders to institute actions on behalf of the company on the one hand, and the curtailing lawsuits by so-called "predatory shareholders" or "professional plaintiffs" on the other hand ... From the legal point of view, s. 148 AktG authorises minority shareholders to bring claims of damages against the members of the management board for the benefit of the corporation, even if the supervisory board or the majority shareholders are unwilling to claim themselves. There are two stages required for a statutory derivative action to proceed. The court must first give leave for it to continue (the first stage). If the court grants that leave, the actual action will then follow (the second stage). For the purposes of the first stage, the claiming shareholders have to go through an approval procedure with the following five requirements:

1. Shareholders must hold a minimum of 1 per cent of the company's share capital or a nominal value of €100,000.
2. The shareholders' shares must have been acquired prior to becoming aware of the violation that could result in a potential claim for damages.
3. A deadline must be sent to the company for instituting action (through either the supervisory board or the management board).
4. The shareholders must have a reasonable suspicion of dishonesty or gross breaches of duty.
5. The action will not primarily be detrimental to the company's welfare.

A façade of effective remedies, but the reality in Germany reflects a different picture

At first glance it seems as if it is quite easy for a company to institute actions against members of the management board for a breach of their duties and to claim damages that the company suffered because of such a breach ...

Legal difficulties in the claim enforcement

Despite numerous efforts of the legislators, in reality the German liability law of management board members contains certain legal obstacles which prevent effective enforcement of claims for damages. For example the criterion of "public interest" is interpreted very broadly by the supervisory board. As a result, this criterion functions like a carte blanche in the decision-making process about whether to initiate a lawsuit. The possibilities which are legally made available for the general meeting do not work effectively as the general meeting is by its nature not in a position to take quick action as it will require the convening of a general meeting, which can be time-consuming and very expensive.

Finally, even the statutory derivative action under s.148 AktG has been shown to be inadequate to promote the enforcement of claims for damages, for two reasons. First, even the most basic requirement to initiate the statutory derivative action (as mentioned above shareholders must hold a minimum of 1 per cent of the company's share capital or a nominal value of €100,000) is very hard to fulfil and thus acts as a major obstacle to instituting statutory derivative actions. Secondly, the company is vested with the power to replace the minority shareholders as plaintiff at any time during the procedure by making use of its substitution right and continuing the proceedings alone. Even when the costs of the proceedings are borne by the company the disappointment of the shareholders is great, and the amount of work they have done is not compensated. Moreover, there is a risk that the company will withdraw the complainant after entering into the procedure …

Lack of knowledge of breaches

The fact that the shareholders are normally not aware of breaches of duties by the management board or do not have sufficient knowledge about the circumstances related to these violations could be another reason for the scarcity of liability lawsuits against management board members in Germany …

Liability risk for the complaining party

It also has to be borne in mind that the judicial enforcement of claims for damages against the management board by the supervisory board could reveal facts that can indicate that the members of the supervisory board themselves were in breach of their duties. Here, in particular, there will always be a question of whether they in fact supervised or governed in a diligent way and monitored the activities of the management board carefully enough. There is always a risk that the members of the supervisory board violated their monitoring obligations prior to the contested breaches of duty by the management board, which means that they, the complaining party, could be exposed to direct liability of their own, according to ss. 116(1) and 93 AktG …

Risk of damaged reputation for the company …

Loyalties

Moreover, it is important to make a few comments regarding loyalty. The fact is that the management of a company is guided by mutual confidence between the management board and the supervisory board, and loyalties between the members of the respective boards, often developed over several years of mutual collaboration. This should not be underestimated. The supervisory board may have no willingness to initiate liability proceedings against members of the management board whom the supervisory board has itself appointed … Becoming a member of the supervisory board after serving on the company's management board is not uncommon in Germany …

Cost risk

Another major reason for not filing actions is cost … This factor affects the shareholders' lawsuit in particular, because the corporation does not bear the costs of initiating the stage one procedures, and, as explained above, if leave to proceed with the statutory derivative action is not granted by the court, the minority shareholder will bear all the costs. So the economic incentive for initiating a shareholders' lawsuit is low, especially as the proceedings are litigated to the benefit of the corporation and, even in case of a successful action, the damages will be paid to the company, with no other benefit to the minority shareholder other than, perhaps, the company's shares being worth more.

Notes and Questions

1. What can be done to improve external governance and monitoring in Germany, particularly to hold members of the management board more accountable for breaches of their duties?
2. How could the market for corporate control be improved? How important is it for good corporate governance in Germany?
3. The challenges that shareholders face in terms of private enforcement are not unique to Germany and are common to most countries. The US and Australia are considered the leading outliers in this regard. Most European countries rely upon public enforcement instead of private enforcement. Is US or Australian-style private enforcement, utilizing class actions and derivate actions driven by contingency fees and litigation funding, something to consider for Germany and other European countries? What other alternatives may exist?
4. Might there be reasons other than economic incentives for shareholders to initiate private enforcement? See Chapter 10 (Japan) and Chapter 11 (Korea).
5. Most major European countries have established corporate governance codes or best practices and stewardship codes that are implemented through a comply-or-explain approach. In the case of Germany, Italy, and Netherlands, the codes are managed by a mixture of public entities, such as the securities regulator, and private entities such as the stock exchange and other private associations. In France and Switzerland, private entities are the custodians, whereas in Spain a public entity assumes that role. Who is best situated to be the custodian of such codes?

3.6 EU Law and Corporate Governance

Although there is no company law at the EU level, with each member state enacting its own corporate and other business laws, the European Commission regularly issues directives on a range of corporate governance issues. These are intended to harmonize company law and corporate governance and create minimum standards throughout the EU. In addition to such binding directives, the European Commission also produces recommendations and research that is intended to influence member states and contribute to further harmonization of EU practices.

Relevant directives in the corporate governance area include the following:

1. Shareholder rights – Directive 2007/36/EC (on certain shareholder rights for listed companies, such as timely access to information on shareholder general meetings).
2. Takeover bids – Directive 2004/25/EC (minimum rules for changes of control).
3. Capital requirements for financial institutions – Directive 2013/36/EU.
4. Transparency/disclosure – Directive 2013/34/EU (requires, inter alia, EU listed companies to file annual corporate governance statement).

In addition to the above, there are directives in related areas such as accounting standards and recommendations and studies on directors, employee share ownership, and remuneration policies. A number of German companies, for instance, have chosen to convert their legal form to a Societas Europaea (SE), which allows a one-tier board and reduced labor representation.

Horst Eidenmüller, Lars Hornuf, and Markus Reps, 'Contracting Employee Involvement: An Analysis of Bargaining Over Employee Involvement Rules for a Societas Europaea' (2012) 12 *Journal of Corporate Legal Studies* 201, at 201

Since 2004, businesses in Europe have the opportunity to incorporate as a European Company (Societas Europaea, hereinafter SE). After a slow start, the SE has become fairly popular. By the end of 2010, approximately 700 SEs had been incorporated, mostly in Germany and the Czech Republic … Clearly important are certain governance features of the SE such as the option available to founders to choose between a one-tier and a two-tier corporate structure. Another relevant governance feature is the SE regime on employee involvement. In many Member States of the European Union, some form of employee involvement in the management of public corporations is mandatory … In Germany, for example, one-third (one-third participation) and even 50 percent (parity co-determination) of the supervisory board members of a joint stock corporation (Aktiengesellschaft) must be employee representatives if the firm employs more than 500 and 2,000 workers, respectively. Now, if such a company merges with a company from another European Member State and forms an SE, under the applicable European rules, negotiations on the employee involvement regime must take place, and shareholders/management may strike a bargain with labour on a new regime that may well look very different from the one in place before the transaction. Hence, the SE is based on freedom of contract with respect to a fundamental corporate governance feature, namely employee involvement in the management of the firm …

It appears that creative agreements on consultation and information rights are widespread, indicating severe inefficiencies of the legal status quo with respect to such rights. Agreements on participation rights that depart from the status quo are rarely concluded. However, the evidence does not suggest that this is because the existing regime is optimal. Rather, endowment effects and reputation costs play an important role: trading participation rights for other benefits is an anathema for employee representatives as they perceive such trade as a dramatic loss that must be avoided. Conversely, shareholders and management refrain from pressing for such trades, as curbing employee participation rights, even by agreement, would be perceived as a signal detrimental to firm value by the general public, i.e. imposing a significant reputational sanction on the firm.

Notes and Questions

1. How might the European Commission affect corporate governance in Europe? Should it contribute to greater harmonization? If so, how should this be accomplished?
2. European companies (SEs) are registered under the corporate law of the EU rather than under the law of a particular member state. Their number has continued to increase, reaching nearly 3,000 by early 2018. Does it surprise you that when German-based businesses become SEs they generally do not change requirements under German law for a two-tier board and labor co-determination? One of the advantages of the SE form is that it generally becomes easier for a business to expand and restructure (including through acquisition or merger) in other EU member states.

3.7 Recent Developments

European companies have not been immune to corporate governance problems. Major companies have been embroiled in bribery schemes, spying on board members, accounting fraud, and skirting environmental regulations.

3.7.1 Scandals

Richard Milne, 'Siemens Woes Show VW a Route out of Trouble,' *Financial Times* (October 14, 2015)

For Volkswagen in 2015, read Siemens in 2007. The similarities and differences between the VW emissions scandal and the bribery affair that shook Siemens, Europe's largest engineering group, almost a decade ago point to how events may turn out at the German carmaker.

Siemens, which makes everything from trains to gas turbines, was emerging from a deep restructuring at the end of 2006 under Klaus Kleinfeld, its ambitious chief executive, when the first bribery allegations surfaced.

Mr Kleinfeld engaged Debevoise & Plimpton, a US law firm, to conduct an internal investigation. The allegations soon led to the exposure of a systemic approach to bribery across continents involving hundreds of millions of euros, shaking the company and German industry.

By April 2007, the position of Heinrich von Pierer, Siemens' chief executive during most of the bribery period and then its supervisory board chairman, had become untenable and he was ousted. Days later, Mr Kleinfeld followed him, pushed out by the board. Neither man was suspected of, nor charged with, any wrongdoing.

But unlike VW, which turned to insiders to replace its chief executive and chairman in the past month, Siemens appointed outsiders to both posts for the first time in its 168-year history.

Peter Löscher, the new chief executive, and Gerhard Cromme, the chairman, wasted no time in tackling the culture at Siemens and negotiating a settlement with regulators, especially in the US. That led to fines of more than $1bn. "We could only have achieved all this, and convinced the US regulators, with new blood," says a senior director from that period.

VW has instead turned to company veterans to deal with a potentially far bigger scandal, with analysts estimating that fines, repairs and lawsuit damages could cost Europe's largest carmaker in the range of $20bn–$50bn.

Matthias Müller, VW's new chief executive, was the carmaker's head of product management and general representative during the crucial years of 2007–10 while Hans Dieter Pötsch, since last week the chairman of the supervisory board, was finance director for 12 years from 2003.

At Siemens, Mr Löscher sought to implement a culture of zero tolerance for corruption with a clear-out of senior executives, the addition of a US lawyer to the management board and even legal action against some former managers.

Mr Müller has also pledged to change VW's culture, which under Martin Winterkorn, his predecessor, seemed to become something akin to a "dictatorship," several executives say. The new chief executive has told workers that he welcomes open discussion and differences of opinion.

But there are doubts that VW's culture can be so easily changed. Unusually, it is run as an informal partnership between management, workers and local politicians (local government holds a fifth of VW's voting shares and two board seats).

The result is that German jobs are protected, particularly in the main plant in Wolfsburg, VW's home town. Productivity and efficiency lag well behind rivals; Toyota produces as many cars as VW with half the employees. "For real change at VW, you have to dismantle this system and I see no real desire for that," says a former supervisory board member. "As long as you have this nexus of workers, politicians and managers, I think VW will be dysfunctional." He points to scandals at VW over purchasing in 1993 and bribery in 2005.

In some ways, VW has followed Siemens' lead, immediately hiring Jones Day, the US law firm, to conduct an internal investigation into the cheating of US emissions tests. In others, VW has responded far quicker than other companies, removing Mr Winterkorn within a week rather than the months required at Siemens.

Siemens' approach was not entirely successful: Mr Löscher was later ejected as chief executive after a long series of operational mishaps. But the Siemens experience shows that outsiders can be more credible in leading a clean-up. VW's record of three scandals in 22 years suggests it needs to do something different.

3.7.2 Board Diversity and Quotas

Board members in European corporations generally remain male and local. Few are run by foreigners, even at the most multinational firms. The trend, however, is for European boards to incorporate greater gender diversity and internationalization. Starting with Norway in 2003, a host of European countries began to require or recommend the appointment of women on boards. Spain followed in 2007, then Belgium, France, Italy, and the Netherlands in 2011, and Germany in 2016. As of January 2017, the mandated quotas are 40 percent in France, 33 percent in Belgium and Italy, and 30 percent in Germany, while voluntary best practices are 30 percent for the Netherlands and Spain. Countries have different methods of handling non-compliance, with France and Norway, for instance, imposing fines.

The mandatory quotas have led to a sharp increase in the gender diversity of boards across Europe. In large companies, the portion of women has almost doubled from 2011 to 2016. In particular, Norway, Sweden, France, and Finland have the highest percentage with over 30 percent of their board seats held by women. Women occupy roughly one-quarter of board seats in Belgium, Denmark, Italy, and the Netherlands. The number of women serving as chairs of the board or CEOs, however, remains significantly lower.

Without a mandatory quota, it has been suggested that the inertia for all-male boards is too strong for internal reform. The UK, which follows a comply-or-explain approach, has achieved considerable progress but less than one-quarter of board seats are occupied by women, placing it on the lower end among European countries. Furthermore, Switzerland, like the US, is one of the few Western countries where best practices do not even exist, and it has the lowest percentage among major European countries. Sweden and Finland, on the other hand, do not even have any specific targets, but still have among the highest proportion of women on boards.

Some evidence suggests that mandating gender diversity has forced boards to improve their overall appointment process for directors by placing it on a more professional basis. A 2006 Harvard Business Review study also found that for gender diversity to be meaningful, a board needed to have three or more women members for significant change to occur.

Notes and Questions

1. How were the corporate governance problems at Siemens and Volkswagen different? Are Anglo-American governance scandals different from European ones?
2. Should countries adopt quotas to spur the appointment of women to boards? Does diversity improve board performance? Some evidence shows that boards that lack diversity have greater corporate governance problems. Does this matter or is diversity important as a social goal in itself?
3. Should gender diversity be required or should it be promoted on a comply-or-explain basis? If companies are mandated to appoint women, what would prevent this from appearing as tokenism or resulting in appointment of a less qualified person based on gender? Should other aspects of diversity be considered such as ethnicity, race, religion, profession, and age?

List of Statutes and Regulators

France

Code de Commerce (2016)
Code monétaire et financier (2014)
Corporate Governance Code of Listed Companies
Autorité des marchés financiers
Euronext Paris

Germany

Commercial Code (2016)
Stock Corporation Act (Aktiengesetz, AktG) (2016)
Securities Trading Act (2016)
German Corporate Governance Code
Federal Office of Justice
Federal Financial Supervisory Authority
Deutsche Börse

Italy

Civil Code (2016)
Consolidated Law on Finance (2016)
Corporate Governance Code
Commissione Nazionale per le Società e la Borsa
Borsa Italiana

Netherlands

Netherlands Civil Code
Act on Financial Supervisions (2016)
Act on the Supervision of Financial Reporting (2015)
Dutch Corporate Governance Code
Netherlands Authority for the Financial Markets
Euronext Amsterdam

Spain

Capital Company Act (2014)

Securities Market Law (2015)

Good Governance Code of Listed Companies

National Securities Market Commission

Bolsas y Mercados Espanoles

Switzerland

The Code of Obligations (2016)

Stock Exchange Act (2013)

Regulations of the Swiss Stock Exchange (2014)

Swiss Code of Best Practice for Corporate Governance

Swiss Financial Supervisory Authority

Swiss Exchange Regulation

SIX Swiss Exchange

4

GLOBAL THEORIES

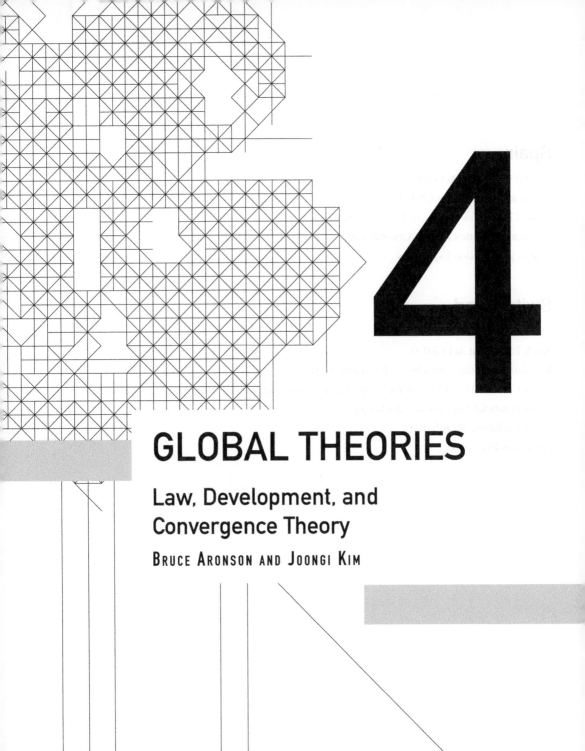

Law, Development, and Convergence Theory

BRUCE ARONSON AND JOONGI KIM

4.1 Introduction

Providing a theoretical framework to analyze corporate governance, particularly from a comparative perspective, has been an evolving challenge. While certain common themes exist, scholars from a wide variety of disciplines ranging from law, finance, business, and sociology have attempted to provide a broader perspective by which to understand comparative corporate governance. Numerous provocative theories have emerged.

First, as governments seek to bolster the growth of capital markets to promote economic development, the role of law in developing deep, liquid capital markets has become a hotly debated topic. One of the more controversial theories that emerged stressed the importance of the law in providing adequate investor protection, which was considered a critical precondition for developing capital markets marked by dispersed ownership. It was further argued not only that the law mattered but that the legal origins of a country particularly mattered. According to this argument, the characteristics of the common law tradition, as represented by the US and UK, provided a superior environment for capital market development compared with civil law countries such as Germany or France. Common law countries with their stronger investor protections offered a better form of corporate governance that would also contribute to higher corporate valuations.

If the law plays such an important role, then the next question concerned the extent to which legal features from one country can be successfully transplanted into another. Whether and how law could be transplanted into a country with a different sociopolitical history, ownership structure, regulatory system, courts, rule of law, and social values became a focus. Whether cross-border legal transplants were sustainable followed as the next challenge.

This recent research, referred to as the "law and finance" literature, has been both highly influential and controversial. Its leading proponents, four economists (LaPorta et al.), are often referred to by their initials "LLSV." Their research has had a wide-ranging effect on global economic development. One notable impact was at institutions such as the World Bank, which utilized this approach in designing their Ease of Doing Business rankings. What type of strategies should be pursued by developing Asian economies that feature concentrated ownership and family control? The impact of the law in improving corporate governance and leading to capital markets development became an important topic to be explored.

Another central debate concerned whether convergence toward a single system was occurring. In 2001, Professors Henry Hansmann and Reinier Kraakman first put forward a highly provocative hypothesis when they suggested an "End of History" in corporate law under which the shareholder primacy model had prevailed. All other systems, they argued, were converging toward this model. Corporate law's fate was akin to Francis Fukuyama's proclamation following the breakup of the Soviet Union and the end of the Cold War that an "End of History" had occurred in political economy such that liberal capitalist democracy had prevailed over socialism. Globalization, harmonization, and capital contributed to an inevitable convergence to a shareholder-oriented model of corporate governance.

Criticism against the legal origins and law matters theory and convergence theory abounds. Some argue that due to different social and political histories, corporate governance evolves differently in various countries. Such a background creates a path-dependent framework in which countries are inextricably embedded. While pressures might exist, and some degree of convergence might occur at the periphery, deep convergence to a single type of corporate governance model was not possible. Others might argue that convergence, particularly toward shareholder primacy, should not be pursued and should be resisted.

This chapter provides background on global theories of corporate governance. It first analyzes the debate surrounding whether law, culture, political history, markets, or legal origins matter more in determining a country's corporate governance. It then explores whether corporate governance is converging and, if so, to what extent.

4.2 Does Law Matter?

Brian R. Cheffins, 'Dividends as a Substitute for Corporate Law: The Separation of Ownership and Control in the United Kingdom' 63 *Washington and Lee Law Review* 1273 (2006), at 1274–80

As the twentieth century drew to a close, corporate law scholarship "found the market" as "contractarian" analysis became the dominant mode of analysis. A key underlying presumption of this economically oriented school of thought was that market dynamics define primarily how directors, shareholders, and others associated with companies interact. Corporate law, the thinking went, had only a supplementary and supportive role to play, namely facilitating efficient contracting. No sooner had legal academics started to push law to the margins when economists began to assert that the extent to which law provides protection for investors is a key determinant of the configuration of corporate governance structures around the world. The claim made was that the "quality" of corporate and securities law does much to determine whether a country will have strong securities markets and a corporate economy dominated by firms with widely dispersed share ownership.

The "law matters" thesis economists have advanced has important normative implications because it suggests countries will not develop a robust stock market or escape from potentially backward family capitalism unless laws are in place that provide suitable protection for investors. Not surprisingly, the thesis has attracted much attention from legal academics. But is "investor friendly" corporate and securities law in fact a necessary condition for a country to develop strong securities markets and a corporate economy where large firms are generally widely held? ...

II. The "Law Matters" Thesis

A. The Theory

Currently, a widely held belief is that corporate law – the rules governing the rights and duties of directors, senior executives, and shareholders – is a variable that does much to explain how strong securities markets and diffuse share ownership can emerge in the face of possible rent extraction, information asymmetries, and the potential inefficiencies of family-oriented management. The basic logic underlying the law matters thesis is that where corporate law is deficient, potential outside investors will be hesitant about buying shares because of fear that corporate "insiders" (large shareholders and/or senior executives) will skim or squander firm profits. Corporate insiders, being aware of such scepticism, will refrain from using the stock market to exit and will opt instead to retain the potentially ample private benefits of control available due to weak regulation. The widely held corporation will therefore not become dominant, regardless of whatever inherent economic virtues it might offer.

The law matters thesis implies that things might well unfold differently if a country has "quality" corporate law. Outside investors, cognizant that the law constrains rent extraction by corporate insiders, will be reassured about the logic of owning tiny holdings in publicly traded companies. Concomitantly, controlling shareholders, aware that the law largely precludes them from exploiting their position, will be favourably disposed towards unwinding their holdings.

Securities law and, more precisely, disclosure regulation are also potentially important. In an unregulated environment, by virtue of information asymmetries, potential investors may well shun corporate equity because they cannot distinguish "high-quality" companies from their less meritorious counterparts. With compulsory disclosure rules in place, investors will find it easier to separate the good firms from the "lemons." As deserving companies begin to receive support from the market, they will begin to carry out public offerings with increasing regularity. As the process continues, a country's securities market will become stronger, and a suitable economic platform will have been established to allow the widely held company to become dominant.

Disclosure regulation can also potentially help to foster ownership dispersion by encouraging dominant shareholders to exit. If the law requires substantial transparency, the odds of detection of improper diversion of corporate assets grow. If corporate insiders are in fact discovered exploiting minority shareholders, adverse publicity, lawsuits, and regulatory sanctions could follow. Apprehension about such outcomes should discourage dominant shareholders from extracting private benefits of control and lead them to contemplate unwinding their holdings.

The law matters thesis offers a message that policymakers potentially ignore at their peril: Countries will struggle to reach their full economic potential unless laws that protect minority shareholders are in place. America's rich and deep securities markets are frequently cited as a key source of innovation and economic dynamism. The law matters thesis suggests that such benefits are only likely to be secured if the correct regulatory environment is in place. Leading proponents of the law matters thesis have acted as consultants for the International Monetary Fund and the World Bank, which in turn have promoted corporate law reform globally with a particular emphasis on protection of minority shareholders. The message has seemingly been heard by policymakers, because governments around the world over the past decade have been strengthening regulations affecting outside investors.

Stephen J. Choi, 'Law and Finance Lessons?' (2008) 22 *Journal of Money and Finance* 29, 70–1, 82–3

V. Preconditions for Strong Investor Protections

A variety of methods are available to countries seeking to improve their investor protections. Countries can improve their securities disclosure and liability laws, focus on specific acts of expropriation such as financial tunneling, reduce the level of red-tape in their business regulations, employ alternative means of monitoring managers and controlling shareholders, and so on.

One approach would be simply to pick and choose among various potential determinative factors that may lead to greater financial development. However, the best approach for a particular country may vary with country-specific factors …

Academic studies confirm the importance of determining the precise laws that will work in a specific country context. Berkowitz, Pistor, and Richard (2003) (BPR) conduct a study on the importance of path dependence in laws. They divide LLSV (1998)'s sample of 49 countries into non-transplant countries (including countries that received their law through a transplant but followed an idiosyncratic development such as the United States) and transplant countries … They report that the coefficients on all the transplant variables except for the direct-receptive transplant dummy variable were negative and significant, consistent with the hypothesis that indirect and unreceptive transplants result in a lower level of legality.

What are the preconditions for a country's regulatory system to commit to protecting investors? Countries may not have the ability to change their legal origin, past status as colonies, or initial endowments or geographical location. However, countries do have the ability to change other factors that may prove even more determinative of long-term financial development and economic growth.

One important and endogenous factor within countries is the internal support among interest groups within the country in favor of investor protections. Internal support increases the probability that formal investor protection laws will work in practice to protect investors. How can a country improve the internal support for investor protections? While there are no easy answers …

VI. Conclusion

The law matters. If nothing else, the law and finance literature reinforces an intuitive but nonetheless important point: providing strong investor protections is important to get investors to part with their money and to pay more for company securities. Investors without adequate protections will either eschew investments or demand high discounts upfront to compensate for the prospective losses from managerial or controlling shareholder opportunism …

The LLSV line of papers is not the only evidence that the law matters. Companies (at least prior to the Sarbanes–Oxley Act) routinely chose to issue securities in the U.S. in part to obtain the benefits of a higher regulatory regime. Similarly, companies in countries weaker investor protections faced large discounts for their securities prices. Perhaps the law matters – just not the specific laws on which LLSV focus …

Rather than attempt to discern the precise elements of the law that matters – which may vary based on country-specific and institution-specific factors – this paper instead asks how countries may structure their law-making institutions to orient themselves toward providing investor protections. At least two avenues of reform are available to a country interesting in restructuring their institutions toward investor protection. First, countries may seek to affect their internal interest group dynamics. Reducing the power of domestic conglomerates, opening up a country to more trade flow and outside financial investment are all methods of increasing the constituencies within a country in favor of stronger investor protections. Second, countries may affect the incentives of their regulators directly. Regulators in a monopoly position may choose to enjoy their monopoly, extracting rents from shareholders and encouraging rent-seeking behavior by firms. Regulators facing some degree of competition may respond with greater attentiveness to investor needs. Providing regulatory choices for issuers and investors may also lessen the opposition of private interest groups (such as controlling shareholders) against reform; only those issuers that desire stronger protections may opt for a high investor protection choice.

Simply transplanting laws from one country to another often does not work. Achieving internal support for investor protections is an important factor in increasing the receptiveness of a country to new laws to protect investors, increasing the likelihood of effective enforcement and greater financial development. Once committed to investor protection, policymakers within countries will have the information and expertise to determine what aspects of the law are best suited to protect investor in their own country-specific situation.

Notes and Questions

1. Does the law matter in creating dispersed ownership and deeper liquid capital markets?
2. How does law matter? How important is the role of the law in investor protection? How important is investor protection? If someone asked your opinion on what factors are important for economic development in transitional economies, what factors would you cite? Would legal protection of minority investors be high on your list?
3. If the law is important, how is it important? Is it an important aid in attracting foreign capital? Does development in transitional economies depend on attracting foreign capital?
4. What should Asian countries do? How should they utilize the law? What type of legal strategies should they develop? Are legal protections for minority investors more important for domestic investors in a transitional economy or for foreign investors? Do their interests coincide?
5. Are market forces more important than law in creating better corporate governance? Under the efficient market hypothesis, the stock price of a company represents the most accurate, real-time measure of the value of a company. The stock price serves as the most powerful form of discipline and incentive for corporations. Other markets include the market for corporate control, market for CEOs and senior executives, market for products and services, and market for open free and fair trade competition across borders (see also Table 2.2).
6. Should governments take a more laissez-faire, market-driven approach or interventionist law-based approach to improve corporate governance? Does it matter if the country is an emerging or advanced economy?

4.3 Legal Origins: Common Law versus Civil Law

David Cabrelli and Mathias Siems, 'Convergence, Legal Origins, and Transplants in Comparative Corporate Law: A Case-Based and Quantitative Analysis' (2015) 63 *American Journal of Comparative Law* 109, 117–22

C. Legal Origins and Related Taxonomies

The core idea of legal families is that the diversity of legal systems around the world is not random but that groups of countries share common features in terms of legal history, legal thinking, and positive rules. Particular relevance is attributed to the distinction between common and civil law countries: common law and civil law are said to "constitute the basic building blocks of the legal order," and this distinction is also seen as the "most fundamental and most discussed issue in comparative law."

In particular, common law and civil law are said to differ in their relevant sources of law and legal methods. In the civil law, the main source of law is statute law, underpinned by academic writings. The main pieces of legislation are "codes," which provide a logical, systematic, and coherent set of rules to be applied by judges in a deductive and legalistic way. The common law, by contrast, is at its core case law: the judiciary reason inductively from case to case, paying close attention to the facts and remaining constantly aware that such reasoning is not strictly logical but is also based on common sense. Thus, in the common law, not only do the judiciary aim to solve individual disputes, but their decisions are a means of developing the law "from below," with previous judgments acting as precedents, some of which will be binding in future cases; hence, the common law is sometimes said to have an advantage in terms of adaptability. Common law judges are also said to be more prepared to display judicial creativity and are praised for being "market-wise," for instance, in guaranteeing "freedom of contract."

Meanwhile, judges in civil law countries are said to reason very differently …

By marrying the "legal families" approach with comparative corporate law, a particular variant of the former – referred to as the "legal origins" theorem in shorthand – has gained a considerable degree of currency, occupying vital territory in the field of comparative law. The principal contention advanced by the "legal origins" theorem was propounded in a series of articles penned by Rafael La Porta and colleagues … La Porta et al. found that corporate law regimes grounded in the tradition of the common law were more protective of shareholders than civilian systems:

> Compared to French civil law, common law is associated with (a) better investor protection, which in turn is associated with improved financial development, better access to finance, and higher ownership dispersion (b) lighter government ownership and regulation, which are in turn associated with less corruption, better functioning labor markets, and smaller unofficial economies, and (c) less formalized and more independent judicial systems, which are in turn associated with more secure property rights and better contract enforcement.

The argument posits that the direct correlation between regimes which protect shareholders and the sophistication of the state of the capital markets and financial development of a jurisdiction means that civil law countries suffer from a weaker level of stock market development. This has developed into a highly influential body of academic literature, particularly via the *Doing Business* reports of the World Bank. The ascendancy of the common law position is said to be attributable to a low level of government ownership and regulation of corporations, less formalized judicial procedures, and the emphasis it attaches to the reasoned and incremental development of corporate law through a highly independent judiciary. Common law regimes are cast as pursuing a market-based approach, where the shareholder's individual interests are to the fore. Moreover, in these countries, capital markets are seen as more developed, so that interest in shares is broader and shareholder ownership is often dispersed. In civil law countries, by contrast, concentrated ownership structures mostly prevail in publicly traded companies. Since management cooperates with the dominant shareholders, relations within the company are more important than control through the markets. This "insider model" is to be explained by the fact that banks and employees hold a strong position. The firm is accordingly run not primarily in the interests of shareholders, but in the interests of all stakeholders in the undertaking. In these countries too, state influence has a large part to play, so that political views are brought to bear inside the companies.

Further distinctions are frequently made. For instance, since the category of non-Anglo-Saxon countries is very broad, it is suggested that one must distinguish between German, Latin (in the sense of the Romance language countries, i.e. Italy, France, Spain, etc.), and Japanese (or Asian) models of corporate governance. In this vein, for example, it may be said that only the German model tends to present a mandatory division between the management and supervisory board, that the Latin and Japanese models are more network-oriented than the German model, and that stock markets are more important in the German and Japanese models than in the Latin model. Another distinction is between the corporate law and corporate governance systems of developed, developing, and transition economies …

The "legal origins" theorem has generated a great deal of controversy. The critiques vary from concerns about the failure of the theory to consider the political determinants of corporate law and corporate governance systems to the adequacy of the methodological approach adopted by La Porta et al. and the assumptions that underpin the conclusions drawn from the empirical results. For example, on the political front, Mark Roe refers to the tendency of governments of a "left-wing" social democratic hue to favor the interests of labor over capital; in such systems, the government eschews corporate laws protecting shareholders as a class in order to prioritize the demands of labor, which leads to greater conflicts between the interests of shareholders and directors/managers. The resulting greater opportunities for vertical agency costs are attributable to the policy preferences of those "left-wing" governments with a social democratic tradition.

Turning to the methodological deficiencies … Studies conducted on the basis of longitudinal time-series coding systems have demonstrated that the evidence for a correlation between legal origins and stock market development is much more tenuous. Moreover, these studies revealed that the level of shareholder protection in civil law regimes has been catching up with common law jurisdictions in recent years. Subsequent research has also identified many coding errors, and when the index is recalibrated to remove them, the correlations found by La Porta et al. simply disappear … Since countries of the same legal origin are often neighboring countries with a similar culture, La Porta et al.'s results may simply show that geographic vicinity and a common culture make it likely that the laws of two countries influence each other. In itself, such a conclusion appears entirely unremarkable. Moreover, historical linkages between countries may have become weaker as a consequence of the convergence of legal and economic systems. Turning to the criticism of the assumptions underpinning the findings reached by La Porta et al., Katharina Pistor propounds three fallacies which lie at the heart of the "legal origins" theorem. First, there is the "extrapolation fallacy" – the unsubstantiated assertion that common law systems with stronger legal protections for shareholders invariably incentivize smaller investors to save their money in shares, leading to a broader investor base and greater capital market development. Second, Pistor advances the "transmission problem," which criticizes the supposed unidirectional impact of legal origin on specific legal provisions in regulations, statutes, and case law, and on more efficient economic outcomes.

Among the multiple factors that contribute to a country's financial development, the importance of the law has been underappreciated. At the same time, many believe that the importance has been overstated.

Stephen J. Choi, 'Law and Finance Lessons?' (2008) 22 *Journal of Money & Finance* 29, 46

In sum, legal origin has a robust correlation with financial and economic development. The robustness of this relationship, however, does not mean that other factors are also not as or more important for development. Studies indicate that initial colonial endowments, ethnolinguistic heterogeneity, and culture may also have correlate with the level of economic development in a country. Moreover, the causal relationship between legal origin and development – while plausible – is not definitive. As a theoretical matter, the differences in the amount of governmental intervention between common law and civil law systems may be overstated. The U.S. employs large statutory regimes (e.g., federal securities regulation) and very interventionist laws (e.g., Sarbanes–Oxley Act). Other factors may also correlate with legal origin that explain much of the variation in the level of development for countries. The importance of legal origin from a policy maker's perspective is also likely overstated.

Notes and Questions

1. What role does "legal origins" play in any country's corporate governance?
2. Does the common law tradition marked by strong investor protections explain the dispersed ownership in the US and UK and the development of capital markets? Should developing countries consciously aim to develop a system of dispersed share ownership rather than concentrated share ownership? Do courts generally protect investors better than legislators, who may be more concerned about redistribution of resources? What about regulators? Is self-regulation by the industry preferred?
3. What is the most effective way for developing countries in Asia, most of which have concentrated ownership, to pursue dispersion and financial market development? Stronger corporate governance? Should the emphasis be investor protection, disclosure, enforcement, "comply or explain," self-regulation, gatekeepers, oversight of controlling owners, stronger boards, or a corporate control market? A hybrid?
4. Should the government take a more interventionist approach or market-driven approach?

4.4 Transplantation to Improve Corporate Governance

Some argue that legal features from one jurisdiction can be selected and then transplanted into other jurisdictions. Legal features are viewed as being fungible and can grow anywhere and are not climate or environment specific. This theory propounds that countries can improve and develop the ideal corporate governance through an ideal mix of transplants.

David Cabrelli and Mathias Siems, 'Convergence, Legal Origins, and Transplants in Comparative Corporate Law: A Case-Based and Quantitative Analysis' (2015) 63 *American Journal of Comparative Law* 109, 124–5

The "legal transplants" theory asserts that it is "socially easy" to lift a rule or system of law from one jurisdiction to another. The theory was developed by Alan Watson in his studies on Roman law. The underlying point made by Watson, which is significant for the case-based project adopted here, is that law is an autonomous phenomenon and can be divorced from the social, cultural, economic, and political background within which it operates. Instead, the legal tradition, rather than those contextual factors, is more important in determining whether the adoption of a particular rule or body of law by one particular legal system from another (a) ought to be pursued in normative terms and (b) will be successful. For that reason, Watson rejects the contention that contextual features ought to be given wider consideration prior to any legal borrowing for fear that the recipient legal system will reject the transplant.

This point is developed further by Roger Cotterrell, who draws a distinction between instrumental law and culturally based law. Unlike family law, which is conditioned by a jurisdiction's social and cultural context, and constitutional and administrative law, which are shaped by its political culture, Cotterrell argues that company and commercial law are relatively culturally neutral in nature, since such laws are inextricably linked to "economic interests rather than national customs or sentiments." For that reason, corporate laws are more easily transplantable than family or succession laws …

However, not all scholars are convinced by Watson's theory. The skeptics can be grouped into two camps, namely the contextualists and the culturalists. First, the contextualists reject the idea that law is an exogenous phenomenon and will be accepted by a host jurisdiction irrespective of its culture and context. For example, Otto Kahn-Freund takes the position that "any attempt to use a pattern of law outside the environment of its original country entails a risk of rejection … [and] its use requires a knowledge not only of the foreign law but also of its social and above all political contexts." The difference between the contextualists and the culturalists is a matter of degree, since the latter take the more extreme position that the notion of legal transplants should be rejected outright. The leading proponent of the culturalist argument is Pierre Legrand, who asserts that "[i]n any meaningful sense of the term, 'legal transplants' … cannot happen." Here the argument is that once received, a rule or system of law is no longer comparable to its original incarnation in the home jurisdiction. Instead, the form and style of the rule or system of law is refined and shaped by the local context, environment, and culture to the extent that it no longer makes sense to talk of the subject of study as a "legal transplant."

Notes and Questions

1. Can corporate law features be transplanted into other countries successfully? What type of features would be more successful than others? What kind of difficulties may arise? Are economic and commercial legal strategies and policy instruments such as corporate law-related features more transplantable?
2. If a country adopts class actions, for instance, does this mean it will work absent a strong private enforcement culture, a capable plaintiff bar and judiciary, and contingency fees?
3. What type of features should Asian jurisdictions seek to transplant? What would be most important and effective? Global institutional investors, centered in the US and the UK, have consistently pressured Asian companies to require independent directors. Is that a corporate governance feature that is likely to work in Asia in the same way as in the US and the UK?

4.5 The Convergence Debate

Another debate surrounds whether corporate governance is in a process of convergence. If convergence is occurring, to what degree? Is it toward a shareholder-oriented model? *Should* corporate governance converge? For all countries? If convergence is occurring, what should countries in Asia do to prepare themselves? Is it functional convergence or formal convergence of corporate law?

Henry Hansmann, 'How Close Is the End of History?' (2006) 31 *Journal of Corporation Law* 745, 745–9

I. Introduction

At the same time, I confess to some hesitancy in returning to The End of History. That essay was written to capture, a bit provocatively, a particular perspective in a debate on convergence in corporate law that was just then gathering steam. It's been fairly successful in that respect. I'm concerned that any effort to amplify or qualify the piece might spoil the role it's come to play. Nevertheless, I'll take the risk and try to offer some further perspective on it ... There are, in fact, at least three different types of claims that our End of History essay might be interpreted as making. I'll label them the normative claim, the efficiency claim, and the factual claim. I'll take them in turn, offering a few thoughts about the content and credibility of each.

II. The Normative Claim

The strongest and clearest claim we make in the essay is a normative or ideological claim. It states that there is increasing consensus among the relevant actors, around the globe, that what we term the "standard shareholder-oriented model" of the business corporation is the most attractive social ideal for the organization of large-scale enterprise.

"Compared to what?" is the obvious question. The Article here sets a limited, but not trivial, standard: compared to (1) a state-oriented model (2) a labor- (or, more broadly, stakeholder-) oriented model, and (3) a manager-oriented model.

By that standard, the normative claim is holding up extremely well. For example, in Japan, long a standard-bearer for the state-oriented model, the Ministry of Economy, Trade, and Industry has just released a "Corporate Value Study" proposing guidelines for takeover defensive tactics that are based on the "corporate value standard" and "the interests of shareholders as a whole," and that are explicitly patterned on Delaware law. In Germany, once the most prominent advocate of the labor-oriented model, we now see academic commentary critical of codetermination as reducing shareholder value. And in the U.S., home of the managerial model, the focus everywhere is on increasing the accountability of officers to corporate boards and the accountability of boards to shareholders.

To be sure, there continues to emanate, particularly from continental Western Europe, a broad disquiet about the standard shareholder-oriented model. The perceived problem, at its core, seems to be that this model gives excessive rein to market forces in general – in the share market, the labor market, the product market, and elsewhere – and that the result is excessive social instability. In part, this seems just protectionist pleading for special interests, favoring workers who have jobs over those who do not, favoring shareholders who hold controlling interests over those who do not, and so forth. To that extent, these concerns are unlikely to maintain broad normative appeal, but rather will be accepted sooner or later as no more than window dressing for continued favoritism toward entrenched interests.

But this disquiet may also reflect a broader concern about social efficiency. For many individuals, social stability may have sufficient value to merit the sacrifice of a substantial amount of productivity as measured, as it conventionally is, in terms of the net value of market transactions. If so, the legitimacy of the standard shareholder-oriented model may suffer in the long term, however much it may be in ascendance now. To probe this possibility a bit deeper, we must turn to the efficiency claim.

III. The Efficiency Claim

The efficiency claim holds that the standard shareholder-oriented model is the most efficient way to organize large-scale industry, and will remain so for as far as we can see. Can the efficiency claim be false if the normative claim is true, even if, for want of a better measure, we take (Kaldor–Hicks) social efficiency as our rough normative standard? The answer could be yes, if the current normative culture is mistaken about what is efficient. Of course, as suggested at the end of the previous section, if that is the case, then the current normative consensus may not be long-lived: we may all agree today that we have reached the end of history normatively, but someday, when we understand the facts better, we are going to change our minds, and the endpoint of history will recede into the distance.

The End of History was a bit cautious about pressing the efficiency claim. It implied, however, that there were good reasons to accept that claim. One reason was survival: firms, and societies, organized along the standard shareholder-oriented model seemed to be outcompeting those that were organized differently. Other reasons went more to logic, and to experience, with particular components of competing models. First, parliamentary institutions behave poorly with respect to markets in aggregating the preferences of a heterogeneous group. Voting control over a firm must therefore be confined to a highly homogeneous group. This makes sharing of voting control between investors of capital and other stakeholders very costly. Second, fiduciary rules are even less suitable as a means of achieving a workable balance between conflicting interests. Hence, imposing affirmative fiduciary duties on management to protect the interests of two or more groups simultaneously is unworkable. Third, thoroughly entrenched managers will too often mismanage or over-invest. Fourth, it is not possible to have state control without imposing on the corporation various objectives that are unrelated to productive efficiency. Since nothing in the foreseeable future seems likely to change these constraints on the organizational forms that are productively efficient, the principal competitors to the standard shareholder-oriented model will remain badly handicapped.

The most serious argument against the efficiency claim has a broader basis, however. As suggested in the previous section, the argument is that the standard shareholder-oriented model involves too steep a tradeoff between material prosperity and social order. It may be fine for Americans, who are intensely individualistic and place an exceptionally strong value on personal liberty. But for other societies, including Western Europe, that place a higher value on stability, the market forces unleashed by the standard shareholder-oriented model may be excessively corrosive of personal expectations and social relations. It is not crazy to feel that a leisurely daily walk to a dependable workplace in the well-preserved medieval city of one's birth is preferable to lower prices on MP3 players. If the current organization of business in a given society perpetuates the dominant role of workers, powerful families, managers, or the state, that may be seen not as a vice but as a virtue – a workable means of reinforcing the society's legitimate structure of authority. It is from this perspective that the end of history claim is weakest.

IV. The Factual Claim

The factual claim holds that, whatever may be the case with respect to ideology and efficiency, practice and law are, as a matter of fact, converging on the standard shareholder-oriented model. Our article implied that the factual claim was true, but carefully avoided offering any timeframe for future convergence.

As it happens, convergence in fact has proceeded quite quickly in the few years since we wrote – even faster than we might have predicted if we'd been so adventurous as to try. Major corporate jurisdictions have adopted a wide range of shareholder-oriented corporate reforms, including stronger public and private enforcement, stricter controls on market manipulation and insider trading, improved disclosure, regulation of both affirmative and defensive tactics in takeovers, and limitations on unequal voting structures. The interesting question here is not whether there is convergence toward the standard shareholder-oriented model, but rather how far it will go and how long it will persist.

Surely the corporate reforms that we see are driven in substantial part by the particular international economic and political context of the past two decades, which is characterized by strong international capital markets ... We've been here before, namely in the decades before the First World War. Those were, in fact, the decades in which the joint stock company, in the same basic form as we know it today, came to be the standard form of organization for large-scale enterprise in all major economies. As Rajan and Zingales have emphasized, war and depression subsequently led to substantial autarchy in the capital markets. That isolation, together with the turmoil of the times, allowed special interests to achieve vested power in corporate structures. It was in this period that nonstandard corporate models arose: employee participation as in Germany, state corporatism as in France and Japan, family dominance as in Sweden, and managerialism as in the United States. Only recently have world capital markets again opened up, and this surely goes far in explaining the recent rapid convergence toward the standard shareholder-oriented model.

If and when, once again, something happens to close down the world's capital markets – paranoia about terrorism, perhaps, or confrontation between great powers – then, even if the standard shareholder-oriented model of corporate capitalism is efficient, leading societies may once again start moving away from it, adopting corporate structures that give the state and/or important private interests more control. Today we see both China and Russia struggling with the tradeoff between state control of enterprise and access to capital on the international markets. Though both have, with occasional backsliding, resolved this tradeoff recently in favor of access to capital, and hence movement toward the standard shareholder-oriented model, it might not take much of a shock for either or both to decide that they prefer strong state control ... As we march toward the end of history, further interruptions of this sort may await us. Or, to put it differently, one's faith in reaching the end of history for corporate law may be closely tied to one's faith in achieving Fukuyama's original End of History in politics ...

Unsurprisingly, the theory of convergence has generated much commentary.

Franklin A. Gevurtz, 'The Globalization of Corporate Law: The End of History or a Never-Ending Story?' (2011) 86 *Washington Law Review* 475, 507–20

III. What Is Important in Measuring Convergence

1. Mandatory versus Permissive Corporate Law

As discussed earlier, one of the enduring cycles in corporate law is the moving convergence on the balance between regulation and deregulation in the protection of minority shareholders. Hence, one does not need familiarity with the voluminous academic literature addressing the topic to recognize the critical importance of the debate over whether corporate law protections of minority shareholders should be mandatory or left for the participants to work out.

The competing tensions here are ideological, political, and practical. The ideological disagreements over mandatory versus permissive corporate law rules reflect differing factual assumptions about the rationality of individuals, i.e., whether people act as rational wealth-maximizing individuals or whether they act on irrational behavioral impulses. The ideological disagreements also reflect different assumptions about the efficiency of markets and the capability of government to avoid inefficient rent-seeking by public officials and other interest groups. Finally, they reflect a philosophical disagreement about the intrinsic value of individual autonomy.

The earlier discussion about cycles of regulation and deregulation illustrates the political tensions that prevent stable convergence regarding mandatory versus permissive corporate law. Corporate managers, for obvious reasons, are generally resistant to regulation that would limit their autonomy. Furthermore, unless a crisis looms, there may be little push by shareholders for mandatory protections because shareholders may underestimate the danger and overestimate their ability to protect themselves. The prospect of regulatory arbitrage – forming the corporation under more relaxed laws – creates special pressure for deregulation in the corporate arena.

The increasing numbers of American and foreign limited liability companies organizing under Delaware law while operating largely or exclusively outside of Delaware highlight the political forces behind deregulation …

Another and earlier example comes from the 1980s. In response to a highly controversial Delaware Supreme Court decision finding that directors had breached their duty of care, Delaware enacted a striking example of permissive legislation in corporate law. The legislature amended Delaware's corporate statute to allow provisions in certificates of incorporation that waive monetary liability for directors who breach their duty of care. Demonstrating convergence in action, this scene later replayed itself in Japan in the 1990s. Following a huge damage award against directors of a Japanese bank who breached their duty of care, the Japanese legislature enacted a provision allowing corporate charters to limit the amount of damages for which directors can be liable.

As explained earlier, however, these political winds can blow in both directions, thereby preventing a permanent convergence in favor of deregulation. Ever since the South Sea Bubble, waves of corporate scandal and crisis have caused large losses for shareholders and triggered broader economic dislocation. The result – from the English Bubble Act's attempt to prevent joint-stock companies without official charter, from issuing transferable shares, to the mandatory corporate governance provisions in the Sarbanes–Oxley and Dodd–Frank Acts – is a political backlash against deregulation and an adoption of mandatory shareholder protections.

Finally, what frustrates permanent convergence is the simple fact that both regulation through mandatory protections and deregulation through contractual freedom have merits and flaws. Practically speaking, finding the "Goldilocks" balance between bust-producing deregulation and growth-stifling regulation has not been an easy undertaking.

2. Authority versus Accountability for Corporate Managers

Drawing on the organizational theories of Kenneth Arrow, Stephen Bainbridge has crystallized a second fundamental tension in corporate law: the tension between the authority and accountability of those in charge of the corporation. Specifically, in order for any organization to function, members of the organization must be given some authority to act; if no one has authority to do anything, nothing gets done. The problem – which economists call the "principal–agent" or "agency cost" problem – is that those with authority to act often misuse their authority. They may engage in disloyal conduct to enrich themselves at the expense of the organization or they may act honestly but misguidedly out of carelessness, bad judgment, or various biases and emotions. As expressed in an old cliché instead of the language of economics, because humans are inherently fallible, "power corrupts." Hence, there is need for mechanisms of accountability, lest authority devolve into the corruption that results from absolute power.

The tension begins with the fact that mechanisms of accountability necessarily impinge on authority. This fact is particularly evident when the mechanism involves a requirement of advance approval. Even when the mechanism involves only after-the-fact consequences, however, the fear of such consequences can reduce the willingness to exercise authority. This may deter desirable as well as undesirable acts. The real problem, however, is not simply that accountability limits authority; it is that mechanisms of accountability generally are not self-executing. Instead, fallible human beings carry out the accountability mechanisms, whether this involves selecting those who will have authority, approving specific actions, or deciding if authority has been misused. Hence, accountability mechanisms essentially transfer authority from one person to another person or group. These transferees, however, may themselves have poor motives or act misguidedly. Of course, one could have other persons impose accountability upon the persons who impose accountability, but then, given this logic, one must repeat this process endlessly ...

We can find examples of these disagreements in the various mechanisms of accountability, including selection, approval, and consequences. Recently in the United States, disagreements about accountability through selection have played out in the controversy over "proxy access," which refers to the right of shareholders in public companies to demand that shareholder nominees for board positions appear on the proxy form distributed by the corporation to its shareholders. While this would seem to be an elementary exercise in democratic governance, critics of proxy access have highlighted conflicts of interest and misguided motives among shareholders demanding proxy access. In other words, critics have pointed to the fallible nature of those who would monitor others through the mechanism of selection.

Actually, proxy battles for control of publicly traded companies are not major drivers of accountability because they rarely occur. Of far more significance is the threat of a change in management following a corporate takeover. Corporate laws in different nations diverge in the manner they govern such acquisitions and management's efforts to thwart them. Indeed, an attempt to harmonize corporate takeover laws in Europe provoked so much controversy that the resulting European Union harmonizing directive allows member nations to opt out of key provisions. This is yet another example of the difficulties of balancing authority and accountability between managers (who have an interest in preserving their positions) and shareholders (who face collective action problems in deciding whether to sell).

The dilemma of how to balance authority and accountability also has produced disagreement among nations about requirements for shareholder approval of management actions and shareholder ability to command management actions. Shareholders in many nations possess more power in these areas than they do the United States.

There is also marked divergence in approaches to achieving accountability by imposing liability on managers for disloyal or ill-advised decisions. In some instances, this divergence is subtle and even concealed under an apparent convergence. For example, the doctrine known as the "business judgment rule," which apparently originated in the United States, has spread worldwide. This doctrine calls for restraint in imposing liability upon directors for disinterested decisions that turn out badly or with which some shareholders may disagree. Hence, at first glance, this would appear to represent an important example of convergence on the fundamental question of balancing authority and accountability through judicial review of business decisions.

A closer examination of case law, however, reveals that a rule calling for restraint in second-guessing board decisions may be applied very differently in different legal cultures. For example, a few years ago, Delaware judges applied the business judgment rule in a highly deferential manner to exonerate directors who had approved payment of $130 million to the fired former president of a company after a one-year term in which he accomplished very little. At around the same time, German judges found a breach of duty, despite applying the business judgment rule, by nitpicking at the decision of the directors of a German company to award a bonus of $17 million to the outgoing CEO, whose actions had played an important role in gaining over $50 billion for the company's shareholders.

Such differences in attitudes may both reflect and reinforce important societal differences whose significance would be masked if one only paid attention to the apparent convergence marked by both courts' purported decision to apply the business judgment rule. There is a wide gulf between executive compensation levels in the United States and in the rest of the world ... Unless there is convergence in broader national attitudes regarding the importance of equality in wealth distribution, one cannot expect convergence in the application of even nominally similar corporate laws addressing the balance of authority versus accountability in executive compensation.

Finding the balance between authority and accountability becomes even more difficult when one considers the process for enforcing liability upon corporate managers. The problem is that the concept of authority calls for managers to decide if the corporation should enforce claims against the managers themselves. Accountability is only achieved, however, if someone else makes enforcement decisions. Yet any other decision maker faces potential problems of suspect motives or significant costs (often paid by the corporation) in order to determine whether liability (or even further investigation) is warranted.

Interestingly, there has been a growing convergence in this area. Many civil law nations have begun to recognize derivative suits brought by shareholders on the corporation's behalf against its directors while also subjecting such suits to minimum shareholding requirements for standing and perhaps to judicial preclearance of the merits of the action. At the same time, the United States, which apparently pioneered the derivative suit, has seen various efforts to curb such litigation, especially by turning the requirement that the plaintiff make a pre-suit demand upon the board into a judicial preclearance of the merits of the suit.

Conclusion

Whether expressly stated or left implicit, a normative agenda underlies the predictions of convergence: if convergence is going to happen anyway because of efficiency, then nations should embrace convergence. Depending upon the nation of the writer, this translates into support of legal exports (you should adopt my nation's corporate laws) or of legal imports (we should adopt another nation's corporate laws).

The theses developed here are intended to prevent an unexamined acceptance of such arguments. Convergence through imitation and transplant is constantly occurring in corporate law, but the points upon which corporate laws converge commonly represent only temporary way stations from which divergence will reappear until there is convergence again at a new point of temporary consensus. Corporate laws do not necessarily converge to more efficient or otherwise normatively superior points, but are influenced by fads and fashions, erroneous assumptions about correlation and causation, and rent-seeking by those favored by the particular points of convergence. This lack of permanent convergence is particularly likely in the difficult contexts of balancing regulation and deregulation or authority and accountability with respect to shareholder protection.

David Cabrelli and Mathias Siems, 'Convergence, Legal Origins, and Transplants in Comparative Corporate Law: A Case-Based and Quantitative Analysis' (2015) 63 *American Journal of Comparative Law* 109, 114–16

It is no exaggeration to say that Hansmann and Kraakman's article generated a formidable reaction amongst comparative corporate law scholars across the world. But many contested their arguments. Some scholars objected that path dependencies still play an important role. As regards the law, this may be the result of fundamentally different legal mentalities between common and civil law countries, and in terms of corporate governance, historical and cultural differences may persist, reflecting different types of market economies. Proponents of "path-dependence" theory argue that the structure of a jurisdiction's corporate governance system and the shape of its corporate laws are conditioned by its cultural, social, economic, and political past. Hence, "history matters," since once a jurisdiction has embarked upon a particular path, legal systems become "locked in" and conditioned by institutions built up within the system over the years. As a result, strong complementarities between different institutions in the system are generated, rendering it difficult and inefficient for that jurisdiction to suddenly shift direction by introducing an altogether novel set of institutions. For this reason, "path-dependence" proponents argue that the uniqueness of corporate governance systems ought to be strengthened and permitted to evolve organically in accordance with the existing legal, political, social, and economic infrastructure. More nuanced positions are also possible. For instance, it could be said that, today, legal systems do not differ primarily because of different legal families, but rather on account of their belonging to a particular regional group. In particular, this may be the case in Europe, where the EU has harmonized some aspects of corporate law and the Europeanization of economic and legal thinking may also have led to convergence on other topics.

Other commentators have been critical on different grounds. Some have been of the view that the effect of regulatory competition amongst jurisdictions runs counter to convergence, leading inexorably to greater divergence amongst legal systems as each jurisdiction competes and engages in a "race to the bottom" to attract incorporations. Further reasons advanced to explain why we ought to be skeptical about the potential for such convergence include cultural constraints, political–economic barriers, and the variations across jurisdictions in the legal rules addressing the protection of shareholders.

In particular, the arguments against convergence theory are closely connected with the divergence in the structure of share ownership of companies one finds in common law and civil law countries. In the capitalist market economies of common law jurisdictions such as the United Kingdom and the United States – which are categorized as "liberal market economies" in the "varieties of capitalism" literature in the field of comparative political economy – the corporate governance system is referred to as an "outsider/arm's length" system of ownership and control. Ownership of the shares of large public corporations quoted on the capital markets in such systems is widely dispersed, with an absence of dominant controlling shareholders. Some scholars have argued that the main focus of corporate laws in such jurisdictions is on protecting shareholders as a class from conduct of managers and directors that is prejudicial to shareholder interests, given that the latter are in a position to further their own interests at the expense of shareholders. As such, the "agency costs" to be tackled here are of a "vertical" nature in dispersed share ownership systems. Furthermore, a large degree of emphasis is placed on corporate disclosure and market control by outsiders. This can be contrasted with "co-ordinated market economies" in the "varieties of capitalism" literature, where the corporate governance system is "insider/control-oriented" in nature. This taxonomy roughly maps onto the corporate law regimes of the civil law jurisdictions where the share ownership of public corporations is concentrated in a single or a few blockholder controlling shareholders. Such systems are characterized by weak minority shareholder protection, a phenomenon which is largely attributable to the ability of controlling shareholders to extract private benefits by virtue of their dominance and control. Since the governance of companies in such "insider/control-oriented" systems is closely co-ordinated between management and the blockholding controlling shareholders, many commentators contend that corporate law protections in civil law jurisdictions are designed to protect minority shareholders. The argument runs that the "agency costs" which arise in civilian "insider/control-oriented" jurisdictions are horizontal, i.e. attributable to a misalignment of the interests of majority shareholders and minority shareholders, rather than a vertical misalignment between the interests of directors and shareholders generally as a class, which is predominant in common law jurisdictions.

The debate as to which of the "outsider/arm's length" or "insider/control-oriented" systems of ownership and control is superior or more efficient has not been resolved: the jury is still out.

Notes and Questions

1. What do you think of the argument for an end-of-history convergence toward shareholder primacy, particularly in terms of the normative, efficiency and factual claims? What aspects of it do you find persuasive? What are its central weaknesses? What effect does globalization have on the debate? What about the influence of equity culture, institutional investors, harmonization of accounting standards, and global gatekeepers?
2. Is formal convergence of corporate law and governance occurring? To what degree is it occurring? If so, how? By corporate law, securities law, case law or codes? Only in particular areas such as boards or independent directors, executive compensation, gender diversity, self-dealing, and private enforcement? Toward an Americanized, shareholder-oriented model? A hybrid model?
3. Is functional convergence of corporate governance occurring whereby governance practice is converging in practice and less so due to law? To what degree is it occurring? If so, how and why? Are market forces driven by institutional investors leading toward functional convergence that may be more influential than formal convergence? (See Chapter 13.)

4. Will convergence lead to a race to the top ("bonding"), race to the bottom, or a stratification of different systems? Will companies seek to list on stock exchanges and countries with higher corporate governance laws and standards to gain reputational benefits and higher valuations? This topic is explored in Chapter 13.
5. Is it a good idea for corporate governance to converge? For all countries?
6. What should countries in Asia do in light of pressures for convergence or divergence?
7. What will prevent convergence or divergence from happening?

4.6 Framework of Analysis

Against this theoretical background, the following chapters will seek to analyze corporate governance in Asia by categorizing and comparing each jurisdiction through the lens of shareholder, stakeholder, and controlling shareholders systems. Each jurisdiction will be explored based upon the various theories propounded with the help of the template of purpose, board function, ownership structure, law and enforcement, and recent developments. Although any method of analysis has its limitations, we believe this framework based upon the traditional classification of corporate governance systems, as modified in this book, is the most useful approach to gain an understanding of the challenges that Asian corporate governance faces.

Topics such as whether law matters and to what degree, the influence of convergence, divergence or path dependence, shareholder versus stakeholder primacy, and the desirability and viability of legal transplants will all be discussed. We hope that such an examination will provide insight regarding how various forces and pressures are pushing and pulling modern corporations in Asia and what direction policymakers should take. Each chapter conveys contextual information concerning each jurisdiction from a comparative perspective in the application of these theoretical concepts. While corporations in Asia continue to evolve, the book seeks to provide a framework of analysis to understand Asia's corporate governance landscape.

PART II

ASIAN CORPORATE GOVERNANCE SYSTEMS

5

AUSTRALIA

Jennifer G. Hill

5.1 Introduction

Australia's system of corporate law originally derives from the United Kingdom, however, over time, significant differences have emerged between the two jurisdictions. UK company law was increasingly influenced by European Union law (though this trend will inevitably wane post-Brexit), and Australian corporate law was influenced by local corporate scandals and by developments in other jurisdictions, such as the United States.

Australia operates under a 'twin peaks' model of financial regulation, under which the Australian Prudential Regulation Authority (APRA) is responsible for regulation of financial institutions and the Australian Securities and Investments Commission (ASIC) has responsibility for business conduct and consumer protection. The Australian Takeovers Panel is the primary forum for resolving takeover disputes in Australia. Since the global financial crisis (GFC), Australia's 'twin peaks' regulatory model has been widely emulated, including by the United Kingdom.

One interesting feature of the Australian corporate governance system is the relationship between hard law and soft law. The primary legislation, the Corporations Act, contains both mandatory and optional provisions. It includes, for example, replaceable (or optional) rules, which corporations may elect to adopt as constitutional provisions. Some provisions are replaceable for private companies, but mandatory for public companies. Listed corporations are also required to comply with the Australian Securities Exchange (ASX) Listing Rules. Other distinguishing features include executive compensation (centering on Australia's version of 'say on pay,' the controversial 'two strikes' rule), and a public enforcement model, under which the regulator, ASIC, can bring litigation for a range of contraventions of the Corporations Act, including statutory directors' duties.

Corporate scandals and collapses have played an important role in prompting corporate law reform, and have affected not only hard law, but also soft law. In 2003, Australia adopted the ASX Corporate Governance Principles, a set of non-prescriptive 'comply or explain' (or 'if not, why not') corporate governance guidelines. At the time, the managing director and CEO of the ASX stated that, by adopting a disclosure-based approach to corporate governance, the ASX was "keen to avoid a U.S. style *Sarbanes–Oxley* legislative solution."[1] The ASX Corporate Governance Principles are underpinned by ASX Listing Rule 4.10.3, which requires

Thanks go to Alan Ngo, Penina Su, and Mitheran Selvendran for excellent research and editing assistance in relation to this project.

[1] Richard Humphry, 'If Not, Why Not?' (speech delivered to the Australian Institute of Directors Forum, Sydney, April 2, 2003) 3.

listed companies to disclose in their annual reports the extent to which their corporate governance practices conform to the ASX Corporate Governance Principles. Where they diverge, the company must "state its reasons for not following the recommendation and what (if any) alternative governance practices it adopted in lieu of the recommendation during that period."

Anita Indira Anand, 'An Analysis of Enabling vs. Mandatory Corporate Governance: Structures Post-Sarbanes–Oxley' (2006) 31 *Delaware Journal of Corporate Law* 229, 230–2

State corporate law in the United States in particular is largely enabling at the state level, providing default rules to which corporations must adhere if they do not choose an alternative arrangement that will govern them. Despite the enabling character of state corporate law, most would agree that Sarbanes–Oxley cannot be characterized as enabling legislation. Thus, this article addresses the conspicuous aspect of U.S corporate governance regulation that is mandatory under Sarbanes–Oxley [SOX] – conspicuous because of the enabling character of state corporate law and because other principal common law jurisdictions have not adopted a similar approach.

While the U.S. regime under SOX is largely mandatory, other jurisdictions have adopted a different governance model. Canada's regime dates back to 1995 when the Toronto Stock Exchange (TSX) issued a list of best practices that Canadian listed firms could voluntarily follow. Disclosure regarding the extent of a firm's compliance with the best practices was required in the firm's proxy circular or annual report ...

The U.K. regime is also partially enabling under the 1998 Combined Code which creates best practice guidelines. Compliance with these guidelines is voluntary, but companies listed on the London Stock Exchange are required to include in their annual report a statement indicating how the company applies the Combined Code's principles. Similarly, the Australian corporate governance regime revolves around the Australia Stock Exchange (ASX) guidance, which presents recommendations on how to achieve best practice in governance. The ASX guidance requires each listed company to provide a corporate governance statement containing disclosure of noncompliance in its annual report.

Thus, in three major common law jurisdictions outside the United States, corporate governance law can be called "partially enabling" where a code of best practices is coupled with a mandatory disclosure obligation. This is distinct from [US] state corporate law, which is, as discussed above, enabling. The seeming popularity of the partially enabling or "best practices" structure presents a puzzle as to why these jurisdictions have adopted a hybrid governance regime and, in particular, what are the benefits and costs of such a regime.

Notes and Questions

1. In a Royal Commission investigating the collapse of HIH Insurance, the Hon. Justice Neville Owen stated – "I am becoming less and less comfortable with the phrase 'corporate governance' – not because of its content, but because it has been so widely used that it may become meaningless." Nonetheless, Owen J. ultimately concluded that the phrase "corporate governance" describes "the framework of rules, relationships, systems and processes within and by which authority is exercised and controlled within corporations. It encompasses the mechanisms by which companies, and those in control, are held to account" (HIH Royal Commission, *The Failure of HIH Insurance, Volume 1: A Corporate Collapse and Its Lessons*, Commonwealth of Australia, 2003, xxxiii). This definition of corporate governance was adopted in the ASX Corporate Governance Principles (p. 3).
2. Does this definition accord with your view of the meaning of "corporate governance"? If not, how would you alter it? The ASX Corporate Governance Principles also state that "[g]ood corporate governance promotes investor confidence, which is crucial to the ability of entities listed on the ASX to compete for capital." Do you consider this to be the main justification of promoting good corporate governance? What other justifications might exist?
3. Why do you think the ASX Corporate Governance Principles might have adopted the term "if not, why not," rather than the more familiar terminology of "comply or explain"? (see ASX Corporate Governance Principles, p. 3).

5.2 Purpose: Shareholder versus Stakeholder

Corporate social responsibility (CSR) has become an increasingly important issue in recent times. International scandals, such as Enron, and the home-grown James Hardie scandal, had a significant impact on corporate policy debate in Australia concerning stakeholders and CSR.

Much of the discussion about CSR took place against the backdrop of the James Hardie corporate scandal, in combination with s. 172 of the UK Companies Act 2006, which explicitly requires directors to have regard to various stakeholder interests in fulfilling their duty to "promote the success of the company for the benefit of its members as a whole." The James Hardie scandal also resulted in a special inquiry, two government reports on the general issue of corporate responsibility, and proceedings brought by ASIC against the executive and non-executive directors of the company.

Shelley Marshall and Ian Ramsay, 'Stakeholders and Directors' Duties: Law, Theory and Evidence' (2012) 35 *UNSW Law Journal* 291, 297

Under the traditional rules of company law, directors' duties are regarded as being owed to the company and to the company alone; and for this purpose the company's interests are equated with the interests of the members collectively. Directors on this view are not entitled, still less bound, to consider the interests of other groups, such as the company's employees, creditors, customers and suppliers, or to have any concern for such matters as the community, the environment, welfare and charity, unless what they do has derivative benefits for their shareholders.

Three important questions can be asked. First, are there any circumstances when the interests of non-shareholder stakeholders can be considered by directors without there being any derivative benefit for shareholders? Second, are there any circumstances when the interests of non-shareholder stakeholders *must* be considered by directors? Third, are there any circumstances when the interests of non-shareholder stakeholders can be given higher priority by directors than the interests of shareholders?

5.2.1 James Hardie: A Mini-Case Study

Jennifer G. Hill, 'Australia: The Architecture of Corporate Governance,' in Andreas M. Fleckner and Klaus J. Hopt (eds.), *Comparative Corporate Governance: A Functional and International Analysis* (New York: Cambridge University Press, 2013), pp. 106, 112

The James Hardie scandal prompted reconsideration of Australia's traditional shareholder-centred approach to corporate law and the issue of corporate social responsibility generally. The saga involved James Hardie Industries Ltd. ("JHIL"), a building company, which manufactured asbestos products in Australia from the early twentieth century until the late 1980s, amid increasing evidence of the dangers of asbestos.

In 2001, JHIL was restructured to quarantine potential asbestos-related compensation claims from the operating businesses. As part of this restructure, JHIL established a foundation ("the Foundation") to cover claims of workers and others suffering asbestos-related illnesses. JHIL issued a media release stating that the Foundation was "fully funded," with sufficient funding to meet all legitimate future tort claims. There was also a complex restructuring of the James Hardie group in which a new Dutch company, James Hardie Industries NV ("JHI NV") was substituted for JHIL as the ultimate holding company in the group. In 2003, it became clear that there was a massive shortfall in the Foundation's funding, and that the restructure would have disastrous consequences for tort claimants. JHIL's directors claimed that under Australian corporate law their primary duty was to the shareholders, and that it would have been impermissible for them to provide additional funds to the Foundation to support liabilities to tort claimants.

The James Hardie events caused ongoing public outrage, which ultimately forced JHI NV to enter into the largest personal injury settlement in Australian history.

Parliamentary Joint Committee on Corporations and Financial Services (PJC Committee), *Corporate Responsibility: Managing Risk and Creating Value* (Commonwealth of Australia, 2006), pp. xiii, 52, 55, 59

The committee heard a number of arguments in relation to whether or not existing requirements in the Corporations Act 2001 allowed company directors to consider broader community interests, and whether any change was required to legislation to either permit, or require, responsible corporate behaviour.

A number of interpretations of the current legislative framework regarding the duties of directors were provided to the committee. At one end of the scale was the view, made prominent in the case concerning James Hardie Industries, that a director would be failing in his or her duties if consideration was given to any factors other than maximising profit. At the other end of the scale, the 'enlightened self-interest' interpretation of directors' duties argues that directors may consider and act upon the legitimate interests of stakeholders other than shareholders, to the extent that these interests are relevant to the corporation.

This 'enlightened self-interest' interpretation is favoured by the committee. Evidence received suggests that those companies already undertaking responsible corporate behaviour are being driven by factors that are clearly in the interests of the company. Maintaining and improving company reputation was cited as an important factor by companies, many of whom recognise that when corporate reputation suffers there can be significant business costs …

[T]he committee does not agree that acting in the best interests of the *corporation* and acting in the best interests of the *shareholders* inevitably amounts to the same thing …

The committee does not support the British approach [ie s. 172], which appears to introduce great uncertainty into the legal expression of directors' duties. For instance, there is no way to forecast those circumstances under which a court might decide that a company's purposes 'consisted of or included purposes other than the benefit of its members.' And what might a court determine those purposes to be? Until such a determination was made with respect to a particular company, directors may not even be sufficiently equipped with basic knowledge about those to whom they owed a duty. Subclause (3) requires directors to have regard to a menu of non-shareholder interests, but gives no guidance as to what form this 'regard' should take, and therefore gives no guidance to directors on what they must do in order to comply …

In many cases, it will be clear that corporate responsibility enhances shareholder value. At the very least, it is clear that rampant corporate irresponsibility certainly decreases shareholder value.

ASX Corporate Governance Council, *Corporate Governance Principles and Recommendations* (3rd edn, 2014)

Principle 3: Act ethically and responsibly

A listed entity should act ethically and responsibly.

Commentary

A listed entity's reputation is one of its most valuable assets and, if damaged, can be one of the most difficult to restore. Investors and other stakeholders expect listed entities to act ethically and responsibly. Anything less is likely to destroy value over the longer term.

Acting ethically and responsibly goes well beyond mere compliance with legal obligations and involves acting with honesty, integrity and in a manner that is consistent with the reasonable expectations of investors and the broader community. It includes being, and being seen to be, a 'good corporate citizen.'

ASIC v. *Healey* [2011] FCA 717 at [14] (Middleton J.)

A director is an essential component of corporate governance … The role of a director is significant as their actions may have a profound effect on the community, and not just shareholders, employees and creditors.

Notes and Questions

1. What do you understand the modern Australian position regarding CSR and the shareholder/stakeholder issue to be? Does a coherent answer emerge to the three questions posed by Professors Marshall and Ramsay above?
2. Neither the PJC nor other reports recommended that Australia go down the path taken under s. 172 of the UK Companies Act 2006. Why not? Do you consider that Australian corporate law, particularly with respect to the James Hardie scandal, would have been improved by the inclusion of a provision like s. 172?
3. How does the modern Australian position regarding CSR compare to the various approaches adopted in other jurisdictions discussed in this book? Do you consider that CSR is better addressed by hard or soft law?
4. UK billionaire John Caudwell described as "immoral" the argument that corporations must reduce the amount of tax paid to the greatest extent possible to fulfil their duties to shareholders (*BBC News*, April 1, 2015). Do you consider that contemporary Australian law would support Caudwell's view?
5. It has recently been suggested that directors who fail to take into account the potential impact of climate change on their company's business may be in breach of their directors' duties (Jessica Irvine, 'Company Directors to Face Penalties for Ignoring Climate Change,' *Sydney Morning Herald*, October 31, 2016). Do you agree? How would you structure an argument in support of such liability?

5.3 Board Function

5.3.1 Board Structure and Independent Directors

The Australian Council of Superannuation Investors (ACSI) publishes an annual survey *Board Composition and Non-Executive Director Pay* on large listed companies that provides an interesting snapshot of contemporary developments relating to board structure and composition. ACSI's 2016 survey found the following:

- ASX100 companies had an average board size of 8.3 members.
- In ASX100 companies, an average of around 85 percent of board seats were held by non-executive directors, over 90 percent of which qualified as independent directors.

The ASX Corporate Governance Principles merely recommend the presence of a majority of independent directors on an "if not, why not" basis. In ACSI's 2016 survey, only one ASX100 company had a board with a majority of executive, rather than independent, directors.

The ASX Corporate Governance Principles also recommend that listed companies should establish a range of committees, including a nomination committee, an audit committee, a committee to oversee risk, and a remuneration committee. Each of these committees should have at least three members, the majority of whom are independent and be chaired by an independent director. The Principles further recommend ensuring that the chair is an independent director, splitting the roles of CEO and chair. Additional mandatory rules relating to audit and remuneration committees apply to certain subcategories of listed companies via the ASX Listing Rules.

Director independence has become a controversial issue in recent times. The ASX Corporate Governance Principles set out a range of specific professional and personal factors that may compromise independence (Recommendation 2.3, Box 2.3). One particularly contentious factor that may compromise independence is if the director is, or is associated with, a substantial shareholder in the company.

ASX Corporate Governance Council, *Corporate Governance Principles and Recommendations* (3rd edn, 2014)

Recommendation 2.3 Commentary

To describe a director as "independent" carries with it a particular connotation that the director is not allied with the interests of management, a substantial security holder or other relevant stakeholder and can and will bring an independent judgement to bear on issues before the board.

It is an appellation that gives great comfort to security holders and not one that should be applied lightly.

Notes and Questions

1. Professor Peter Swan has strongly criticized the shift to independent directors in Australia, claiming that it has caused a massive destruction of shareholder value in the top 200 listed companies. One reason he cited was that, as a result of the specific definition of "independence" under the ASX Corporate Governance Principles, independent directors have negligible ownership interests in their own companies. This research has been challenged by numerous groups, with the Australian Institute of Company Directors (AICD) stating that "We would also suggest it goes against the view of just about every investor group and corporate governance group in the country." How convincing do you find Professor Swan's arguments against independent directors? Do you agree that directors should have "skin in the game" and that the Australian definition of independence is defective in failing to recognize this?

2. How effective do you think remuneration committees are likely to be in combating the danger of managerial power in relation to executive pay?
3. Another controversial contemporary issue relating to boards is that of gender diversity. According to ACSI's 2016 survey, over the past fifteen years the proportion of board seats held by women at ASX100 companies has trebled, increasing to more than 25 percent in 2015. Yet, in spite of this improvement, representation of women in executive and board leadership roles is still relatively low. Australia has chosen not to adopt binding quotas to ensure gender diversity on boards. Rather, board diversity-related issues appear in several of the ASX Corporate Governance Principles, including Recommendation 1.5, which states that a listed company should have a diversity policy against which it can "set measurable objectives for achieving gender diversity" and disclose progress toward those goals in its annual report. The AICD has called on all boards to ensure that 30 percent of their directors are women, and has urged S&P/ASX200 companies to meet this target by the end of 2018. Is this enough? What other regulatory techniques might be more effective?

5.3.2 Shareholder Activism

Shareholder power is distinct from, but closely linked to, shareholder activism. The GFC created a legitimacy problem for business. It highlighted some of the dangers of unconstrained managerial power and raised the issue of whether shareholders should be granted stronger powers (and encouraged to use those powers more effectively) as an independent corporate governance technique. A number of regulatory developments, including in the area of executive compensation, have arguably shifted the balance of power between the board and shareholders in the latter's favor. Institutional investors have been particularly important, however, other activists, such as corporate social responsibility activists, have also played a role in Australia's corporate governance ecosystem.

Geof Stapledon, 'The Development of Corporate Governance in Australia,' in Christine A. Mallin (ed.), *Handbook on International Corporate Governance: Country Analyses 2nd edn* (Cheltenham, UK and Northampton, MA: Edward Elgar, 2011), pp. 330, 338–41

Institutional share ownership in Australia grew from about 45–50 per cent in the 1990s to approximately 64 per cent by 2009 …

Before 1990, institutional investors' role in corporate governance in Australia was confined largely to tendering – or not tendering – their shares to hostile takeover bidders. Since 1990, however, institutional shareholders have played a steadily increasing role in mitigating agency costs. They have produced and promoted best-practice guidelines covering board structure and composition, executive and director remuneration, auditor independence and a range of other matters; participated actively in debates about corporate and securities law reform; intervened occasionally at individual companies, for instance through behind-the-scenes pressure to shake up an underperforming board, or through a public campaign for greater investor protection; and shown a greater propensity to exercise their voting rights since the late 1990s. However, Australian institutional investors are not monolithic. Although they share similar views on some matters of general principle, different institutions commonly take different approaches to corporate governance issues. This reflects the fact that they are competitors in the investment management industry.

The increased influence of institutional investors in Australian corporate governance is partly explained by the advancement of proxy advisory firms ...

The proxy advisers are probably best known for their impact on executive remuneration. By analysing companies' remuneration practices and disclosures, and providing recommendations in relation to the 'say on pay' advisory vote, they have stimulated an increased level of dialogue between companies and their institutional shareholders on pay issues, and drawn attention to questionable remuneration practices. Several large companies have experienced a majority 'against' vote on the say-on-pay resolution, and this has normally led to remuneration arrangements being changed for the future ...

Where there is a large non-institutional blockholder on a company's share register, the scope for institutional investors and their proxy voting advisers to minimize agency costs is reduced ...

Nevertheless, even in blockholder-controlled companies, institutional investors and their proxy voting advisers can play a significant monitoring role. Institutional investors' exercise of voting rights, together with corporate law and stock exchange listing rules that prohibit related parties from voting on transactions in which they are interested, can reduce the potential for minority shareholders' interests to be ignored by the blockholder.

5.3.2.1 The Reincorporation of News Corp: A Mini-Case Study

Based on Jennifer G. Hill, 'Subverting Shareholder Rights: Lessons from News Corp.'s Migration to Delaware' (2010) 63 *Vanderbilt Law Review* 1

In 2004, News Corporation (News Corp.) announced its intention to move from Australia to Delaware, to obtain primary listing on the New York Stock Exchange and to seek inclusion in the Standard & Poor's 500 Index. The reincorporation proposal involved incorporation of a new parent company in the United States and was to be implemented by schemes of arrangement, which under Australian law, required both court and shareholder approval. Although News Corp. argued that the move to Delaware was prompted by legitimate commercial goals, including the ability to gain greater access to US capital markets, critics argued that the main goal of the move was to strengthen managerial power vis-à-vis shareholder power.

The original reincorporation proposal prompted a revolt by a number of institutional investors, concerned that the move to Delaware would significantly diminish their rights under Australian corporate law. Two such institutions, ACSI and Corporate Governance International Pty Ltd, with the support of several major international institutional investors, launched a campaign, urging News Corp. to transplant certain key shareholder protection and corporate governance best practice provisions under Australian law into its prospective Delaware charter.

News Corp. ultimately made a number of concessions to the institutional investors' corporate governance demands. One particularly controversial matter involved defensive board conduct, such as use of a poison pill, in response to a hostile takeover offer. Poison pills, which are an accepted feature of the US corporate law, are not permissible in Australia, and the institutional investors wanted the News Corp.'s Delaware charter to include an explicit provision stating that the board of directors had no power to adopt a poison pill. News Corp. agreed to a restriction on the board's power to issue a poison pill. However, this restriction was not placed in the corporation's charter, as had been sought by the institutional investors, but rather in a board policy.

News Corp.'s concessions quelled the corporate governance revolt by institutional investors, and the reincorporation proposal was overwhelmingly approved at a general meeting of the company in October 2004. Yet, the institutional investors' revolt reignited after the company's move to Delaware. In November 2004, in the same week that the reincorporation became fully effective, News Corp. announced that it had adopted a poison pill, but that, in accordance with its new board policy, the pill would expire in one year, unless approved by shareholders. However, that did not occur. In August 2005, News Corp. announced that its board had extended the poison pill for two years beyond its original expiration date, without the approval of shareholders. Although Rupert Murdoch argued that News Corp. had never promised to make its board policy unalterable, a group of twelve mainly Australian and European institutional investors filed legal proceedings against News Corp. and its directors in the Delaware Court of Chancery in *UniSuper Ltd. v. News Corp.* [2005] WL 3529317 (*UniSuper* case). The institutions sought to invalidate the extension of the News Corp. poison pill and any subsequent extensions, unless authorised by shareholder vote. In spite of a motion by the defendants to dismiss the case, in late 2005, Chancellor Chandler ruled that the plaintiffs' action could proceed.

Notes and Questions

1. To what extent does the News Corp saga challenge an assumption under the "law matters" hypothesis that a high level of corporate governance homogeneity exists across common law jurisdictions?
2. What are the implications of the News Corp saga for convergence and transplant theory?
3. At the time when shareholders approved News Corp's Delaware reincorporation in late 2004, Australia's financial press was divided as to the significance of the institutional investors' corporate governance campaign. Some journalists portrayed the campaign as a major victory for the institutions, whereas others viewed News Corp's concessions as inconsequential and a mirage. With the benefit of hindsight, which interpretation of events do you think is more accurate?
4. In the *UniSuper* case, the plaintiffs argued that the board policy concerning poison pills adopted as a concession by News Corp constituted a binding contract. The defendants, on the other hand, argued that any contract would be contrary to Delaware law as an impermissible constraint of centralized managerial authority. Why do you think Chancellor Chandler considered this to be a "troubling" aspect of the defendants' argument from a policy perspective in relation to reincorporation in Delaware?

5.3.2.2 David Jones: A Mini-Case Study

In 2013, a leading Australian retailer, David Jones, became the target of shareholder activism after it was revealed that two of its directors had purchased shares in the company in controversial circumstances. The share trades, which the company's chair approved, were within a "window period" under the company's share trading policy. Nonetheless, they occurred one day after rival, Myer, had approached the David Jones board with a confidential merger of equals takeover offer, and three days before the release of positive quarterly sales data, resulting in a significant increase in David Jones's share price.

ASIC launched an investigation over insider trading concerns, but ultimately decided that there was insufficient evidence to take enforcement action. Shareholders, however, made their displeasure very clear. Although the chairman apologized for the controversy, many shareholders regarded the matter as "unfinished business." At the company's annual general meeting in November 2013, there was a significant "no" vote (of around 39.5 percent of shares voted) against the company's remuneration report and in February 2014, the two directors and chairman announced that they would resign as part of a "board renewal process." In April 2014, David Jones issued a revised securities trading policy.

Notes and Questions

1. What are the corporate governance lessons from the David Jones controversy?
2. If you were advising a company's board of directors on its share trading policy, what information would you suggest that it include in the light of the events at David Jones?

5.3.3 Shareholders and Executive Remuneration

Australia introduced reforms to executive pay after both the corporate scandals at the beginning of the century and the GFC. Following the collapse of Enron in the United States, and HIH and One.Tel in Australia, the Corporations Act was amended in 2004 to include s. 250R(2), which requires an annual non-binding shareholder vote on the directors' remuneration report, modeled on an analogous 2002 UK provision.

Executive pay also became a focal point during the GFC. In 2008, Australian Prime Minister Kevin Rudd attributed the crisis to "extreme capitalism," characterized by "[o]bscene failures in corporate governance which rewarded greed without any regard to the integrity of the financial system." Of Australia's regulatory responses to the GFC, the most controversial was the so-called "two strikes" rule.

Jennifer G. Hill, 'Images of the Shareholder: Shareholder Power and Shareholder Powerlessness,' in Jennifer G. Hill and Randall S. Thomas (eds.), *Research Handbook on Shareholder Power* (Cheltenham, UK and Northampton, MA: Edward Elgar, 2012), pp. 53, 66–8

One sphere where the role of shareholders has changed radically is that of executive pay. This area was traditionally off-limits to shareholders. However, in recent times, many jurisdictions around the world, including the United States, the United Kingdom and Australia, have accorded shareholders stronger participation rights in relation to executive pay. This trend reflects the view that shareholder approval can be a useful check and balance on board power in the area of executive pay, and is designed to restore 'trust' in financial markets.

Although the trend at first sight suggests convergence, there are interesting variations in use of shareholder consent as a regulatory technique in relation to executive pay across jurisdictions. 'Say on pay' comes in different flavors when it comes to stringency and shareholder power levels.

In 2011, Australia introduced a distinctive brand of say on pay, colloquially known as the 'two strikes' rule. This rule derived from the Australian Government

Productivity Commission's influential report on executive pay following the global financial crisis. The Productivity Commission recommended the two strikes rule, as a means of increasing board responsiveness to significant 'no' votes by Australian public shareholders under the pre-existing non-binding say on pay provision, 250R(2) of the *Corporations Act*.

Under Australia's two strikes rule, a listed corporation is required to put a spill resolution to shareholders if there have been two consecutive shareholder 'no' votes of 25 percent or more on the directors' remuneration report. If this spill resolution is successful, all of the company's directors are then required to submit to re-election by the shareholders within 90 days.

Australia's two strikes rule arguably casts shareholders in the role of quasi-regulator. It essentially creates an internal 'enforcement pyramid,' under which shareholders are given more leverage and the ability to escalate pressure on an unresponsive board. Sanctions available to shareholders range from the essentially symbolic non-binding first strike to replacement of the entire board. The two strikes rule is also a powerful example of regulatory 'shaming' in operation. A second strike can be embarrassing and damage the reputations of both the company and its directors.

The two strikes rule, like say on pay generally, has proven controversial. There are two recurring, and inconsistent, criticisms of shareholder voting in relation to executive pay. A common refrain is that shareholders lack expertise and are insufficiently sophisticated to understand and identify flawed compensation schemes. Another argument, however, views shareholders as partially responsible for perverse incentives in executive pay, and any increase in their powers as the policy equivalent of letting the fox guard the henhouse …

Contemporary corporate governance literature stresses the importance of distinguishing between law on the books and law in action, so it is important to assess the actual operation of the two strikes rule. Since its adoption, Australian shareholders have actively used their strengthened protest powers. In the 2011 annual meeting season, 106 companies received a first strike, and in 2012, 22 companies received a second strike. Three of those second strike companies failed the consequent spill resolution … In the 2013 season, prominent department store company, David Jones, received a first strike, and Cabcharge suffered a third consecutive strike, having survived its first spill resolution.

To date, no Australian board has failed to survive a final spill motion. However, the threat of removal of directors has prompted clear changes to board policy in a number of cases …

There are several important points emerging from Australia's two strikes rule. One is that ownership structure matters. The two strikes rule is designed for widely dispersed shareholding, and cannot work effectively where there is a majority shareholder who can block any spill motion. Secondly, the two strikes rule has increased the influence of proxy advisory firms, with strikes at a number of companies occurring on the recommendation of, for example, ISS Proxy Advisory Services. Finally, shareholders are increasingly using the two strikes rule to discipline boards for non-pay related matters. Examples of this phenomenon include successful 2013 strikes against David Jones, which was a direct response to shareholder dissatisfaction about corporate governance lapses, and against Fairfax Media's remuneration report, which was orchestrated by mining magnate, Gina Rinehart, after she unsuccessfully attempted to join the board.

Michael Smith, 'Boards Face Investor Backlash on Pay,' *Australian Financial Review* (November 6, 2015), p. 40

The annual general meeting season is only warming up but there have already been eight strikes against companies as investors and super funds flex their muscle over executive pay and bonuses.

Downer EDI and Macmahon Holdings this week both received a vote of more than 25 per cent against their remuneration report …

Other companies to receive a strike over the last month include glove and condom maker Ansell, UGL, Samson Oil & Gas, Mortgage Choice, Pacific Brands, medical device group ImpediMed.

Boards are under more scrutiny than ever around executive pay.

It is too early to say whether the latest strikes are part of a broader rebellion against high executive salaries but proxy advisers, fund managers and super funds tell Chanticleer they are still not happy with the complexity of remuneration reports and bonus structures.

Vas Kolesnikoff, head of Australian and New Zealand research at ISS, who voted against Downer's remuneration report because of a $1.24 million retention payment to a key executive, says he is seeing higher votes against boards than in previous years.

The impact of capital raisings on remuneration structures, where executives are compensated for the dilution of their holdings, will also be a contentious issue.

The role of superannuation funds is also shaping up as a game-changer. Company directors find it a pain answering to yet another group of interested parties but they know they ignore the increasingly well-organised super funds at their peril …

There is the danger it all goes too far. Many directors privately warn that they are spending more time managing remuneration than the actual job of running a company and various operational issues.

Notes and Questions

1. How does Australia's "two strikes" rule work in practice?
2. The US adopted its first "say on pay" provision under the Dodd–Frank Act 2010 that provides for a non-binding shareholder vote not less than once every three years for reporting companies. In the United Kingdom, the Enterprise and Regulatory Reform Act 2013 introduced reforms, which provide shareholders of quoted companies with a binding vote on future remuneration policy that must be approved by ordinary resolution at least every three years (or earlier if any amendments are proposed). Following this shareholder approval, the board must not make remuneration payments unless they are consistent with this policy or have been independently approved by shareholders. How does Australia's "two strikes" rule compare, in terms of regulatory stringency, to the US and UK approaches to remuneration? To what extent does the approach in each jurisdiction constrain board powers in relation to remuneration?

5.4 Ownership Structure

Chapter 1 of this book included an extract from the OECD's *Corporate Governance Factbook* (2015) on the ownership structure of listed companies. In that extract, the OECD identified Australia as one of three countries that are generally characterized as having predominantly dispersed ownership structures (while noting, however, that dispersed ownership had decreased in these countries between 2008 and 2012).

Vivien Chen, Ian Ramsay, and Michelle Welsh, 'Corporate Law Reform in Australia: An Analysis of the Influence of Ownership Structures and Corporate Failure' (2016) 44 *Australian Business Law Review* 18, 21–2

Australia is commonly categorised as a country with dispersed corporate ownership structures, similar to those of other Anglo-American countries. Nevertheless, studies indicate that share ownership in Australia is more concentrated than in the UK and US, placing it in an intermediate position between dispersed ownership and concentrated ownership countries. There is also a consistent pattern of increasingly concentrated share ownership in Australia, attributed to increasing institutional shareholdings. Differences in the methods used across studies, however, raise the need for caution with regard to the comparability of the data.

One of the main methods used to examine share ownership dispersion draws from the classic Berle and Means approach of examining the proportion of companies controlled by block-holders. Wheelwright's study in 1953 examined 102 of Australia's largest companies. Companies were considered as manager-controlled where there was an absence of block-holdings of 5% or more by single shareholders. The study found that a third of the 102 companies were controlled by managers. A subsequent study of 299 large Australian manufacturing companies found that 11% were manager-controlled. Ownership dispersion in the US was significantly higher than in Australia, with 40% of the 200 largest companies controlled by managers. In a more recent study, Stapledon found in 1996 that 97% of Australian companies listed on the All Ordinaries Index had block-holders of at least 5%. In contrast, only 20% of UK listed companies had block-holders of at least 5%.

The disparity between Australian share ownership structures and those of the UK and US is also seen in La Porta et al.'s study. Their study of ownership dispersion was based on a threshold of 10% or more of the company's voting rights. Eighteen out of 20 of the largest US companies were found to be widely held, while 16 out of 20 UK companies were similarly widely held. In contrast, merely 11 out of 20 of Australia's largest listed companies were widely held.

An alternative measure of ownership dispersion examines the proportion of shares owned by the top 20 shareholders. Studies indicate an increasing concentration of corporate ownership in Australia over time. The 20 largest shareholders in 100 of Australia's largest companies held, on average, 37% of shares in 1957. The top 20 shareholders were found to hold, on average, 43% of shares in manufacturing companies from 1962 to 1964. A study of listed companies observed an increase to almost 52% in the first half of the 1970s. More recent data indicates that average holdings of the 20 largest shareholders had increased to 72% by the early 1990s.

A third measure of ownership dispersion focuses on the proportion of companies listed on the stock exchange. Mitchell et al highlight the potential inaccuracy of generalisations based on listed companies given significant differences across countries in relation to the proportion of the total number of companies listed on stock exchanges. Comparisons with the US and UK indicate that Australia has a substantially smaller proportion of companies listed on the stock exchange. Studies in the mid-1990s suggest that Australia had approximately a third of its largest companies listed. In contrast, almost all of the largest US companies and two thirds of the UK's largest companies were listed on the stock exchange. As the ownership and control of unlisted companies typically reflects concentrated ownership, the significant proportion of unlisted companies in Australia further supports the divergence of Australian ownership structures from those of dispersed ownership systems.

In short, the evidence suggests that Australia's shareholding structures are more concentrated than those of the UK and the US. Further, the concentration of ownership has increased correspondingly with institutional holdings. Stapledon's study found that institutions were the largest or only substantial shareholders in 24% of listed companies in 1993. By 1996, this had increased to 34%. At the same time, studies suggest that holdings by individual shareholders in Australia have decreased over time.

Notes and Questions

1. Does this article accord with the OECD's depiction of the corporate ownership structure in Australia? What are the regulatory implications of the developments in this regard discussed in the article?

5.4.1 Market for Corporate Control

Geof Stapledon, 'The Development of Corporate Governance in Australia,' in Christine A. Mallin (ed.), *Handbook on International Corporate Governance: Country Analyses 2nd edn* (Cheltenham, UK and Northampton, MA: Edward Elgar, 2011), pp. 330–1

The threat of a hostile takeover offer being made for the shares in the company they manage can serve as an incentive to senior executives to run the company efficiently. If they do not do so, and such a bid materializes and is successful, the executives run the risk of being fired.

The likelihood of a suboptimally managed company becoming a target of a hostile bid is likely to be a factor, partly, of the efficiency of the market for corporate control in the company's country of domicile. Australia has a reasonably efficient market for control, by comparison with most other developed economies. Dignam found that, in the 10 years from 1992 to 2001, there were 401 completed mergers and acquisitions (M&A) transactions involving Australian listed companies as targets, of which 75 (18.7 per cent) were hostile. Comparing Australia to the United Kingdom and the United States, Dignam concluded that Australia's market for corporate control was comparatively weak. He found that only 29 of the 401 M&A transactions (7.2 per cent) were successful hostile bids, compared to just over 20 per cent for the UK during 1988–98, and 21 per cent for the US during 1980–94. Nonetheless, contrasted with most other developed economies, such as Japan and the countries of continental Europe, it is clear that Australia's incidence of hostile bids overall, and of those that succeed, places the country at the upper end of the scale in terms of a developed market for corporate control.

Jennifer G. Hill, 'Subverting Shareholder Rights: Lessons from News Corp.'s Migration to Delaware' (2010) 63 *Vanderbilt Law Review* 1, 22–6

Significant differences exist between the United States and other common law countries, including Australia, with respect to the balance of power between shareholders and directors in takeovers …

Under U.S. law, assessment of directors' defensive conduct in takeovers is the province of state law and courts. Delaware law, in spite of the potential for intense scrutiny of directors' defensive tactics following the *Unocal* decision, continues to accord great deference to board decisions under a paradigm in which the board occupies a "gatekeeper" role. Although views differ on whether this gatekeeper paradigm in fact promotes shareholder interests, the assumption that board access to defensive tactics is a vital antidote to coercive bids continues to have strong traction in U.S. corporate law scholarship.

In the United Kingdom, takeover disputes are resolved not by the courts but by a specialized non-judicial body, the Panel on Takeovers and Mergers (the "UK Panel"), which is responsible for administering the City Code on Takeovers and Mergers (the "City Code"). The operation of the U.K. Panel reflects a self-regulatory approach to takeovers and has served as the blueprint for reform in numerous jurisdictions, including Australia, Hong Kong, Ireland, and South Africa. The U.K. approach has thus far been characterized by an extremely low incidence of tactical litigation compared to the United States …

In contrast to Delaware's deference to board discretion, the City Code seriously restricts the ability of the board to engage in defensive tactics and implement entrenching mechanisms. It elevates shareholder decisionmaking power during a takeover, an approach which also underpins recent European Community developments in takeover law. A central feature of the City Code is the "frustrating action" principle, which prohibits directors, in the absence of shareholder approval, from taking any action that may result in frustration of a bona fide offer or in the shareholders being denied the opportunity to decide an offer on its merits. Some scholars argue that differences in the prevailing paradigms in the U.K. and U.S. context are attributable to the stronger influence of institutional investors under the U.K. self-regulatory regime than in the United States, where the balance of power is firmly tilted towards management.

Australia's takeover laws also diverge from the Delaware approach and have been described as "unique" and "widely regarded as some of the most restrictive among capitalist economies." They are explicitly based on policies of equality of opportunity and protection of minority shareholders …

Australian law moved closer to U.K. law in 2000, when responsibility for the resolution of takeover disputes shifted from the courts to the Australian Takeovers Panel. Although Australian courts traditionally adopted a fiduciary duty analysis to assess directors' defensive conduct, the Australian Takeovers Panel diverged sharply from this approach by implementing its own "frustrating action" policy. This policy focused on the effect, rather than the purpose, of directors' conduct in response to a takeover, and limited permissible action by the board in the absence of shareholder consent. It constituted a major shift in the balance of power between the board and shareholders during a bid under Australian law.

Emma Armson, 'Lessons for the Australian Takeovers Panel from the United Kingdom' (2014) 29 *Australian Journal of Corporate Law* 295, 310–13

The UK Panel's key roles involve setting, administering, monitoring compliance with and enforcing the detailed rules contained in the UK Code, as well as its 'spirit' and General Principles …

Unlike the UK Panel, the Australian Panel does not act of its own volition, but instead decides applications brought before it. Its key role is to make a declaration of unacceptable circumstances and orders where appropriate. The panel may make a declaration where it appears that circumstances are unacceptable having regard to (i) their effect on control or an acquisition of a substantial interest in a company (ii) the purposes of the takeover provisions set out below, or (iii) if they are likely to give rise to a contravention of the provisions on takeovers, compulsory acquisitions, takeover rights and liabilities, substantial shareholdings or tracing beneficial ownership …

Takeover disputes are resolved by the Australian Panel based primarily on the purposes of the takeover provisions. These purposes set out the underlying policy of ensuring that acquisitions take place in an 'efficient, competitive and informed market,' target shareholders have enough information, reasonable time to make a decision and are afforded a 'reasonable and equal opportunity to participate in any benefits' under a takeover bid, and an appropriate procedure is followed prior to the use of the compulsory acquisition provisions. The purposes are implemented in the takeover provisions in Ch 6 of the Corporations Act …

The Australian Panel comprises legal and commercial experts in takeovers, and relies on less formal procedures than a court. Proceedings are generally conducted based on written submissions, with parties only rarely appearing before the panel in oral conferences. Matters are decided by a 'sitting Panel' comprising three members, from a current total of 41 part-time members.

Notes and Questions

1. Why do takeovers occupy such an important role in corporate governance and regulation?
2. What do you consider the benefits (or disadvantages) to be of using a specialist panel to resolve takeover disputes, rather than the courts?
3. In what ways does Australia's Takeovers Panel differ from its UK equivalent?
4. In recent years, there has been a dramatic increase in the use of schemes of arrangement, rather than hostile takeover bids, to effect changes in corporate control in Australia.

5.5 Law and Enforcement

A contributing factor in the complexity of Australian corporate governance is the interaction between the general law and statutory law in the context of directors' duties. Like the UK Companies Act 2006, the Corporations Act codifies a number of directors' and officers' duties (ss. 180–4). However, unlike its UK equivalent, which supplants directors' general law duties, the Australian version explicitly preserves directors' general law duties.

Australia's corporate law regime is also unusual in terms of enforcement. It relies heavily on a public enforcement model, whereby ASIC is the main enforcement mechanism for breach of statutory directors' duties under the civil penalty regime in Part 9.4B of the Corporations Act.

Australia provides a striking contrast in this regard to the UK and the US, which rely upon private enforcement mechanisms. The primary mechanism for enforcement of directors' duties in the UK is through shareholder derivative suits, although historically these have been rare. In the United States, although derivative suits are common, directors, particularly non-executive directors, are effectively insulated from the financial consequences of breach of directors' duties (except where breach of loyalty is involved) by, for example, the business judgment rule and exculpation clauses in corporate charters.

The duty of care and diligence under s. 180(1) of the Corporations Act has become one of the most important, and controversial, duties owed by directors. In recent years, ASIC has brought a number of high-profile cases alleging breach of this duty by company directors. These cases demonstrate that Australian directors, in contrast to their US counterparts, face the real possibility of liability for breach of duty of care and diligence. This was not always the case. Historically, the standard of care for directors was relatively lax. However, in 1959, Menzies J. of the High Court of Australia (writing extracurially) stated that it should not to be thought that "honest, diligent muddling will be tolerated" and "what is expected of directors will tend to become the measure of what is required of them." Menzies J.'s comments ultimately proved to be prophetical.

It has been said that dicta in a prominent decision in the mid 1990s, *Daniels* v. *Anderson* (1995) 37 NSWLR 437 represented a "quantum shift" in raising the legal expectations of Australian directors and officers with regard to the duty of care. Australian case law in this area has been influential internationally; it has been cited judicially in Hong Kong, Singapore and the UK. However, unlike the UK, where breach-of-duty actions are exceedingly rare, there are numerous examples of such actions in Australia as a result of public enforcement under the civil penalty regime.

Michelle Welsh, 'Realising the Public Potential of Corporate Law: Twenty Years of Civil Penalty Enforcement in Australia' (2014) 42 *Federal Law Review* 217, 220, 224–6, 230, 234

The questions considered [in this article] are: whose interests should the public regulator represent when it is tasked with the responsibility of enforcing the statutory directors' duties that largely codify fiduciary and common law duties? Given that the duties are owed by directors to their company, should the regulator represent the interests of the company and its shareholders – who have suffered a loss as a result of the alleged contravention of the directors' duties – or should it represent the interests of the members of the larger community? In these situations, what are the interests of the larger community? …

The argument advanced in this article is that despite the fact that the statutory directors' duties codify what are in effect private rights between directors and the companies they control, the primary role of a public regulator is *not* to utilise the enforcement mechanisms at its disposal in order to obtain compensation for companies which have suffered a loss. Rather, the regulator's role is to act in the public interest. This interest is best served if the regulator utilises the enforcement mechanisms strategically to encourage individuals, who would otherwise be inclined towards non-compliance, to alter their behavior and comply with the statutory directors' duties …

[The civil penalty] regime greatly expanded the role of public enforcement following contraventions of the statutory directors' duties. Traditionally the company and, in limited circumstances, shareholders had standing to enforce contraventions of the directors' duties. The civil penalty regime introduced in 1993 gave ASIC standing to take civil enforcement action following suspected contraventions of the statutory directors' duties …

This civil penalty regime allows ASIC to issue court-based proceedings against directors who are suspected of breaching the statutory directors' duties, and to seek declarations of contravention, pecuniary penalties, disqualification and compensation orders. Any compensation order made is for the benefit of the company to which the contravening conduct relates. Proceedings for a declaration of contravention and civil penalty orders are treated as civil proceedings for the purpose of the application of the rules of evidence and procedure, and the standard of proof is on the balance of probabilities …

Regulatory theory and in particular, responsive regulation theory, posits that it is possible for public regulators to exercise enforcement mechanisms in a manner that encourages increased levels of compliance. Responsive regulation provides insights into how regulatory regimes should be constructed and how regulators should utilize the enforcement mechanisms to achieve this aim. It requires regulators to utilize these mechanisms in certain strategic ways that are focused on securing maximum voluntary compliance, rather than being focused on obtaining compensation for past losses …

ASIC has achieved a high degree of success with its civil penalty applications that allege that a contravention of the statutory directors' duties has occurred. In 29 of the 33 finalised cases ASIC obtained a declaration of contravention and civil penalty orders against at least one of the named defendants. ASIC was not successful in four of the 33 finalised cases.

Notes and Questions

1. Professor Welsh argues that ASIC, as a public regulator, should not be focused on obtaining compensation for past losses on behalf of investors. Do you agree with this normative argument?
2. The article notes that ASIC "does not have the ability nor the resources to detect every contravention." Does this have any implications for the type of cases that ASIC will decide to pursue in the courts?
3. In early 2018, the Australian government announced that it would significantly increase the penalties for corporate and financial misconduct, including under the civil penalty regime. See Australian Government, the Treasury, *Boosting Penalties to Protect Australian Consumers from Corporate and Financial Misconduct* (April 20 2018). Do you think higher penalties act as an effective deterrent?

5.5.1 The *James Hardie* Litigation

Jennifer G. Hill, 'Evolving Directors' Duties in the Common Law World,' in Adolfo Paolini (ed.), *Research Handbook on Directors' Duties* (Cheltenham, UK and Northampton, MA: Edward Elgar, 2014), pp. 3, 14–19

The *James Hardie* litigation traversed several courts between 2009 and 2012. Key decisions were *ASIC v Macdonald (No 11)* in the Supreme Court of New South Wales, *Morley v ASIC* in the New South Wales Court of Appeal, and finally *ASIC v Hellicar* in the High Court of Australia.

At first instance in *ASIC v Macdonald (No 11)* … Gzell J held that JHIL's issuance of the final ASX announcement to the effect that the Foundation was 'fully-funded' was misleading or deceptive, thereby contravening the Corporations Act.

The non-executive directors were found to have breached the statutory duty of care and diligence under section 180 of the Corporations Act on the basis that they knew, or should have known, that unequivocal public statements of this kind could result in legal liability, harm to the company's reputation, and market backlash … Gzell J held that JHIL's non-executive directors, together with the chief executive officer ('CEO'), chief financial officer ('CFO') and the joint company secretary/general counsel, had breached the statutory duty of care and diligence under the Corporations Act. The judge subsequently imposed a five year disqualification order and a pecuniary penalty of A$30,000 for each of the non-executive directors …

Gzell J's finding that JHIL's board had approved a draft version of the final ASX announcement at its meeting on 15 February 2001, while consistent with the board minutes, directly contradicted the evidence of JHIL's directors …

The JHIL directors not only denied authorising the draft ASX announcement, but also asserted that they *would* not have authorised an unqualified announcement, thereby reinforcing ASIC's claim that the announcement was indeed misleading or deceptive. The judge held that approval of the draft ASX announcement was part of the directors' monitoring function, rather than a matter of 'operational responsibility.'

Several possible liability safe harbours were unavailable to the non-executive directors on the particular facts of the case. Since the directors denied approving the draft ASX announcement, they did not seek to rely on the business judgment rule. Reflecting a trend in contemporary Australian corporate law, Gzell J also held that delegation was unavailable to insulate directors from liability. In his view, '[m]anagement having brought the matter to the board, none of them was entitled to abdicate responsibility by delegating his or her duty to a fellow director …'

A final volte-face in the *James Hardie* litigation occurred in 2012, when the High Court of Australia considered the matter. In *ASIC v Hellicar*, the High Court unanimously allowed ASIC's appeal, and restored Gzell J's first instance decision that the non-executive directors and company secretary/general counsel had breached their statutory duty of care and diligence …

ASIC v Hellicar represented a major victory for ASIC and other government regulators, as well as a cautionary tale for directors. The *James Hardie* litigation as a whole represents a watershed in Australian corporate law. Previously, Australian corporate law, like its US counterpart, tended to maintain a clear divide between conduct and decision rules, particularly in relation to non-executive directors. Although the leading decision on directors' duty of care and diligence, the mid-1990s case of *Daniels v Anderson*, contained strong dicta about the responsibilities of all directors, ultimately these aspirational statements were not [at that time] matched by liability for non-executive directors.

5.5.2 The *Centro* Litigation

The extracted articles that follow discuss cases involving the Centro Group, namely: (1) *ASIC* v. *Healey* (2011) 196 FCR 291 (*Centro Liability Decision*); and (2) *ASIC* v. *Healey [No 2]* (2011) 196 FCR 430 (*Centro Penalty Decision*). Two US commentators described the *Centro Liability Decision* as a "wake-up call from down under." Whereas that decision was considered by many to be too harsh on the defendant directors, the *Centro Penalty Decision* was widely criticized in the financial press for being too lenient.

John Lowry, 'The Irreducible Core of the Duty of Care, Skill and Diligence of Company Directors: *Australian Securities and Investments Commission v Healey*' (2012) 75 *Modern Law Review* 249, 249–50, 254

The decision [in *Centro Liability Decision*] is the latest development in the trend seen both in Australia and the UK towards imposing greater accountability on directors in discharging their duties of care, skill and diligence. It also highlights the fundamental importance of financial disclosure both as a regulatory tool and as a key component for ensuring that the markets can effectively monitor the performance of corporate management ...

The proceedings were brought by ... ASIC against the CEO, the CFO, the non-executive chairman and five other non-executive directors of the Centro group of companies. ASIC sought declarations that each of the defendants had breached their statutory duty of care and diligence owed to the Centro companies and thereby contravened relevant provisions of the (Australian) Corporations Act 2001 (Cth) in approving consolidated financial accounts for the Centro group for the financial year ending 30 June 2007. The consolidated financial statements had incorrectly classified A$1.5 billion in debt as non-current liabilities (when they were in fact current liabilities) and failed to disclose US$1.75 billion in guarantees ... This was in circumstances where both Centro management and Centro's auditor, PricewaterhouseCoopers (PwC), had previously reviewed the financial statements and the directors' report and had failed to identify any such errors. It was held by Middleton J that each of the directors had breached their duty of care and diligence in relation to the relevant Centro companies and had failed to take all reasonable steps to ensure compliance with the financial reporting obligations ...

The key question for Middleton J was whether directors of substantial publicly listed companies are required to apply their own minds to, and carry out a careful review of, the proposed financial statements and the proposed directors' report in order to determine that the information they contain is consistent with the director's own knowledge of the company's affairs. Closely linked to this question was whether the defendant directors had omitted to raise material matters that should have been known to them. The point was made by the judge that the case before him 'is not about a mere technical oversight' given that the information not disclosed was material to the risks facing the companies: '[t]he importance of the financial statements is one of the fundamental reasons why directors are required to approve them and resolve that they give a true and fair view.'

Jennifer G. Hill, 'Centro and the Monitoring Board – Legal Duties versus Aspirational Ideals in Corporate Governance' (2012) 35 *University of New South Wales Law Journal* 341, 353–6

The *Centro Liability Decision* clearly reflects the upward trajectory of the duty of care and diligence in Australia since the early 1990s, when a series of cases in the areas of insolvent trading and the duty of care provided the first judicial indication that legislative changes and increasing community expectations meant that more would be required of Australian directors than had historically been the case. These cases stressed that the law would no longer tolerate the passive or incompetent director, and that directors must have sufficient financial competence and knowledge of the company's affairs to enable them to reach an informed opinion as to the company's financial capacity …

However, the overall doctrinal message of the *Centro Liability Decision* changes significantly when viewed in combination with the *Centro Penalty Decision*. Whereas the *Centro Liability Decision* found that the executive officers and non-executive directors had all breached their duties of care and diligence, the later decision distinguished between the defendants in terms of the penalty outcomes of those contraventions. In the *Centro Penalty Decision*, Middleton J made detailed declarations of contravention against all defendants. He imposed a fine of A$30,000 on Centro's former CEO, and a two year managerial disqualification order on its former CFO. However, no penalties were imposed on the six non-executive directors.

Once Middleton J had determined breach of the duty of care and diligence in the *Centro Liability Decision*, the focus shifted, in the *Centro Penalty Decision*, to consideration of a different set of mitigation techniques, including exoneration provisions in the *Corporations Act*, which assumed centre stage. These provisions grant the court power to excuse a person from breach where the person acted honestly and ought to be excused, having regard to all the circumstances of the case …

Justice Middleton could have decided that Centro's non-executive directors were exonerated from liability by virtue of these provisions. Yet he did not. Rather, he held that the non-executive directors had contravened the *Corporations Act* and, accordingly, the Court should make declarations of contravention, but that no further penalty would be imposed upon them.

Notes and Questions

1. Do you consider that the decision in the *Centro Liability Decision* was too stringent and the decision in the *Centro Penalty Decision* was too lenient? What might explain the same judge adopting seemingly divergent approaches in these two cases?
2. In both the *Centro* and *James Hardie* litigation, certain matters were regarded as "non-delegable" by the directors. Is this realistic in modern public corporations? How might the law determine which tasks can be delegated and which cannot?
3. In a number of recent cases, ASIC has adopted a "stepping stone" approach to duty-of-care liability. Under this approach, ASIC has brought proceedings under s. 180(1) of the Corporations Act against directors, on the basis of their failure to prevent contraventions of other provisions of the Act by the company itself. Not surprisingly, this form of liability, which greatly expands the risk of breach of the duty of care for company directors, is very controversial. Is this form of liability consistent with a monitoring role for directors?
4. It should be noted that ASIC's prominent public enforcement role under the civil penalty regime is complemented by some private enforcement mechanisms. For example, in 2000 a new statutory derivative suit under Part 2F.1A of the Corporations Act was introduced to overcome traditional obstacles to shareholder actions. Yet, such actions are relatively rare, possibly due to reluctance by courts to grant applicants an indemnity against costs from the company. On the other hand, there has been a surge in class actions in Australia over the last decade or so. The development of class actions as a private enforcement mechanism was facilitated by the rise of litigation funding, which performs a similar function to contingency fee arrangements in the US.

Statutes and Regulators

Statutes, Rules, and Codes

Corporations Act 2001 (Cth)

Australian Securities Investments Commission Act 2001

Australian Securities Exchange (ASX) Listing Rules

ASX Corporate Governance Council, *Corporate Governance Principles and Recommendations* (3rd edn, 2014) [at the time of this book going to press, a fourth edition of this text is under consideration. If adopted, it will contain some significant changes to the third edition; see fourth edition consultation draft, at www.asx.com.au/documents/asx-compliance/consultation-draft-cgc-4th-edition.pdf]

Regulators

Australian Securities and Investments Commission (ASIC)

Australian Prudential Regulation Authority (APRA)

Australian Securities Exchange (ASX)

6

HONG KONG

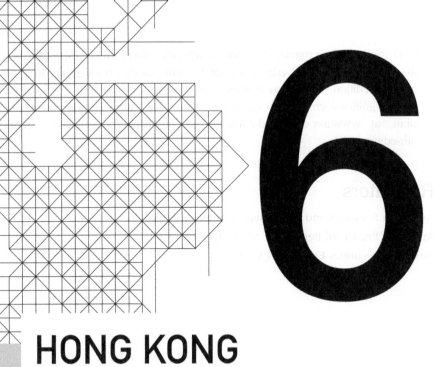

S. H. Goo and Yu-Hsin Lin

Since the 1990s, Hong Kong has been working hard to improve its corporate governance system. Although a common law jurisdiction, its stock market differs from the NYSE and LSE, as there has always been a large concentration of ownership which brings a set of different agency problems, namely expropriation of minority interests rather than managerial abuses. But at the same time, there is an increasing number of mainland state-owned enterprises (SOEs) in the market which brings all types of agency problems, namely managerial abuses, expropriation of minority interest, and the failure to pursue shareholder value maximization. To add to the complication, 85 percent of the listed companies are not incorporated in Hong Kong, which means that many provisions in the Companies Ordinance do not apply. Thus, the regulators including the exchange and the Securities and Futures Commission (SFC) have to think outside the box to come up with effective measures to improve corporate governance. By and large, they have succeeded in crafting a system that is comparable to the international standards. However, room for further improvement remains in the effective enforcement of those standards.

6.1 Board Function

6.1.1 Division of Corporate Powers

In general, Hong Kong follows the shareholder primacy approach. Directors are required by law to act in the interests of the shareholders of the company. The board structure of Hong Kong companies follows the UK and US model where there is a unitary board in charge of monitoring the management.

The Model Article for Public Companies Limited by Shares only provides a starting point in understanding the division of powers and the role of the board in companies. The Hong Kong Corporate Governance Code and Corporate Governance Report (CG Code) provides a better illustration of the role of the board in practice where the board generally plays the role of supervising management and may delegate authority to the managers. Where the articles already conferred management rights to the board, the management power of the board is still subject to the control of shareholders by supermajority or special resolutions.

6.1.2 The Role of Independent Directors

In 2004, the Stock Exchange of Hong Kong (SEHK) introduced new requirements under its listing rules with regard to board independence under which listed companies had to have at least three independent non-executive directors (INEDs) and

The work presented in this chapter was financially supported by a grant from the Research Grants Council of the Hong Kong Special Administrative Region, China, Project No. CityU11606017.

at least one of the INEDs had to have appropriate professional qualifications or accounting or related financial management expertise. A subsequent amendment required listed companies to have INEDs represent at least one-third of the board by December 31, 2012.

In addition, the CG Code sets out the principles of good corporate governance, and two levels of recommendations: (a) code provisions; and (b) recommended best practices. Issuers must state whether they have complied with the code provisions set out in the CG Code and give considered reasons for any deviation in their interim reports and annual reports.

Under the CG Code, the INEDs should be expressly identified as such in all corporate communications that disclose the names of directors (A.3.1). The recommended best practice provides that serving more than nine years could be relevant to the determination of a non-executive director's independence. If an INED serves more than nine years, any further appointment should be subject to a separate resolution by shareholders. The board should set out why they believe the individual continues to be independent and should be re-elected (A.4.3).

Hong Kong Institute of Directors, *Guide for Independent Non-Executive Directors*, July 2012

The challenges faced by Hong Kong's independent directors grow out of a corporate governance setting where boards typically are controlled by the founding family or otherwise dominated by a close-knit shareholding group, where the presence of independent directors on the board is mainly the result of the Listing Rules of Hong Kong Exchanges and Clearing Limited and where directors in these positions because of legal and business realities often question whether they are adding any value or feel powerless to voice contrary opinions or effect positive changes.

Douglas W. Arner, David C. Donald, Say Hak Goo, Richard Weixing Hu, Chen Lin, Bryane Michael, Frank M. Song, Wilson H. S. Tong, Chenggang Xu, Dariusz Wojcik, and Simon X. Zhao, 'Assessing Hong Kong as an International Financial Centre' (April 1, 2014), University of Hong Kong Faculty of Law Research Paper No. 2014/012, at 123–7

The effectiveness of independent directors has been widely questioned

Experiences – not training or education – serves as a key predictor of a director's performance. As such, instead of mandating training, the SEHK (or the Companies Registry) should work with organisations such as the Hong Kong Institute of Directors (HIKoD) to promote apprentice schemes and a flexible job market for corporate directors. The data suggest that a directorship in Hong Kong still relies

Figure 6.1 A directorship in Hong Kong is still something to do after retiring from a "normal" job

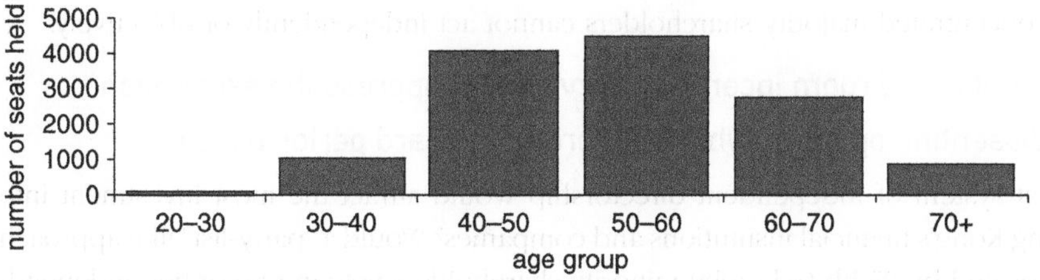

Source: webb-site.com
The data show the distribution by age of directorships held in Hong Kong's companies. Of the 13,249 directors' seats up for grabs, about 500 are held by individuals who have lived beyond Hong Kong's expected life expectancy of 72.

on experience and contacts built up over a long career. Figure 6.1 shows the age in 2013 of directors in Hong Kong's listed companies. The average age sits at around 55 years old (the age when many used to contemplate retirement) ...

The best way to encourage the professionalization of today's cohort of company directors ... consists of making corporate directorship into a self-regulating profession. As the SEHK has already sought to regulate the experience and performance standards of directors through the CG Code, the SEHK should create an ad hoc committee with the terms of reference for creating such a profession. A first step could be creating an apprentice system for young investor-managers keen on serving as a director on a larger company. The standing committee would decide on methods of training, evaluation, job "matching" and so forth ...

The best directors balance multiple board appointments with the strains of over-commitment. For Hong Kong, the data suggest that 6 directorships serves as the maximum for Hong Kong's very effective directors ... Companies should seek to attract the most (or most influential) directors – who in turn take on several directorships. However, beyond 6 directorships, the data suggest these directors become too busy and their returns start to fall. Numerous proposals to limit the number of board directors sit on focus on the "busyness" part of a director's ability to handle such appointments – without looking at the "skill" part ... This suggests either independent directors who hold more seats are very much superior to their non-independent colleagues – or more likely serious under-supply and over-demand for excellent independent directors. Proposals aimed at limiting directorships would cause serious under-supply in the market for directors.

Another – extremely valid – question concerns whether independent directors actually work. The Hong Kong media points to independent directors who resigned rather than face the difficult problems faced by their companies. On the other hand, a host of academic evidence ... supports the fact that independent directors "work" rather than the alternative. On the other hand, Webb (2011) makes an excellent point when he notes that independent directors who require the votes of concentrated majority shareholders cannot act independently or objectively.

Current board room incentives perversely suppress the expression of dissenting opinions which can promote board performance

What system of independent directorship would attract the most investment into Hong Kong's financial institutions and companies? Would a "party-list" like approach advocated by Webb (whereby minority shareholders vote in one or two independent directors) encourage or repel foreign and local investors? The data show that independent directors increase firm value – but we do not know if such statistical findings would translate into portfolio managers' dollars. Figure 6.2 – if representative at all of true local preferences – suggest that reserving some independent director spots for minority shareholder election might be popular among investors …

Such an approach would improve corporate governance – and thus investment prospects of Hong Kong as an international financial centre for three reasons. First, the extent data shows that truly independent directors do improve a company's investment prospects. When companies really need outside capital, they tend to desire truly independent directors. Second, "dissenting opinions" by independent directors during board meetings and AGMs help serve as the empirical fodder for changing long-term codes of corporate governance. Webb wants independent directors to have their own section in annual reports and to have the right to submit reports to the SFC. Even if they do none of these things, their deliberations will publicly identify weak parts of Hong Kong companies' corporate governance …

Figure 6.2 "Party-list" board elections needed given extreme concentration among Hong Kong corporate shareholders

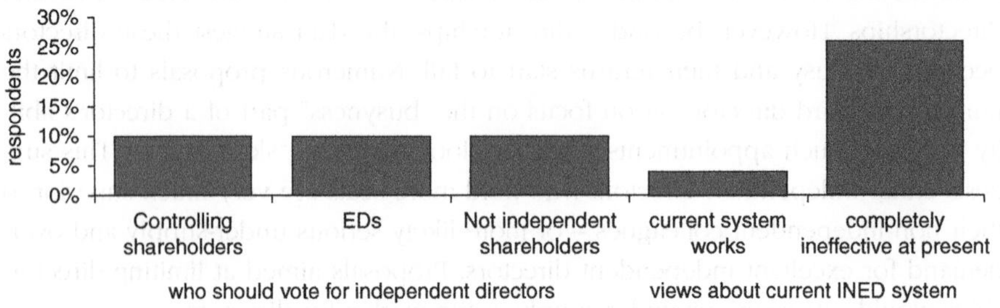

Source: webb-site.com

The data show the results of a 175-person poll conducted by David Webb's website. Such results may show bias, as his newsletter subscribers likely reflect his interests and preferences. Nevertheless, they are the only data we have on investors' preferences.

Third, such a proposal would improve the system without affecting the economic interests of majority shareholders. Even 33% directors would have relatively little say during board meetings – and no voting power at AGMs. As such, their deliberations would likely generate a fair amount of public discussion, without actually impairing the interests of Hong Kong's concentrated shareholders in the short-term.

Notes and Questions

1. How can independent directors address the agency problems presented in a family-controlled company?
2. Widespread concern remains over the independence of independent directors where the controlling shareholders dominate the nomination and election process. How can the process be improved?
3. The definition of independent directors does not address the personal relations they may have with controlling shareholders, insiders, or CEOs. How can the law effectively address this issue? Discuss whether the *ex post* judicial review of independence in the US should apply to Hong Kong.
4. Is nine years too long for an independent director? Should there be a limit on how many companies a person can serve as an independent director? Should they be given a section in the annual report to express their views?
5. What do you think of the apprentice system for young investor-managers to train future outside directors?
6. Should shareholders not among the top 10 percent be allowed to nominate directors?

6.1.3 Fiduciary Duties

Directors' duties include duty-of-care and fiduciary duties. In the past, directors' duties were governed by common law and generally followed UK case law. In light of the codification in UK, Hong Kong codified directors' duty of care in 2014 and restated the minimum objective standard as adopted in the common law. The objective standard for duty of care is "the general knowledge, skill and experience that may reasonably be expected of a person carrying out the functions carried out by the director in relation to the company." This objective test provides a minimum standard of care and cannot be adjusted downward to accommodate someone who is incapable of attaining the basic standard. But for a director appointed due to some special knowledge, skill or experience, a higher standard of care will apply.

Although duty of care has been codified, fiduciary duties are still governed by case law. The main reason is the reluctance to accept the UK "enlightened shareholder value" (ESV) approach to the duty to promote the success of the company.

During the consultation process, it appears that respondents misunderstood the ESV approach as requiring directors to be responsible to all stakeholders in addition to shareholders.

Notes and Questions

1. Do you think the statutory statement of directors' duty of care, skill, and diligence brings much-needed clarity to the law and offers invaluable guidance to directors on what is expected of them?
2. Should the Companies Ordinance go further to codify directors' fiduciary duties? Should the UK's ESV approach be adopted?

6.2 Ownership Structure

6.2.1 The Dominance of Family-Controlled and Foreign Companies

A unique feature of the stock market is its domination by companies with concentrated ownership. Listed companies are either Hong Kong or PRC companies dominated by controlling families, or PRC companies dominated by the state (PRC SOEs) or a small number of Hong Kong companies controlled by the Hong Kong government. Only a small percentage of the companies listed in the stock exchange are widely held corporations. This brings unique challenges in regulating the corporate governance and other aspects of listed companies.

According to *The Economist*, in 2015, the top fifteen families controlled assets worth 84 percent of GDP. Companies controlled by controlling families are less likely to have managerial abuses, as the directors and managers are often appointed by the controlling shareholders who will monitor their performance. Thus, the usual corporate governance issues of managerial abuses, and the mechanisms widely used in the US and UK in widely held corporations are not usually relevant. Controlling shareholders are more likely to expropriate minority shareholders through related party transactions, change of control transactions, or excessive remuneration.

Likewise, in a small number of PRC SOEs, the state has a close monitoring role and managerial abuses will be less likely. But the state may use the company assets for objectives that the state pursues and not necessarily for the benefit of other shareholders. Where the state does not exercise control, ironically, the usual managerial abuses one sees in a widely held corporation in the US and the UK are likely to happen. For these companies, the mechanisms used in the US and the

UK against managerial abuses may be of reference value. With the number of PRC SOEs listing increasing over the years, these mechanisms become more and more relevant.

David Donald, 'Hong Kong's Economic Structure: The Corporate Control Context,' in *A Financial Centre for Two Empires: Hong Kong's Corporate, Securities and Tax Laws in Its Transition from Britain to China* (Cambridge: Cambridge University Press, 2014), p. 54

Two salient economic characteristics

The dominance of substantial shareholders

The history of Hong Kong … has cut a path of development in which private ordering by both British and Chinese merchants greatly controlled the shape of the Hong Kong economy, society and government, which let the regulatory actions and interventions of government minimal … Britain and the Commonwealth were the sources for the development of much of Hong Kong's common law, meaning that the doctrines and principles found in this body of law are not always well adapted to the local circumstances of Hong Kong. While this relationship is no longer binding post-1997, the path dependence of Hong Kong's history is very strong in this regard. On the other hand, the relationship with China has been a constant in Hong Kong's history that varied in shape and intensity as a factor of the state of political affairs in China … We thus understand that the Region called Hong Kong presents a very complex phenomenon – absorbing and adapting British institutions while reacting and adjusting itself in relation to China's, Asia's and indeed global developments.

In this political–economic climate, and particularly during times when its domestic market was largely disconnected from mainland China, Hong Kong business leaders spun out webs of control in corporate groups that came to dominate the relatively isolated local economy in many areas and serve as bases for larger regional and global business expansion … The investment of leading local companies in mainland China has both accelerated the economic integration of the two areas and increased the size of some local corporate groups. The result of this developmental path has been to create both a salient characteristic of the Hong Kong economy … and a resulting type of legal risk: in the relatively small local economy within Hong Kong, important sectors are dominated by a few corporate groups controlled by dominant owners, often founding families. The minority shareholders investing in these listed companies that remain dominated by controlling families or, indeed, the PRC government must be adequately protected …

... The presence of dominant shareholders in Asian companies, including those of Hong Kong, has been well documented ... However, relative to most other jurisdictions in the analysis, these authors also found low use of pyramid structures and dual class share structures, techniques that can be employed unfairly to achieve greater control than the shareholding in question might otherwise lend its owner. In fact ... use of dual classes of shares with different voting rights is prohibited on the SEHK.

... [I]n spite of this correlation between shareholding and higher pay, executive compensation in Hong Kong remains low by international comparison. On the basis of the member companies of the Hang Seng Index (HSI) for which pre-tax information on chief executive officers (CEOs) is available, the average annual CEO pay for 2011 was just over US$2.9 million, a sum that would make the average CEO of Hong Kong's largest listed companies roughly the 420th most highly paid US CEO according to Forbes 2012 rankings.

A stock market dominated by companies formed under foreign law

A second type of legal risk arises from Hong Kong's character as an international financial centre for mainland China ... Hong Kong, as a Region of China with a freely exchangeable currency and solid rule of law, offered a window to international finance. Mainland Chinese private and state-owned companies have entered Hong Kong to use its stock exchange as a source of external financing. Companies owned directly or indirectly by the PRC, state-owned enterprises (SOEs), have since 1993 listed 'H-shares' in Hong Kong while maintaining another listing in Shanghai or New York ... If we take 1990 as the year when 'the China dimension' of the SEHK began in earnest, we see that the market capitalization of the SEHK has increased 33–fold, from HK$650 billion to HK$21.87 trillion in 2012 ...

A result of this international expansion is that, at the close of 2012, only about 15 per cent of the companies listed on the SEHK were incorporated in Hong Kong. The law where a company is incorporated governs the basic structure of its governance, including the distribution of powers between shareholders and directors, and the duties to which each of these groups are subject. Securities law add provisions on mandatory disclosure and prohibit certain kinds of activities (insider dealing and market manipulation), while exchange listing rules can create contractual duties of disclosure and board composition ... The current national distribution of listings on the SEHK, however, means that the protections afforded investors under Hong Kong company law would not be available for about 85 per cent of the listed companies if Hong Kong did not take measures to correct this ... [This] throws out a significant regulatory challenge for the securities law and the listing rules of Hong Kong. This is particularly true because the PRC SOEs that comprise about 11 per cent of the listed companies and over 20 per cent of the SEHK market capitalization are not only incorporated under PRC law, but are also generally dominated indirectly by the state through a majority shareholding. They are very large companies with very powerful controlling shareholders. At the close of 2012, four of the top five companies by market capitalization listed on the SEHK were SOEs.

David Donald, 'Hong Kong's Economic Structure: The Corporate Control Context,' in *A Financial Centre for Two Empires: Hong Kong's Corporate, Securities and Tax Laws in Its Transition from Britain to China* (Cambridge: Cambridge University Press, 2014), p. 152

Hong Kong company law has established three mechanisms to deal with this problem. First, SEHK examines the law of a jurisdiction before allowing its companies to list on the SEHK, so that a certain level of quality – whether it takes the shape found in Germany or Bermuda – is a prerequisite for listing. Second, the SEHK requires that companies adjust their internal governance before and during listing through commitments made in the listed company's articles of incorporation (certificate, by-laws, *statut*, or *Satzung*). Third, an outreach section of the Hong Kong Companies Ordinance applies a package of 'shareholder protection' mechanisms (including derivative and unfair prejudice actions, and right to inspect records) to companies listed on the SEHK, regardless of where they are incorporated.

David Donald, 'Hong Kong's Economic Structure: The Corporate Control Context,' in *A Financial Centre for Two Empires: Hong Kong's Corporate, Securities and Tax Laws in Its Transition from Britain to China* (Cambridge: Cambridge University Press, 2014), p. 97

Governance relevant information summarized for the dominant corporate groups

The [foregoing] analysis of 15 major corporate groups with companies listed on the SEHK has revealed three types of ownership patterns:

Companies with controlling family shareholders, such as Cheung Kong, companies whose controlling shareholder is the government of China, such as China Mobile, and as the exception, widely held companies such as HSBC. As Table 6.1 makes clear, classic 'Berle and Means' corporations are restricted to the financial sector, and government control is heavily concentrated in the commerce and industry sector, with the 18 per cent holding of Temasek as the non-Chinese exception.

Following the traditional line of thinking on economic development, we would expect that family companies and state-held companies would evolve towards the higher, more American form of a company with widely dispersed shareholdings and professional managers. However, when we examine the information available

Table 6.1 Shareholding types for groups examined

Shareholding structure	Financial sector	Property sector	Commerce and industry
Controlling family (over 30%)		Cheung Kong Hang Lung Henderson New World Sun Hung Kai	Hutchison Jardine Matheson Swire
State control (over 30%)	BOC Standard Chartered (18%)		China Mobile China Resources CITIC Group
Dispersed (all under 10%)	HSBC BEA		

Figure 6.3 Changes in controlling shareholdings (2003–12)

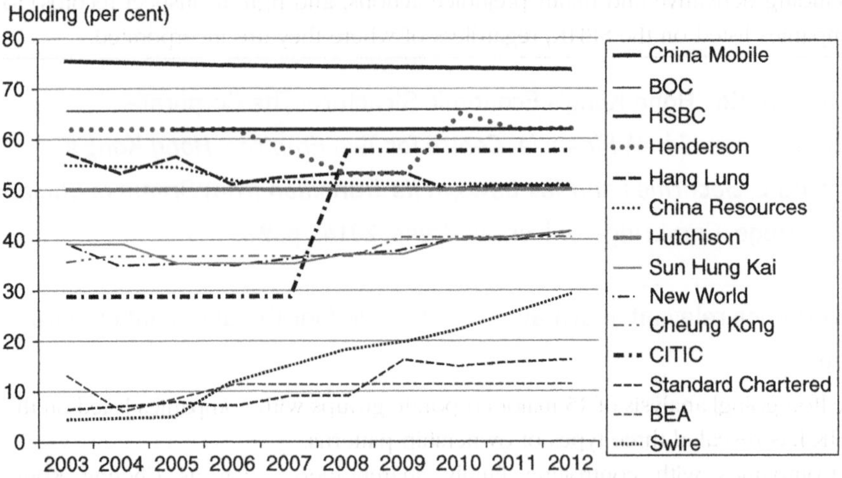

Notes: Majority share changes of listed firms (2003–12). Data taken from the annual financial statements of the companies plotted.

for the lead listed company in the groups discussed, we see a trend towards concentration of holdings rather than towards dispersal. Figure 6.3 shows the concentration trend in shareholding for the major corporate groups analysed in this chapter over the decade from 2002 to 2013 ... This could be a result of controlling shareholder repurchases following the GFC, when outside investors began to lose confidence and reinforcing a controlling position was cheap, or it may indicate that

Table 6.2 Controlling shareholder: board control overlap

Shareholder structure	Family holding	Government holding	Widely held
Shareholding or related party is chairperson	Cheung Kong Hang Lung Henderson Hutchison Sun Hung Kai Jardine	China Mobile (ministerial connection)	BEA (minority, founding shareholder)
Shareholder or related party is CEO	Cheung Kong Henderson Sun Hung Kai Jardine	China Mobile (ministerial connection)	BEA (minority, founding shareholder)
Shareholder or related party is executive director	Cheung Kong Hang Lung Hutchison Henderson Sun Hung Kai New world Jardine	China Mobile (ministerial connection)	BEA (minority, founding shareholder)

the Berle and Means corporation will not be the goal of listed companies in Hong Kong, which is an important fact to consider when building up the Hong Kong regulatory framework with American style protections against strong management. Rather than import such measures, Hong Kong should concentrate on increasing the public float of listed companies, perhaps by increasing the current 25 per cent threshold,[1] and strengthening the protections offered against the abusive acts of controlling shareholders.

In a listed company, exit is always a viable option, but this is not something an international financial centre should encourage, as it thrives by attracting such shareholders from the entire global market. Thus, controlling shareholder domination of the board is not something that is often desirable. Table 6.2 shows that based on the 2012 annual reports for the 15 corporate groups examined, the overlap between controlling shareholders and board control existed primarily in the family operated property development concerns, and in Jardine and Matheson. Going forward, it may be advisable for rules on the information to be provided about directors to better bring out collateral ties (such as ministerial or administrative agency ties) for the board members of an SOE.

1 SEHK Listing Rules, Rule 8.08 (1)(a): "at least 25% of the issuer's total number of issued shares must at all times be held by the public."

Douglas W. Arner et al., 'Assessing Hong Kong as an International Financial Centre' (April 1, 2014), University of Hong Kong Faculty of Law Research Paper No. 2014/012, at 118–19

Figure 6.4 shows a number of studies which look at the extent to which these concentrated owners enrich themselves through self-serving dividend and salary payment practices. While we know the concentrated shareholding decreases shareholder value and deters investment in Hong Kong's companies, we cannot make policies which remedy concentration-related market distortions in Hong Kong's equities markets. Investors in Hong Kong's companies' share also cannot know the extent of

Figure 6.4 Do Hong Kong's majority owners benefit excessively?

Issue	Description
Self-serving salary payments	Cheung et al. (2003) find that even 5% stake or more in a large Hong Kong company means executives get paid more.
Self-serving dividend payments	Chen et al. (2005) find evidence for increased dividend payments as concentrated ownership increases. They view this as expropriation of other investors.
Self-serving short-termism	Carney and Gedajlovic (2002) find evidence for lower capital expenditure and earnings manipulation among companies with high ownership concentrations.
Earnings manipulation	Leung and Horowitz (2003) find that highly concentrated ownership correlates with less disclosure related to each of the firms' operating business segments.
Other self-dealing	Zhang (2008) finds that dividend payments correlate with higher equity valuations – suggesting that investors pay a premium to be able to get their money back. Cheung et al. (2003) find concentrated ownership leads to reductions in firm value.

Insiders may also take the company public when a public valuation will likely bring large premiums over the book value of assets and then go private again when the market undervalues shares. We do not discuss such self-serving profit-taking as no rigorous academic research exists on this trend.

beneficial ownership concentration in the shares they buy (with some exceptions which we address below). With knowledge about the underlying concentration of beneficial ownership in the shares that institutions and individual purchase, they can engage in activism or hedge the risks that such concentration might bring.

6.2.2 Market for Corporate Control

A fair amount of merger and takeover activity exists within groups or by controlling shareholders as part of their restructuring. There is also an increasing number of PRC-outbound M&As (much of which passed through Hong Kong):

> As a general rule, investments into China tend to be private M&A investments, often using a combination of Hong Kong and offshore vehicles to acquire large, but often non-controlling stakes, in PRC businesses in need of capital or expertise. Chinese outbound investments can take a myriad of forms, but frequently utilise Hong Kong holding companies or, if capital-raising is required, Hong Kong listed companies.[2]

Hostile takeovers are rare, however. So there is no active market for corporate control in Hong Kong. This largely follows corporate Asia, where companies tend to be family-run and controlled, therefore deals have to be on an agreed basis (see Larry R. Lang, *Mergers and Acquisitions in Hong Kong* (Hong Kong: Pearson Education (Asia), 2000, preface, pp. vii–viii).

6.2.3 Conflicts of Interests and Related Party Transactions

Many related party transactions exist within groups, many of which are perfectly legitimate, but others are transactions by which controlling shareholders expropriate from the minority shareholders.

Under the Listing Rules, there are basically two types of related party transactions. Notifiable transactions use quantitative tests that establish the relative size of the transaction to the issuer to determine the level of shareholder disclosure or involvement required. They cover share transactions, disclosable transactions, major transactions, very substantial acquisitions, very substantial disposals, and reverse takeovers. For share transactions, all that is required is a notification to the SEHK and publication of an announcement in the newspapers. For disclosable transactions, there is an additional requirement of sending circular about the transaction to shareholders. For all other transactions, further requirements of shareholder approval and accountant report must be met.

2 www.globallegalinsights.com/practice-areas/mergers-and-acquisitions/global-legal-insights–mergers-and-acquisitions-6th-ed./hong-kong

Connected transactions use an objective analysis to determine whether persons connected with the issuer have an interest in the transaction (which therefore creates the risk of conflict of interest) to determine the level of shareholder disclosure or involvement required. They are transactions which involve the issuer and connected persons. The rules are detailed and designed in response to the complicated family and other arrangements in place in Hong Kong. Unless exempted, all connected transactions have to be (i) in writing (ii) announced as soon as practicable (iii) approved by independent shareholders (iv) set out in a circular to shareholders, and (v) reported in issuer's annual report.

Related party transaction should in theory be entered into for the benefit of the companies. However, evidence suggests otherwise due to controlling shareholders' conflict of interest. There have been various consultation papers calling for the statutory backing of listing rules. In the end, only the disclosure of price-sensitive information (PSI) by listed companies, was replaced by Part XIVA (s. 307A–307ZA), of the Securities and Futures Ordinance (SFO). A breach of the Part XIVA attracts civil remedies but is not a criminal offence.

Douglas W. Arner et al., 'Assessing Hong Kong as an International Financial Centre' (April 1, 2014), University of Hong Kong Faculty of Law Research Paper No. 2014/012, 113–15

Reducing self-dealing by connected parties through whistleblowing

Connected party transactions clearly reduce shareholder value in Hong Kong. Figure 6.5 shows the reduction in market premia (the difference between a listed

Figure 6.5 Connected party takeovers and asset sales destroy about 25 percent of the value of Hong Kong companies at turn of the century

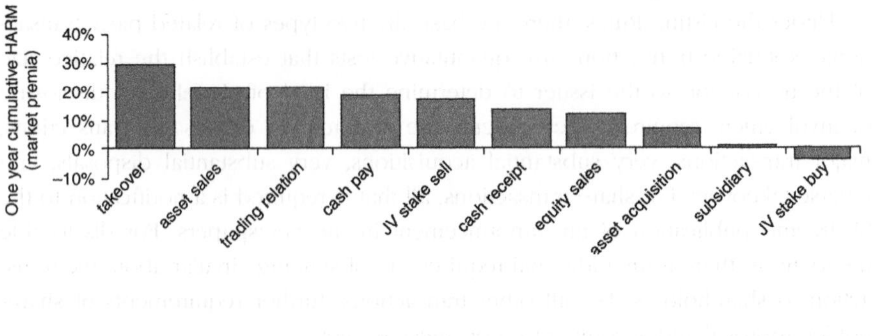

Source: Cheung et al. (2004) at Table 4A

The data show the reduction in market premia (measured by market values divided by the book value of the firm's assets) in 328 regulatory filings. The authors correlate type of transaction with associated change in market premia one year on.

Figure 6.6 Lack of information on connected party transactions causes Hong Kong share prices to go down about 20 percent within ten days from event

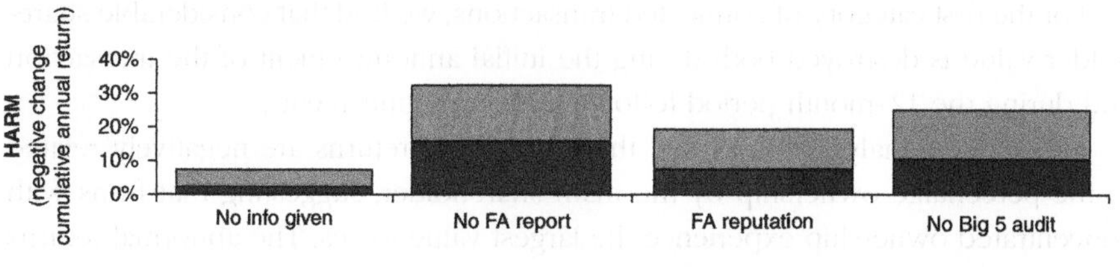

Source: Cheung et al. (2004) at Table 5B

The data show the decrease in market adjusted cumulative annual returns for a number of Hong Kong companies. Correlation analysis determined the decrease in these returns – after controlling for market factors – when companies provided no information on a transaction, and when they do not provide a financial adviser report, for difference in the reputation of the financial adviser involved in the transaction, and when no Big 5 auditor provided assurance over the transaction. The dotted part of the block shows the extra explanatory power the authors got when they controlled for the specific type of transaction (e.g. takeover, asset sale).

company's market capitalization and its book value) ... When connected parties engage in takeover (M&A) activity, firm value decreases by about 30%. Asset sales between connected parties tend to reduce firm value (as measured by the market premium over book value) by about 20%. Such transactions suggest tunneling – as most transactions should aim to increase (rather than decrease) firm value ...

Now the SEHK Listing Rules contain some of the most comprehensive connected party transactions rules in the world [Chapter 14A], and the Companies Ordinance requires disclosure of connected party transactions involving the directors of non-listed companies. [Companies (Directors' Report) Regulation, s. 10] ... Figure 6.6 shows the reduction in firm value (expressed in positive numbers as a harm) due to several informational constraints related to connected party transactions. When the company provided no public information about a connected party transaction, cumulative annual returns on average fell by about 10%. When the financial advisor involved in transaction provided no report, firm value fell ... by about 30%.

Cheung, Yan-Leung, P. Raghavendra Rau, and Aris Stouraitis, 'Tunneling, Propping, and Expropriation: Evidence from Connected Party Transactions in Hong Kong' (2006) 82(2) *Journal of Financial Economics* 343–86, at 345–6

We classify the connected transactions in our sample into three broad categories – a priori likely to result in expropriations (asset acquisitions, asset sales, equity sales, and cash payments to directors), transactions that are likely to benefit the listed firm (cash receipts and subsidiary relationships) and transactions that may have been driven by strategic rationales (takeover offers and joint ventures, joint ventures stake acquisitions and sales).

For the first category of connected transactions, we find that considerable shareholder value is destroyed both during the initial announcement of the transaction and during the 12–month period following the announcement …

Multivariate analysis shows that these abnormal returns are negatively related to the percentage ownership by the main shareholder, suggesting that firms with concentrated ownership experience the largest value losses. The abnormal returns are also negatively related to proxies for information disclosure. Firms that do not provide an assessment of the deal by an independent financial advisor and firms whose auditors are not one of the Big 5 auditing firms experience a negative market reaction, while firms with Level II and III ADRs experience a positive market reaction. In contrast, we find limited evidence that the proportion of independent non-executive directors on the board and the presence of audit committees affect the market reaction.

The likelihood of undertaking connected transactions is higher for firms whose ultimate owners can be traced to mainland China. Furthermore, conditional on undertaking a connected transaction, the likelihood of poor information disclosure, and the likelihood of undertaking transactions that violate the exchange's listing rules are both higher for firms with mainland Chinese ultimate owners and for firms with concentrated ownership …

Finally … we find limited evidence that the market anticipates the expropriation by discounting firms that undertake connected transactions. On average, these firms trade at positive industry-adjusted market-to-book ratios, and do not earn consistently negative abnormal returns during the 12–month period preceding the deal.

Notes and Questions

1. Discuss the corporate governance challenges faced by family-controlled firms.
2. The level of executive compensation is relatively low as compared to other jurisdictions. We can reasonably suspect that the low level of executive compensation results from effective monitoring by family-controlling shareholders. Yet, in line with the new trend in regulating executive pay and requiring disclosure around the world, a remuneration committee chaired by an INED and composed of a majority of INEDs is required. Do you think a remuneration committee is suitable?
3. What are the regulatory challenges faced by a jurisdiction where almost 90 percent of listed companies are incorporated in a foreign jurisdiction? How should the regulatory gap be addressed?

6.3 Law and Enforcement

6.3.1 Private Enforcement

Enforcement of listing rules is primarily carried out by the SEHK. But the sanctions for breach that SEHK can impose are not serious, including private reprimand, public criticism, public censure, suspension of trading, and cancellation of listing. The SEHK cannot impose civil or criminal sanctions such as fines.

A shareholder may bring a private action either in the form of a statutory derivative action if the listed issuer is incorporated in HK, a common law derivative action if incorporated overseas and has a place of business in HK, or a petition for unfair prejudice remedy if incorporated in HK or incorporated elsewhere but has a place of business in HK.

Linklaters (Samantha Thompson et al.), *Comparison of Hong Kong and UK Corporate Governance Considerations in Hong Kong Corporate Governance: A Practical Guide* (London: White Page, 2014), p. 181

Private actions in Hong Kong have been limited to derivative suits and unfair prejudice suits. As of 2014, only 33 statutory derivative actions have been filed since the provisions were introduced into the Companies Ordinance in 2004. They have had a success rate (i.e., leave has been granted to proceed) of about 45%. The decisions appear reasonable and judges have expressed a desire to hear challenges to allegedly bad governance if a plausible argument is made.

... In almost all (12/14) actions in which leave has been granted, the defendant director was also a substantial shareholder. The actions were not based on shareholder action against a professional manager. Controlling shareholders present a real problem. As mentioned above, the Hong Kong courts have recently applied unfair prejudice relief to listed companies for the first time, and this could be very meaningful for the markets. The case *Luck Continent Ltd v Cheng Chee Tock Theodore* ... had unusual facts. It was filed by a majority, not a minority, shareholder, Luck Continent Ltd, which had acquired the listed company CY Foundation Group Ltd through a reverse merger. The unfairness occurred because a shareholder with more than 25% of the shares blocked a special resolution to amend the company's articles, which were in breach of the Exchange's listing rules, thereby forcing the company to stay in suspension from the exchange, with concomitant damage to its share price. The court found that there was a tacit agreement – in the form of an "agreement with the Exchange made for the benefit of both the company and its shareholders" between the company and the shareholders that the company should comply with the SEHK listing requirements, and thus equity demanded such agreement be enforced. As such the company's continuing failure to meet the listing rules (as caused by the blocking shareholder) unfairly prejudiced the plaintiff's legitimate interests, and the court ordered that the company's articles of association be amended to allow for removal of directors by majority vote …

A short term proposal for Hong Kong regulations is that courts should accept and extend the *Luck Continent* decision to guarantee adequate policing of the markets against controlling and minority shareholders, and not primarily by one between professional managers and dispersed shareholders.

6.3.2 Public Enforcement against Market Misconduct

Controlling shareholders and directors are often in possession of confidential information that may also be price sensitive. To prevent them from taking advantage of such information, not only does a statutory requirement under Part XIVA to disclose such information now exist, but there are also provisions in the SFO to regulate insider dealing and other forms of market misconduct such as market manipulation and price rigging. The enforcement against market misconduct has been mainly carried out by the SFC.

David C. Donald and Paul W. H. Cheuk, *Hong Kong's Public Enforcement Model of Investor Protection* (January 26, 2017), Chinese University of Hong Kong Faculty of Law Research Paper No. 2017–01, at 36–8

Actions against market misconduct

The SFC is also the primary enforcer of rules against market misconduct, primarily insider dealing and various forms of market manipulation … Beginning in 2006, the SFC began a "pragmatic shift in … enforcement activities … to send a potent message when breaches occur … to take action which drives changes in behavior." This meant that raw numbers of enforcement actions decreased while the number of high profile, labor-intensive cases increased.

For example, in 2008 the SFC exercised a hitherto dormant power provided under SFO s 385 to intervene in a scheme of arrangement proceeding through which PCCW Ltd (a company dominated by Richard Li, son of Hong Kong wealthiest man, Li Ka-shing) sought to squeeze out its public shareholders at an historically low price and delist voluntarily from the SEHK. Although a scheme designed by Li and his allies to manipulate voting rights was approved at the CFI, the SFC took it to the Court of Appeals, where it was held unfair, which rendered approval for the roll up transaction invalid.

In 2011, the SFC charged a Cayman Island company listed on the SEHK, Hontex International, with publishing misleading statements regarding its accounts in a securities prospectus. The SFC used SFO s 213 to obtain an order that Hontex must make a repurchase offer to all damaged shareholders at a value of HK$1.03 billion. The SFC also revoked the license of Hontex's lead manager (sponsor) for the listing, Mega Capital (Asia), levied a HK$62 million (US$8 million) fine, and proceeded to issue new rules that would expressly subject such sponsors to a regime of duties and prospectus liability.

Under this enforcement policy, actions for insider dealing have also been brought against persons connected with Citic Pacific Ltd and ABN Amro Asset Management (Asia) Ltd. In 2012, the Court of Appeal upheld conviction of an officer of Morgan Stanley Asia Ltd in a case for insider dealing, although the defendant managed to get a reduced prison sentence of six years. The fine was also reduced from HK$23.3 million in appeal to around HK$1.7 million, but only in order to compensate for loses sustained by investors; in subsequent proceedings the SFC obtained restoration orders requiring the former managing director to compensate a total of over HK$23.9 million (US$3 million) to 297 affected investors to restore their pre-transaction positions

S. H. Goo and Anne Carver, 'Civil Remedies: Market Misconduct Tribunal (MMT),' in S. H. Goo et al., *Corporate Governance: The Hong Kong Debate* (Hong Kong: Sweet & Maxwell Asia, 2003), ch. 8

For the SFO, market manipulation was a criminal offence. However, sophisticated market practices and techniques had made it difficult to obtain sufficient evidence to prove market manipulation to the criminal standard of beyond a reasonable doubt. Many offenders were able to escape punishment or liability. Thus, the SFO provides an alternative civil route under the jurisdiction of the MMT to the existing criminal route in dealing with market manipulation. In other words, market manipulation will be subject to both a civil action before MMT in addition to a criminal offence.

In addition, the MMT will take over the jurisdiction of the existing Insider Dealing Tribunal to handle insider dealing ... A number of other specified market misconduct activities are also subject to civil action before the MMT, such as stock market manipulation, false trading in securities or future contracts, price-rigging in securities or futures markets, disclosure of information about prohibited transactions in securities or futures contracts, and disclosure of false or misleading information inducing transactions in securities or futures contracts. [SFO 245] All these types of misconduct and market manipulation and insider dealing are now referred to as "market misconduct" ...

The advantage is that the civil standard of proof of "a balance of probabilities" is used in determining whether market misconduct has been established ... [SFO, 252(7), 387]

The other advantage is the range of sanctions the MMT can impose, which include the following [SFO, 257(1)]:

(a) a "disqualification" order to disqualify a director from being a director of any listed company for a period of up to five years

(b) a "cold shoulder" order (ie a person is denied access to market facilities) for a period of up to five years

(c) a "cease and desist" order (ie an order not to breach the provisions of market misconduct again)

(d) order disgorgement of people plus compound interest thereon

(e) order payment of legal costs and investigation expenses, incurred by the government and the SFC or the FRC; and

(f) refer to any body of which the person who has engaged in market misconduct is a member for possible disciplinary action.

Criminal Offences: The Court

[A]s an alternative to civil proceedings before the MMT, the SFO also provides a criminal route for dealing with market misconduct activities where there is sufficient evidence to meet the criminal standard and it is in the public interests to bring prosecution before the courts. [para. 23] The US, the UK and Australia all have dual criminal and civil routes for dealing with market misconduct, and this factor has influenced the government in choosing this option.

The penalties under the SFO are also substantially increased to the maximum penalty of 10 years' imprisonment or a fine of up to HK$10 million for conviction on indictment, and HK$1 million and three years' imprisonment for summary conviction. [SFO 303] However, the rule against double jeopardy applies so that a person cannot be tried in both the MMT and the courts for the same market misconduct.

The offences of market misconduct mirror the civil actions in the MMT. In other words, all the market misconduct under the civil route are also criminalized, if not already so. Thus, insider dealing becomes a criminal offence ...

Choosing Between Civil and Criminal Route

Before 2012, the SFC would make the initial decision whether to refer a matter to the Financial Secretary for possible referral to the MMT or to refer the matter to the Secretary for Justice for criminal prosecution. However, the Financial Secretary and the Secretary for Justice could redirect the case to the other regime if he or she disagreed with the SFC's referral. An amendment was made in 2012 to remove the uncertainty that could arise from this arrangement. Now, if it appears to the Commission that market misconduct has or may have taken place, the Commission may institute proceedings in the Tribunal concerning the matter (s 252(1)), provided consent is obtained from the Secretary for Justice (s 252A(1)). The Secretary for Justice may refuse consent if a criminal charge under Part XIV is being contemplated for the same conduct (s 252A(2)).

The Investigative Powers of SFC

Currently, the SFC can review the books and records of a listed company or members of its group when it appears to the SFC that misconduct in the management of the company exists ...

> (a) ... [The SFO has the] ... power to ask for an explanation for which it was made, the circumstances under which it was prepared or created, and the details of any instructions given in connection with the making of that entry. [SFO, s. 179]
>
> (b) ... The SFO now enhances the SFC's powers ... by enabling it to seek records and documents relating to the affairs of a listed company or its group companies from those third parties. [SFO, s. 179]

Insider Trading

Insider dealing has been a problem in Hong Kong and weak enforcement has been cited as a cause.

James Early and Alex Pape, *Why HK Needs to Get Tougher on Insider Trading before China Does* (December 7, 2015), at www.ejinsight.com/20151207-why-hk-needs-to-get-tougher-on-insider-trading-before-china-does

---

Hong Kong: a 'paradise' for insider trading

Although Hong Kong's stock exchange is 100 years older than Shanghai's, it didn't see its first insider trading prosecution until 2008. Prosecutions in Hong Kong started rising in 2013 after the SFC implemented a special task force, but this may not be enough considering China's newfound momentum. Hong Kong needs to do more.

Both markets still suffer from rampant insider trading, but Hong Kong's reputation depends on its being the clean, well-regulated brother of mainland China – a trusted bastion of capitalism and proper order.

Hong Kong – a city The Economist magazine dubbed "a paradise" for insider trading – faces a sluggish stock market, demographic challenges, slow GDP growth, and worries about China's gradual encroachment. At a time like this, it can't afford to fall behind its northern neighbor.

Besides, isn't enforcing the law something any government should be doing in earnest anyway? …

Rules and penalties: China vs Hong Kong

In both Hong Kong and China, the rules themselves have been gray …

Despite – or perhaps because of – the fact that equity ownership in Hong Kong's stock market is concentrated among large family investors, insider trading wasn't formally restricted in 1991. It was not criminalized until 2003, and Hong Kong's debut insider trading conviction didn't occur until five years later. (By contrast, insider trading became illegal in the US in 1933.)

Hong Kong's procedures make sense: Insider trading charges are investigated by the SFC and then either referred to the Market Misconduct Tribunal (MMT) for civil cases, or a court for criminal cases, but not both.

Yet there are clear reminders that an aggressive stance against insider trading is not favored by everyone: In 2008, an appeals court removed the MMT's right to compel evidence and right to impose fines greater than the culprit's ill-gotten profits.

Penalties in China and Hong Kong are weak compared to those in the US and UK …

… Hong Kong's MMT can no longer impose fines; Hong Kong courts can, but only up to HK$10 million; they can also assign prison terms of up to 10 years, but this is rare.

It's not hard to see one reason why insider trading is so common: The negative consequences simply aren't that bad.

Arguably, loss of face is the more serious deterrent in many cases. For an investor who could potentially make massive amounts of money by trading on non-public information, the threat of disgorging ill-gotten profits, being temporarily blocked from one's profession and paying a relatively modest fine is an insufficient deterrent.

Big fines and jail sentences – which stand a reasonable chance of being enforced – are necessary to deter big insider traders.

Why enforcement is so weak

But soft punishments aren't the biggest problem. Enforcement is.

Academic evidence shows that enacting insider trading laws in a new market isn't enough to lower that market's implied cost of equity (a lower cost of equity increases share prices). Cost of equity drops only after the first prosecution of insider trading.

Like most criminals, inside traders are pragmatic: Regardless of what the law says, if they don't think they'll be caught, they'll commit the crime.

So although enforcement – in both Hong Kong and China – has taken small steps toward improvement, why has it been so slow overall?

Lack of resources is the simplest reason. This is a prioritization issue underneath, directly arising from different views on who, or what, is injured by insider trading, on what constitutes criminal or immoral behavior, and from cultural views that often value providing favors and enhancing interpersonal relationships above adherence to seldom-enforced laws.

Logistically, Hong Kong's insiders own so many shares that separating legitimate from illegitimate insider trades can be difficult.

And about half of Hong Kong's equity trading is done from offshore, yet Hong Kong has no extradition provisions for insider traders. It's hard to prosecute someone who's not there …

Hong Kong can't compete with the size, growth or momentum of its northern neighbor, but it has the clear advantage in legitimacy and trust – an advantage it's wise to protect. And Hong Kong is rightfully a paradise for many things. Insider trading should not be among them.

SFC, 'Court Finds Two Solicitors Engaged in Insider Dealing and Fraud or Deception,' (January 15, 2016), at www.sfc.hk/edistributionWeb/gateway/EN/news-and-announcements/news/doc?refNo=16PR5

In January 2016, the courts issued a landmark judgment on enforcement. The court found two solicitors engaged in insider dealing and fraud or deception.

The Court of First Instance today found that two solicitors, Mr Eric Lee Kwok Wa and Ms Betty Young Bik Fung, and Eric Lee's sister, Ms Patsy Lee Siu Ying, contravened the SFO by insider dealing in the shares of Asia Satellite Telecommunications Holdings Ltd (Asia Satellite) and engaged in fraud or deception in transactions involving securities of Hsinchu International Bank Company Ltd (Hsinchu Bank).

The court's decision is a landmark ruling on the interpretation of section 300 of the SFO which prohibits the use of fraudulent or deceptive schemes in transactions involving securities.

The SFC … alleged the defendants made a total profit of $2.9 million in these transactions. The SFC alleged that, in relation to Hsinchu Bank transactions in September 2006:

- Betty Young obtained information about a tender offer for Hsinchu Bank shares while working as a lawyer seconded to a client of her employing law firm;
- the client she was seconded to intended to make the tender offer and she was working on the offer;
- the information about the offer was non-public, confidential and materially price sensitive;
- subsequently, Betty Young bought Hsinchu Bank shares and tipped off Eric Lee and his sisters to buy the shares before the announcement of the tender offer; and

- this amounted to fraud or deception under section 300 of the SFO because Betty Young owed duties to her employer and their client including the duty to refrain from using such information for personal gain.

The SFC further alleged that, in relation to Asia Satellite transactions in February 2007:

- Eric Lee obtained information about the proposed privatization of Asia Satellite shares when the law firm he worked for advised on this transaction;
- that information was non-public, confidential and materially price sensitive;
- subsequently Eric Lee tipped off Betty Young and his sisters to buy Asia Satellite shares before the announcement of the proposed privatization; and
- this amounted to insider dealing under section 291 of the SFO.

The court found that these allegations were proven against Betty Young, Eric Lee and Patsy Lee.

The court ruled that there was not enough evidence to prove the allegations against Stella Lee. Nevertheless, the court may exercise its power under section 213 of the SFO against her to remove the illicit profit from her and restore the victims in the transactions. The court may make orders under section 213 against people who are knowingly or otherwise involved in a contravention of the SFO.

In addition, listed issuers are also required to file a copy of their disclosure materials on an application to list securities and ongoing disclosure with the SEHK and the SFC. The SFC has power under the Listing Rules (Cap. 571V) to direct the SEHK to suspend trading in the issuer's securities or cancel the listing, where the disclosures contain materially false, incomplete, or misleading information.

Shareholders cannot sue for breach of listing rules, or enforce the SFO. They must rely on the SEHK to enforce the listing rules, and the SFC to enforce the SFO. While they may sue for pecuniary loss suffered where there is market misconduct, a breach of listing rules is not per se market misconduct, except rule 13 on disclosure of price sensitive information which has become Part XIVA of the SFO.

The SFC also has power to bring actions under s. 213 SFO for certain remedies for breach of the SFO. The orders that the court can make are "entirely free-standing"; the court can make orders even though allegations of contravention have not been dealt with by the MMT or the criminal court.

Notes and Questions

1. Should Hong Kong adopt a provision similar to s. 777 of the Australian Corporations Law which allows a person aggrieved by a failure to comply with the business rules or listing rules to apply for a court order to comply and enforce the rules?

6.3.3 Shareholder Activism

As the cost of litigation is high in Hong Kong, legal enforcement by shareholders is rare. It is often carried out by the regulator. Shareholders will usually take the "Wall Street walk" and sell their shares. However, institutional shareholders are increasingly playing an active role in activism. Even though institutional shareholder activism remains rare, it needs to play a bigger role.

'Recent Shareholder Activism in Asia Could Signal Changing Attitudes,' *Skadden* (January 2016)

In fact, in some situations Hong Kong's regulatory regime allows minority shareholders in Hong Kong-listed companies to enforce corporate governance standards. This is exemplified by the saga of the proposed acquisition by GOME Electrical Appliances Holding Limited of certain assets from GOME Electrical's controlling shareholder and founder ... Given that the deal involved an acquisition from a substantial shareholder, the transaction required independent shareholder approval under the Hong Kong Stock Exchange's listing rules (i.e., the controlling shareholder and parties associated with him could not vote on the deal). In October 2015, GOME Electrical announced that the terms of the transaction had been revised to reduce the aggregate consideration payable by it for the proposed acquisition by nearly 20 percent of the originally proposed amount.

According to GOME Electrical's rationale for the revised terms, the company and the vendor had "received valuable feedback from a number of independent shareholders regarding the acquisition" since the original announcement. This feedback may well have included a clear indication that the transaction stood little chance of being approved by the independent shareholders on the terms originally proposed.

James Early and Alex Pape, 'Why Hong Kong Should Embrace Active Investors' (November 10, 2015), at www.ejinsight.com/20151110–why-hong-kong-should-embrace-active-investors

The place: the Bank of East Asia boardroom. Huddled around chairman David Li Kwok-po – whose family holds a controlling stake – is a who's who of powerful Hong Kong bankers, as well as a son of Li Ka-shing.

The topic: a braggadocious investor 13,000 kilometers away telling the world that the bank's board is incompetent or worse. Paul Singer, whose New York hedge fund accumulated a HK$1.6 billion (US$210 million) stake in the bank, is upset about a planned HK$6.6 billion private placement to Japan's Sumitomo Mitsui Banking Corp. Bank of East Asia Ltd. doesn't need the capital, Singer insists, and he publicly questions the board's motivation for the move.

The backdrop is important: Bank of East Asia has been a dismal investment, underperforming the Hang Seng Index over the previous one, five and 10 years. Since 2007, earnings have grown 61 percent, but earnings per share have advanced just 14 percent.

Part of the cause? The number of shares has ballooned from 1.6 billion to 2.3 billion. The bank explained the Sumitomo deal, announced in September, as preparatory for Basel III capital requirements. The bank's 11.6 percent core Tier 1 capital ratio was healthy, though, so Singer saw a more nefarious reason for the placement: the Li family's control of the bank was threadbare; a sale to a friendly party would help secure their grip on the company. Implicit in such boardroom thinking, common in Hong Kong and Asia generally, is that minority shareholders will suffer their dilutive mistreatment silently.

Activist investors, however, don't keep silent: prominent in their playbook is making a very loud, very public ruckus. Loud, public fights may seem too brazen for the Hong Kong market. Controlling tycoons certainly hope so. But underlying Singer's brassy ploy is a simple truth that David Li – and numerous other company leaders – cannot ignore. His responsibility is not to maintain control. It is to maximize shareholder value.

Challenge on the horizon

The Bank of East Asia story is not unusual in Hong Kong. "The vast majority of Hong Kong-listed companies have a controlling shareholder, either a family or a government," local investor activist David Webb said, "so there is little scope for activism at the investor level." Hong Kong famously ranks No. 1 – ahead of Russia and Malaysia – on The Economist magazine's crony capitalism ranking, which measures the tendency of those in economic control (billionaire tycoons) to use power, politics and favors to charge higher-than-fair prices or squeeze competition out of industries.

From villain to superhero

Activist investors have been around since the 1980s, when they were better known as corporate raiders, who developed a reputation for gutting weak companies for a quick profit. Unfortunately, that perception – especially in Asia – hasn't kept up with their evolution over the past three decades. These days, activists are closer to Good Samaritan superheroes than villains. For one thing, their time horizon has lengthened. Established activist funds lock in their clients' investment for one or two years, much longer than the typical hedge fund lock-up period of a few months …

Activists generally want what's best for the company. Their reach has grown. Fewer than 1 percent of hedge funds are activists, Hedge Fund Research figures show, yet they claimed 20 percent of hedge fund inflows last year … Singer's Elliott Capital directs US$25 billion, enough to strike fear in the hearts of even colossal firms like Bank of East Asia, whose directors see a very serious investor behind what otherwise might seem a paltry US$232 million investment. To date, though, activist investing remains a primarily American phenomenon ... And that's the first reason that activists are turning their attention east: the American markets are beginning to feel saturated ...

And there's the second reason: welcome to Asia, where shareholder underperformance – Hong Kong is the cheapest major market in the world – and conflicts of interest have long been the norm.

Cold reception

Activists will encounter neither a warm welcome nor a friendly environment in Hong Kong. First of all, only about 15 percent of companies primarily listed on the Hong Kong exchange are actually Hong Kong entities. Most are legally domiciled in the British Virgin Islands, the Cayman Islands or Bermuda.

Litigation can become complex quickly. Even after winning a judgment or court order in Hong Kong, shareholders may need to do the same in the relevant offshore domicile, which the company likely selected for its propensity to thwart external pressures.

Potentially worse is the short-term trading mentality of Greater China investors. Activists typically take a relatively small stake and rely on other shareholders' solidarity ... to gain approval for their views. The shorter an investor's time horizon, though, the more likely he is to view himself as a renter rather than an owner. Renters don't concern themselves with structural improvements, rezoning plans or other considerations that lead to long-term value creation ...

Unstoppable force

These obstacles won't stop the activists. Despite all the hurdles, Singer is more likely to be a forerunner than an anomaly. Pushed by the need for more fertile pastures and pulled by the unharvested grassland of underperforming conglomerates, activists are coming to Hong Kong. In doing so, they might shake the market out of its slump and attract better, more productive, longer-term investors in their wake.

In the US, the prospect of an activist campaign keeps American CEOs alert. This is in the best interest of everybody. CEOs stay focused on creating value for shareholders.

Shareholders earn a healthy return on their investment. The job of regulators becomes easier, as managers have more compelling fears than an audit. Hong Kong managers don't face the same threat. Smaller firms may fear private takeovers, but few private equity firms have the capital to challenge a company as large as Bank of East Asia. Those that do typically employ a large amount of debt, and a decent slug of the profits they earn investors is eaten up by fees.

Activist investors, though, needn't take a large stake, use debt or charge exorbitant absolute fees to win. The typical activist assumes a stake less than 5 percent of the target company's equity. (Singer held just 2.5 percent of Bank of East Asia's shares.) The first move is often a private, friendly offer of suggestions to management. We'd expect most Hong Kong managers to ignore these suggestions. The private, friendly suggestions are made earnestly, but they're proof that the activist tried to be cordial.

If they don't work, the activists begin to unveil their arsenal of weapons. They've spent hundreds of hours researching the company and evaluating paths toward value creation. They likely know the financials, competitors and industry dynamics better than most board members. They've hired experts on corporate law and often have enough cash to chase the company to any offshore domicile. And they've already met with other major investors, such as banks and pension funds, and likely convinced at least several that a change in company policy – or management – is best for shareholders. That last tactic is key, because activists don't control enough shares to be powerful alone; they rely on other investors joining their cause. One of the best possible outcomes in Hong Kong is for activists to provide a channel for subtler investors to voice grievances.

Asian market etiquette generally forbids outright conflict between investor and manager. Activists break with this tradition. Joining them puts existing institutional investors in a sensitive but undeniably healthy position. When an activist campaign goes public, institutional investors will be forced to make a choice. They can remain silent, essentially siding with incumbent management. That's fine if they agree with management, but if management is clearly wrong or inept, visible passivity potentially makes institutional investors appear spineless or conflicted. Or they can side with the activist investors, provoking uncomfortable but necessary conversations with the management team, but potentially creating higher share prices.

Hong Kong should embrace, and not fear, activists

As far as the Hong Kong market has come, it is still undeniably Chinese in its controlling ownership structures and often conflicted ownership culture. It is unsurprising that this situation has persisted so long. Entrenched families have the incentives and the means to maintain their power.

The Hong Kong legal system favors big business, and Hong Kong decorum hinders criticism from minority shareholders. Activism will force the Hong Kong shareholder system to decide its priorities. And things are already changing: in June, a court agreed with Singer that Bank of East Asia's board had failed in its duty to review the Sumitomo Mitsui transaction adequately, and the bank is now considering some business and board changes.

This is how activism's healthy pressure should work. The public company was never meant to be a clubby bureaucracy or an instrument of power. Activist investors will insist that Hong Kong executives, board members and investors remember this.

Let's hope they listen.

Notes and Questions

1. Do you think there will be more activism in Asia in the near future?
2. What is special about activism in Hong Kong? What are the downsides?
3. What can be done to promote more activism, particularly by institutional investors?
4. Is the lack of resources really a critical problem in enforcement?

6.3.4 Gatekeepers

Hong Kong relies on external auditors, company secretaries, and lawyers as gatekeepers. There has also been concern for auditors' immunity and independence. In an attempt to provide an independent oversight on auditors' independence, the government established the Financial Reporting Council (FRC) in 2006 and has proposed to further reform it.

S. H. Goo and Anne Carver, 'Immunity for Auditors of Listed Companies,' in S. H. Goo et al., *Corporate Governance: The Hong Kong Debate* (Sweet & Maxwell Asia, 2003), pp. 145–6

Auditors are in a very good position to detect fraud or irregularity, and those who wish to serve the public interest by reporting their concerns to the regulatory authority may face a civil claim at common law, for example, for negligence or breach of confidentiality, or suffer professional embarrassment and financial penalty. Potential liability to defamation is also a major concern.

To remove the risk of such adverse consequences, the SFO provides auditors of listed corporations with a statutory immunity from liability under the common law, if they choose to report to the SFC suspected fraud and other fraudulent or improper practices of which they become aware in the course of their auditing work. [para. 14.7, SFO s. 381] It does not impose upon them any duty to report.

In determining whether there are circumstances suggesting that fraud, misfeasance or other misconduct has been committed, the auditor is entitled to take a subjective opinion. This is because, as the accountancy profession pointed out, unless an auditor is personally involved in or possesses first-hand knowledge of fraud, misfeasance or other misconduct, he or she must necessarily rely on personal judgment or interpretation of circumstantial evidence, such as books and records of the listed corporation, in determining whether to make a report to the regulator. [para. 14.8]

... There is currently a review being undertaken ... whether auditors should be regulated by an independent body, whether auditors should be allowed to provide non-auditing services to the same company for which auditing services are provided, and whether there should be mandatory rotation of auditors every few years.

FSTB, 'Executive Summary,' *Proposals to Improve the Regulatory Regime for Listed Entity Auditors – Consultation Paper* (June 2014)

---

1. [omitted]
2. The existing regulatory regime for listed entity auditors is not consistent with international standards and practices that the oversight of the regulation of listed entity auditors should be independent of the profession itself. As a result, Hong Kong is not eligible to be represented on IFIAR which is an influential international organization in the regulation of auditors ...
3. [omitted]
4. For the new regulatory regime for listed entity auditors, we propose that the relevant professional body, namely HKICPA, will perform the statutory functions of registration, setting of CPD requirements and setting of standards on professional ethics, auditing and assurance with respect to listed entity auditors, subject to oversight by the independent auditor oversight body, namely FRC. We further propose to vest in FRC disciplinary and inspection functions and powers with regard to listed entity auditors, in addition to its existing investigatory function and powers.

Notes and Questions

1. What type of reforms are necessary for the FRC?
2. Should auditors be granted immunity to report fraud? Should they have a duty to report it?
3. How can the HKICPA and FRC effectively monitor and regulate auditors?

Laws and Regulations and Regulators for Public Companies

Law and Regulations Relating to Companies

Companies Ordinance (Cap. 622)

Companies (Winding up and Miscellaneous Provisions) Ordinance (Cap. 32)

Companies (Model Articles) Notice (Cap. 622H)

Laws and Regulations Relating to Listed Companies

Securities and Futures Ordinance (Cap. 571) (SFO)

Hong Kong Stock Exchange Main Board Listing Rules

Hong Kong Stock Exchange Growth Enterprise Market Listing Rules

Codes and Guidelines Relating to Public Companies

Codes on Takeovers and Mergers and Share Buy-backs

Corporate Governance Code and Corporate Governance Report (Appendix 14 of Main Board Listing Rules)

Regulators

Securities and Futures Commission (SFC)

Stock Exchange of Hong Kong

Companies Registry (also, CR has the power to enforce Companies Ordinance)

7

INDIA

UMAKANTH VAROTTIL

7.1 Introduction

Since the liberalization of its economy in 1991, India has embraced globalization and has sought to attract higher levels of foreign investment. Toward this end, India's government and regulators have used corporate governance as a tool and important signaling mechanism. Although corporate governance as a concept was unheard of until the 1990s, it has become the mainstay of the corporate sector. Market developments have been accompanied by sweeping legislative and regulatory reforms that have fundamentally altered the scene. India offers a suitable case study for understanding the significance of corporate governance to an emerging market and the impact of reforms.

Since the middle of the previous century, corporate law in India consisted of the Companies Act 1956 and rules issued thereunder by the government through the Ministry of Corporate Affairs (MCA). Corporate governance and securities regulation received impetus in 1992 following the establishment of India's securities regulator, the Securities and Exchange Board of India (SEBI). SEBI established a set of corporate governance norms in 2000 in the form of Clause 49 of the Listing Agreement ("Clause 49"). A new Companies Act 2013 was enacted that substantially enhanced corporate governance requirements. Clause 49 was recently substituted by the SEBI (Listing Obligations and Disclosure Requirements) Regulations, 2015 ("Listing Regulations").

The frenetic phase of reforms coincided with corporate governance developments around the world. One theme that resonates throughout the analysis in this chapter is the extent to which corporate governance in India has been influenced by developments elsewhere. In the initial phase of reforms, India formally converged with Western standards in that the governance norms were largely imported from countries such as the US and the UK. However, recent reforms involving the enactment of the Companies Act 2013 and the Listing Regulations have been occasioned due to local requirements that explicitly recognize the concentration of shareholdings in Indian companies. The formal convergence of corporate governance norms based on the Western model has given way to divergence to take into account specific governance problems faced by Indian companies. Local factors have had an important role to play in shaping corporate governance norms.

Although a common law country, India maintains concentrated ownership, more reliance on codification than judge-made law and is stakeholder-oriented. Among its other unique characteristics, India requires at least one woman on listed company boards, has significant shareholder activism, and has the strongest corporate social responsibility provisions in Asia.

7.2 Purpose: Shareholder versus Stakeholder

The evolution of corporate law and governance norms in India across the shareholder–stakeholder spectrum provides for interesting analysis wherein the intellectual tensions have come to the fore.

Umakanth Varottil, 'The Evolution of Corporate Law in Post-Colonial India: From Transplant to Autochthony' (2015) 30 *American University International Law Review* 253

3. *Enabling Other Stakeholders*

The question whether companies should be run for the benefit of their shareholders or whether the interests of other stakeholders must be taken into account is a vexed one, and directly attracts the controller-stakeholder agency problem …

Hitherto, directors of Indian companies had negligible guidance under company law as regards their duties and liabilities … This somewhat unsatisfactory situation has been mended in the Companies Act, 2013 which is rather explicit about directors' duties. The new provisions not only provide greater certainty to directors regarding their conduct, but also enable the beneficiaries as well as courts and regulators to judge the discharge of directors' duties more objectively.

… [Section 166(2) of] the Companies Act, 2013 extends the stakeholder principle further while codifying directors' duties. It provides:

> A director of a company shall act in good faith in order to promote the objects of the company for the benefit of its members as a whole, and in the best interests of the company, its employees, the shareholders, the community and for the protection of environment.

Even if there was a doubt under previous legislation as to the extent to which stakeholder interests are to be considered by directors of a company, it has been put to rest in the new legislation. In other words, shareholders are not the only constituency that deserves the attention of directors; other constituencies such as employees and even the community and the environment are to be considered by the directors.

…

[T]he Companies Act, 2013 in India has preferred to adopt the pluralist approach by providing recognition to both stakeholders and shareholders, without necessarily indicating a preference to either. Despite the superficial similarity between the English and Indian legal provisions on directors' duties, there is a vital distinction in that shareholders continue to occupy a pivotal position in England, whereas in India they are only one among a number of constituencies that command the attention of directors....

In all, we find diverging philosophies in corporate governance that operate in India and its colonizer. Viewed from the agency problems paradigm ... while shareholders continue to hold the attention of corporate managements in the U.K., other stakeholders are entitled to the wider protection of corporate law in India.

Notes and Questions

1. The stakeholder approach has been solidified since the 1960s when corporate law began adhering to avowed socialist ideals. Significant corporate transactions such as a scheme of compromise or arrangement (such as an amalgamation) were permitted only if they were not prejudicial to public interest. The legislative activity during this era was supported by innovation in judicial decision-making that stretched the contours of corporate law to fit within the "socialist" theme underlying the times. In a significant ruling, the Supreme Court of India observed:

   > The traditional view of a company was that it was a convenient mechanical device for carrying on trade and industry, a mere legal frame work providing a convenient institutional container for holding and using the powers of company management ... This doctrine glorified the concept of a free economic society in which State intervention in social and economic matters was kept at the lowest possible level. But gradually this doctrine was eroded by the emergence of new social values which recognised the role of the State as an active participant in the social and economic life of the citizen in order to bring about general welfare and common good of the community ... The adoption of the socialistic pattern of society as the ultimate goal of the country's economic and social policies hastened the emergence of this new concept of the corporation ... But, one thing is certain that the old nineteenth century view which regarded a company merely as a legal device adopted by shareholders for carrying on trade or business as proprietors has been discarded and a company is now looked upon as a socio-economic institution wielding economic power and influencing the life of the people.[1]

   This approach seeks to extend corporate law and governance beyond that of a private matter between a company and its managers and shareholders and into one that has broader

[1] *National Textile Workers' Union* v. *P. R. Ramakrishnan*, AIR 1983 SC 75, para. 4, per P. N. Bhagwati, J.

societal implications. Do you think the approach is excessive and muddles the discourse on corporate governance? What are the problems of considering the company as carrying a public character? Are principles of corporate governance equipped to address such ideas?

2. The "public" character of a corporation has been provided for under the Companies Act 2013 primarily in the form of explicit duties imposed on directors. Note the differences between India's pluralistic approach toward stakeholders and the enlightened shareholder value approach followed by the UK. Which is the more reasonable approach? Or, does the adoption of the approach depend on the economic, political, and social circumstances prevailing in the appropriate country? Are there any underlying legal and institutional differences between the UK and India? If so, what are they?
3. In the US, while the shareholder value approach has been traditionally accepted, for example in *Dodge* v. *Ford Motor Co.*, 170 NW 668 (Mich. 1919), constituency statutes in various states confer powers to directors to take into account the interests of non-shareholder constituencies. Compare and contrast India's pluralistic approach with the constituency approach in various US states.
4. According to the "legal origins" thesis, although common law systems are generally understood to be shareholder-oriented, India has expressly adopted a stakeholder approach. While common law systems tend to rely on judge-made law in the development of their jurisprudence, India has largely relied on a codification process. As seen later, greater reliance is placed on public enforcement of corporate law rather than private enforcement. To that extent, does India begin to resemble civil law jurisdictions? Or, is that too simplistic an analysis? For example, India has neither adopted a two-tier board structure nor co-determination.
5. In the pluralistic approach followed by Indian corporate law to address the interests of non-shareholder constituencies, there could potentially be conflicts among the interests of various stakeholders. While shareholders' interests are generally homogeneous (except for differences between controlling shareholders and minority shareholders), stakeholders could possess vastly differing interests. How do boards prioritize those interests?
6. Moreover, shareholders' interests are more tangible and measurable than stakeholder interests. Shareholder interests are represented largely by financial parameters of a company that indicate corporate performance (with the most common resultant indicator being the share price of a company) as well as other indicators that may represent corporate governance. How can directors measure stakeholder interests that are somewhat more intangible and subjective in nature?
7. What kind of remedies can non-shareholder constituencies exercise against breach of directors' duties? India follows the UK approach whereby directors owe their duties to the company and not directly to shareholders or other stakeholders. Hence, do stakeholders have any *locus standi* to bring claims against companies or boards for breach of duties to act in their interests? What is the merit in possessing rights that may not be justiciable in a court of law? Does this not reduce the efficacy of the stakeholder approach to corporate governance?

7.3 Board Function

The board of directors operates as a centerpiece of corporate governance, and hence its composition and role acquire tremendous importance. As in many other countries, board independence has become a key tool. Since 2000, India has mandated the requirement of independent directors on corporate boards of listed companies. Prior to the Companies Act 2013, considerable criticism existed that independent directors did not function in an effective manner as the concept was primarily imported from legal systems such as the US and the UK and were unlikely to operate in India where concentrated shareholding was the norm and other institutions to support independent directors (such as efficient capital markets and stringent audit mechanism) were absent. However, the Companies Act 2013 has introduced extensive measures that elaborate on the appointment, roles, responsibilities, and liabilities of independent directors that have radically altered the relevance of board independence.

This section first examines the roles of independent directors and then it looks at issues pertaining to executive compensation, whose ramifications in companies with controlled shareholdings are substantially different from those with dispersed shareholding.

Vikramaditya Khanna and Shaun J. Mathew, 'The Role of Independent Directors in Controlled Firms in India: Preliminary Interview Evidence' (2010) 22 *National Law School of India Review* 35

While Indian listing standards require that the boards of listed companies include independent directors, neither the listing standards, nor the Companies Act, prescribe a particular role for independent directors vis-à-vis the executives, promoter-affiliated directors or the public shareholders, or define the contours of their liability with any real precision ... [O]ur project intends to understand firsthand what the role of independent directors in India is today and what these groups think such role should be going forward.

While our interview research remains preliminary ... we have already observed some interesting results:

(i) All of the independent directors viewed their role principally as that of strategic advisors to the promoters.

(ii) Relatedly, most independent directors did not perceive their role to be that of a "watchdog" over the promoters and management. Reasons cited by directors against such a role ranged from the practical (lack of time or resources or training) to the philosophical (not good for board collegiality and functioning). Moreover, many of them believed that any legal requirement imposing such a role would be highly inappropriate given that the current scope for independent director liability was perceived to be very high (and included a bona fide, nontrivial risk of criminal liability), sometimes arbitrarily imposed, and not offset by adequate remuneration and directors and officers insurance coverage.

...

(iv) Particularly in light of the liability risk, every one of the directors and advisors we interviewed found independent director compensation to be grossly inadequate and incommensurate to the attendant risks.

(v) Most of the independent directors described the boardroom environment as being receptive of their viewpoints, particularly in the [post-Satyam era] ... While many of these situations involved the proposal of new strategic initiatives, rather than conflict situations, directors did share experiences in which independent director opposition to a promoter's plan caused a reconsideration or even abandonment of such plans.

(vi) Many of the independent directors agreed that selecting independent directors through an independent nominating committee could help counteract the promoter's influence on independent directors, although most agreed this would only operate to a very limited extent.

...

Our findings also highlight the very strong and universal desire of independent directors to have relatively clear guidance on their duties together with some constraints on liability.

Vikramaditya Khanna and Umakanth Varottil, 'Board Independence in India: From Form to Function?,' in Dan W. Puchniak, Harald Baum, and Luke Nottage (eds.), *Independent Directors in Asia: A Historical, Contextual and Comparative Approach* (Cambridge: Cambridge University Press, 2017)

V. Recent Reforms and the Increasingly Functional Approach to Board Independence

The corporate law reform process in India has been underway for nearly two decades. However, it acquired a greater sense of urgency more recently due to corporate governance scandals such as the massive fraud of over US$ 1 billion at Satyam Computer Services Limited, a leading company in the information technology (IT) sector. The need was felt, among other things, to strengthen the corporate governance regime in India, of which board independence is an important component.

...

The recent reforms represent a turning point in the evolution of corporate governance in India and they usher in greater stringency in governance norms, accompanied by further reliance on independent directors as a key institution. The reforms elaborate on the roles, responsibilities and liabilities of independent directors and appear to be moving independent directors in India towards being more functional than formalistic. While this is welcome in many respects, these changes need to occur carefully because they risk putting large burdens on independent directors, which may in turn deter the more capable candidates from accepting these positions. After all, if our goal is to have careful and skillful people monitor controllers then we are likely to scare such people away from the position of independent director by having wide ranging liability and broad obligations on them for activities they may not be able to easily prevent or control....

4. *The Role of Independent Directors*

The criticism that the previous regime neither elucidated the role of independent directors nor specified the constituency that required their attention has been addressed, to some extent, in the 2013 Act ...

a. Monitoring Role: Minority Shareholder Interests

The role of independent directors includes safeguarding the interests of all stakeholders, particularly the minority shareholders, balancing the conflicts among various stakeholders, and also acting as a moderator or arbitrator in cases of conflicts between management and shareholders. More specifically, independent directors now have a greater role to play in matters such as related party transactions wherein they are required to ensure that the board adequately deliberates over these matters and acts in the interests of the company. This is even more relevant because related party transactions tend to be rampant in jurisdictions such as India with concentrated shareholding, which makes their oversight and regulation crucial.

[Schedule IV] ... imposes a higher onus on independent directors, and would require them to participate in the affairs of the company more closely in order to be able to discharge this monitoring role. How that might be achieved when the board meets only a handful of times a year is yet to be elucidated.

Another aspect that receives clarity is that independent directors are now expressly required to pay attention to the interests of minority shareholders. This is crucial given the agency problems between the controlling and the minority shareholders. The new regime requires independent directors to take on a more active role on significant transactions such as mergers, corporate restructuring or related party transactions where the minority interests may be at stake....

6. *Reviewing the Independent Director's Position Under the New Regime*

...

First, the new regime may be considered too prescriptive. By stipulating the features of board independence in microscopic detail, it leaves much less room for independent thought and discretion to be exercised by individual directors. The invasion of corporate regulation into the boardroom might arguably increase the cost of doing business and affect entrepreneurialism and innovation ...

Second, the higher obligations under the new legal regime might hinder competent individuals from taking up independent directorships on corporate boards. For instance, the regime makes the duties and liabilities of independent directors fairly significant. Meaningful levels of remuneration do not complement this. Since the remuneration levels for independent directors in India are considerably lower than international standards, highly skilled individuals might be unlikely to take the risk or put their reputation at stake to serve on corporate boards ...

Third, as a procedural matter, the implementation could give rise to difficulties although the intention of greater stringency is understandable. Corporate governance norms are dynamic in nature and require reconfiguration periodically to keep pace with the changing business climate. Usually, while the basic governance framework is dealt with by statute, the details are contained in codes of conduct that are more flexible in nature. However, the 2013 Act results in many items being made less flexible because they are contained in legislation which is more difficult to change nimbly ... The question remains whether there has been a knee-jerk reaction to recent scandals that may adversely impact genuine businesses during the times ahead.

N. Balasubramanian, Samir Kumar Barua, and D. Karthik, 'Corporate Governance Issues in Executive Compensation: The Indian Experience (2008–2012)' *Indian Institute of Management Bangalore Working Paper No. 426* (2013), at http://ssrn.com/abstract=2337861

2.2 Influence of Ownership Structure

There have been comparatively fewer studies reflecting the situation in countries like India, with their predominantly concentrated ownership structures in the hands of promoters or other block holders such as financial institutions. In such cases, the boards' role in pay determination at the top cannot be similar to that of their U.S./U.K. counterparts, although their responsibilities (given the broad convergence in their respective legislative and regulatory frameworks) may not be very dissimilar ... The Companies Act 2013 (Sec. 178), however, mandates (for the first time) nomination and remuneration committees for public limited companies, including listed companies ...

In the Indian context, one should substitute the promoter or dominant controller for the chief executive [in the US], who will almost always be from the promoter groups or their families; in the limited number of cases where non-family-group professionals are appointed as chief executives, they are likely to hold the job at the pleasure of the promoters. Executive compensation in such cases will, in general, be a function of the size of the shareholding of the promoters – the larger or more dominant they are, the (potentially) higher will be their compensation; conversely, the smaller the shareholding power, the less likely the chances of their compensation being much higher than the market. Rent extraction in this area is thus strongly driven by the extent of the share ownership of the promoter group.

...

One other dimension of ownership-related impact on executive compensation in India also needs to be noted. Especially in the case of some family-controlled companies, there appears to be a practice of pegging the pay of family members in top executive positions at relatively modest levels. Whether this practice is used as a signalling mechanism to contain other pay aspirations in the higher echelons of the managerial hierarchy, or because of the immateriality of executive pay in their total earnings from the company or the group, or even as part of image-building to reflect equitable and responsible corporate behaviour are all issues that have not yet been fully explored ...

3 Compensation Approval and Disclosure Regimes

In most parts of the developed world, executive compensation in corporations is determined by the board of directors (primarily the compensation committee) of the company, subject to any regulatory restraints and requirements. In several other jurisdictions including India, the board can only recommend individual directorial compensation for approval to the shareholders in a general meeting, although in practice, given the absentee shareholder apathy and the indifference to such matters, this is merely a formality ...

3.2 Appointment and Compensation

It is the prerogative of the board (on the recommendation of its nominations committee, where one exists, and possibly with the help of head-hunters and compensation consultants) to appoint a person as a director at a mutually agreed compensation; the appointment is subject to the approval of the shareholders. Indian law requires the appointment of every director (including a managing director) along with complete details of the remuneration package including perquisites to be tabled separately and approved individually at shareholders' meetings. This has been the case for several decades now and is one of the areas where Indian requirements have been ahead of many other countries including the U.S. ...

As mentioned earlier, director compensation levels in India since political independence in 1947 were severely constrained "in public interest" for a long time;

since economic liberalisation in the 1990s, these unrealistic individual limits have been virtually eliminated …

There are other legal provisions that allow for executive compensation payments at reduced levels in case of the absence or the inadequacy of profits to support the levels of pay that were determined when the profits were adequate.

3.3 Shareholders and Executive Compensation

In India, the compensation arrangements of every director (including executive directors, who are our main focus in this study) whenever contracted and/or paid have to be approved by the shareholders in a general meeting … In itself, this is a happy situation that compares favourably with that in several other more developed markets where shareholders are yet to obtain a binding right to have such a say …

7.3.1 Tata Motors: A Mini-Case Study

In 2014, Tata Motors, which is part of the Tata Group, sought shareholder approval for the payment of executive compensation to three top executives of the company, including to the heirs of a former managing director. Approval was required because the compensation exceeded prescribed limits due to the inadequacy of profits of the company for the relevant years. This required a special resolution of 75 percent majority of shareholders present and voting. Strikingly, in a shareholders' meeting held in July 2014, Tata Motors failed to obtain the requisite 75 percent majority, due to which the management's proposal for payment of executive compensation was defeated. Although the promoters supported the payment, the resolution was opposed by about 64 percent of the company's public shareholders in the institutional category and about 30 percent public shareholders in other categories.

This episode signals that payment of executive compensation is not a matter of course, especially for companies with inadequate profits. Even though Tata Motors' proposal was supported by some proxy advisory firms, it was nevertheless defeated by shareholders as being inconsistent with the performance of the company. This suggests that shareholders (particularly institutional shareholders) are becoming active when it comes to decisions such as executive compensation. In the Tata Motors case, the proposals for executive compensation involved professional managers rather than promoters.

Tata Motors returned to shareholders in January 2015 by highlighting that the remuneration was in line with industry standards. This time, however, shareholders accepted the company's line of argument and approved the compensation. In all, this episode underscores that shareholder approval of executive compensation cannot be taken for granted, and in the context of greater shareholder activism, such a "say on pay" requirement could operate as a significant check against excessive levels of compensation.

Notes and Questions

1. Family businesses are dominant in the Indian context, even in publicly listed companies. How does one take into account cultural and social links between individuals when considering if a director is independent? Can these factors be addressed through legislative or regulatory definitions of board independence? Or, should be they be considered by courts in specific facts and circumstances.
2. In companies with concentrated shareholding, what is the optimal method of appointing independent directors? Given that such directors are expected to not only monitor management but also controlling shareholders, the current method of majority voting is ineffective because controlling shareholders can appoint and remove independent directors. Should India adopt a method that minimizes the role of controlling shareholders in the appointment and removal of independent directors? If so, consider what those alternative methods may be.
3. Literature on independent directors suggests that their appropriate role can be bifurcated into a strategic advisory role and monitoring management (and controlling shareholders). Are these exhaustive of the types of roles that independent directors can play? Can you think of any other roles?
4. A company could have a single controlling shareholder or a group of them. Controlling shareholders could be one or more business families or the state or a multinational corporation. Should the roles of independent directors differ in each case? If so, why?
5. How would you compare the duties and liabilities of independent directors of Indian listed companies with those of other countries surveyed in this book? Are they too onerous such that they carry the unintended consequences that more able and experienced individuals may be disincentivized from joining corporate boards?
6. What type of issues are likely to arise while considering executive compensation to directors and senior management of listed companies with concentrated shareholding? Balasubramanian, Barua, and Karthik hint that companies with business families as controlling shareholders might pay modest executive compensation given that they can take profits out of the company through other means such as dividend. What might those methods be? Do corporate governance norms address them? However, anecdotally, some large Indian listed companies have paid their controlling shareholder-managers significant sums as executive compensation. What explains this phenomenon?
7. India has tight controls and procedures on "say on pay," and hitherto had stringent caps on the amount of compensation (pegged to a percentage of profits). Does shareholder approval requirement for executive compensation resolve the issues pertaining to excesses in compensation? What if controlling shareholders can vote for the payment to themselves and ensure the passage of the resolution for say on pay? Should the amount of compensation be capped, or be left to market forces to determine?

7.4 Ownership Structure

That concentration of shareholdings in Indian listed companies is the norm is beyond doubt. The following studies have sought to ascertain the level of shareholdings held by controlling shareholders:

1. Chakrabarti showed average promoter shareholdings in Indian companies in 2002 to be at 48.1 percent.[2]
2. Mathew's 2007 study found that the average promoter stake in the top 100 companies listed on the Stock Exchange, Mumbai (also known as BSE) was 48.09 percent, while in the top 500 listed companies it was 49.55 percent.[3]
3. Balasubramanian and Anand's subsequent study of shareholding patterns in Indian companies during the period 2001 to 2011 evidences that the trend is in the direction of more concentration rather than dispersion. They found that the median holdings of promoters in the top 50 companies had risen from 42.94 percent in 2001 to 56.24 percent in 2011, and in the top 100 companies from 48.83 percent to 54.21 percent.

However, a recent study indicates the loosening of concentration among promoters in that there has been dilution in their stake. It found that the average promoter shareholding was 49.22 percent in the top 50 companies, 52.17 percent in the top 100 companies and 54.62 percent in the top 500 companies.[4]

Comparing the data with the previous studies discussed above, it is clear that the promoter holdings in 2015 are more concentrated than those in 2007, but they are less concentrated compared to 2011. This indicates that while there was a trend of further concentration during the period between 2001 and 2011, there has been some level of dispersion thereafter.

There is more to it than absolute ownership percentages. Controlling shareholders bolster the power of concentrated ownership through other mechanisms such as cross-holdings, pyramid structures, and tunneling. These phenomena are quite common in the Indian corporate context.

[2] Rajesh Chakrabarti, 'Corporate Governance in India: Evolution and Challenges' (2005), at http://ssrn.com/abstract=649857

[3] Shaun Mathew, 'Hostile Takeovers in India: New Prospects, Challenges, and Regulatory Opportunities' [2007] *Columbia Business Law Review* 800, at 833.

[4] Umakanth Varottil, 'The Nature of the Market for Corporate Control in India,' in Umakanth Varottil and Wai Yee Wan, *Comparative Takeover Regulation:* Global and Asian Perspectives (Cambridge: Cambridge University Press, 2017).

N. Balasubramanian and R. V. Anand, 'Ownership Trends in Corporate India 2001–2011: Evidence and Implications' *Indian Institute of Management Bangalore Working Paper No. 419* (2013), at http://ssrn.com/abstract=2303684

Ownership Patterns in India

Corporate ownership in India is predominantly concentrated in the hands of domestic individuals and promoter groups, multinational parents, or the state. Much of the family and other domestic holdings could be traced back to the days of the British Managing Agencies ... The Indian state was the other major dominant shareholder in a number of large corporations when as part of national policy, state owned enterprises were set up to reach commanding heights in the Indian economy; many of these are now publicly traded corporations as a result of the government's privatisation initiatives. The third group responsible for concentrated ownership in the country is the foreign multinational sector: many international corporations have identified India along with China as the future economic power engines of the world and set up shop in the country. With several sectors of the economy gradually opening up for foreign participation, this sector may grow substantially in the near future....

Inter-corporate Ownership – Pyramids and Groups

The acceptance of the principle that corporations may own shares in other corporate entities was to have a monumental influence on the development and growth of what we know now as corporate groups and conglomerates ...

... [Corporate groups] offer a fertile ground for potential tunneling by their controlling owners and managers through transfer of resources, profits, cash and even opportunities between firms in which their cash flow rights vary, Such abusive related party transactions take the form of interest free loans and advances, inter-corporate deposits and purchase and sale of goods and services at rates disadvantageous to the company where the group cash flow interests are lower than the other parties' where they are higher ...

...

In Summary

In line with the trends in other developed markets, non-institutional retail shareholdings are on the wane in the country. During the study period, they declined substantially almost halving from their 2011 levels ...

Foreign companies in this study have strengthened their entrenchment with median holdings running over 50% right through. Government policy changes opening up several business sectors for majority foreign direct investment may be a contributing factor for the decline in the number of listed companies.

Table 7.1 The corporate sector in India (1957–2011)

March 31	Limited by shares			Unlimited liability companies	Companies limited by guarantee	Foreign companies
	Non-government companies	Total companies	Total companies			
1957	74	29,283	29,357	–	1,364	551
1961	142	26,007	26,149	–	1,169	569
1971	314	30,008	30,322	–	1,270	543
1981	851	61,863	62,714	176	1,478	300
1991	1,167	22,3285	224,452	317	2,117	489
2001	1,266	56,7834	569,100	461	2,918	1,141
2011*	1,316	713,239	714,555	437	3,600	3,127
*Public	988	58,658	59,646			
*Private	328	654,581	654,909			
listed companies			NSE 1,657BSE 5,000+			

Source: Table 2.4 and Statement XI (pp. 18, 87) 55th Annual Report on the Working & Administration of the Companies Act, 1956: Year ended 31 March 2011; Ministry of Corporate Affairs, Government of India; Listed companies from websites of respective stock exchanges

Government companies in this sample witnessed a decline in non-institutional shareholdings over the study period, with institutional holdings showing corresponding increases. In case of management controlled companies in this sample, the increase in institutional holdings and the corresponding decrease in non-institutional holdings has not been as sharp as the changes in the other three categories.

Implications for Governance

Implications for management controlled companies are no less daunting, albeit for different reasons. Just because the managers are not substantial owners, the risk of their indulging in similar tunneling initiatives is no less important. Such companies' boards and directors would likely need to be even more vigilant since such structures come with the negatives of concentrated ownership and control structures, often without the positives that family controlled entities bring to the table.

The growing institutional investor holdings, again, can be a mixed blessing. It can help improve investee companies' governance through meaningful engagement and also use its voting clout to preempt any abusive initiatives perceived as not being in the interests of absentee shareholders. On the other hand, unscrupulous controllers may find it convenient to canvas support from the fewer institutional investors, directly or through their masters. Good stewardship practices both in-house and opposite investee companies may minimize the risks of the latter.

... Some key measures, among them, notably, the restraint on promoters voting on resolutions where they stand to benefit, have already been initiated through legislation and regulation; their impact will of course depend upon speedy and effective compliance monitoring.

Notes and Questions

1. Controlling shareholders continue to hold dominant shareholding in listed companies. However, recently there appear to be some indications of dilution. What impact is this likely to have on a market for corporate control in India? If there are at least a few listed companies with either minimal or no promoter shareholding, they could be exposed to the possibility of hostile takeovers. Could this operate as a governance-enhancing mechanism?
2. As we have seen, phenomena such as pyramiding and tunneling are common in the Indian markets. Hence, the regulation of related party transactions (RPTs) becomes crucial. Hitherto, India had weak regulation of RPTs. Such transactions only had to be disclosed in the financial statements of the company, and no prior approval or review by the board of directors or audit committee was necessary. Under the Companies Act 2013, RPTs now require the prior approval of the board. Moreover, significant RPTs also require shareholder approval wherein an interested shareholder is precluded from voting, requiring a "majority of the minority" vote. Will such measures be effective?

7.5 Law and Enforcement

To implement corporate governance norms, legal systems have utilized two broad approaches. One relates to the use of a voluntary code of corporate governance. At the other end of the spectrum lies the mandatory approach whereby a policymaker or regulator prescribes a set of rules that all companies covered by them are required to comply.

After occasional experimentation with the voluntary approach, Indian legislators and regulators have opted for the mandatory approach to enforce corporate governance norms. This approach is consistent with India's legal system and institutional culture. Historically, government regulation has been the cornerstone for implementing laws and regulations pertaining to businesses. Moreover, the existence of strong controllers and the relative lack of sophistication of market players make the voluntary method less appropriate. The flip side of this approach is that it makes corporate governance norms rigid and its implementation somewhat mechanical that may not be desirable for the development of markets.

Umakanth Varottil, 'The Evolution of Corporate Law in Post-Colonial India: From Transplant to Autochthony' (2015) 30 *American University International Law Review* 253

D. Corporate Law Enforcement Machinery

It is simple at first blush to attribute the growth to India's legal system through civil liability and its enforcement through the judiciary. This would be consistent with the "legal origins" notion of investor protection due to India's colonial legal heritage. India not only has a sufficiently robust substantive law on investor protection, but the independent judicial system drawn from the common law tradition allows for judges to mold the law to suit specific circumstances and thereby adapt to the dynamicity in the capital markets.

However … the efficacy of India's legal system as a tool for enforcing corporate and securities laws necessitates a more nuanced treatment. Counter-intuitively, India's common law legal system operating through the judiciary has not played a vital role in the development of the capital markets through the imposition of civil liability upon issuer companies or the compensation of investors for losses due to misstatements. Despite the existence of substantial rules for civil liability and compensation and the presence of an elaborate court system, the associated conditions for the judiciary to make an impact on corporate law and investor protection are conspicuous by their absence. The Indian court system is plagued by delays, costs, and other inefficiencies. Nearly 32 million cases are pending before different levels within the Indian judiciary thereby causing a significant strain on the system.

Cases can on average take 15 years to achieve final outcomes. For this reason, civil liability and compensation of investors' losses have almost never been utilized to any meaningful extent in India as a tool for enforcing corporate law.

...

Recognizing the need for private enforcement of corporate law, the Companies Act, 2013 has introduced a statutory shareholder class action mechanism. In order to obviate the delays faced before the regular court system, the legislation proposes the establishment of a specialized body in the form of the National Company Law Tribunal ("NCLT") that will hear shareholder class actions and other corporate law disputes. Nevertheless, I am not sanguine about their effectiveness due to the lack of institutional factors necessary for their utilization. For example, India follows the English rule on costs, whereby the loser pays the reasonable costs of the opponent as ordered by the courts. This may act as a disincentive to shareholders to bring suits even if they have a strong case on the merits. Moreover, in India the costs are not limited to attorneys' fees. Because investor actions are brought before the regular civil courts, plaintiffs usually have to pay stamp duty and court fees, which may be significant in some states. Contingency fees are one way to motivate entrepreneurially minded attorneys to take on riskier suits ... [C]ontingency fees are prohibited in India thereby disincentivizing plaintiff attorneys from taking on riskier suits. Although the establishment of the NCLT will eliminate some of the costs such as stamp duty and court fees, the lack of institutional factors that promote a class action culture make it unlikely that private enforcement will obtain the necessary fillip.

...

While India began briefly with the "comply-or-explain" approach, it quickly migrated to a mandatory approach towards corporate governance, which has since continued ... The push towards mandatory rules in India has therefore become complete.

Notes and Questions

1. What are the interest groups that may have been influential in the evolution of India's corporate governance norms? What explains the radical change in approach, especially with reference to the enforcement provisions?
2. Is the voluntary comply-or-explain approach unlikely to be effective in India? In the case of a mandatory approach, who should enforce the corporate governance norms? Should it be the regulator or the courts? Is public enforcement preferable or private enforcement? Concomitantly, should the focus of the regulations be on the victims of corporate wrongdoings (i.e. affected minority shareholders) or on the perpetrators (i.e. errant managers or controlling shareholders)?

7.6 Special Features

This section considers three issues representing features that are somewhat unique to India. The first looks at board composition with a specific focus on diversity. The second examines shareholders as a constituency and how activism is becoming a key tool in the hands of shareholders of Indian companies. The third looks at corporate social responsibility, which has taken on a quasi-mandatory tone in India, an approach that makes India stand out from the rest of the world.

7.6.1 Board Diversity

Board diversity has acquired considerable prominence in recent times. Although the concept of diversity has various hues, one manifestation relates to gender diversity and the requirement for women directors. What began as a useful management strategy has acquired regulatory overtones. Several countries have incorporated gender diversity into their corporate governance regimes. Some, Norway being at the forefront, have sought gender diversity as a mandatory requirement. Others have either required disclosure and transparency measures or even extended comply-or-explain mechanisms. India has opted to follow the mandatory approach by requiring large companies to have at least one woman director.

N. Balasubramanian and Nirmal Mohanty, 'Gender Diversity on Boards' NSE Quarterly Briefing No. 10 (July 2015), at www.nseindia.com/research/content/resQB10.pdf

---

I. Introduction

Since directors with diverse backgrounds and experiences tend to look at problems and solutions from wider perspectives, diversity in boards has been widely considered as an important contributor to improved decision-making. True, greater diversity could potentially disrupt cohesion; but the associated cost may be worthwhile if it leads to better decisionmaking.

Gender diversity is a subset of the broader concept of diversity …

Gender diversity in boards is predicated on two grounds. The first relates to social equity and human rights. Corporations and their boards do not operate in a vacuum. The societal prejudices do permeate organizations. Like in most other countries, the Indian society has traditionally assigned a secondary and often inferior status to women compared to men. This prejudice is reflected in the poor

Table 7.2 Women on Indian boards (as at April 1, 2015)

Sr No.	Number of	Total
1	Covered companies	1,451
2	All directors in covered companies	9,384
2–A	Women directors in covered companies	1,186
3	All directorships in covered companies	11,917
3–A	Women directorships in covered companies	1,470
4	% Women directors out of total directors (2–A/2)	12.6
5	% Women directorships out of total directorships	12.3

...
Source: Prime Database

representation of women in corporate boards. Fortunately, significant increase in higher education, particularly in professional education for women has augmented the available resource pool of women candidates suitable for senior managerial positions. Nevertheless, the progress has been excessively slow ...

The second ground for gender diversity is a business case. In other words, it is also in the commercial interest of companies to have greater gender diversity on their boards ...

III. The Indian Scenario

The Companies Act of 2013, Section 149 (1) requires every company of a prescribed class to have "at least one woman director"; the prescribed class comprises all listed companies (with some exceptions ...). As regards listed companies, this provision is reflected in the Clause 49 (II) (A) (1) of the Listing Agreement. Also, SEBI had mandated that the appointment of woman directors to the board must happen no later than April 1, 2015. If the listed companies remain non-compliant after April 1, 2015, stock exchanges have been mandated by SEBI to levy monetary penalties starting June 30, 2015 ...

Corporate sector's response to the mandate

Our analysis is based on Prime Database data on woman directors as on April 1, 2015. These data are available for 1,451 NSE-listed companies. Out of these 1451 companies, 147 companies (10.1%) did not have any woman on their board. Overall, women represented an estimated 12.3% of total directorships.

Afra Afsharipour, 'The One Woman Director Mandate: History and Trajectory,' in Indian Institute of Corporate Affairs (ed.), *Corporate Governance in India: Change and Continuity* (New Delhi: Oxford University Press, 2015), at http://ssrn.com/abstract=2686991

3. INDIA'S BOARD DIVERSITY REQUIREMENT: IMPLEMENTATION CHALLENGES

The reach of the one woman director requirement was expected to be vast. According to some reports, almost 1000 directorship positions would need to be filled in listed companies alone to comply with the mandate. Other reports placed this number in the many thousands given the large number of firms listed on the BSE and NSE. Early reports after passage of the Act provide support that many companies were beginning to search for women directors prior to the effectiveness of the MCA and SEBI rules in Spring 2015. Despite these early efforts, there have been significant challenges with implementing the mandate.

Challenges with the Pipeline

Initial reactions to the requirement brought up concerns about the pipeline of women executives at Indian firms. Various reports show that compared to other leading economies in Asia, the representation of women in the labor force in India is the lowest in the region … Thus, there were concerns about whether India had a sufficiently qualified number of women with senior executive experience who could serve as board members.

…

There are several challenges that affect the pipeline of women executives to board positions. One challenge is that financial services firms churn out the highest number of women leaders in India. However, internal policies at leading investment banks restrict executives from taking external board memberships that can generate a conflict of interest. Moreover, the banking industry produces the greatest number of women CEOs in India, yet these women currently cannot be tapped because regulatory norms prohibit them from having an interest in any other company.

Even more significant are the challenges that arise from traditional gender norms and societal expectations in India that place significant burdens on the familial and household responsibilities of women. Many women's groups have expressed the general sentiment that the lack of Indian women in senior positions are due to "archaic cultural stereotypes on the roles of men and women in society," such as the notion that women's primary responsibility is to take care of the family, as well as to gender gaps in literacy and in the numbers reaching higher education …

These realities led experts to express concern that the corporate sector's response to the requirement would be to seek women directors who are already serving on other boards. It appeared, at least at first, that many of the same women were initially being tapped for board positions …

Implementation Shortcomings

Despite the lofty aims of the one woman director requirement, corporate India as a whole did not move quickly toward compliance. Various reports indicated that by the end of 2014, almost 37% of companies listed on the NSE had not appointed a woman director. Even with significant advance notice of the compliance deadline, analysts estimate that nearly 600 companies announced the appointment of a woman director in the last two days before the April 1, 2015 deadline. In addition, some companies, including some very large state-owned firm, failed to comply with the deadline. Early figures from analysts estimated that approximately 13% of companies listed on the National Stock Exchange of India (NSE) failed to appoint a woman director as of April 1, 2015 … The last minute push to appoint woman directors raises legitimate concerns about whether companies have adopted "a check-the-box attitude" …

The lack of compliance resulted in threats by SEBI that it would take action against non-compliant companies … In early April 2015, SEBI directed the stock exchanges to impose fines on non-compliant firms …

… [M]any have also expressed a concern that companies would fill directorships with family and friends rather than developing the experience and talent of women who have no prior experience on boards …

Nevertheless, reports indicate that many of the women directors appointed to company boards were family members of the promoter or non-independent directors … Early evidence suggests that many companies … appointed to Indian corporate boards women who were relatives of company promoters, thus undermining the diversity rationale behind the law.…

What Next?

The authors proposed several policies to increase the pipeline of women directors in India. First, improve the process of identifying women directors. This will increase the available talent pool by helping to bring competent women in the non-business sphere to the board's attention. Second, firms should develop a director training and development program for mid-career women with high potential, competence, and willingness to be on boards. Additionally, existing executive directors can be groomed during their tenure to be independent directors in non-competing industries. Third, enhance the supply of potential women directors with education and networking organizations such as those seen in the West.

Others have also advocated for SEBI to amend its listing rules to require that the one woman director in listed companies must also be an independent director.

Notes and Questions

1. Are you persuaded by the business reasons for gender diversity on corporate boards? Are there any other compelling reasons you can think of?
2. The empirical results pertaining to the effectiveness of gender diversity in corporate boards is mixed with no evidence of a causal relationship between diversity and corporate performance. Is it prudent to press ahead with diversity through legislative measures?
3. What is the suitable method for implementing gender diversity? Is the approach of mandatory quotas a suitable one? Would a comply-or-explain approach be preferable?
4. How does one address the issue of tokenism? To plug any loophole, do you think it would be better to provide that women directors who are to be appointed to satisfy the quota requirements must either be independent or must fulfill other competence criteria? How does one enforce these requirements?

7.6.2 Shareholder Activism

India is one of the few Asian countries that has seen a significant rise in shareholder activism. Legal and market reforms have sought to confer greater power in the hands of shareholders. The presence of activist institutional shareholders such as private equity funds and hedge funds has already caused an upheaval in some corporate boardrooms in India.

While these developments pave the way for a transformation in the tenor of the governance debate, shareholder activism encounters certain structural and institutional weaknesses within the Indian markets. The dominance of controlling shareholders in most Indian companies operates to dampen the effects of shareholder activism. The legal system and institutions in India are not conducive to rendering timely and cost-effective remedies to shareholders who adopt a litigation strategy to counter managements that are perceived to act inimical to shareholder interests.

Umakanth Varottil, 'The Advent of Shareholder Activism in India' (2012) 1 *Journal on Governance* 582

VII. Evaluating the Impact of Shareholder Activism

A. *Distilling the Evidence*

The present study finds palpable anecdotal evidence that indicates a greater role on the part of activist shareholders in India since 2011 than that witnessed in the past. This is due to the efforts of the corporate regulators to enhance shareholder participation in corporate decision-making through various measures such as e-voting, e-meetings and the imposition of a stewardship role on institutional investors such as mutual funds. Apart from being nudged by the regulators, certain activist investors themselves have taken on the mantle of influencing corporate governance in companies in which they have invested. The emergence of a strong set of informational intermediaries in the form of proxy advisories signals a new era in shareholder activism in India …

While some general trends in India can be gleaned from anecdotal evidence, there is little track record to build any empirical evidence yet. Although there are empirical studies carried out in other markets, they remain equivocal about the positive impact of shareholder activism on corporate governance …

On the other hand, it has been argued that the significant costs generated by shareholder activism cannot justify the limited benefits it confers.

…

While the anecdotal evidence indicates the strong emergence of shareholder activism in India, the empirical evidence regarding its impact on corporate governance in other markets is mixed. Given this situation, the benefits of shareholder activism as a measure to boost corporate governance in India must be accepted with some caution.

B. *Effect on Controlled Companies*

In insider economies such as India, due to the influence of controlling shareholders, activist investors would not find it easy to alter the outcome of decisions made at shareholders' meetings. This may in turn reduce the incentives of activist investors to adopt stances that operate to act as a check on management. As a corollary, controlling shareholders are less likely to be deterred by the actions of activist shareholders.

…

Hence, if there is some ambivalence regarding the effectiveness of shareholder activism generally, then its positive effect on controlled companies that populate the Indian corporate setting is only likely to be minimal.

… [W]e find that while shareholder activism does influence corporate governance in several ways, not the least by publicizing governance failures and drawing attention to specific issues that may be of relevance to the investing community, we are far from finding any empirical correlation between shareholder activism and corporate governance. If that link is not clear in developed markets such as the US with companies that have diffused shareholding, we must accept shareholder activism in insider economies like India that have controlled companies with some amount of caution. While it would be rash to argue against activism, its impact must not be overstated.

7.6.2.1 TCI VERSUS COAL INDIA: A MINI-CASE STUDY

This instance relates to the corporate dispute that unfolded in early 2012 between Coal India Limited (CIL), a government company that is listed on stock exchanges in India, and the Children's Investment Fund Management (UK) LLP (TCI), a hedge fund that held 1 percent shares in CIL. TCI sought to remove the Indian government's intervention in CIL's affairs (although the government held 90 percent shares in CIL) and the board's independent management of the company. TCI also raised a number of specific issues. For example, CIL was refusing to sell products at market prices due to heavy government influence. Not satisfied with the responses received from CIL, TCI initiated action against the company and its directors, and it also simultaneously issued a notice initiating arbitrations under the provisions of the bilateral investment treaties (BITs) that India had entered into with the UK and Cyprus.

Around the world, TCI has a remarkably successful track record in forcing managements to change their policies in response to its activist stance. However, in India it was unable to replicate this, as it decided to exit from its investment in CIL in October 2014 due to which the legal action was dropped. While this case study indicates that investors are not hesitant in initiating legal action against companies on matters relating to corporate governance, it also signifies the difficulties in succeeding in such actions, including due to the inadequacies of legal remedies for investors in the Indian context.

Notes and Questions

1. How likely is shareholder activism to operate in companies with dispersed shareholding and those with concentrated shareholding? Where are they likely to be more effective, if at all?
2. Anecdotal evidence suggests that activist investors have not enjoyed as much success in Asian markets such as India as they have been able to in Western markets. What could be the possible reasons for this? Are institutional, cultural, and social factors likely to play a role?
3. Could activist investors pursue agendas that may contrast with the interests of passive minority shareholders? Could activism engender short-termism among managers that may not be in the long-term interests of shareholders? Do you agree with these criticisms?
4. India is one of the few Asian countries that have witnessed the proliferation of active local proxy advisory firms. These firms provide advice to shareholders (particularly of the institutional variety) on how to exercise their corporate franchise on portfolio companies. The publication of their recommendations also assists small non-institutional shareholders. Do such proxy advisory firms bridge the information asymmetry among companies, institutional investors, and non-institutional shareholders? Consider whether proxy advisory firms themselves are independent gatekeepers or whether they could be susceptible to conflicts of interest.

7.6.3 Corporate Social Responsibility

Although the concept of corporate social responsibility (CSR) has acquired tremendous prominence in the business world, the manner in which it has been introduced in India is unique. CSR generally refers to the requirement of companies to carry out their business activities in a sustainable and socially responsible manner. However, in India companies are foisted with a legislative mandate to do so. Although it falls short of a mandatory legal obligation, it is nevertheless a significant responsibility on the part of large Indian companies, including spending a percentage of their profits toward specified CSR activities.

Afra Afsharipour and Shruti Rana, 'The Emergence of New Corporate Social Responsibility Regimes in China and India' (2014) 14 *UC Davis Business Law Journal* 175

IV. India's New Corporate Social Responsibility Regime

Charitable giving has long been a priority for many Indian corporations. Some of the largest business houses in India, such as the Tata Group, have had a sustained focus on corporate philanthropy. Long before any discussion of CSR as a legal requirement, some of India's largest conglomerates established separate philanthropic funds and welfare programs or initiatives as a form of charity to indicate the virtues of the company or the organization … Some scholars have even argued that business responsibility in India is rooted in Gandhi's trusteeship model with companies seen as trustees who manage resources on behalf of society.

…

4. Amendment of the Companies Act

In 2010, the MCA began to move toward incorporating CSR, and a more mandatory version of CSR, into a proposed Companies Act …

… [T]he MCA indicated that it would introduce mandatory CSR requirements into the Companies Bill …

Over the next several years, the MCA fluctuated between imposing mandatory CSR requirements into the Companies Bill and adopting CSR recommendations with a "comply-or-explain" approach, eventually settling on a compromise approach. The compromise approach arose after significant criticism of the mandatory spend provision in the draft Companies Bill …

A. The Requirements of the Companies Act, 2013

Under the Companies Act, CSR is considered to be a board-level activity. Every company with a [specified minimum net worth, turnover or net profit] during any financial year must constitute a CSR Committee of the Board consisting of three or more directors, out of which at least one director must be an independent director. The Act empowers the CSR Committee with (i) formulating and recommending to the Board, a CSR Policy which must indicate the activities to be undertaken by the company; (ii) recommending the amount of CSR expenditure to be incurred on such activities; and (iii) regularly monitoring the CSR initiatives of the company. The Board must then take into account the recommendations made by the CSR Committee and approve the CSR policy of the company.

Under the Act, the Board must "ensure that the company spends, in every financial year, at least two per cent of the average net profits of the company made during the three immediately preceding financial years, in pursuance of its Corporate Social Responsibility Policy." If a company does not have adequate profit or is not in a position to spend the prescribed amount on CSR, the regulation would require the directors to provide disclosure and give suitable reasons in their annual report, with a view to checking non-compliance.

While there was much debate over whether to have made the CSR spending provision in the Act mandatory, the final consensus was to approach spending through a "comply or explain" framework. Thus, while there is no penalty for failing to spend on CSR, there are penalties for failing to report on CSR activities conducted or failing to explain why CSR spending was not carried out. Failure to explain is punishable by a fine on the company ...

The Companies Act does not purport to define CSR, but it does include a detailed schedule of CSR activities that companies "may" undertake ...

B. *Shortcomings of India's Emerging Corporate Social Responsibility Model*

The potential for CSR reforms in India is enormous. There are several important concerns, however, with the Indian government's approach to CSR. First, the mandatory spend provision indicates a more philanthropic model of CSR rather than the broader stakeholder model. Instead of approaching CSR from a holistic viewpoint that addresses the activities of companies in a variety of areas, the Companies Act provides a limited scope for CSR activities and arguably reduces CSR to an ineffective 2% spending provision. Second, the Act has come under criticism that the government is attempting to force companies to do what should be the state's job, such as providing education. Third, the government seems to be seeking to capitalize on the cultural values of Indian firms, yet answers the CSR debate with the same solution that it has used, thus far with mixed success, with respect to corporate governance reforms – i.e., in large part locating responsibility for CSR activities in the board of directors ...

The regime for CSR under the Companies Act has many detractors. The vision of CSR espoused in the Act certainly falls short of an expansive stakeholder view of CSR. Experts have questioned whether the Act's requirements render CSR a more "check-the-box" obligation ...

Critics have noted that the 2% spend provision is essentially fruitless and will not necessarily render a business socially responsible. For example, given the vagueness in the definition of CSR under the Companies Act and the scope of CSR activities in the MCA's final rules, a corporation in a line of business that causes significant detrimental environmental impact could spend the mandatory funds on building a school in an un-impacted rural area rather than on ensuring that it decreased its adverse environmental impact. The local-community focus of the CSR requirement of the Companies Act may render CSR activities as simple window-dressing without significant changes to potential social and environmental damage that a company may inflict ...

In connection with the criticism that the vision of CSR in the Companies Act is rather limited, commentators have also lamented that such CSR activities are essentially a privatization of the state's role and responsibility in many areas ... In other words, businesses cannot substitute for the state in solving India's massive social problems.

Notes and Questions

1. What factors may have played a role in India embarking upon a quasi-mandatory approach toward CSR finding a place in basic company law? What interest groups may have been involved, and do you think the compromise that has been struck is a viable one?
2. Is a minimum spending requirement on CSR activities an appropriate method of implementation? Does it not amount to mere symbolism, and a type of obligatory corporate philanthropy? Are CSR and corporate philanthropy the same, or are they two different concepts that have become conflated?
3. Under the relevant rules, CSR excludes "activities undertaken in pursuance of the normal course of business of the company." Does this not appear somewhat paradoxical in that companies' normal business conduct will not be taken into account for CSR? Does it matter that the Companies Act focuses on CSR as a matter of expenditure of funds by companies rather than as a matter of conduct or corporate behavior? How does one reconcile the need for companies to be socially responsible in their ordinary course of business and undertake further responsibilities in the form of philanthropy?
4. In considering the disclosure of CSR practices, what types of reporting requirements would be appropriate so as to inform the investors and other stakeholders of the company's actions?
5. What type of governance structure would be appropriate for considering CSR matters? For example, the Companies Act 2013 requires large companies to have a CSR committee of directors. What role should those directors perform?

Statutes and Regulators

Statutes

Companies Act 2013

Securities and Exchange Board of India Act 1992

Securities Contracts (Regulation) Act 1956

SEBI (Listing Obligations and Disclosure Requirements) Regulations 2015

Regulators

Ministry of Corporate Affairs, Government of India

Securities and Exchange Board of India

Stock Exchanges (primarily BSE Limited and the National Stock Exchange of India Limited)

8

SINGAPORE

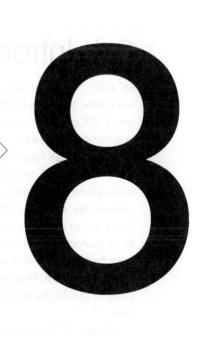

Dan Puchniak

8.1 Introduction

In 1965, Singapore was a poor developing country with no significant natural resources. Today, its GDP per person is double Japan's and significantly higher than every G7 country. This remarkable feat presents a conundrum for conventional comparative corporate governance theory – which has been derived primarily from Anglo-America's corporate governance experience.

When viewed through an Anglo-American lens, Singapore's remarkable success appears to confirm conventional corporate governance theory. Singapore is consistently ranked as having the best corporate governance in Asia. Singapore has a strong common law legal system and has historically led the Commonwealth in its protection of minority shareholder rights. Singapore's listed companies have long had boards which are dominated by "independent directors." In sum, based on these features, Singapore appears to be a shining example of a successful transplant of the Anglo-American-cum-global model of "good" corporate governance to Asia.

If one drills down a bit deeper, however, in many respects, Singapore is the antithesis of the Anglo-American model. In Singapore, the state is the largest shareholder of public listed companies – an anathema to the Anglo-American model. Singapore's listed companies are dominated by controlling block shareholders, whose shareholdings have become even more concentrated as its wealth has reached world-leading heights – the opposite of what the prominent Anglo-American law and finance theory would predict. Singapore's market for corporate control is nascent and shareholder activists are virtually non-existent – two features which form the core of "good" corporate governance in the Anglo-American model. Singapore has one of the world's most efficient and least corrupt governments, which effectively regulates its corporate governance and financial markets – but, at the same time, its lacks a Western-style democracy.

In short, in many respects, Singapore turns the conventional wisdom of the Anglo-American model for "good" corporate governance on its head. In turn, to understand Singapore's phenomenal corporate governance and economic success, it is essential to understand the idiosyncrasies of Singapore. This may sound obvious, because it is. However, it is contrary to much of the leading comparative corporate governance theory which suggests a universal, one-size-fits-all approach. Singapore corporate governance appears both deceptively familiar and intriguingly unique.

8.2 The Purpose of Singapore Corporate Law and Governance

Raffles Town Club Pte Ltd v. *Lim Eng Hock Peter and others* [2010] SGHC 163 (High Court, Singapore)

Raffles Town Club Pte Ltd (RTC), which owned and operated a social club, sued its former directors for breaching their directors' duties. At the material time, the defendants were the only directors and shareholders. RTC claimed that the former directors had wrongfully caused RTC to pay themselves excessive directors' and consultancy fees amounting to approximately S$15 million.

The High Court dismissed RTC's claim. It found that because RTC was solvent and the defendants were the only shareholders of the company, the defendants' interests and the company's interests were one and the same. Since the defendants in their capacity as RTC's directors and shareholders approved the directors' and consultancy fees, they could not be held liable to the company for breaching their directors' duties. On appeal, the Court of Appeal upheld the decision.

...

It is trite law that the Defendants, as directors, owe a duty as fiduciaries to the company to act honestly and in the best interests of the company. The first question I asked myself was, "Whose interests are the company's interests?" In *Walter Woon on Company Law* (Tan Cheng Han SC, gen ed) (Sweet & Maxwell, 3rd Rev Ed, 2009) ("*Walter Woon*"), the learned authors write:

> A company is not a monolith consisting of bland interchangeable digits. Rather, it is an entity with many stakeholders. The interests of these stakeholders, while to some degree are aligned, are often at variance between themselves. There are the members, whose personal interests are not subsumed within the corporate structure. There are employees, whose interests are tied up with the prosperity of the company. Then there are the creditors of the company, who generally can look only to the company for the payment of the sums due to them.

Certainly, one of the tests used when considering the validity of a commercial transaction is whether the transaction benefited the company as a commercial entity. Thus, when a decision is made to plough profits back into the company rather than pay them out as dividends or bonuses, it reflects a decision to prefer the interests of the company as a commercial entity over the interests of the shareholders and employees as individuals. It does not mean, however, that this is the only possible interest that a company might have.

In a capitalist environment which encourages entrepreneurship such as ours, the Court should not view every transaction which does not positively result in profitable returns to the company as a commercial entity with suspicion. Thus, the learned authors of *Walter Woon* recognised … that the "collective interests of the members of the company can also be equated with the interests of the company …" It was never in dispute that RTC was solvent at all material times … Thus, the Plaintiff's interests here should be equated with the interests of its shareholders since the Plaintiff has neither shown that the company was at all near becoming insolvent, nor that there are other creditors in the picture whose interests have to be protected in the event that the company becomes insolvent.

Raffles Town Club Pte Ltd v. _Lim Eng Hock Peter and others_ [2013] 1 SLR 374 (Court of Appeal, Singapore)

Dillon LJ, who delivered the other majority judgment, said (at 288): 'An individual trader who is solvent is free to make stupid, but honest commercial decisions in the conduct of his own business. He owes no duty of care to future creditors. The same applies to a partnership of individuals. A company … likewise owes no duty of care to future creditors. The directors indeed stand in a fiduciary relationship to the company, as they are appointed to manage the affairs of the company and they owe fiduciary duties to the company though not to the creditors, present or future, or to individual shareholders … The shareholders, however, owe no such duty to the company. Indeed, so long as the company is solvent the shareholders are in substance the company.'

Dan W. Puchniak and Tan Cheng Han, 'Company Law,' in _Singapore Academy of Law Annual Review_, 145, Teo Keang Sood (ed.), Academy Publishing (2015), at http://journalsonline.academypublishing.org.sg/Journals/Singapore-Academy-of-Law-Annual-Review-of-Singapore-Cases/e-Archive/ctl/eFirstSALPDFJournalView/mid/512/ArticleId/1137/Citation/JournalsOnlinePDF

In *Ho Kang Peng*, the Court of Appeal acknowledged that while the bribes that were paid to a third party were intended to benefit the company financially (at least in the short term), and a court would generally be slow to interfere with commercial decisions made by directors, a director would not be regarded as having acted bona fide in the company's best interests where such director had engaged in dishonest activity. The best interests of a company do not involve only profit maximisation, and certainly is not profit maximisation by any means. It was as much in the interests of the company to have its directors act within their powers and for proper purposes, to obtain full disclosure from its directors, and not to be deceived by its directors. There could be no doubt that a director who caused a company to pay bribes and, therefore, ran the risk of the company being subject to criminal liability was not acting in the company's best interests. This was a risk that no director could honestly believe to be taken in the interest of the company. The court also said that by continuing a highly irregular and improper practice which the director understood had been initiated by the previous management under a different form without inquiring why it was made, whether it would implicate the company, and whether proper sanction had been obtained, the director had failed to exercise the diligence and care that a reasonable director ought to have exercised, this being another aspect of the duty a director owes to his company …

This decision is a welcome one. It provides a timely reminder that directors ought to take into account what would benefit the company over a longer horizon and that profit maximisation should not be the only focus of corporate boards. It also sets a strong rule that engaging in acts that expose a company to criminal liability will not be regarded as acting in a company's best interests. At the same time, the decision reiterates the importance of directors exercising proper supervision and due diligence in the discharge of their duties instead of blindingly following existing practices.

In *Airtrust (Singapore) Pte Ltd v Kao Chai-Chau Linda* [2014] 2 SLR 673, the High Court applied the principle laid down by the Court of Appeal in *Yong Kheng Leong v Panweld Trading Pte Ltd* [2013] 1 SLR 173 that if all of a company's shareholders assent to a director's breach of fiduciary duty then there is no need for a formal shareholder resolution to relieve the director from liability. In this case, however, the High Court found that it was unclear whether all of the shareholders had indeed assented. As such, it could not be assumed that the director's liability would be relieved without a formal shareholder resolution …

It is noteworthy that the High Court rejected the argument that the assent of all of the shareholders could be assumed based solely on the fact that the case involved a family-run company in which the patriarch, who was the controlling mind of the company, would have suggested to the shareholders to assent. This finding is welcome because failing to require clear evidence of assent would unjustifiably risk relieving a director of liability when in fact such relief may have been opposed by the shareholders had a formal resolution been attempted. It must be remembered that in such cases, if there is any uncertainty as to whether shareholders have assented, a formal resolution can always be passed.

Ho Kang Peng v. *Scintronix Corp Ltd (formerly known as TTL Holdings Ltd) [2014] SGCA 22* (Court of Appeal, Singapore)

In fact Oh's [defendant director] evidence was candid and points quite clearly to the purposes and nature of the Payments. The following exchanges in cross-examination are telling:

Q Mr Oh, do you agree that such payments are illegal?
A Because it's – personally for my view, because we go there to do business, my – our main goal are to earn money.

...

Q Mr Oh, you're not answering my question. Are these payments proper, are these payments illegal?
A Whether it's proper or not, but I feel that in China, mostly they do it this way. If not – if not we would not have any business.

...

Q Mr Oh, do you think it is correct practice for a listed company to pay money to get business?
A If it was agreed between the partners, as I've said, if it's in China, especially in China.

No doubt, Oh's answers were really his personal perceptions regarding doing business in China which are nothing more than obvious generalisations. More importantly, Oh seemed to accept that the purpose of the Payments was to procure business for the Company.

The Appellant [defendant director] himself also made similar concessions under cross-examination which he sought to qualify immediately thereafter:

Q ... Don't you think it is wrong to pay money to get business from someone?
A I did not felt [*sic*] that it was wrong because in China, this is very common for us to pay people money to procure business.

Notes and Questions

1. According to Singapore company law, prima facie, directors' duties are owed to the company. Directors do not normally owe duties directly to shareholders, creditors, employees, or any other corporate stakeholders. Do you think that this approach improves the efficiency of Singapore corporate governance?
2. As a general rule, in a solvent company, directors are required to consider the interests of shareholders (both present and future) as a general body in discharging their duties owed to the company. In most cases, this amounts to considering if the transaction benefits the company as a commercial entity.
3. The Companies Act expressly allows directors to take account of the interests of employees when they discharge their directors' duties. Moreover, case law suggests that directors may consider the interests of the corporate group and other stakeholders when making corporate decisions. In addition, when a company is on the brink of insolvency, the interests of the company become tantamount to the interests of the present and future creditors in the context of directors fulfilling their duties to the company.
4. It would be fair to say that Singapore company law, at its core, is based on a shareholder primacy model. Shareholders have the right to remove directors from a public company at any time. Generally, directors are legally bound to act in the best interests of the company – which is most often equated with the interests of the shareholders as a whole. The Singapore company law, however, has come to recognize that other stakeholders play an important role in the company and allows for them to be taken into consideration by directors in discharging their duties owed to the company.
5. Ultimately, the goal of Singapore corporate law appears to be ensuring the long-term success of the company – which is sometimes referred to in Singapore as the interests of 'enlightened shareholders' (i.e. those shareholders who understand that profit maximization in the long term often requires ensuring that the interests of all corporate stakeholders are taken into account on an ongoing basis).
6. However, Singapore's "shareholder primacy" model differs considerably from the Anglo-American model, as listed companies are dominated by controlling shareholders – who are normally either the government or family-controlled firms.
7. Would it be correct to classify companies in which the Singapore government is the largest shareholder as being based on the "shareholder primacy" model?
8. Is the approach taken by Singapore courts in their enforcement of corporate law more reflective of Singapore's Commonwealth heritage or Asian culture?
9. Should cultural norms be given weight or taken into consideration when defining the purpose or function of a country's corporate law and governance system?

8.3 Board Function and Shareholder Power in Singapore

Luh Lan and Umakanth Varottil, 'Shareholder Empowerment in Controlled Companies: The Case of Singapore,' in Jennifer G. Hill and Randall S. Thomas (eds.), *Research Handbook on Shareholder Power* (Cheltenham, UK and Northampton, MA: Edward Elgar, 2015), p. 572

B. Strategies for Addressing the Agency Problem

We divide the strategies relating to the controller-minority agency problem into two categories: (1) participative strategy, and (2) controlling strategy. Participative strategy is aimed at enhancing the rights of the minority shareholders in controlled companies such that they can exert greater power to minimize the agency problem. Controlling strategy is aimed at moderating the powers of the controlling shareholder such that checks and balances can be imposed on their private benefits of control, thereby minimizing the agency problem. The two strategies perform opposite roles to achieve an equilibrium ...

III. PARTICIPATIVE STRATEGY

Shareholders in Singapore companies wield significant powers, and arguably much more so than shareholders in US companies. For example, shareholders in Singapore companies can appoint directors with a simple majority of votes at a shareholders' meeting. Likewise, shareholders are entitled to remove directors by a similar majority. This right of removing directors is an absolute one, and can be exercised even where there is no 'cause.' Hence, it is not possible for directors to establish a secure staggered board of the type prevalent in several Delaware companies. Shareholder approval is also required for several other matters such as disposal of a significant asset or business of a company, payment of executive compensation to senior managers, a merger of the company, and the like.

Under the Companies Act ('the Act') in Singapore, shareholders [holding at least 10 percent of shares] are also entitled to convene meetings to carry out these and other actions ... If the board of the company does not oblige, then the shareholders may themselves proceed to convene a meeting if they command a majority among those who have requested the meeting. Shareholders holding 5 percent voting rights in the company may also propose resolutions that the company must put to vote. The powerful nature of these rights enables the shareholders to monitor the management effectively and to reduce the agency costs between them …

The SGX has also implemented recent reforms (SGX 2013). These reforms require all companies listed on the SGX to hold their meetings in Singapore (ibid.). This requirement arose on account of foreign companies holding their shareholders' meetings in other countries although their primary listing is on SGX and it came to the fore on account of corporate governance scandals in a number of Chinese companies listed on SGX (Jindra 2012). The SGX has also now mandated that all resolutions be put to vote by way of a poll. This is to ensure transparency in the voting process, and to eliminate the other possibility of voting through a show of hands. While the mandatory poll requirement is understandable due to the goals of transparency, it does not provide much comfort to minority shareholders in controlled companies. In a poll, each share has one vote, and hence the controlling shareholders will be in a position to determine the outcome of any resolution due to their large shareholding. The process of voting by poll entrenches the controlling shareholders further rather than providing a greater opportunity to minority shareholders …

Apart from eliciting greater participation of outside shareholders in corporate decision-making, the Code of Corporate Governance in Singapore encourages boards of companies to engage with shareholders in an active and constructive manner (Tan et al. 2006; Anandarajah 2013). Shareholders are also urged to convey their expectations to the boards that can help set the tone for the governance of the company, thereby imposing a role that is akin to stewardship on shareholders in Singapore. While shareholders cannot be compelled to take on a more active role or exercise their votes at meetings, the Code follows a "comply or explain" approach in exhorting companies and shareholders to engage more effectively on matters of corporate performance and governance.

Despite regulatory efforts to encourage greater shareholder participation and to engender a culture of shareholder engagement among companies, the empirical (or even anecdotal) evidence of shareholder activism is scant in Singapore …

Shareholders can be motivated to participate with greater vigor if disclosure and information mechanisms enable them to adopt an informed decision. While there are stringent disclosure requirements that impose an obligation on the companies to notify shareholders of decisions to be taken at meetings, there is considerable scope for improvement in the quantity and quality of information disclosed to shareholders as well as in the enforcement of disclosure obligations (Tjio 2009). In developed and some emerging markets such as India (Varottil 2012), such informational disparity is generally sought to be corrected through intermediaries such as proxy advisory firms that have played an influential role in spurring shareholder activism. Such a market for proxy advisory firms is nascent, if not non-existent, in the Singapore markets …

One effort that stands out in the Singapore markets is that of the Securities Investors Association Singapore (SIAS), which leads the shareholder rights' movement through investor education and other forms of protection of minority shareholder rights (Jindra 2012; Low 2004). While the SIAS has been active in holding investor conferences and other measures to educate the investing public, and also in holding conciliatory efforts between listed companies and their investors, it does not adopt an aggressive stance against listed companies such as by initiating litigation on behalf of investor members (Jindra 2012). Although SIAS's role is significant as a facilitator of shareholder empowerment, its level of success is determined by its ability to persuade managements of listed companies to enhance corporate governance and take into account the interest of the minority shareholders …

In reviewing the effectiveness of the participative strategy in Singapore, we find that shareholders have been conferred considerable rights in Singapore and these are comparable (or even superior) to shareholder rights in other countries such as the US. Primary among these rights include that of appointing and removing all of the directors of a company … Despite these regulatory efforts that seemingly grant greater power to minority shareholders in Singapore companies, such minorities are powerless when it comes to altering the outcome of decisions in companies. This is because decisions are largely left to the managers who operate within the shadow of the controlling shareholders who wield significant powers, including hiring and firing the board members and senior managers of the company.

The lack of power of minority shareholders in controlled companies explains the relative lack of an activist culture among shareholders in Singapore companies …

All of these suggest that the participative strategy is likely to go only some way in resolving the controller-minority agency problem that is endemic in Singapore companies. Instead, the focus must necessarily shift to a strategy that differentiates between controlling shareholders and minority shareholders and seeks to dilute the excessive dominance of controlling shareholders.

IV. CONTROLLING STRATEGY

The controlling strategy has various facets, some of which operate *ex ante* and others operate *ex post* …

A. *Ex ante* Mechanisms

… In Singapore, such controlling strategy is employed most directly in SGX's Listing Rules that regulate related party transactions (referred to by SGX as 'interested person transactions' (IPTs)) involving listed companies. The regulation of IPTs attains significance in controlled companies, as such transactions constitute primary methods of tunneling and expropriation of minority shareholder interests.

... IPTs are subject to a multipronged regulation. *First*, a company must immediately make an announcement of an IPT that is equal to or exceeds 3 percent of the group's latest audited net tangible assets. The announcement must include a statement as to whether the audit committee is of the view that the transaction is on normal commercial terms, and is not prejudicial to the interests of the company and the minority shareholders. *Second*, the company must obtain a prior shareholder approval for an IPT that is equal to or exceeds 5 percent of the group's latest audited net tangible assets. In doing so, an interested person or any of its associates are precluded from voting on the resolution. Therefore, what is required is a disinterested shareholder vote, or a "majority of the minority." Where shareholder vote is sought for, the circular to the shareholders must include the details of the IPT, its rationale, and an opinion from an independent financial adviser stating whether the transaction is on normal commercial terms and whether it is prejudicial to the interests of the company and the minority shareholders. The SGX therefore regulates IPTs through the two instruments: (1) disclosure, and (2) disinterested shareholder approval.

The disinterested shareholder approval requirement deserves attention as it directly engages with the controller-minority agency problem that is prevalent in controlled companies. By disenfranchising the controlling shareholders on decision-making relating to IPTs, it confers greater power on minority shareholders. In the case of IPTs, it removes the decision-making power from the hands of the controlling shareholders and places it with the minority shareholders. While minority shareholders usually suffer from collective action problems, the fact that their decision will determine the outcome of an IPT will likely propel them to action. Even if small retail shareholders continue to suffer from collective action problems, the larger institutional shareholders will possess the necessary incentives to participate in the decision-making process.

While the disinterested shareholder voting for IPTs forms the most significant tool in the controlling strategy, it is applicable for very large transactions and may not directly address systematic tunneling through smaller IPTs over a sustained period of time. In Singapore, transactions below $100,000 are ignored ...

In addition to the specific regulation of IPTs through the SGX, the general principles of corporate law in Singapore impose restrictions on self-dealing transactions. These restrictions are targeted at the board rather than the shareholders. However, they have some role to play in addressing the controller-minority agency problem as directors are often either the controlling shareholders themselves or their representatives. Hence, the regulation of board conduct may indirectly affect the conduct of the controlling shareholders ... A paradigmatic example of such regulated self-dealing transaction involves the diversion of corporate opportunities by the directors to themselves or to entities in which they have a substantial interest. The courts have been willing to step in where it can be shown that there has been a diversion of corporate opportunity (Woon 2009; Tan 2011).

While the imposition of stringent fiduciary duties on directors operates as an effective check against self-dealing, its coverage is ultimately limited to directors acting in that capacity and does not encompass controlling shareholders. Under Singapore law, controlling shareholders do not generally owe fiduciary duties either to the company or to the minority shareholders. Of course, there are some exceptions to this rule, but these are very limited. Except for IPTs which are regulated by the SGX and certain exceptional circumstances where controlling shareholders are obligated to act in the interests of the company or a class of shareholders, they can otherwise act in their own interests. The absence of an overarching fiduciary duty on controlling shareholders provides a limited role to courts …

B. *Ex post* Mechanisms

While the *ex ante* mechanisms deal with the substantive corporate and securities laws that address the controller-minority agency problem, the *ex post* mechanisms involve the enforcement of those laws. On the one hand, there could be public enforcement through the imposition of civil or criminal penalties initiated by regulatory authorities. In Singapore, while the Accounting and Corporate Regulatory Authority (ACRA) enforces the provisions of the Act, the Monetary Authority of Singapore (MAS) and the SGX enforce the provisions of securities laws that are primarily contained in the Securities and Futures Act (SFA) (Tjio 2009; Jindra 2012). Public enforcement can be an important tool for investor protection, primarily to ensure disclosures and market efficiency. Anecdotal evidence suggests the existence of a robust public enforcement machinery in Singapore … Public enforcement mechanisms concentrate on the wrongdoers rather than the victims.

On the other hand, private enforcement mechanisms confer remedies upon minority shareholders in case they are subjected to expropriation or other abusive conduct on the part of the managers or controlling shareholders. *Ex post* private enforcement protections grant minority shareholders some form of redress, although they may also indirectly operate as a deterrent against abusive conduct by the controlling shareholders. Singapore law offers a sophisticated and effective framework that facilitates minority shareholder actions. The legal regime has developed systematically through statutory mechanisms as well as effective judicial intervention …

1. Oppression action

Section 216 of the Act confers shareholders with the ability to bring an oppression action if the affairs of the company are being carried on in a manner that is oppressive to such shareholders or if an act or conduct of the company unfairly discriminates or is otherwise prejudicial to the shareholders bringing the action. An oppression action is a direct action in that it can be pursued by minority shareholders against the controlling shareholders (or the company). By emboldening the minority shareholders, the oppression remedy seeks to address the controller-agency problem ...

Since the principal outcome of an oppression action is to grant the minority shareholders with an exit opportunity, the relevance of this remedy is largely confined to private companies or unlisted public companies. The utility of this remedy breaks down in the context of a public listed company as the minority shareholders do have an exit opportunity through the market that exists for the company's shares ...

2. Derivative action

Apart from a direct action such as an oppression claim, shareholders may also bring a derivative action on behalf of the company. It is common for such a derivative action to be brought against a director who has breached a fiduciary duty. It is not possible to bring a derivative action against controlling shareholders as they owe no fiduciary duty to the company. Hence, derivative actions are generally an integral part of the strategy that helps address the agency problem between the shareholders and the managers. Although it is not directly beneficial in the context of the controller-minority agency problem, it may have some role to play in disciplining managers who are either controlling shareholders themselves or their representatives. Given the inextricable linkages between controlling shareholders and managers in controlled companies, derivative actions may have an incidental impact in addressing the controller-minority agency problem.

Singapore has two concurrent mechanisms that allow minority shareholders to bring derivative actions. The first is a statutory derivative action and the second is the common law derivative action ...

While derivative actions (whether statutory or common law) have become a key prong of the minority protection regime in Singapore, their utility as part of the controlling strategy remains in doubt for several reasons. *First,* they apply only to rein in the conduct of directors and managers and they may only have an incidental effect on controlling shareholders, although the latter can be liable as shadow directors if the board is accustomed to act in accordance with the directions of the controlling shareholders. *Second,* their efficacy is confined to unlisted companies and private companies that are generally devoid of an exit option for their shareholders. There is no track record of the utilization of the derivative action mechanism to address the controller-minority agency problem in Singapore. Given that the company derives the benefit of the derivative action, there is no incentive (particularly for small shareholders) to incur the cost of bringing an action.

Moreover, the legal system in Singapore does not lend itself to collective action in litigation. Although a class action can be brought under the current law, the incentives that generally create a market for class actions are not present in Singapore. The costs of litigation are prohibitive in nature, the "loser pays" principle applies to limit risk-taking on the part of the plaintiff shareholders, and the plaintiff bar that is usually incentivized to bring class actions does not exist in Singapore as lawyers are prevented from charging contingency fees due to the prohibition against champerty. Hence, the necessary environment for individual or class actions on behalf of shareholders has not existed in the same manner as it does in the US (Loke 2010; Jindra 2012). Recently, there have been some calls for the government to review the age-old doctrine prohibiting champerty and maintenance to allow greater access to justice for the poor (Ho 2013). If third-party funding of litigation is permitted in Singapore, it remains to be seen if more shareholders from listed companies will be encouraged to utilize statutory derivative action to discipline the management, and in turn, the controlling shareholders.

To conclude, Singapore does have a robust set of *ex post* protections available for minority shareholders … However, these *ex post* protections so far have been aimed at small companies that are not listed …

V. CONCLUSIONS AND WAY FORWARD

[T]he idea of shareholder empowerment must be viewed with an altogether different lens in controlled companies compared to the more conventional approach that is indifferent to shareholding structures. In such companies, the use of a participative strategy that empowers minority shareholders can only have a partial impact as it is stonewalled by the dominant voting power of the controlling shareholders. Instead, we argue, the focus in controlled companies must be on moderating the powers of the controlling shareholders through what we have referred to as the controlling strategy. A combination of the two strategies is likely to generate an optimal outcome. Reliance solely on minority shareholder empowerment, which is becoming the norm in companies with dispersed shareholding, is bound to be ineffective …

Our normative approach points us towards the need for a different set of proposals in considering shareholder empowerment in controlled companies. Specifically, the participative strategy in controlled companies may consider alternative voting mechanisms to strengthen the position of minority shareholders. These include the cumulative voting system for the appointment of directors where minority shareholders are guaranteed the choice of a proportion of the board depending upon their percentage of shareholding in the company. Similarly, the controlling strategy may need to place greater emphasis on the role and duties of controlling shareholders. The current position of negligible fiduciary duties on controlling shareholders must give way to a more refined set of duties that apply at least in the case of significant transactions between controlling shareholders and the company. A suitable instance of such a significant transaction is a squeeze-out of the minority shareholders where the controller-minority agency problem is most acute …

Meng Seng Wee and Dan W. Puchniak, 'Derivative Actions in Singapore: Mundanely Non-Asian, Intriguingly Non-American and at the Forefront of the Commonwealth,' in Dan W. Puchniak et al., *The Derivative Action in Asia: A Comparative and Functional Approach* (Cambridge: Cambridge University Press, 2012), p. 323

For readers looking for Asian exceptionalism, this … will disappoint. The current rise of shareholder litigation in Singapore lends little support to the tired trope of the reluctant Asian litigant. Familial bonds and face-saving settlements appear to play no more of a role in Singapore than they do in the West in preventing shareholder litigation in closely held family companies or potentially embarrassing disputes. The monolithic view of Singapore as a paternalistic Asian nanny state that discourages the individual enforcement of shareholder rights also rings hollow in the face of the evolution of its derivative action and other shareholder remedies. Indeed, with a view to bolstering the private enforcement of directors' duties and strengthening individual minority shareholder rights, Singapore's parliament implemented a statutory derivative action, and its courts expanded the scope of its oppression remedy, long before most other Western common law countries. In short, although 'Asian culture' undoubtedly plays some role in Singapore society, there is little evidence that it has had a meaningful impact on the evolution or use of its derivative action or other minority shareholder remedies

What the Singapore story lacks in Asian exceptionalism, it more than makes up for in its Commonwealth heritage and economic pragmatism. The evolution of the derivative action in Singapore has closely tracked developments in other leading Western common law countries. From the time of Singapore's independence, court acceptance of the infamously nebulous English rule in *Foss v. Harbottle* substantially limited the ability of minority shareholders to make use of the common-law based derivative action. Following the trend in leading Western common law countries, Singapore's courts allowed for the expansion of the oppression remedy to deter corporate controllers from abusing their power and to provide a remedy for minority shareholders who suffered such abuse …

In a similar vein, the decision of Singapore's parliament in 1993 to model the statutory derivative action on the equivalent provision in the Canadian Business Corporations Act exemplifies the continuing and definitive role of Singapore's Commonwealth heritage on the development of its shareholder remedies. It also exemplifies Singapore's economically pragmatic approach of trying to stay on the cutting edge of shareholder rights in the common law world, as it implemented the statutory derivative action long before most other Western common law countries ...

Just as Singapore's derivative action is rooted in its Commonwealth heritage and economic pragmatism, it is also intriguingly 'non-American.' There has not been a single reported derivative action brought against a director of a public listed company in Singapore ... Singapore's dearth of derivative actions against public listed companies should not surprise. For better or worse, like most other countries, Singapore lacks the high-powered financial incentives that drive attorneys to pursue derivative litigation vigorously against public listed companies in the United States. In addition, unique to Singapore, its statutory derivative action applies only to non-listed companies ..., which means that shareholders have to overcome the rule in *Foss* if they want to bring an action on behalf of a public listed company – an idiosyncrasy that originally was cautiously pragmatic but now appears to be excessively conservative, and is likely to be amended in the near future.

The corporate governance context in which Singapore's derivative action exists is also intriguingly non-American. To start, Singapore's public market for shares is considerably more concentrated than in the United States. Singapore's lack of dispersed shareholdings raises questions about the highly influential and controversial legal origins theory, which paints all common law countries (especially economically successful ones) with the same brush and suggests a causal link between common law minority shareholder protections, dispersed shareholdings and economic prosperity. Indeed, Singapore's strong common law heritage, concentrated shareholdings and recent acclamation as the world's most efficient economy turn the legal origins theory on its head. Add to this Singapore's dearth in truly independent directors, its absence of a vigorous market for corporate control and the government's role (through its sovereign wealth fund) as the market's most important shareholder, and the Singapore story may even force the stubborn few who still have blind faith in the American model to open their eyes to other possibilities.

Notes and Questions

1. The Singapore Companies Act was amended in 2014 to extend the statutory derivative action to cover all Singapore-incorporated companies – whether listed or unlisted. Unfortunately, however, the amendment does not appear to extend the statutory derivative action to foreign-incorporated companies. Even after this amendment, it appears that the common law derivative action – and, in turn, the much-criticized fraud on the

minority test – will still have some relevance as it will be the only avenue for shareholders in foreign-incorporated companies to pursue a derivative action. The possibility of shareholders in foreign-incorporated companies wanting to pursue a derivative action in Singapore is far from remote. Singapore's two leading cases on the common law derivative action were both brought by shareholders in foreign-incorporated companies (see *Sinwa SS (HK) Co Ltd* v. *Morten Innhaug* [2010] 4 SLR 1; *Ting Sing Ning* v. *Ting Chek Swee* [2008] 1 SLR 197).

2. Why do you think that the focus of comparative corporate law around the world has tended to be on "participative strategies" when it would appear that for most countries "control strategies" are likely more important?
3. Does the fact that there are stronger legal rights for shareholders in Singapore than in the United States make Singapore's corporate law uniquely shareholder friendly?
4. Why has Singapore not witnessed a rise in shareholder activism in the same way as many other countries in the West and Asia?
5. Would Singapore's corporate governance benefit from an amendment of the law requiring prior approval from disinterested shareholders for *all* "interested person transactions"?
6. Why is it almost impossible for minority shareholders to succeed in a claim for oppression in a listed company in Singapore?
7. Will there be a substantial increase in shareholder litigation in Singapore due to the recent change in the Companies Act which extends the right to bring a derivative action to shareholders in listed companies?
8. Should controlling shareholders be subject to a fiduciary duty?
9. Should an alternative voting mechanism such as cumulative voting be explored as well?

8.4 State-Owned Enterprises and the Singapore Model

Tan Cheng-Han, Dan W. Puchniak, and Umakanth Varottil, 'State-Owned Enterprises in Singapore: Historical Insights into a Potential Model for Reform' (2014–15) 28 *Columbia Journal of Asian Law* 61

INTRODUCTION

It is easy to forget that a few decades ago state-owned enterprises (SOEs) were generally viewed as inefficient quasi-government departments which posed no meaningful competitive threat to privately-owned corporations. In fact, as recently as a decade ago, many pundits posited that SOEs were on the verge of extinction …

Over the last decade, however, the renaissance of SOEs has made comparative corporate law seem more like the beginning of time rather than the end of history. In this new era, SOEs have made a valiant return from the precipice of extinction and now compose a substantial portion of the world's most powerful corporations …

… The success and sustainability of China's SOEs has been vigorously debated both within China and internationally. In the midst of this debate, however, a somewhat surprising view appears to be emerging: that Singapore's SOEs (also referred to in Singapore as government-linked companies or GLCs) may provide a good model for reforming China's SOE Model. In fact, very recently, the Chinese government decided that by 2020 the Singapore GLC Model would be replicated in China 30 times over – making this proposed reform potentially one of the most important corporate governance initiatives of our time.

… Ultimately, this article concludes that the Singapore GLC Model is so closely intertwined with Singapore's idiosyncratic history and unique regulatory culture that, although the model has been extremely successful within Singapore, transplanting it to China (and we suspect, most likely, anywhere else) could be difficult.

In the process of arriving at this conclusion, this article further illuminates two broader points that cut to the core of comparative corporate law theory. First, as alluded above, the success of the Singapore GLC Model and China's ambition to emulate it challenge notions that corporate governance systems are converging towards a market-oriented (American) model of the shareholder-centric corporation. Indeed, an examination of the historical evolution of the Singapore GLC Model illustrates that a highly successful economy and system of corporate governance can be built on a foundation of corporations that have the government (and not only private free-market actors) as their ultimate controlling shareholder …

Second, the success of the Singapore GLC Model challenges the basic conception that private enterprise rather than the state is necessarily more efficient at allocating capital to its most productive use …

I. THE ATTRACTION OF THE SINGAPORE MODEL

… Today, Singapore is one of the richest countries in the world … With virtually no natural resources, effective governance has been the key to Singapore's success.

This has not gone unnoticed. For the past eight years, the World Bank has recognized Singapore as having the best regulatory and economic environment in the world for doing business. Transparency International consistently ranks Singapore in the top five countries in the world for having the lowest level of corruption. The *Wall Street Journal* and the Heritage Foundation consistently rank Singapore in the top few countries in the world with respect to economic freedom. The Asian

Corporate Governance Association has repeatedly ranked Singapore as having the best corporate governance in Asia.

At first blush, Singapore's leading regulatory, free-market and corporate governance rankings suggest that it may be a poster child for the American-cum-global model for good corporate governance-which is built on the notion that the dispersedly-held, shareholder-centric, Berle–Means corporation is the zenith of efficiency. If one drills down a bit below the rankings, however, it quickly becomes apparent that Singapore's corporate governance model is distinctly un-American at its core. In fact, the dispersedly-held, shareholder-centric, Berle–Means corporation virtually does not exist in Singapore.

To the contrary, Singapore's corporate governance system is built almost entirely on companies owned by concentrated block-shareholders. In fact, over ninety percent of Singapore's publicly listed companies have block shareholders who exercise controlling power. In addition, empirical evidence suggests that as Singapore's wealth has increased, its concentration of shareholdings has also increased ... Even more incongruent with the American, market-oriented, shareholder-centric model, is that listed companies in which the government is the controlling shareholder (i.e., GLCs) account for thirty-seven percent of the total stock market capitalization in Singapore. As such, the Singapore government is by far Singapore's most powerful shareholder ...

... [S]tudies have shown that far from Singapore GLCs trading at a discount to their peers, capital markets in fact value GLCs more highly than non-GLCs. One study estimated this premium at twenty percent after taking into account other variables that might affect firm value such as industry effects, size and monopoly power, profitability (it being the case that GLCs are generally more profitable), and bankruptcy risk.

Another study corroborated this by finding that GLCs on average exhibit higher valuations than those of non-GLCs after controlling for firm specific factors ... This study concluded that on average GLCs provided superior returns on both assets and equity and are valued more highly than non-GLCs. GLCs also did better in many performance measures and did not appear to be worse off in other measures. As such, they were more highly valued. Interestingly, this study also found that GLCs in general managed their expenses better than non-GLC companies. The lower expense-to-sales ratio among GLCs indicated that GLCs were more profitable because they ran leaner operations. Such a finding demonstrated that GLCs in Singapore were different from the generally inefficient nationalized firm run by governments. In addition, more recent studies suggest that GLCs have implemented better corporate governance practices than non-GLCs – which bodes well for their future sustainability and economic performance.

The question that arises is why Singapore GLCs were exceptional in this regard and whether such exceptionalism is transplantable. In this article, we suggest that

Singapore's history around the time of self-governance and eventually independence, in particular her political and social circumstances, was a major factor in the development and governance of her GLCs. Of particular importance was the tenuous hold that the People's Action Party (PAP), which has governed Singapore since independence, had on power …

…

CONCLUSION: REFLECTING UPON THE EVOLUTION OF GLCs IN SINGAPORE

As evident from the preceding discussion, Singapore adopted a unique trajectory towards growth that was spearheaded by her GLCs. The success of GLCs in Singapore can be attributed to a number of factors that have been entrenched within the country's governance system as a result of her historical experience. We argue that any attempt to replicate the Singapore model in other jurisdictions such as China ought to take into account these historical underpinnings …

History reveals the operation of certain characteristics that are specific to GLCs in Singapore. *First*, Singapore is a city-state and an international financial center. While corporate governance measures are shaped by investor preferences, particularly those placed by global financial investors of repute, their enforcement (both public and private) is considerably strong in Singapore. The stellar reputation of Singapore and her companies, whether privately-owned or government-owned, in the overall corporate governance standings in Asia is therefore entirely understandable.

Second, despite the dominant ownership and control of the government, GLCs are professionally-managed with limited interference from the government. Temasek's policy is to ensure that independent boards on portfolio companies provide the requisite strategic direction and monitoring so as to benefit shareholders, including the minority shareholders …

Third, the broad themes of public governance in Singapore have also been transposed to its GLCs. Professionalism in management and governance, executive compensation practices that ensure attraction of the best talent and a zero-tolerance policy towards corruption are hallmarks of governance both in Singapore's public sector as well as her GLCs. Not many countries have achieved the level of talent, effectiveness and efficiency in their public governance to make it a potential asset in the highly competitive global market for corporate governance, which seems to be apparent in the interface between the Singapore government and her GLCs.

Fourth, the existence in the 1950s and 1960s of a contested democratic political environment appeared to play a significant role in fostering good political governance in Singapore which was in turn transposed to her GLCs. The PAP was clearly aware of how the Labour Front government lost support as a result of negative public perception brought about partly by allegations of corruption against a member of the cabinet. The PAP therefore sought to cast itself in the 1959 elections as the party of honest and efficient government. Having won convincingly, it had to live up to its promises or risk being punished in subsequent polls ...

Fifth, the fact that the PAP's legitimacy is deeply intertwined with Singapore's economic performance creates a structure in which Temasek has clear incentives to ensure that GLCs are effectively governed for the benefit of all shareholders. This suggests that conventional comparative corporate governance theory, which assumes that controlling shareholders are incentivized primarily to extract private benefits of control, does not seem to apply in full force to Temasek. As such, to understand Temasek and how it exerts controlling power over the governance of GLCs, requires a uniquely Singaporean lens to illuminate the historical foundations of the principles of economic pragmatism and political stability that have moulded its effective governance ...

... This suggests that corporate structures and institutions are likely to be shaped very closely by existing structures, which are not amenable to material change due to rent seeking and interest group politics. Moreover, as our study underscores, political and cultural factors play an important role in shaping corporate governance structures and practices. Having said this, it is entirely possible that over time, Singapore's dominant form of corporate governance could evolve sufficiently to resemble the market-oriented model of a shareholder-centric corporation. Even so, it is perhaps a fallacy to assume that there is a "resting point" for corporate governance structures. A "converged" system of corporate governance may itself evolve over time into something materially different ...

... Finally, we ... do not seek to argue by implication that Singapore should continue to rely on GLCs as major drivers of her economy. While her historical circumstances suggest a strong path dependency towards strong state involvement in the economy, it is and will remain an open question whether this should still be the case or if it is time for the government to further distance itself from the commercial sphere.

Notes and Questions

1. What distinguishes Singapore from Japan and, to a certain extent, the other high-growth Asian economies is the extent to which its economy has continued to grow after catching up with developed Western economies. Currently, the GDP per person in Singapore is approximately double that of Japan. Singapore's ability to not only catch up, but also to surpass, other developed economies has made the "Singapore model" the focus of significant attention. In addition, the fact that Singapore lacks a Western-style democracy and its government is Singapore's largest shareholder has increased the interest in the "Singapore model." Should Singapore maintain its "Singapore model"? Should other countries imitate or draw lessons from it?

2. Why is it significant that Singapore's shareholder structure has become even more concentrated as Singapore has become one of the world's wealthiest countries?
3. What about Singapore may make the enforcement of corporate governance measures easier to execute than in most other countries?
4. Why do you think that SOEs have succeeded in Singapore when they have failed in so many other countries?
5. Why might private benefits of control not be as much of a problem in government-linked companies in Singapore than in other controlling shareholder-dominated companies?
6. What does the success of the 'Singapore model' tell us about the convergence theory and path dependence theory?

8.5 Independent Directors and the Importance of Shareholder Identity in Singapore

Dan W. Puchniak and Luh Lan, 'Independent Directors in Singapore: Puzzling Compliance Requiring Explanation' (2017) 65(2) *American Journal of Comparative Law* 265–333

Introduction

At first blush, the story of the rise of independent directors in Singapore appears conventional, if not mundane. In 2001, in the wake of the Asian financial crisis, Singapore needed to bolster its corporate governance. It did what every responsible, well governed country in Asia was supposed to do: look to the West (or, more precisely, to Anglo-America) for corporate governance solutions.

At that time, the American independent director stood out as perhaps the most recognizable global symbol of good corporate governance … From this perspective, Singapore's decision in 2001 to implement a U.K.-inspired Code of Corporate Governance (2001 Code), which required the adoption of American-style independent directors on a "comply or explain" basis, appeared highly conventional. As history would have it, however, it turned out to be anything but.

In fact … Singapore's embrace of American-style independent directors made it a corporate governance outlier … [T]he widely held belief that the American concept of the independent director has been transplanted around the world is a myth. The reality, which our review of the rules governing independent directors in 245 corporate governance codes from eighty-seven jurisdictions reveals, is that only a handful of jurisdictions have ever adopted the American concept of the independent director (i.e., where directors who are independent from management only – but not substantial shareholders – are deemed to be independent). Instead, most jurisdictions have merely adopted the term "independent director" from the United States, while significantly modifying the American concept by requiring directors to be independent from management and significant shareholders in order to be considered independent. This modification is critical, as it alters the core function of the independent director from being a corporate governance mechanism designed primarily to monitor management on behalf of dispersed shareholders to one designed primarily to monitor controlling shareholders on behalf of minority shareholders.

At least from the perspective of agency theory, in most jurisdictions it makes perfect sense to modify the American concept of the independent director by requiring independence from significant shareholders … [D]irectors who are independent from management and significant shareholders (i.e., the un-American concept of independent directors) can potentially add significant value in a block-shareholder environment by monitoring controlling shareholders and thus mitigating private benefits of control.

… This presents us with the first puzzle that this Article seeks to solve: Why would Singapore's highly skilled regulators deviate from the seemingly logical and well-trodden path of other controlling shareholder-dominated jurisdictions by transplanting the American concept of the independent director into Singapore's controlling-shareholder environment and maintaining it for over a decade?

Strange as this decision may be, the response of listed companies in Singapore to it presents an even more intriguing puzzle. Rather than shun the 2001 Code's seemingly ill-defined and functionally irrelevant American-style independent directors, listed companies in Singapore embraced them with vigor – which is the opposite of what agency theory and leading corporate governance scholars would have predicted. In fact, shortly after the 2001 Code went into force in 2003, an overwhelming 96% of Singapore-listed companies reported full compliance with the Code's recommendation that one-third of the board be composed of American-style independent directors. Not long after that, 98% of Singapore-listed companies reported full compliance, with a majority of all directors in Singapore reportedly being "independent." These extraordinary statistics present us with the second intriguing puzzle that this Article seeks to solve: Why did listed companies in Singapore embrace seemingly functionally irrelevant American-style independent directors, and what role (if any) have these directors played in Singapore corporate governance?

To add a final twist to this bemusing regulatory tale, after more than a decade of near-perfect compliance, Singapore has recently decided to abandon its promotion of American-style independent directors. The 2012 Code of Corporate Governance (2012 Code), which went into full force at the start of 2015, requires independent directors to not only be independent from management, but also from shareholders holding more than 10% of the company's shares. This presents us with the final puzzle that this Article seeks to solve: Why, after more than a decade of near-perfect compliance, has Singapore decided to abandon American-style independent directors, and what impact (if any) may this have on the future of corporate governance in Singapore?

... [W]e offer an abridged account of our solutions to these three puzzles upfront ... With respect to the first puzzle ... historical evidence suggests that Singapore's seemingly illogical decision to adopt the American-style independent director and maintain it for over a decade was the product of strategic regulatory design (not ignorance) ... Adopting American-style independent directors in the 2001 Code allowed Singapore to send a critical signal of "good" corporate governance to international markets in the wake of the Asian financial crisis. In addition, maintaining American-style independent directors throughout the 2000s all but ensured that Singapore would have a high proportion of "independent directors" and near-perfect compliance with its Code without fundamentally altering its unique and functionally efficient state- and family-controlled corporate governance system ...

With respect to the second puzzle ... After putting agency theory aside and understanding Singapore's unique institutional and shareholder environment, however, the functionality of American-style independent directors in listed companies in Singapore becomes clear. Interestingly, it appears that the functionality of American-style independent directors in Singapore varies depending on the identity of a company's controlling shareholder. In family-controlled firms (family firms), American-style independent directors sometimes appear to leverage their close relationship with family controllers to serve as effective mediators who resolve disputes between family-member shareholders and/or act as trusted advisers to the family chairman.

In contrast, in state-controlled companies ... American-style independent directors appear mainly to fill the gap in managerial monitoring that exists because of the unique institutional constraints that the Singapore government has placed on its own controlling-shareholder power to limit its involvement in directly monitoring or managing government-linked companies. Moreover, in family firms and government-linked companies, the adoption of American-style independent directors functions as a firm-level signal of good corporate governance, while at the same time does not erode the ultimate control of controlling shareholders in such firms.

With respect to the third puzzle ... First, scandals in non-Singapore-based companies listed on the Singapore Exchange (SGX) appear to have been a significant driver of the recent reform. In the late 2000s in Singapore, there was an exponential increase in "S-chip" companies (i.e., companies that are listed on the SGX but whose operations and controlling shareholders are located in mainland China, or PRC-controlled firms). Remarkably, within a few years, PRC-controlled firms went from being inconsequential to accounting for one-third of the value of IPOs and 20% of total listings on the SGX. PRC-controlled firms, however, were riddled with corporate governance scandals, which typically involved wealth tunneling by mainland Chinese controlling shareholders to the bane of minority (both individual and institutional) shareholders in Singapore. These scandals exposed weaknesses in Singapore's American-style independent director system, spurring the reform …

Second, an examination of the 2012 Code's fine print … suggests that the reform has been carefully crafted to ensure that Singapore's largely successful government-linked company corporate governance structure will remain firmly intact. In addition, the reform has been skillfully tailored so as not to fundamentally disrupt the governance of Singapore's largely successful family firms. This again suggests that the reform may have more to do with signaling and less to do with functional reform than appears at first blush.

…

Part IV: Uniquely Singaporean But With Comparative Lessons That Abound

… More specifically, at least three aspects of the independent director in Singapore highlight its idiosyncratic nature. First, as our research above reveals, Singapore's adoption and maintenance of the American independent director into its controlling-block shareholder environment made (and arguably still makes) it a corporate governance outlier …

Second, Singapore's status as a small city-state suggests that many of the most salient aspects of the rise and function of the independent director in Singapore may not be readily generalizable. The ability of Singapore's regulators to use informal mechanisms to effectively mitigate private benefits of control in local companies has almost certainly been facilitated by the small, tight-knit nature of Singapore's business community. Moreover, the small size of Singapore's pool of talented independent directors is another distinct feature that has had a significant impact on the regulation of independent directors in Singapore …

Third, Singapore's unique regulatory architecture and institutional environment also suggest that the rise and function of the American independent director in Singapore may be exceptional. Indeed, as explained in detail elsewhere, the regulatory architecture governing government-linked companies – which ironically makes the American concept of the independent director fit neatly into Singapore's controlling-block shareholder environment – appears to be uniquely Singaporean and would likely be difficult for other jurisdictions to replicate. As explained above, Singapore's efficient and meritocratic government has played an important role in the rise of the independent director in Singapore. This is also an aspect of Singapore's independent director story that distinguishes it from other jurisdictions – particularly from developing jurisdictions which tend to have a keen interest in the Singapore model.

Despite the undeniably Singaporean character of the rise and function of the independent director in Singapore, this analysis teems with comparative lessons that appear to challenge some of the core understandings about independent directors and, more generally, comparative corporate law. First, it suggests that comparative corporate law pays insufficient attention to the precise identity of shareholders – not merely whether they are generally dispersed or concentrated – as a determinant of how independent directors … actually function … Ultimately, this suggests that understanding the precise identity of controlling shareholders (i.e., who they are and, in turn, what drives them) is imperative for accurately understanding the function and effectiveness of independent directors and potentially many other corporate governance mechanisms.

Second, this analysis suggests that the definition of independence has received far too little attention. It is astounding that firms specializing in (and being paid for) corporate governance advice, which influences the allocation of trillions of dollars of investment capital, have often erroneously assumed that American-style independent directors have been (or should be) transplanted around the world – entirely overlooking how the definition of independence varies in critically important ways among jurisdictions (and even within jurisdictions over time). It is also surprising that some of the most often cited literature on independent directors – particularly cross-country empirical analyses – have also almost entirely disregarded the critical differences in the definition of independence and/or often erroneously assumed the global ubiquity of American-style independent directors. Similarly, the failure of prominent international organizations, such as the World Bank, to take account of differences in the definition of independence among jurisdictions is disconcerting. As the Singapore story illustrates, how independence is defined is critically important and must be carefully considered.

Third, the rise of the independent director in Singapore is a reminder of the importance of signaling as a driving force in both the regulation and adoption of independent directors – something which has largely been overlooked. Interestingly, it appears that Singapore has been able to credibly signal good corporate governance by merely formally adopting independent directors without fundamentally altering the manner in which its companies function …

Notes and Questions

1. The fact that the US concept of the independent director has only been adopted by a handful of countries is contrary to the conventional wisdom that it has been transplanted around the world. This may suggest that countries have tended to mold the US concept of the independent director to fit their controlling shareholder environments (i.e. countries dominated by controlling shareholders have required independent directors to be independent from the company's controlling shareholder – rather than merely management – so that they can effectively monitor the controlling shareholder). This straightforward "functional explanation," however, appears to account for only part of the story. It is curious that most countries which have altered the US definition of independence have nevertheless maintained their majority voting systems for electing directors – essentially nullifying the functional effectiveness of the expanded definition of independence for policing controlling shareholders.
2. Over the last decade, the comparative corporate law literature has come to realize that most listed companies in the world, aside from many of those in the United States and United Kingdom, are dominated by controlling shareholders. The literature still tends to paint all controlling shareholders with a similar brush. Singapore, however, illustrates that controlling shareholders are diverse. Such diversity may impact significantly how they function and the strategies that should be used to regulate them.
3. What do the scandals in PRC-controlled firms in Singapore suggest about how we should view the influence of culture in corporate governance in Asia?
4. What lessons, if any, can the rise of independent directors in Singapore teach us about the challenges of understanding corporate law comparatively?

Regulations and Statutes

Companies Act, 2006, c. 50

Code of Corporate Governance (Monetary Authority of Singapore, 2012)

9

CHINA

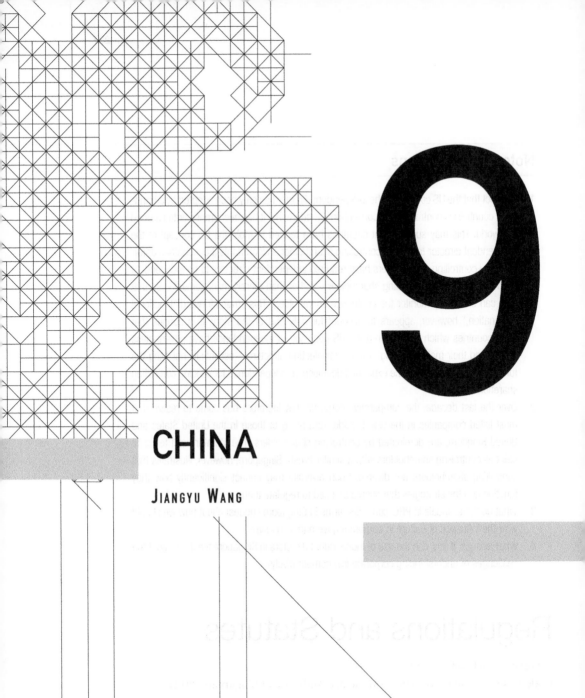

Jiangyu Wang

9.1 Introduction

Corporate governance became a highly fashionable topic in China when a listed company, popularly known as YinGuangXia, was disclosed by the media to have committed an RMB745 million fraud through massive fabrication of sales receipts and false disclosures perpetrated by a few "core" insiders. This case caused losses to thousands of minority shareholders and is considered one of the biggest corporate scandals in PRC history. It revealed some fundamental weaknesses in the management, regulation, and supervision of the country's enterprises. Since the early 2000s, corporate governance has been one of the government's priorities. In the following years, government agencies issued numerous laws and normative documents to standardize the corporate governance practice of Chinese enterprises.

On paper, Chinese corporate governance follows a generally westernized framework, including a shareholders' meeting, board of directors, supervisory board, manager, and accompanying fiduciary duties. However, "Chinese characteristics" of corporate governance exist. First, China has a hybrid system of corporate governance institutions, borrowed from both the Anglo-American model and Germanic–Japanese model. In terms of internal governance, the typical organizational structure of a company comprises three tiers of control, namely the shareholder's meeting, the board of directors, and the supervisory board. Partially as a solution to the agency problem stemming from the separation of ownership and control in modern corporations, Anglo-American jurisdictions install independent directors on the board, Germanic–Japanese jurisdictions provide a supervisory board or *kansayaku*, but listed companies in China must have both. As observed by Tan and Wang:

> The coexistence of the supervisory board and the independent directors demonstrates a strong feature in the mentality of China's corporate reform, namely, an approach of "crossing the river by feeling the stone," because, although the reformers were eager to learn from foreign experience, they were unsure as to which model was suitable to China. As such, legal institutions from both the "insider" model and the "outsider" model were transplanted into Chinese soil without a proper evaluation of their suitability.[1]

A second feature is the political impact of dominant state ownership on the governance of companies. Most of those companies were converted from traditional

[1] Lay-Hong Tan and Jiangyu Wang, 'Modelling an Effective Corporate Governance for China's Listed State-owned Enterprises' (2007) 7(1) *Journal of Corporate Law Studies*.

state-owned enterprises (SOEs) and are considered to be under the control of the government or even the Chinese Communist Party. Indeed, the "grabbing hand theory" suggests that the government uses SOEs "to serve political and social objectives, which has a negative impact on the firm's economic performance." Some view this theory as overly simplistic, as the state might have a larger stake in converting the SOEs into normal, commercial entities. Another strand of literature, the "helping hand theory," maintains that the government may "generate a positive effect on firm performance because [it helps] secure scarce resources in the quasi-market economy and mitigate agency problems in firms with poor corporate governance."[2]

The state typically exercises its "grabbing hand" or "helping hand" through related party transactions. Although controlling shareholders in any system may try to obtain private benefits of control or support SOEs ("propping up"), this is a particular issue in China due to the prominence of SOEs and their political control. China has initiated a regulatory scheme to attempt to limit the number and impact of such transactions by requiring the approval of independent directors.

Third, local context also plays an important role in the corporate governance of Chinese companies. Hamilton points out that it is fundamentally wrong to characterize Chinese private firms by holding them up against similar firms of Western capitalism without considering the cultural aspects. Embedded in its own hierarchical and harmonious cultural tradition, "the Chinese family firms is [*sic*] in fact … a 'political infrastructure' in which 'power differentials' … lie behind the disparities in economic roles and rewards in the family business."[3]

In short, although Chinese law on paper produces the same kind of companies, different political, economic, and social contexts, respectively and collectively, make corporate governance of Chinese companies distinctive in many respects. The governance practice of Chinese enterprises is an evolving process the direction of which has been shaped by many factors. This chapter not only outlines the general allocation of corporate powers among various governance and management institutions in a company – including the shareholders' meeting, the board of directors, the supervisory board, and the management – but also places the legal framework of corporate governance in China in its political, economic, and social context.

[2] Eric Chang and Sonia Wong (2004), 'Political Control and Performance in China's Listed Companies' (2004) 32 *Journal of Comparative Economics* 617, 618.

[3] Gary Hamilton, *Commerce and Capitalism in Chinese Societies* (London and New York: Routledge, 2006), p. 224.

Notes and Questions

1. What are the Chinese characteristics of corporate governance? How do they compare to local context or characteristics in other Asian countries?
2. The extraordinary economic growth model in East Asian countries has been characterized as the East Asian model (EAM), which is essentially a model for "state-led development." Is government ownership of, and political influence over, many important industries and companies a positive or negative characteristic of Chinese corporate governance? Is it good for economic growth and development?
3. What problems do the hybrid model of corporate governance address? Is it likely to be successful? Should China continue to maintain a hybrid model, or should it focus on one type of model? Do other countries in Asia also have a "hybrid" model?

9.2 Purpose: Striking a Balance between the State, Shareholders, and Stakeholders

The history of China's corporate law has been a journey, meaning it has been under constant change. In the course of its development, Chinese company law has been the fusion of three interests: state interest, shareholder interest, and stakeholder interest. The 1993 Company Law ("CL 1993") was a statute mainly for SOEs and their corporatization. Significant amendments to the Company Law were introduced in 2005 ("CL 2005"), which aimed to transform the law from a restrictive statute into an enabling statute by affording more legal protection for minority shareholders. In addition, the amendments introduced ideas of "social conscience" into China's corporate law regime. The Company Law was further revised in 2013 ("CL 2013") to cancel the minimum registered capital requirements and facilitate company registration rules. Although it is not clear whether China is marching toward a stakeholder model, the Company Law fairly clearly aims to facilitate the representation of the interests of the state, the shareholders, and the stakeholders.

Jiangyu Wang, *Company Law in China: Regulation of Business Organizations in a Socialist Market Economy* (Cheltenham, UK and Northampton, MA: Edward Elgar, 2014), pp. 23–43

1.5 THE CONCEPT, PURPOSES AND PRINCIPLES OF COMPANIES AND COMPANY LAW IN CHINA

...

1.5.3 2005 Revision of the Company Law: Marching toward rule of law in the corporate world?

The 2005 revision of the Company Law is a breakthrough in the development of China's corporate law. This is not to say that the new Company Law has established a regime which is totally different from the former one; instead, the new law represents an accelerated movement in an ongoing trend toward developing a rule-based, investor protection oriented, transparent legal system for modern business companies in China ...

General Applicability: From a Law for State-owned Enterprise to a General Law for All Types of Companies

... The 2005 law becomes a more general corporate statute by deleting the many provisions of the 1993 law that gave special privileges or protection to SOEs. As Wang Baoshu observes, about 14 Articles in the old law specially designed for SOEs were abrogated by the new law, although the special section on wholly state-owned companies remains. For example, the 1993 Company Law only permitted CLS or state-owned LLC to issue corporate bonds (Article 159). In so doing, the new law does away with the decades-long practice of discriminating against privately owned companies.

Deregulation: From Government Control of Enterprise to Freedom of Enterprise

The most significant change in the new law is that it represents a movement from restrictive to enabling statute, thus shifting the regulatory philosophy from tight government control to deregulation. Under the new law, the freedom of enterprise, which means the enterprise and the entrepreneurs are free to operate the business and dispose of corporate resources, has gained considerably larger room. This shift is demonstrated in the following aspects:

Relaxed incorporation requirements: In the regulation of business incorporation, the new law has largely completed the process of moving from an approval system to a registration system ...

Relaxed registered capital requirements: CL 1993 required a minimum registered capital between RMB100,000 and RMB500,000 for setting up domestic

LLCs, making incorporation unaffordable for many. The new law replaces this capital spread with a standard minimum capital of RMB30,000 and makes the corporate form available to more investors. It also expands the means of capital contribution, bringing in more varieties of noncash assets that can be used as investment ...[4]

More discretionary and enabling rules, and expanded corporate power: CL 1993 is often described as a restrictive statute which tended to impose heavier regulation on companies. It was full of restrictive phrases "should," "must," "must not" which compelled companies to do or not do specified things. Under CL 1993, the articles of association, a company's constitution, were not treated as a living document, as they had to copy the mandatory provisions of Company Law. In a stark contrast, CL 2005 grants tremendous power to the articles of association and allows shareholders to stipulate rules of conduct in the articles by changing the discretionary provisions of the Company Law. For example, under the old law, corporate profits had to be distributed strictly in proportion to the shareholders percentage of capital contribution in the company. The new law now allows shareholders to specify in their articles any manner of profit distribution agreed to by the shareholders. Indeed, "[t]here are virtually no provisions related to management that cannot be altered or expanded in a manner determined by the shareholders in their articles of association" ...

1.6 COMPANY LAW IN THE CONTEXT OF CHINA'S POLITICAL, SOCIAL AND LEGAL CULTURE

In understanding China's Company Law one must also understand the unique political-legal environment in China. In China's one-party political system, the ruling party has the basic instinct to put everything, including business corporations, under its political control. Although in the Reform Era, the party has long realized that independent commercial enterprises are the key to achieving economic growth and has sought to return autonomy to enterprises through the implementation of a variety of civil and commercial laws. Furthermore, the socialist nature of the political-legal system also requires business firms to sacrifice a certain degree of freedom of enterprise to cope with the state's official ideology and the regulators' policy agendas. In summary, as one commentator advises, "[f]oreign investors who wish to set up enterprises in China should take note of [the uniquely Chinese definition of the business corporation as a hybrid economic–political–sociocultural institution] and be prepared to interact closely with the Communist Party of China (CPC) and other government-affiliated organizations, and to provide their willingness to comply with the official interpretation of corporate social responsibility."

[4] The 2013 Company Law removed the minimum registered capital requirement for establishing companies and replaced the paid-up capital requirement with a subscribed capital system. In addition, the incorporation formalities were tremendously simplified.

1.6.3 Corporate Social Responsibility

Corporate Social Responsibility (CSR) has emerged as an issue of increasing social and business importance in corporate China. The concept of CSR was invented in the West long before China arose as a central part of the global production network. In recent years, CSR has caught considerable attention in China, leading to an emerging normative framework. The Company Law even has a specific provision on CSR. Article 5 of the law stipulates: "When engaging in business activities, a company must abide by laws and administrative regulations, observe social morals and business ethics, act in good faith, accept supervision by the government and the public, and bear social responsibilities."

A more recent initiative by the government is the promulgation of the Guiding Opinions on Practicing Social Responsibility by Central Enterprises by the State-owned Assets Supervision and Administration Commission (SASAC) (hereinafter the CSR Opinions), in which the SASAC ordered China's centrally-administered SOEs to play a leading role in CSR. It provides a broad definition of CSR that covers environmental protection, energy and resources conservation, work safety, labor protection, consumer rights, maintaining market order, upholding business ethics and philanthropy, shareholder value, and job creation. Apparently, these are often mutually conflicting objectives which are difficult to implement by one enterprise.

The CSR movement in China appears to be a top-down process at this stage. At first, it was a response of the business community to a call from the central leadership to adopt a new approach to project called the "scientific development concept," and to build a "harmonious society" in China. It is also a response of China's export industries, especially the textile and apparel industry, to "sharp foreign criticism about conditions in [China's] factories amid claims that its cheap exports come at the expense of the environment and workers' safety and pay." In spite of Article 5 of the PRC Company Law, it is still an open question whether CSR should be a concern for company law. Even though CSR should be pursued by companies, it imposes moral rather than legal obligations on corporate behavior. In brief, perhaps Chinese company laws should not even consider codifying and enforcing CSR.

Notes and Questions

1. Corporate law in China is increasingly becoming less restrictive. Why is this? Is it because a country's corporate law would inevitably become more enabling than restricting as it moves up the ladder in economic development?
2. Why does the Chinese Company Law codify the role of the Chinese Communist Party, China's ruling party? Would this in any way restrict the ease of doing business in China, especially from the perspective of foreign investors?

3. Chinese Company Law also codifies corporate social responsibility (CSR). In the West, CSR is promoted as a means to encourage companies to engage in useful social activities in addition to, or apart from, their main goal of profit maximization. What is the purpose of CSR in China?

9.3 The Legal Framework

The Company Law provides a common structure for business corporations, which possesses the five core structural characteristics including legal personality, limited liability, transferable shares or equity interest, centralized management under a board structure, and shared ownership by contributors of capital. In 2005, the Company Law abandoned most of the restrictive rules on company incorporation and operation, and introduced new rules in line with international practice. In addition, business companies are also subject to a wide range of other business laws and rules, including the self-regulatory rules of the stock exchanges.

The corporate governance structure of a typical Chinese company adopts a two-board system and comprises the general shareholders' meeting (also known as the general assembly), a board of directors, a supervisory board (or supervisory committee), and a (general) manager (chief executive officer). The general shareholders' meeting is called the "power organ" (*quanli jigou*) of the company, suggesting that the shareholders in China are more powerful than in some other jurisdictions.

Lin Zhang, 'Adaptive Efficiency and the Corporate Governance of Chinese State-Controlled Listed Companies: Evidence from the Fundraising of Chinese Domestic Venture' (2010) 10 *UC Davis Business Law Journal* 151, at 156–62

I. The Status Quo of Corporate Governance in the SCLCs

The current SCLCs (state-controlled listed companies) are the transformative results of traditional SOEs ... The three principal corporate governance institutions in China may further illustrate this understanding of control-based model: the shareholders' meeting, the board of directors, and the supervisory committee.

A. The Shareholders' Meeting

In China, the shareholders' meeting occupies a central position in corporate governance, as it is viewed as the supreme governing organ of the corporation. In terms of the latest Company Law of the PRC which came into effect in 2006 [CL 2005], the shareholders' meeting holds the following comprehensive decision-making powers: (1) determine corporate operation guidelines and investment plans; (5) review and approve the corporate fiscal budgets and final account report on an annual basis; (6) review and approve the corporate plans regarding allocating profits and making up for losses; … (9) make decisions regarding corporate mergers, divisions, dissolution and liquidation … By this listing, it appears that the shareholders' meeting of a corporation in China retains substantial managerial powers, some of which are usually delegated to the board of directors in the United States and other western countries. This arrangement increases the likelihood that a majority shareholder will control the operation of the corporation to a considerable degree …

B. The Board of Directors

Under the [CL 2005], the board of directors plays the role of executive branch of the shareholders' meeting in a corporation. It is mainly responsible for the enforcement of operation decisions made by the latter. The state has achieved control over the board of directors by means of personnel arrangements. Generally speaking, in an SCLC, the chairman and the vice chairman of the board of directors and the director who is concurrently the chief executive officer ("CEO") are actually recommended to their post by local CPC committees. The CPC's shortlists of recommendations for these positions are then forwarded to local governments and their state-owned asset management commissions. Next, the state-owned asset management commissions require the state holding corporations, who are the principal shareholders of the SCLCs, to convene the shareholders' meeting of the SCLCs in order to formally appoint the candidates from the shortlists. Moreover, in terms of local government regulations, the chairmen of the board of directors usually act as vice CPC secretaries of the SCLCs, while the vice chairmen act as CPC secretaries. In addition, many directors in the SCLCs are former officials of disbanded departments of the government.

The independent directors of the SCLCs also represent the voice of the state. According to the "Guidelines on the Establishment of the Institution of Independent Directors in Listed Companies" issued by the CSRC [China Security Regulatory Committee] in 2001 ("2001 Guidelines on Independent Directors"), the shareholders' meeting elects the independent directors. Therefore, in the SCLCs, the state as the majority shareholder actually controls the selection of the independent directors. Consequently, independent directors maintain their ties with the government and act on behalf of the state.

C. The Supervisory Committee

In China, the principal function of the supervisory committee in a corporation is to monitor the behavior of directors and managers in the shareholders' interest. The members of the supervisory committee in the SCLCs tend to be drawn from two sources. First, state holding corporations, as majority shareholders, select external shareholder supervisors in the shareholders' meeting. Generally, these external shareholder supervisors are retired government officials, renowned economists and accountants who have close relationship with the authorities. Second, within the corporations, the secretaries of the CPC's corporate disciplinary committees and the labor representatives also constitute shareholder supervisors. These two sources clearly convey the two main purposes of the supervisory committees of the SCLCs. First, the committee is applied to further internalize the oversight of competent government departments over the operations of the SCLCs, thus assuring the maintenance and growth of state assets and the implementation of state policies. Second, the CPC's disciplinary committees can exercise their traditional function within the corporations as the primary organs of managerial discipline through their personnel overlap with the supervisory committees. Therefore, the corporate institution in charge of management supervision in the SCLCs is also firmly held by the state. Even if it has not obviously taken effect in practice, this additional control by the state is another issue worthy of consideration.

Notes and Questions

1. What roles do shareholders, directors, and supervisors play in corporate governance in China?
2. The CL 2005 has adopted the cumulative system. While the Company Law itself does not seem to make the cumulative system mandatory, the Code of Corporate Governance for Listed Companies in China requires that "cumulative voting should be adopted in listed companies that are more than 30 per cent owned by controlling shareholders." A 2012 study found that, 840, or 89.3 percent of the total 941 of the companies listed on the Shanghai Stock Exchange adopted in principle the cumulative voting system in their articles of associations. Out of the 840 companies, only 93 companies established working rules that made the operation of the cumulative system possible, and only 24 companies used the cumulative system in their 2012 board election. However, from a mathematical perspective, the largest shareholder held more than 75 percent of the total ownership in half of the 24 companies, rendering the cumulative voting system meaningless. See Qian Yulin, 'The Transplant and Practice of Cumulative Voting System in China: Empirical Observations based on the Listed Companies' (2013) 6 *Faxue Yanjiu* [*Chinese Journal of Law*] 119–30. Is the cumulative voting system really useful in terms of protecting minority shareholders' rights? Under what conditions can it work toward that goal?
3. Are there real checks and balances in Chinese companies?
4. Compare the supervisory committee, also known as the supervisory board, in China's state-owned companies, to the supervisory board in public companies (Aktiengesellschaften) in Germany. Do they have the same or similar functions, powers, and duties?

9.4 Functions of the Board and Independent Directors

The powers and responsibilities of the board of directors provided in the PRC Company Law seem to suggest that the board of directors in Chinese companies, like its counterpart in more mature jurisdictions, plays a central role in corporate governance. This, however, is not necessarily the case. Legally, the functions of the board are constrained by the statutory powers conferred upon the shareholders' meeting. In practice, the independence of the board of Chinese companies, especially those of SOEs, has been undermined by the fact that the company may either be controlled by the majority shareholder (which is the state for SOEs) or by the "key persons" who are powerful individuals.

What is interesting about corporate governance in China is that it adopts both the supervisory board (from the civil law system) and independent directors (from the common law family) to monitor the directors and executives. The original design of the two-board structure was meant to establish checks and balances within the company by having the supervisory board monitoring the management board (the board of directors). The supervisory board system appeared to be a failure at least from the perspective of the 1993 CL. Disappointed at the ineffectiveness of the supervisory boards, the CSRC issued, in August 2001, *Guidelines on the Introduction of the Independent Directors System in Listed Companies.*

Despite the debates about the effectiveness of independent directors, directors have played a role in improving corporate governance in China. Certain limits on their impact remain.

Jiangyu Wang, *Company Law in China: Regulation of Business Organizations in a Socialist Market Economy* (Cheltenham, UK and Northampton, MA: Edward Elgar, 2014), pp. 170–87

6.3.9 Separation of Powers between the Board and the General Meeting

Looking at the allocation of decisional power in Chinese companies with a critical eye, one may not find a clear separation of powers between the board of directors and the general meeting. In contrast, the shareholder-centered nature of corporate governance in China has produced a 'mixture of competences' in the allocation of functions and powers between the board and the general meeting. For example, the general meeting is in charge of 'determining the company's business strategy (*jingying fangzhen*) and investment plans (*touzi jihua*),' while the board has the power to 'decide on the company's business operation plans (*jingying jihua*) and investment proposals (*touzi fangan*).' It is not clear where to draw a line between 'business strategy and investment plans' and 'business operation plans and investment proposals.' The authority to decide profit distribution rests exclusively in the hands of the general meeting, although the board has the power to initiate dividend distribution plans.

Giving shareholders' general meetings so much power to intervene in the running of the company's business is a distinctive feature of corporate governance in China, especially in light of the international trend of resting the management of the business and control of the company in the directors. What explains the far-reaching statutory powers granted to the general meeting? It is summited that the purpose behind these powers is to favor the majority shareholder, which, in the Chinese context, is often the State. The powers of the general meeting could only be exercised collectively through voting by the shareholders, and the passage of a resolution must be supported by at least a simple majority of the voting rights based on the percentage of the equity interest held by the shareholders. Since the State is the single or largest shareholder in the SOEs, giving some key decisional powers to the shareholders' meeting, which is usually controlled by the majority shareholders, could desirably undermine the independence of the board to prevent the latter from making decisions that are not in the interest of the State. On the other hand, since the State as a shareholder retains only the most important powers on fundamental corporate decisions, it does not need to involve itself in making decisions for the day-to-day management of the company. However, the general meeting's possession of such comprehensive powers does not necessarily entail better protection of the minority shareholders. In fact, the interests of minority shareholders are often overlooked in such a system.

…

6.4.4 Evaluating the Chinese System of Independent Directors

Now almost all of China's over 2,300 listed companies have installed independent directors on their boards. On average, each company has three such directors. Has the system proven to be effective, or at least more effective than the supervisory board? …

However, in spite of the debate on the link between board composition and corporate performance, countries undergoing institutional transitions still compete to appoint independent directors to corporate board. Since the independent director system was implemented in 2002, China has accumulated only four years of experience in this area. It is hence too early to evaluate the effectiveness of the system in that country …

A joint survey by the Association of Board Secretaries of Listed Companies of Shanghai and Shanghai Jinxin Institute of Securities Research conducted in 2003, two years after China's formal launch of the independent director system, demonstrated that independent directors helped improve corporate governance, especially in terms of bringing professional expertise and protecting minority shareholders. The empirical research of the Research Center of Corporate Governance Center of Nankai University shows that, the degree of perfection of independent directors has an obviously positive relationship with the profitability, market valuation, and financial security of listed companies. It has a negative relationship with the scale of illegal activities of companies. Although the data is still limited and rudimentary, it is increasingly recognized that independent directors can make a difference in firm governance and performance in China.

6.4.5 Explaining the (Limited) Efficacy of Independent Directors in Chinese Companies

Compared with the total failure of the supervisory board, the independent director system has been regarded – albeit with limited empirical evidence – as conducive to good corporate governance. At least in theory, this limited success can be explained from the following perspectives.

First of all, any meaningful – no matter how limited – check and balance imposed on the management of China's listed companies is supposed to have positive effect on corporate governance, as poor governance practices in those companies are rampant ...

In the state-owned companies, the state, after all, is only an abstract owner. It is common in China that the agents appointed by the State to manage the companies, who were civil servants and government officials before appointment, do not always align their own interest with that of the state. Thus the agency problems in China's listed SOEs are featured with the "absence of effective ultimate principal." This has led to one model of insider control, namely the so-called *guanxiren kongzhi* [key-person-control]. The key person is usually the chief-executive officer (CEO), chairman of the board, or a senior executive manager of the company. Appointing them, the government often loses control of their activities. As a result, the key-person usually becomes the super-sovereign and the sole commander of the company. Having virtually the ultimate decision-making power over all corporate affairs, he is in fact endowed with the power of control, execution, and supervision. In other cases – no matter whether the company is an SOE or a private enterprise, if the key-person is appointed and controlled by the parent company, he acts solely as the representative of the controlling shareholder, having no or little regard to the proprietary rights of minority shareholders. The board of directors comprising of insiders, selected by the key-person on behalf of the state or the controlling shareholder, cannot effectively monitor the activities of the key-person.

It is reasoned that, at least from a theoretical point of view, the independent directors, not working in the company on full-time basis and hence less subject to the control of the key-person, would impose constraints on the exercise of power by the key-person ...

6.4.6 Limits on The Effectiveness of Independent Directors

Although the independent director system is, overall, more effective than the supervisory board, the surveys mentioned above all point out that there was a tremendous gap between the current performance of independent directors and the expectation of the public ...

Independence

The biggest problem is still how independence is to be maintained. Although independent directors are outsiders, their independence is somehow constrained by their nomination. The *CSRC Guidelines for Independent Directors* prescribe that they should be nominated by the board of directors, the supervisory board, or a shareholder or shareholders who separately or jointly own more than one percent stake in the outstanding shares of the company, and elected by the shareholders' meeting. It is however difficult to believe that the CSRC is not aware of the high concentration of ownership as well as the dysfunction of supervisory boards in China's listed companies. The survey of the China Securities Daily shows that 67.5 percent of the independent directors were nominated by the board of directors, while 27.5 percent were directly nominated by the controlling shareholders. Further, 52.5 percent of the independent directors under survey said that their remuneration was determined by the company's "senior management executives," while 37.5 of those under survey revealed that it was the "controlling shareholders" who decided their remuneration. Clearly, for a significant portion of the independent directors, their constituency is the controlling shareholders.

Will this constituency base affect the independence of the outside directors? Although those directors appear to be more independent than the inside directors, they are far from being "independent" as one should expect from an outsider who is really free from the influence from inside the company. One independent director pointed out that, in many listed companies, the controlling shareholders wished that independent directors be satisfied to serve as "ornaments" of the corporate Christmas tree, "raising just their hands." Not surprisingly, 65 percent of the independent directors under the survey of the China Securities Daily indicated that they never said "no" in the meetings of the board of directors. A full 100 percent of them indicated that they did, at least "occasionally," vote "yes" when they should have voted "no" based on the merit of the proposal.

The legal framework, designed by the CSRC, has created the problems which undermine the effectiveness of independent directors. The CSRC is certainly aware of the extensively reported problems of high-ownership concentration and key-person control in China's listed companies. Nevertheless, it still imposes no restrictions on the power of the controlling shareholders to nominate independent directors, and grants no special privilege to minority shareholders who are the major victims of the agency problems associated with the key-person control model.

The independence of independent directors is further undermined by the *guanxi* based cultural environment which is still pervasive in contemporary Chinese society. *Guanxi* requires one to show respect for the feelings of – or "give face" to – others, especially to one's friends. As one commentator observes:

> In the Chinese culture with a history of several thousand years, the concept of "saving face for friends" or "giving no cold face to friends" is so persistent that it has huge impact on every interaction between people. Affected by this special cultural environment, it is inevitable that an independent director would be very reluctant to offend his friend, namely the chairman or CEO of the company, although the chairman or CEO has committed something which is detrimental to the interest of the company and its shareholders.

Access to Corporate Information and other Facilities

Apart from independence, the access to corporate information for independent directors is limited – or controlled by the management of the company. A survey conducted in 2004 demonstrated that about 90 percent of the independent directors relied primarily on the corporate management to obtain information, through either the brochure produced by the company or briefing by senior management executives of the company. That is to say, very few independent directors had actually employed the tools granted by the law, such as proxy contest, the right to hire external independent auditors, or direct communication with the company's employees or other stakeholders, to supervise the corporate management.

Regarding independent director's access to information, the legal regime does not offer much help. The *CSRC Guidelines for Independent Directors* mandate that listed companies must provide independent directors with adequate access to corporate information. It is further required that, "when the independent director perform his/her duties, the relevant persons concerned in the listed company shall cooperate actively and shall not turn down the independent director's proper request, nor shall they hinder the independent director's work or conceal the information." In addition, "the company shall make the necessary working facilities available to the independent directors for them to perform their duties."

The key question here is whether these requirements can be enforced … When the corporate management is determined to withhold negative information from conscious independent directors who have doubts about the disclosure of corporate information, those directors normally have no other choice than offering a resignation. They cannot resort to China's corporate law regime, including the *CSRC*

Guidelines for Independent Directors, as the system provides no legal solution if the listed company refuses to provide information. Clearly, when the requirements are not associated with enforcement measures, their legal effects are essentially minimized.

Similarly, although the *Guidelines* require the company to provide the necessary facilities for the independent directors to perform their duties, they do not specify the consequences of violation by the company. For instance, though the *Guidelines* provide that the independent directors can appoint outside auditing or consulting institutions to review the financial affairs of the company, this provision is unlikely to be implemented if the management of the company does not cooperate by bearing the necessary auditing or consulting cost. In a high-profile case in 2004, which is also believed to be the first case in which the independent directors challenged the management of the company, the four independent directors of Lianhua Gourmet Power Co., a company listed in the Shanghai Stock Exchange, requested the management to retain independent outside auditors to review the illegal use of RMB 949 million of the listed company's funds by its largest shareholder. The request was simply ignored by both the management and the controlling shareholder, resulting in a situation which is characterized as "*buliao liaozhi*" in Chinese, meaning "settling a matter by leaving it unsettled."

Liability of Independent Directors

The independent directors are assigned a number of rights and duties by the *Guidelines*. From the legal perspective, rights and duties must be associated with liabilities. In other words, the directors face certain legal consequences should they fail to perform their duties. With regard to duties, the *Guidelines* requires that:

> The independent directors shall bear the duties of good faith and due diligence and care towards the listed company and all the shareholders. They shall earnestly perform their duties in accordance with laws, regulations and the company's articles of association, shall protect the overall interests of the company, and shall be especially concerned with protecting the interests of minority shareholders from being infringed. Independent directors shall carry out their duties independently and shall not subject themselves to the influence of the company's major shareholders, actual controllers, or other entities or persons who are interested parties of the listed company.

But what are the legal consequences if the independent directors fail to fulfill their duties? The *Guidelines*, again, do not specify the consequences of violation, except that an independent director shall be removed if he or she fails to attend the board's meeting in person three times consecutively. Of course, an independent director is also subject to the legal liabilities imposed by the Company Law on any director who violates his duty of good faith and loyalty.

… [P]roblems include, most notably, the lack of true independence of the independent directors and the weak enforcement measures in relation to violation of the legal rules giving powers and privileges to independent directors.

Notes and Questions

1. The CSRC's 2001 *Guidelines* provide that listed companies should revise their articles of association to provide for independent directors. At least one of these should be an accounting professional. For listed companies, independent directors were to constitute at least one-third of the board by June 30, 2003. See generally Donald C. Clarke, 'The Independent Director in Chinese Corporate Governance' (2006) 31(1) *Delaware Journal of Corporate Law* 125–228, at 190–7.
2. Can a director or supervisor represent a company or bind the company to a contract, under China's Company Law? Why?
3. Can independent directors be truly independent in a system dominated by controlling shareholders such as the government? If not, what are the real functions of independent directors?
4. What has been done by the Chinese authority to ensure the independence and effectiveness of independent directors? Is the system useful in China at all? What can be done to improve the system?
5. Audit, nomination, and remuneration committees are recommended but not required in China. Should they be mandated?

9.5 Ownership Structure

Lin Zhang, 'Adaptive Efficiency and the Corporate Governance of Chinese State-Controlled Listed Companies: Evidence from the Fundraising of Chinese Domestic Venture' (2010) 10 *UC Davis Business Law Journal* 151, at 156–62

[T]he current SCLCs in China are the transformative results of traditional SOEs. Even if they have issued shares to the public during the process of privatization, the ownership structure of these enterprises is still characterized by the substantial concentration of shares in the hands of the state. Given the scarcity of available data, it is not possible to show the ownership structure of each SCLC in China to directly prove the above proposition. However, Table 9.1 provides empirical evidence regarding the majority shareholders of the SCLCs in the steel sector. These enterprises are thus used as a proxy to reflect the concentration of state shares in Chinese listed companies. According to Table 9.1, all of the largest shareholders of the twelve SCLCs producing steel and iron were state "holding corporations," which are, in turn, wholly state-owned. The appointments to the corporate leadership positions in the holding corporations are made by state-owned asset management commissions and CPC committees. Moreover, almost all of the candidates for these

Table 9.1 The largest shareholders in the SCLCs in the steel sector in China in 2001

Corporation	Largest shareholder	Amount of shares held by majority shareholder	Percentage of shares held by majority shareholder
Anyang Iron & Steel	Anyang Iron & Steel Group Corp	870,490,259	64.70
Baoshan Iron & Steel	Bao Steel Group Corporation	10,635,000,000	85.00
Guangzhou Iron & Steel	Guangzhou Iron & Steel Group Corporation	352,969,735	51.44
Handan Iron & Steel	Handan Iron & Steel Group Corporation	996,553,100	67.04
Hangzhou Iron & Steel	Hang Steel Group Corporation	479,587,500	74.32
Hongxing Iron & Steel	Jiuquan Steel Group Corporation	515,000,000	70.74
Laiwu Iron & Steel	Laiwu Iron & Steel Group Corporation	715,182,000	82.09
Lingyuan Iron & Steel	Lingyuan Group Corporation	178,500,000	57.58
Ma Anshan Iron & Steel	Ma Steel (Group) Holding Corporation	4,082,330,000	63.24
Nanjing Iron & Steel	Nanjing Iron & Steel Group Corporation	357,600,000	70.95
Tangshan Iron & Steel	Tangshan Iron & Steel Group Corporation	915,772,382	67.64
Wuhan Iron & Steel	Wuhan Steel Group Corporation	1,770,480,000	84.69

positions have worked for related government agencies. Therefore, state holding corporation leaders are seldom held accountable for the economic performance of their enterprises and their subsidiaries, at least as long as they do not deteriorate too dramatically. Their obligations are to guarantee the implementation of state and local policies in those entities. With the state holding corporations as their majority shareholders, the state has tight control over the SCLCs in the shareholders' meeting. Even if the equity division reform of 2005 has made state shares tradable on the secondary market, it has not shaken the state's position in the SCLCs as the largest shareholders due to political considerations and vested interests.

Notes and Questions

1. Should Chinese SOEs pursue "corporatization" to improve corporate efficiency while maintaining government ownership or "privatization" to increase ownership by private shareholders. What are the positive and negative aspects of each approach? How do you think China should proceed?
2. Can the state, or precisely, the state shareholder, be simply treated as the majority shareholder in SOEs and subject to the Company Law with respect to corporate governance?
3. According to the OECD, in 2016, SOEs accounted for 47 percent of the total market capitalization of all listed companies in China.

9.6 Law and Enforcement (External Governance)

Jiangyu Wang, *Company Law in China: Regulation of Business Organizations in a Socialist Market Economy* (Cheltenham, UK and Northampton, MA: Edward Elgar, 2014), pp. 23–43, 220–39

Revolutionary changes were brought by CL 2005 to strengthen corporate governance and shareholders protection ... The most significant development is probably the addition of the statutory right to file derivative lawsuits to defend their and the company's interests ... The legal provisions concerning private enforcement contained in the [CL 1993] were vague and rudimentary, and for all intents and purposes unenforceable. The shift of the focus of shareholder protection from public enforcement to private enforcement represents arguably the single most important rule of law development in China's corporate law system. Judicial protection would enable minority shareholders to monitor the management in a more efficient way and ensure more careful and faithful corporate decisions. Compared with the Old Law, the new rules are clearer, more practical, and more enforceable, and thus more likely to bring about effective and just settlement of corporate legal disputes.

…

Derivative Action under the Company Law

Under the Company Law two litigation techniques are now available to shareholders to vindicate their interests in the company, especially when fiduciary duties are breached by the key players in a company, such as the directors, supervisors, senior management executives, and sometimes even the controlling shareholders. The techniques are the direct suit and derivative suit rules designed for shareholders to bring legal actions against those key players in accordance with the Company Law.

…

[T]he introduction of derivative suits by the [CL 2005] is a major breakthrough in the development of shareholders' protection in China … Suffice it to say that, since derivative suits 'operate to deter mismanagement by imposing the threat of liability [on the key players in the company],' they provide a strong incentive for key players to act in the interest of the company and the shareholders, so as to reduce agency costs and enhance corporate governance. Further, from the perspective of private enforcement, derivative actions are practically the only legal tool possessed by shareholders to deal with insider wrongdoing. When insiders (the key players including the directors and senior executives) breach their duties to the company, the company itself will rarely take action against them as the company is actually controlled by the insiders. Giving shareholders the standing to sue the insiders is then the best choice to redress the injury to the company.

…

The mechanism for derivative suits is chiefly provided in Article 152 of the Company Law, which, over the years, has been supplemented by and elaborated upon by SPC interpretations, court decisions, and writing of judges and influential scholars. It is useful to reproduce the long and awkward-sounding Article 151 here:

> If a director or senior management executive is in the circumstances specified in Article 150 [of the Company Law] hereof, the shareholders in the case of a limited liability company, or the shareholders, in the case of a joint stock limited company, who hold one percent or more of company shares individually or aggregately for more than 180 consecutive days, may request in writing the supervisory board or the supervisor (in the case of a limited liability company without a supervisory board) to file a lawsuit with a people's court. If a supervisor is in the circumstances specified in Article 150 hereof, the aforementioned shareholders may request in writing the board of directors or the executive director (in the case of a limited liability company without a board of directors) to file a lawsuit with a people's court.

> If the aforementioned supervisor board, supervisor, board of directors or executive director refuses to bring a lawsuit after receipt of the written request of the shareholders as specified in the preceding paragraph, or fails to bring a lawsuit within 30 days of the date of receipt of the request, or if the matter is urgent and the company will suffer irrecoverable losses if a lawsuit is not instituted at once, the shareholders specified in the preceding paragraph shall have the right to bring a lawsuit in a people's court directly in their own name for the interests of the company.
>
> If any other person infringes upon the lawful rights and interests of the company and thereby causing losses to the company, the shareholders specified in Paragraph One of this Article may bring a lawsuit in a people's court in accordance with the provisions of the preceding two paragraphs.

Obviously, a shareholder who wishes to initiate a derivate suit must satisfy a number of procedural requirements. Those related to the cause of action, the plaintiff's standing to sue, status of the company in the lawsuit, demand on board, and litigation expenses will be examined in the following sections.

8.3.2 Cause of Action

The cause of action for statutory derivative suits against directors and senior executives is provided in Article 150 of the Company Law, which states: 'If a director, supervisor or senior management executive violates the provisions of laws, administrative regulations or the corporate charter in his performance of duties relating to his position in the company, thereby causing losses to the company, he shall be liable for compensation.'

Article 150 covers a wide range of duties of the key players, including, but not limited to, their fiduciary duties of loyalty and due care provided in Articles 148, 149, and other relevant rules. Generally speaking, Article 150 establishes a fault liability in tort law, under which the key players shall make compensation when '(1) there must exist the fact that the company is injured; (2) the injury must be the result of the wrongdoer's acts of breaching of the provisions of the laws, administrative regulations and the corporate charter in his execution of company duties [which includes certainly the breach of fiduciary duties]; (3) there must be a causal link between the illegal acts and the injury; and (4) the wrongdoer must be at fault, which means he was either intentional or negligent in performing the harming acts.' A textual reading of Article 150, however, suggests 'a derivative action should not be allowed against directors, supervisors and/or senior officers if they caused losses to the company while not in the course of performing company duties.'

Paragraph 3 of Article 152, which offers shareholders the right to launch derivative suits against third parties, might cause confusion in practice. Since any third party other than the directors or senior executives could harm the interests of the company in various ways, 'any other person' might be broadly construed to be the company's controlling shareholder, a creditor who refuses to perform on a contract signed with the company, or an outsider who has inflicted harm upon the company. If the company refuses to sue, the shareholders, subject to fulfilling the preconditions examined below, can sue for the interest of the company. Insofar as the controlling shareholder is concerned, paragraph 3 should be read together with Articles 20 and 21 of the Company Law, which provide, respectively, that the shareholders, including the controlling shareholder, should be liable to compensate the company for any losses caused by their abuse of their limited liability and the company's independent legal personality or by their misconduct in related party transactions ...

...

8.3.5 Preconditions: Demand and Board Control of Derivative Litigation

Given that a derivate suit is about the interests of the company and the recovery, if any, will also go to the company, it is only logical that the company should be given an opportunity to review the claim and decide whether to bring suit before a shareholder is allowed to launch a derivative action. Article 152 thus provides that shareholders may not file derivative suit unless they first make demand on the board of directors or the supervisory board. The demand requirement entails the following specific rules:

1. A demand should be made on the supervisory board (or the supervisor in an LLC without a supervisory board) if the shareholder sues the directors or senior executives.
2. A demand should be made on the board of directors (or the executive director in an LLC without a board of directors) if a supervisor is the named defendant in the suit.
3. The supervisory board (or supervisor) or the board of directors (or the executive director) to whom the demand is served has 30 days to respond after receiving the demand. If they decide not to proceed with a lawsuit, the shareholder is then entitled to bring a derivative suit.
4. The demand is excused if the matter is urgent and a delay in lodging a lawsuit would cause irreparable injury to the company.

Although the demand requirement is procedural in nature, Chinese courts have been treating it as a substantive rule in derivative litigation. That is, the courts are rather stringent about requiring the plaintiff to fulfill the preconditions. In *Xu Hongwei v Beijing Printing Group Ltd.* (2007), the plaintiff, a minority shareholder, filed a derivative action against the controlling shareholder. The plaintiff-shareholder alleged that, because the company, under the defendant's instructions, had moved the major assets of the company from its registered place of business, an urgent situation had thus emerged, and so there was no longer the need for him to fulfill the preconditions by making demand on the either board. The court unhesitatingly dismissed the claim on the grounds that the plaintiff was not able to prove that the situation was 'urgent enough' to waive him having an obligation to meet the preconditions of Article 152 of the Company Law. In *Hantang Co. v Chen Shihua, et al.* (2006), the first derivative suit involving a foreign party tried by the Beijing Number Two Intermediate Court after the [CL 2005] took effect, the plaintiff, a major shareholder of a company, sued against three directors of the company, alleging that they defrauded the company in a related-party transaction. Although the factual elements of fraud were quite clear, the court nevertheless quickly dismissed the plaintiff-shareholder's claim on the grounds of its failure to meet the preconditions of making demand.

Notes and Questions

1. Why was China's judiciary (behind which is of course the Chinese party-state) hostile to shareholders' litigation? What caused the change in the 2005 amendments to the Company Law to allow the derivative action?
2. Why does China require the shareholders to meet certain preconditions before they can bring derivative action? What are the pros and cons of those preconditions, from the perspective of investor protection?
3. What should China do to strengthen private enforcement? Should it adopt a class action type of system? Can it allow class action in corporate litigation, given China's rather unique sociopolitical system?
4. Hui Huang found that out of fifty derivative actions brought between 2006 and 2010 almost all of them involved small limited liability companies. Only a small number of cases apparently have been brought against large, listed companies. What does this say about the effectiveness of derivative actions in Chinese corporate governance?

9.7 Special Features

9.7.1 The Parallel Governance Structures in SOEs

Most SOEs have been corporatized into companies with a modern structure, and hence they are subject to the Company Law and other relevant laws. In theory, the players in the SOEs, including the state-shareholder and other shareholders, the general manager and their deputies, the chair and directors of the board, and the supervisors, are entitled to exercise the rights and obliged to perform the obligations provided in the Company Law. In a rule of law country, it may appear that SOEs only need to act within the four corners of corporate law and securities law and have to comply with, at least on the surface, their formalities and rules. However, this is far from the state of affairs, given the political control of SOEs by the party-state.

Existing literature on corporate governance and control in SOEs has largely focused on the legal framework, looking at the interactions among the shareholders, directors, supervisors, and managers, as if the rights and duties with respect to their relations are mainly or only provided in the Company Law. In fact, legal corporate governance and political governance coexist in the control and operation of Chinese SOEs, and, in most cases, the informal, non-legal, rules in political governance prevail over the legal rules in the corporate and securities laws.

Jiangyu Wang, 'The Political Logic of Corporate Governance in China's State-Owned Enterprises' (2014) 47 *Cornell International Law Journal* 631, 648–60

III. The Twin Governance Structures of SOEs

B. Political Governance in SOEs

[A]n SOE is controlled by the Party-state through the following four mechanisms: (1) the fundamental discipline of the CPC requires all Party members to comply with the Party line; (2) the CPC decides the appointment and promotion of the top executives of SOEs; (3) Party cells within the SOEs convene meetings to make important decisions for the company and to ensure the operation of the company is consistent with the Party line; and (4) SOE executives accused of wrongdoing are investigated by the CPC and punished under Party discipline …

Party Organizations' Participation in SOE Decision-Making

Each SOE has at least one Party organization, known either as the Party Group (*dangzu*), Party Committee (*dangwei*), Party Subgroup (*dangzhibu*). The functions of the Party cells in SOEs are defined in the CPC Constitution as follows:

> In a state-owned or collective enterprise, the primary Party organization acts as the political nucleus and works for the [better] operation of the enterprise. The primary Party organization guarantees and supervises the implementation of the principles and policies of the Party and the state in its own enterprise and backs the meeting of shareholders, board of directors, board of supervisors and manager (factory director) in the exercise of their relevant functions and powers according to law …

The responsibilities and powers of the Party organization in an SOE are more explicitly stated in the 1997 CPC Notice on Party Building in SOEs, which requires the Party organization to supervise the enterprise in order to ensure that the CPC line is faithfully implemented, and authorizes it to "participate in the decision-making on material and important matters of the SOE and provide support to the factory leader/general manager, shareholders' general meeting, board of directors and supervisory board to perform their duties according to law." Accordingly, the board of directors or general manager is required to "consult and respect the opinion of the Party organization" before making any important decisions, and brief the Party organization on the implementation of said decision. Further, the trade unions, youth leagues, and, to some extent, the workers' congress of the SOE are under the leadership of the Party organization.

...

CPC Controlled Personnel Appointment in SOEs

The primary principle of the Party-state's personnel system is the *Dangguan Ganbu Yuanze* (the Principle of Party Control of Cadres), under which the CPC dominates the appointment of all state officials in China. The CPC, through its Organization and Personnel [system], maintains the nomenclature system that covers cadre selection and appointment in all state-related institutions in China. It is a unified management system that "reaches into almost every important nook and cranny in the public sector of the Chinese system." Through this formidable nomenclature system, the CPC controls the appointment, ranking, promotion, transfer, and removal of all but the lowest ranking state officials.

Personnel in SOEs, especially top leaders such as the chairperson and deputy chairperson of the board of directors or the senior corporate executives, are managed and openly appointed by the CPC organizational departments. Each SOE is placed in the political system of the Party-state and given a bureaucratic ranking; the personnel management of SOE leaders is managed by the organizational department of that bureaucratic level. Specifically, the Joint Opinions of the CPC Central Organization Department and the SASAC Party Committee articulates the following principles with respect to personnel appointment in SOEs:

a. The Party Controls Cadres system requires the Party organization's participation in the appointment, management and supervision of all SOE officers above the middle level ...
b. In principle, a balance should be maintained between the principle of Party Control Cadres and the requirements of China's corporate laws that authorize the board to appoint managers and the general manager to appoint lower-level officers. Technically, the selection of personnel can adopt market-based mechanisms to recruit the most competent and competitive candidates.

c. The appointment of senior corporate executives should follow these steps: (1) the Party organization department's examination of the qualifications of the candidates; (2) the Party Committee's full deliberation of the candidates; and (3) the appointment of the candidates by the board of directors based on the recommendation of the Party Committee, following all legal procedures and formalities.

Notes and Questions

1. What are the two structures of corporate governance in SOEs in China? What's the purpose for maintaining the political structure?
2. Do the parallel structures hinder efficiency in Chinese SOEs?
3. China has vowed to reform its SOEs to make them equal, normal, and competitive players in a real market economy. To a large extent, this may be required by the new generation of trade agreements. Given the current party-state-controlled governance system, what can be done to achieve this goal?
4. Describe the difference between legal governance and political governance. How does the governance of Chinese SOEs compare with Singaporean GLCs?

9.7.2 The Problem of Related Party Transactions and Their Regulation

Provisions in the Company Law do not directly address related party transactions. Article 21 of the Company Law prohibits a company's controlling shareholders, actual controllers, directors, supervisors, and senior executives from using their positions to harm the interests of the company. These key persons have a connection with the company and are related parties. They shall be liable for compensation if their related party transactions cause losses to the company. The Company Law grants legal remedies to the company, which may also be pursued by other shareholders through the mechanism of derivative action.

In practice, courts do not appear to play a significant role in this regard as judicial decisions concerning related party transactions are rare. Regulatory measures, including information disclosure, are currently the major tools to address such transactions in China. According to the national Securities Law and the CSRC's Administrative Measures on Information Disclosure by Listed Companies, the following information concerning a related party transaction shall be disclosed: (1) the voting results of the board of directors; (2) the time at which the underlying agreement is signed; (3) the time and place of the transaction's execution; (4) the relationship between all related parties; (5) the subject of the transaction, pricing policies, main provisions of the agreement; (6) the purpose of the transaction; (7) the impact of the transaction on listed companies; and (8) the prerequisites if the transaction is based on a conditional agreement. In addition, disclosure reports should also be furnished by the company's independent directors and relevant intermediaries who render services to the company. Further, the board has to explain why this related party transaction is beneficial for the company.

The regulatory rules on related party transactions are often inseparable from the rules on corporate internal control. Internal control rules may eliminate the room for unfair related party transactions from inside the company.

Yan Tong, Mingzhu Wang, and Feng Xu, 'Internal Control, Related Party Transactions and Corporate Value of Enterprises Directly Controlled by Chinese Central Government' (2014) 1(1) *Journal of Chinese Management* 3–5

Internal controls have not been mandatorily required to be implemented in Chinese listed firms until 2006 due to a series of regulatory changes.

First, China experienced the split share structure reform (the Reform hereafter) in 2006. After the Reform, the [CSRC] issued 'Measures for the Administration of Initial Public Offering and Listing of Stocks,' which requires internal controls for listed companies for the first time. According to this regulation, companies in the initial public offering (IPO) process must have a sound and effective internal control system that should guarantee the reliability of financial reports, compliance with laws and regulations, efficiency and effectiveness of business operations. The efficiency of the internal control system should be assessed by public certified accounting with an assurance report on internal control. This regulation issued by the CSRC should be complied by all the IPO firms no matter whether they are SOEs or non-SOEs.

The second regulatory change in 2006 was 'Comprehensive Risk Management Guidance for CSOEs' (the Guidance hereafter) issued by the [SASAC]. SASAC performs investor's responsibilities for [centrally-owned state-owned enterprises (CSOEs)], i.e. supervising the preservation and increment of CSOEs' corporate value as well as managing the state-owned assets of the enterprises by regulations. The Guidance for CSOEs requires that their internal control system should help risk management and include all the major business processes, such as strategy, investment, marketing, accounting, producing, etc.

Third, the Ministry of Finance, CSRC and other three commissions issued 'The Basic Internal Control Norms for Enterprises' in 2008 and 'The Enterprise Internal Control Guidelines' in 2010 (the Guidelines hereafter). Listed companies in Shanghai and Shenzhen stock exchanges have to comply with these two sets of regulations from 2012. Unlisted firms of large and median sizes are also encouraged to comply with the Guidelines. Similar to the internal control objectives in CSRC's regulations, five components should be structured in the internal control system of a firm, including control environment, risk assessments, information and communications, control activities and monitoring.

The internal control quality of listed firms and CSOEs is regulated by the government using the above-mentioned Guidance and Guidelines. Because most of the CSOEs have one or more listed companies, CSOEs must abide both the Guidance and the Guidelines by preparing internal control reports for the Ministry of Finance and risk management reports for SASAC. Some recent evidence shows that the quality of the internal control of CSOEs is different from that of other listed firms. For instance, the internal control of CSOEs is more efficient than that of other listed firms …

Notes and Questions

1. Many Chinese companies are still SOEs, while many of the so-called privately owned companies also have their roots in China's state-owned economy, as they were converted from SOEs through corporatization or privatization. Does this make related party transactions more prevalent in China than in other jurisdictions?
2. Why does China still mainly rely on the regulators, such as the CSRC, Ministry of Finance, and even sometimes the tax authorities, to deal with the problem of related party transactions, rather than the courts? This is not uncommon in developing countries. It has been argued that developing economies often have to use regulatory tools rather than judicial means to tackle market failures. Do you agree with this proposition?

Corporate governance was introduced with the aim of improving the management efficiency of SOEs in China. This objective set the initial conditions for corporate governance and, to a large extent, predetermined the Chinese characteristics of corporate governance. Progressively, more Western elements have been introduced into the corporate governance system in China. As a result, anyone who looks at the law on paper would not have much difficulty in recognizing the convergence between corporate governance in China and other jurisdictions, although the corporate governance framework in China remains eclectic, with its fusion of the Germanic legal tradition, Anglo-American legal tradition, and Chinese legal tradition.

The biggest divergence between China's corporate governance and that of the mature market economies lies in the control of the governance of SOEs by the Chinese party-state. The parallel governance structures of corporate governance, featuring tight control by the Chinese Communist Party, make it difficult, if even possible, for the state enterprises to operate solely based on commercial considerations when they do business.

Statutes and Regulations

Company Law of the People's Republic of China (Rev. 2013)

Supreme People's Court Judicial Interpretation on the PRC Company Law (I) (Rev. 2014)

Supreme People's Court Judicial Interpretation on the PRC Company Law (II) (Rev. 2014)

Supreme People's Court Judicial Interpretation on the PRC Company Law (III) (Rev. 2014)

Securities Law of the People's Republic of China (Rev. 2014)

Administrative Measures for the Initial Public Offering and Listing of Shares (Rev. 2015)

Administrative Measures for the Disclosure of Information of Listed Companies (2007)

Guidelines on the Articles of Associations of Listed Companies (Rev. 2016)

Code of Corporate Governance for Listed Companies (2002)

10

JAPAN

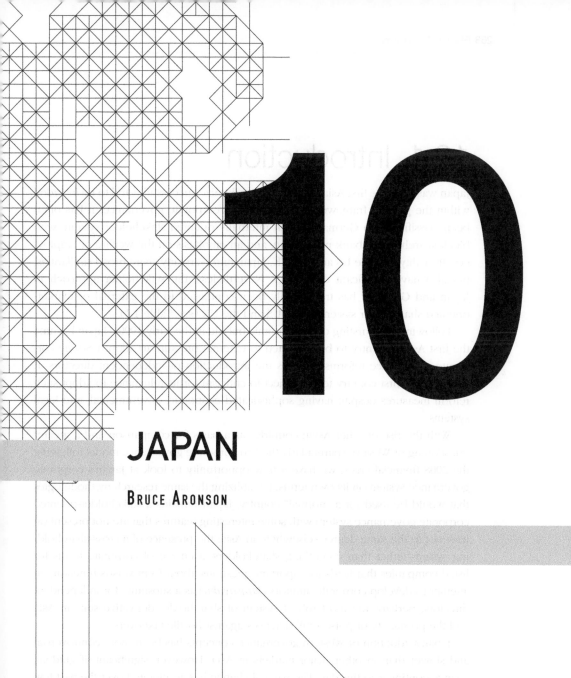

Bruce Aronson

10.1 Introduction

Japan was both the first Asian country to modernize successfully and to be included within the general framework of comparative corporate governance. It has often been classified with Germany, as an internally oriented stakeholder system, with block shareholders, bank monitoring, and an emphasis on the welfare of employees. In reality, like the US and the UK, Japan and Germany share broad similarities, but also have significant differences. Nevertheless, the stakeholder approach in Japan and Germany has traditionally been contrasted to the external or market-oriented shareholder system of the US and the UK (see Table 1.1).

Following the bursting of its economic bubble in the early 1990s, Japan became the first Asian country to be subjected to external pressure to adopt US-style corporate governance reforms, such as the introduction of independent directors. It was also the first country to be subject to criticism for its reluctance to adopt such reform measures despite having sophisticated economic, governmental, and legal systems.

With the rise of other Asian countries as a basis for comparison and a greater questioning of Western (particularly the US) corporate governance model following the 2008 financial crisis, we have a new opportunity to look at Japan's corporate governance system on its own terms, i.e. utilizing the same research methodologies that would be used for a "normal" country. Japan remains a stakeholder-oriented corporate governance system with some interesting features that are not present (at least not to the same degree) elsewhere in Asia: the presence of a cross-shareholding system rather than controlling shareholders, a choice of corporate forms for listed companies that leads to important questions about form versus function, an attempt to develop corporate auditors (***kansayaku***) as a substitute for independent directors, perhaps the most robust system of shareholder derivative suits in Asia and the popularity of poison pill defenses against hostile takeovers.

Japan's adoption of Western governance concepts has been more controversial and slower than in other major markets in Asia. However, significant, if gradual, change continues to this day. The pace of change has accelerated over the past few years due to (a) a new emphasis on corporate governance reform as part of the Japanese government's growth strategy under Abenomics and (b) the high compliance rate with respect to UK-inspired soft law codes, i.e. the recently enacted stewardship code and corporate governance code.

10.2 Purpose: Stakeholder System

10.2.1 Japan's Postwar Model

Masahiko Aoki, 'Conclusion: Whither Japan's Corporate Governance?,' in Masahiko Aoki, Gregory Jackson, and Hideaki Miyajima (eds.), *Corporate Governance in Japan: Institutional Change and Organizational Diversity* (Oxford: Oxford University Press, 2007), pp. 427–48, 429

In order to highlight the changes taking place in Japan's corporate landscape in the past decade or so, let us first quote the stylized features of the preceding system – which we will refer to as the ***traditional J-system*** for the sake of referential convenience. They are:

- Top management (the representative directors) of the corporate firm was ranked as the pinnacle of the career ladder for its permanent employees. The Board of Directors, almost exclusively composed of insiders, functioned as a substructure of top management.
- One of the main objectives of management was to provide steadily growing benefits to its permanent employees in the form of seniority wages, promotion opportunities, bonus and severance payments, fringe benefits and so on, subject to a reasonable level of profits (the so-called *"J-firm"*).
- The main bank was the major supplier of funds to the corporate firm. Other financial institutions and investors expected the main bank to be a principal monitor of the firm (the so-called "delegated monitoring"). The main bank did not overtly intervene with the management of firms in excellent/normal corporate-value state. But the control right was expected to shift to the main bank in a critical corporate-value state, which was to decide whether to bail out and restructure the firm at its own cost, or liquidate it (the so-called "contingent governance").
- The government regulated the banking industry to assure rents to individual banks according to their market shares. It also intervened, if necessary, to bail out financially distressed banks or arrange for their acquisition by healthier banks (the so-called "Convoy system") …
- One-party rule by the LDP was taken for granted. Under such political stability, triadic coalitions among LDP politicians, interest groups and ministerial bureaucrats were formed in parallel along various industrial, occupational and professional lines to protect mutual vested interests of the incumbents. The

mediation among these coalitions was struck by LDP leaders in cooperation with top bureaucrats of the Ministry of Finance (MOF) (the so-called "bureau-pluralism" or "compartmentalized pluralism").

The traditional J-system characterized by these features started to ebb even in the 1980s. However, it was only after the bubble burst that changes became evident.

Notes and Questions

1. Aoki famously described a new, stylized "J-form" for Japanese companies that did not follow the standard contractual model of the firm in Western or at least Anglo-American literature on the theory of the firm. He and other Japanese economists focused on the example of Toyota and generalized the Japanese term "Toyota Production System" (*Toyota kanban hōshiki*) into "just in time" and "lean" manufacturing.
2. Does a system of coordinated stakeholders such as employees, main banks, and corporate groups result from Japanese cultural practices and preferences or is such a system rational in the Japanese context? A number of business school scholars speculated in a "varieties of capitalism" literature about whether a new Japanese form of "government-coordinated economy" could transform into a "liberal market economy."
3. Although Japan's postwar system became fixed in popular perceptions of Japan, it appears that in Japan's prewar period employment and corporate finance systems were significantly more market oriented. What does this say about the cultural argument for Japan's postwar system?
4. A commonly cited feature of Japan's postwar system absent from the above excerpt is horizontal coordination among *keiretsu* group firms. It is explored from a comparative perspective in the following reading.

10.2.2 Comparative Explanation of Japan's Postwar Model

Ronald Gilson and Mark Roe, 'Understanding the Japanese Keiretsu: Overlaps Between Corporate Governance and Industrial Organization' (1993) 102 *Yale Law Journal* 871–906, at 874–5, 905–6

We shall argue here, our system's characteristics color the lens through which the first comparative studies viewed the rest of the world. Analysis of American corporate governance has always sought to solve the problem of separation of ownership and control: who will monitor management in light of dispersed shareholdings. Favored candidates for this monitoring role have shifted from outside directors to the market for corporate control, and, most recently, to institutional investors. As a result, the primary focus in comparative studies of Japanese corporate governance has been the role of the main bank. Conventional wisdom among American scholars has been that the Japanese system solves the corporate governance problem – who monitors management – through continuous monitoring by a financial intermediary, rather than through intermittent and often disruptive monitoring by capital markets. Relying on this analysis, reform proposals have identified institutional investors as having the potential to provide Japanese-style monitoring in the American system.

To date, comparative analyses of the Japanese corporate governance system have assumed that the central *purpose* of the Japanese system, like that of the American system, is solving the Berle–Means monitoring problem. We argue that the Japanese system serves a function in addition to the monitoring of management. Our Japanese model reflects not only the need for *corporate governance,* the traditional factor American scholars have identified as shaping corporate structures, but also the need to support production and exchange – what we will call *contractual governance.* To be sure, complex multi-level monitoring is part of the production process, but this monitoring is motivated not just by financial institutions seeking a return on capital, but also by product market competition. Bank monitoring thus should not be seen in isolation, but as one specific (although important) kind of a wide range of contractual monitoring types in Japan. An empirical observation informs this perspective: although financial institutions hold one-half of Japanese public firm stock, often in highly-concentrated blocks, another quarter of Japanese stock is held by other corporations, often suppliers or customers …

Too many efforts to understand the Japanese system have suffered from Berle–Means blinders. Hidden by the focus on main banks is the fact that one-third of the cross-ownership is held by industrial companies. We hypothesize that cross-ownership reduces the risk of opportunism when parties make large relational investments. The management of any factor that defects, by trying to raise price inordinately, to skimp on quality, or to miss the next technological step in the industry, will face a coalition of stockholders. Fear of such a confrontation deters defection. Product market competition keeps the system from lapsing into a conspiracy of passivity.

Industrial cross-ownership has not previously been emphasized as a key element of the Japanese corporate system, and we believe this connection is important. Indeed, we suspect that some of the main bank interventions can and should be seen not just as the pure intervention of the residual equity holder (or large creditor) to protect its investment – the American model – but as the intervention of factor providers. The bank monitors directly by providing credit and indirectly by serving as agent for the other factors. The bank assumes this agency role partly because of its stock ownership in the other factors …

Notes and Questions

1. Although the internal monitoring role of main banks and their shareholding in client companies received great attention as features of the Japanese postwar model, Gilson and Roe focus instead on cross-shareholding by industrial companies. What is their claim about how this system would work? If it acts as a kind of corporate governance system, how would enforcement work? Would this system work for the bulk of Japanese companies, or only for those companies, like Toyota, that are engaged in strong international competition?
2. Japanese law specialists debate whether the stylized post-war system described by Aoki, and accepted by Gilson and Roe, actually existed in Japan. Due to inconsistencies in the definition and application of concepts like *keiretsu*, Mark Ramseyer of Harvard Law School has claimed that the entire "system" is a myth. See e.g. Yoshiro Miwa and J. Mark Ramseyer, *The Fable of the Keiretsu: Urban Myths of the Japanese Economy* (Chicago, IL: University of Chicago Press, 2006). A more popular academic view is that the postwar system was never completely as described and many of its important elements quickly began to change. See e.g. Curtis Milhaupt, 'On the (Fleeting) Existence of the Main Bank System and Other Japanese Economic Institutions' (2002) 27 *Law and Social Inquiry* 425–37.

10.3 Board Function

10.3.1 Choice of Corporate Form in Japan: Corporate Structures and Fiduciary Duties

Bruce Aronson, Souichirou Kozuka, and Luke Nottage, 'Corporate Legislation in Japan,' in Parissa Haghirian (ed.), *Routledge Handbook of Japanese Business and Management* (Abingdon, UK: Routledge, 2016), pp. 103–5

The twin concerns of economic competitiveness and attractiveness to investors resulted in numerous corporate law amendments in the decade from the mid-1990s that contained two separate, and sometimes contradictory components: providing corporate management with greater flexibility than traditionally granted under

Japan's Commercial Code to finance and structure corporate activities (e.g., permitting spinoffs, stock options, etc.) and, to a lesser degree, providing greater protection for the interests of shareholders (e.g., the debate over a legal requirement for 'outside' directors in the 2000s). Most reforms enhanced management flexibility, so were welcomed by big business groups (such as *Keidanren*) and easily undertaken. Measures to protect shareholders, generally opposed by business groups, constituted a minority of the reforms and were undertaken at a much slower pace.

Numerous amendments to reform specific corporate law provisions of Japan's Commercial Code during the decade from the mid-1990s to the mid-2000s culminated in the enactment of a new Companies Act in 2005 ...

One distinguishing feature of Japanese corporate reform was allowing companies to select among a number of different corporate structures. The Companies Act provided a new array of structuring options for smaller private entities. Since 2002 public companies were given a choice: they could retain the "traditional" Japanese corporate form with the German-inspired features of a ***kansayaku*** board (board of audit) and a representative director as the CEO, or adopt a new option of an "American-style" structure that replaced the board of audit with three committees on the board of directors (audit, compensation, and nomination committees, with a majority of outside directors required for each committee) and a new class of executive officers headed by the chief representative officer.

In addition to these two choices of a company with ***kansayaku*** board and a company with nomination and other committees ("company with committees"), the 2014 amendment to the Companies Act added a third option: a company with audit and supervisory committee. This new form essentially replaced the traditional ***kansayaku*** board with a "one-committee" system; it requires only an audit committee, with a majority of outside directors, as a committee of the board of directors.

Corporate legislation was supplemented by extensive amendments that overhauled existing securities laws in 2006 (renamed the Financial Instruments and Exchange Act (FIEA) in 2006). The FIEA contains several provisions relevant to corporate governance, primarily related to information disclosure and reporting requirements. It required, for example, a new system of quarterly reporting for listed companies.

Reform legislation in Japan can thus be characterized as representing gradual, but significant, evolutionary change. During the first decade of reform this approach disappointed some critics ...

The U.S. model did, in fact, serve as the main inspiration during the first decade of reform in Japan, as seen, for example, in the structural option of an "American-style" company with nomination and other committees that was provided to Japanese companies. However, following the 2008 financial crisis the U.K. approach, featuring mainly "soft law" corporate governance codes with "comply or explain" disclosure provisions for listed companies, has gained increasing influence over the U.S. "hard law" approach ...

Notes and Questions

1. The choice of corporate form for large corporations in Japan beginning in 2002 – an "enabling" version of corporate law – attracted the attention of comparative law scholars. A similar approach was taken in Taiwan (see Chapter 12), Italy, and Portugal.
2. Questions about the formal structure of corporations in Japan, focusing on the question of the necessity of a legal requirement for outside directors, dominated discussion of governance reform in Japan for fifteen years. However, as discussed below, the actual functioning of the board may well be more important than its formal structure.

10.3.2 *Kansayaku* as a Possible Substitute for Independent Directors

Bruce Aronson, Souichirou Kozuka, and Luke Nottage, 'Corporate Legislation in Japan,' in Parissa Haghirian (ed.), *Routledge Handbook of Japanese Business and Management* (Abingdon, UK: Routledge, 2016), p. 107

Kansayaku are an important feature of Japanese companies, as some 97.8% of listed companies have retained their structure of a company with *kansayaku* board, but their actual role remains controversial. Although many countries in Asia have some kind of audit or supervisory board, only in Japan has corporate law reform sought to strengthen their function to serve as a possible substitute for independent directors. For example, the *kansayaku*'s term of office has been gradually extended to four years, longer than the two years for directors, in an effort to protect the *kansayaku* from CEO pressure and ensure their independence.

Kansayaku are required only for a company with *kansayaku* board. In a "large" public company, there must be three or more *kansayaku*; and at least half of them must be outside *kansayaku*. Their traditional authority under the Companies Act is to "audit" for illegality (*ihōsei*); there is also a debate concerning the extent to which *kansayaku* should go beyond instances of illegality to audit for acts that are unsound or not in the best interests of the corporation (*datōsei*). The *kansayaku*'s role has been criticized by foreign investors as being essentially a compliance function, as they lack the legal authority to supervise management: they have a duty to attend board meetings and to intervene when necessary, but have no right to vote and also cannot fire the company president.

Kansayaku do, however, have important powers of their own, including the power of investigation and inquiry at their company, and also at their company's subsidiaries, and the right to request a court injunction when a manager (director) commits an unlawful act. In addition, each *kansayaku* can exercise his or her powers individually, and some of the *kansayaku* are full-time insiders with thorough knowledge of the company.

Kansayaku often claim that their role in practice is generally becoming broader than compliance and is focusing more on risk management, although it is difficult to measure or judge actual practice. In recent years *kansayaku* have been assigned an important role in controlling conflicts of interest (such as approval for limiting the liability of directors). On the other hand, the board was also given a more specific role in the *kansayaku*'s traditional field of compliance. Under the Companies Act the board of directors must make decisions on the establishment of a company's internal control system, and under the FIEA such board decisions must be publicly disclosed.

Asian Corporate Governance Association, 'The Roles and Functions of *Kansayaku* Boards Compared to Audit Committees,' at 3–4 (October 2013), at www.acga-asia.org/upload/files/advocacy/20170330102329_21.pdf

1. Introduction

The argument is often put forward that *Kansayaku* are a substitute for an Audit Committee – a view we do not share because the powers and functions of the two entities, although overlapping to some extent, are quite different in important respects.

Our conclusion from assessing the evidence is that a genuinely independent and well-run Audit Committee has the potential to strengthen board governance and oversight of management more effectively than the *Kansayaku* system. Audit Committees are usually composed of all or a majority of independent directors and chaired by one … Being directors with the right to vote, Audit Committee members have the ability to exert direct influence on board decisions. Because of this, they have greater authority and ability than *Kansayaku* to influence the integrity of financial reporting, the independence of the external accounting auditor, and the robustness of a company's internal controls, internal audit practices, and risk management systems. In recent years, some Audit Committees have taken on additional tasks such as reviewing the implementation of whistleblowing systems.

In contrast, *Kansayaku* are not fully part of the board's formal decision-making and approval process, and do not have the authority of directors (although they do sit in on board meetings and in some companies act as trusted advisers to the president/CEO). Much of the work of the full-time *Kansayaku* is taken up with "business audits," which in many respects task him or her to act more like a quasi-compliance officer who makes sure the company is adhering to laws and regulations. While *Kansayaku* also carry out "accounting audits," this role largely involves setting audit policy, overseeing the work of the external accounting auditor, listening to reports by the full time *Kansayaku*, and mechanically checking the company's financial position ...

On balance, however, we believe that both in terms of structure and actual practice, the powers of *Kansayaku* Boards are weaker than those of Audit Committees ... Paradoxically, in one way the weakness of the system derives from the fact that most of the formal powers given to individual *Kansayaku* are so strong and confrontational in nature – for example, the right to conduct independent investigations, to command directors to cease actions or to sue directors – that, in reality, they are almost never exercised ...

Notes and Questions

1. Little data exists concerning the actual function of *kansayaku* in practice. Accordingly, debates about the role of *kansayaku* tend to revolve around their legal powers and anecdotal examples. Top management at some Japanese companies insist that despite the *kansayaku's* lack of voting power at board meetings, a negative comment by a *kansayaku* will derail a proposal and management does not really distinguish between outside *kansayaku* and outside directors.
2. Is it fair to compare only the roles of *kansayaku* and independent directors? A broader view comparing companies in the US and Japan might conclude that Japanese companies' overall lack of investment in personnel and resources for risk management in individual business units and throughout the organization represents a weakness in Japanese corporate governance, rather than the role of *kansayaku* at corporate headquarters.
3. In 2012 the *kansayaku* professional association, a nonprofit organization, changed its recommended English translation of the Japanese word *kansayaku* from "Corporate Auditor" to "Audit & Supervisory Board Member," with a corresponding change from "Board of Auditors" to "Audit and Supervisory Board." The stated reason was that "In addition to the audit function, the importance of a 'kansayaku's' function in supervising the activities of management, which is performed in collaboration with the Board of Directors, has been recently emphasized."

10.3.3 Board Function over Structure: Case Studies on the Role of Boards and Independent Directors in Japan (Toyota versus Sony)

Bruce Aronson, 'Case Studies of Independent Directors in Asia,' in Dan Puchniak et al. (eds.), *Independent Directors in Asia: A Historical, Contextual and Comparative Approach* (Cambridge: Cambridge University Press, 2017), pp. 439–44

The debate over board function and structure and the role of independent directors was epitomized by a popular comparison between Toyota and Sony. The chairman of Toyota, the champion of traditional Japanese manufacturers, stated at a conference of the International Corporate Governance Network in 2001 that Toyota would stick to its own well-established system that did not include any outsiders. Sony, the first company to introduce executive officers separate from directors in 1996, was an early adopter of the new "American-style" board committee system. Some commentators have attributed the gradual and voluntary nature of Japanese corporate governance during the 2000s to a "Toyota effect" – the well-publicized economic success of Toyota under the traditional governance system, in contrast to the struggles of Sony, acting as a disincentive for Japanese companies to increase the number of outside directors or adopt the new board committee structure.

However, the following case studies of Toyota and Sony illustrate that either corporate governance structure can encounter difficulties, and that actual board and management functioning is arguably more important than board structure. In addition, focusing on contrasting board structures can result in oversimplification, since both companies have adapted over time to improve their board functioning in response to corporate governance issues …

Toyota

Toyota is Japan's largest company by revenue, a substantial employer, and arguably the most respected corporation in Japan. It is emblematic of Japanese manufacturing quality, with practices such as "just in time" and "lean" manufacturing being rendered in Japanese simply as the "Toyota Production System (*Toyota kanban hōshiki*)." The traditional board structure of all directors being experienced insiders representing different departments of the company [was] emphasized in Toyota's case by its emphasis on the role of senior managing directors (one from each department) acting as "bridges" connecting the board and management. This traditional structure did gradually evolve by, for example, a reduction in the number of directors in 2003.

The big impetus for more substantial reform was Toyota's recall problem related to unintended sudden acceleration that began in 2009 … In February 2010 problems with sudden unintended acceleration and other issues resulted in a recall of over six million vehicles in the United States and over eight million worldwide within a two-week period …

The fallout included additional recalls (totalling 10 million vehicles in the U.S. and 14 million worldwide) … ongoing investigations and enforcement … including the largest civil fine in the [US government] agency's history (U.S. $16.375 million), a spate of private lawsuits, and frantic efforts by Toyota to deal with the sudden crisis. A resulting criminal suit in the U.S. against Toyota was settled in 2014 for a payment of 1.2 billion dollars. Toyota eventually recovered economically …

Ensuing corporate governance reforms, announced in March 2011 and March 2013, included both executive and organizational changes. Outside directors were added to Toyota's board for essentially the first time in the company's history …

In 2015 Toyota also began to internationalize its top management team by promoting three non-Japanese to senior managing officer positions within Toyota Motor Corporation itself rather than merely in overseas subsidiaries …

Sony

Hopes were high for Sony when it became one of the early adopters of Japan's new, optional "American-style" board committee system of governance in 2003. In addition to a majority of outside directors, Sony announced early on that it would voluntarily conform to the New York Stock Exchange's definition of independence in determining its outside directors. Strengthening the monitoring function by the use of outside directors was the goal emphasized by foreign investors. But an equal, and perhaps more important, goal for Japanese companies was to formally introduce an executive officer system. This would speed up decision-making by delegating authority for daily operations from the board to officers, add transparency by moving authority formerly held by the president to the three committees, and make it easier for large multinational Japanese companies who have global networks to more readily manage their overseas operations.

Sony's biggest business challenge began in the early 2000s. All of Japan's formerly successful household electronics companies began facing increasing pressures …

For over a decade Sony's management was not up to the challenge. Sony was widely criticized for operating in "silos," i.e., each division worrying about its own products and employment without regard to overall corporate goals or strategy. Sony appointed a non-Japanese CEO, Howard Stringer, to lead the company from 2007–2012, to no avail.

A number of governance issues were raised with respect to Sony's board and the performance of its majority of independent directors. First, is the failure to monitor performance … Second, unsuccessful executives were … in effect, allowed to designate their successors – a serious problem at traditional Japanese companies that the committee structure, with its nomination committee dominated by independent directors, was designed to avoid. Finally … [a]s of 2012, only one of 10 independent directors had any relevant industry experience, only one independent director was new to the board … despite ongoing failures, and as seven of the 10 independent directors were also on at least three other boards, which raises the issue of their time … commitment to … Sony's operations.

[Sony finally began a successful turnaround in 2016–17]

Notes and Questions

1. Toshiba. Toshiba is another iconic name in Japan that encountered corporate governance problems. Toshiba occupied an interesting place in Japanese corporate governance by essentially developing an alternative hybrid system based on the "US-style" company with committees structure. It was intended as a "best of both worlds" system that made the committee structure more practical and effective for Japanese companies. The biggest feature of Toshiba's system was its insistence on the important role of former company officials (who do not formally qualify as independent or even as "outside" directors) to interact with truly independent directors to monitor management and cause effective board functioning.

   However, in 2015 Toshiba had its own scandal as it was discovered that the corporation had padded its profits by US$1.2 billion (150 billion yen) over the past six years. Following the scandal, Toshiba switched to a system with a majority of independent directors on the board. But another scandal emerged in December 2016 concerning multibillion dollar losses and accounting fraud at its US Westinghouse Electric unit that placed the survival of the entire company in question.
2. Prominent companies with different board structures in Japan have all experienced corporate governance scandals. Are these isolated cases, or do they suggest that corporate governance structure is not as important as has been assumed during long years of debate in Japan? If you think that the structure itself might not be so significant, then what is important for achieving "good" corporate governance in the Japanese context or elsewhere?

10.4 Ownership Structure

10.4.1 Cross-Shareholding

Tokyo Stock Exchange, 2016 Share Ownership Survey (2017), at 3

Table 10.1 Distribution percent of market value owned by type of shareholder (units: %)

Survey year	Govt. & local govt.	Financial institutions	City & regional banks	Trust banks	Investment trusts	Annuity trusts	Life insurance cos.	Non-life insurance cos.	Other fin. institutions	Securities companies	Business corps.	Foreigners	Individuals
1970	0.6	31.6	15.8	–	2.1	–	10.0	3.7	2.1	1.3	23.9	4.9	37.7
1975	0.4	35.5	19.0	–	2.2	–	10.2	4.4	2.0	1.4	27.0	3.6	32.1
1980	0.4	38.2	19.9	–	1.9	0.4	11.5	4.6	2.3	1.5	26.2	5.8	27.9
1985	0.3	39.8	20.9	–	1.7	0.8	12.3	4.1	2.4	1.9	28.8	7.0	22.3
1990	0.3	43.0	15.7	9.8	3.7	0.9	12.0	3.9	1.6	1.7	30.1	4.7	20.4
1991	0.3	42.8	15.6	9.7	3.4	1.0	12.2	3.9	1.4	1.5	29.0	6.0	20.3
1992	0.3	42.9	15.6	9.9	3.2	1.2	12.4	3.8	1.2	1.2	28.5	6.3	20.7
1993	0.3	42.3	15.4	10.0	2.9	1.4	12.1	3.7	1.1	1.3	28.3	7.7	20.0
1994	0.3	42.8	15.4	10.6	2.6	1.6	12.0	3.7	1.1	1.2	27.7	8.1	19.9
1995	0.3	41.1	15.1	10.3	2.2	1.8	11.1	3.6	1.0	1.4	27.2	10.5	19.5
1996	0.2	41.9	15.1	11.2	2.0	2.4	11.1	3.6	0.9	1.0	25.6	11.9	19.4
1997	0.2	42.1	14.8	12.4	1.6	3.8	10.6	3.5	0.9	0.7	24.6	13..4	19.0
1998	0.2	41.0	13.7	13.5	1.4	4.7	9.9	3.2	0.8	0.6	25.2	14.1	18.9
1999	0.1	36.5	11.3	13.6	2.2	5.0	8.1	2.6	0.9	0.8	26.0	18.6	18.0
2000	0.2	39.1	10.1	17.4	2.8	5.5	8.2	2.7	0.7	0.7	21.8	18.8	19.4
2001	0.2	39.4	8.7	19.9	3.3	6.0	7.5	2.7	0.7	0.7	21.8	18.3	19.7

Table 10.1 (cont.)

Survey year	Govt. & local govt.	Financial institutions	City & regional banks	Trust banks	Investment trusts	Annuity trusts	Life insurance cos.	Non-life insurance cos.	Other fin. institutions	Securities companies	Business corps.	Foreigners	Individuals
2002	0.2	39.1	7.7	21.4	4.0	5.8	6.7	2.6	0.7	0.9	21.5	17.7	20.6
2003	0.2	34.5	5.9	19.6	3.7	4.5	5.7	2.4	0.9	1.2	21.8	21.8	20.5
2004	0.2	32.0	5.2	18.4	3.8	3.9	5.2	2.2	1.0	1.2	22.1	23.3	21.3
2005	0.2	30.9	4.7	18.0	4.3	3.5	5.1	2.1	1.0	1.4	21.3	26.3	19.9
2006	0.3	30.7	4.6	17.6	4.6	3.5	5.3	2.2	1.0	1.8	20.8	27.8	18.7
2007	0.4	30.5	4.7	17.3	4.8	3.5	5.4	2.2	0.9	1.5	21.4	27.4	18.7
2008	0.4	32.0	4.8	18.8	5.0	3.5	5.3	2.1	0.9	1.0	22.6	23.5	20.5
2009	0.3	30.6	4.3	18.4	4.7	3.4	5.0	2.0	0.9	1.6	21.3	26.0	20.1
2010	0.3	29.7	4.1	18.2	4.4	3.2	4.5	1.9	1.0	1.8	21.2	26.7	20.3
2011	0.3	29.4	3.9	18.6	4.5	3.0	4.3	1.8	0.8	2.0	21.6	26.3	20.4
2012	0.2	28.0	3.8	17.7	4.5	2.5	4.1	1.6	0.8	2.0	21.7	28.0	20.2
2013	0.2	26.7	3.6	17.2	4.8	2.1	3.7	1.4	0.7	2.3	21.3	30.8	18.7
2014	0.2	27.4	3.7	18.0	4.8	1.8	3.6	1.4	0.7	2.2	21.3	31.7	17.3
2015	0.1	27.9	3.7	18.8	5.6	1.5	3.4	1.3	0.7	2.1	22.6	29.8	17.5
2016	0.1	28.4	3.5	19.6	6.3	1.3	3.4	1.2	0.7	2.2	22.1	30.1	17.1
High(Year)	0.9(1986)	44.1(1988)	20.9(1985)	21.4(2002)	6.3(2016)	6.0(2001)	12.8(1986)	4.8(1979)	2.6(1987)	2.3(1988)	30.3(1987)	31.7(2014)	37.7(1970)
Low(Year)	0.1(1999)	26.7(2013)	3.5(2016)	7.3(1986)	1.4(1998)	0.4(1982)	3.4(2016)	1.2(2016)	0.7(2016)	0.6(1998)	20.8(2006)	2.7(1978)	17.7(2016)

Note: The number of Trust Banks are included in that of City & Regional Banks in and before the 1985 Survey.

Hideaki Miyajima and Fumiaki Kuroki, 'The Unwinding of C-Shareholding in Japan: Causes, Effects, and Implications,' in Masahiko Aoki, Gregory Jackson, and Hideaki Miyajima (eds.), *Corporate Governance in Japan: Institutional Change and Organizational Diversity* (Oxford: Oxford University Press, 2007), pp. 79–80, 116–19

1. Introduction

The ownership structure of Japanese firms used to have the following characteristics: shares were highly dispersed, managers and foreigners owned only limited stakes in companies, and substantial blocks of shares were held by corporations and financial institutions. Cross-shareholding, or intercorporate shareholding between banks and corporations, and among corporations, was extensive, and played an in important role in distinguishing, at least until the early 1990s, Japan's ownership structure from that of other countries. Evolving from the postwar economic reforms, Japan's unique ownership structure had become well established by the late 1960s, mainly because top managers considered it to be effective in warding off hostile takeover threats. The remarkable stability of this ownership structure may explain why it lasted for almost three decades.

Cross-shareholding has also played a key role in supporting Japanese management and growth-oriented firm behavior in the postwar period. It encouraged the patterns of stable shareholding that have allowed managers to choose growth rates that deviated from the stock price maximization path and to adopt steady dividend policies that were insensitive to profit (with important implications for governance). Furthermore, the joint ownership of debt and equity by banks purportedly enhanced corporate performance by improving their monitoring of client firms and helping to mitigate asset substitution problems. The high level of ownership by non-financial institutions has also had a significant influence on the monitoring of Japanese companies.

The ownership structure that took root during the postwar period has undergone dramatic changes over the past decade, however. Foreign investors began to increase their stakes in Japanese companies in the early 1990s, especially in larger firms. And more recently, the ratio of shares held by stable shareholders (*antei kabunushi*) began to plummet from previous heights …

Why did the stable ownership structure begin to unwind in the late 1990s? The banking crisis was a crucial factor that directly led to the termination of many cross-shareholding arrangements between financial institutions and firms. After 1995, and especially since 1997, when the banking crisis came to the surface and grew acute, it became increasingly irrational for corporations to hold bank (financial institution) shares due to the high holding risk. Major commercial banks also began to sell off shares after the crisis mainly because of the need to secure funds to dispose of non-performing loans and to respond to BIS regulations. Because cross-shareholding is a mutual relationship, once one side decides to sell its partner's share, it is natural that the partner will respond and the unwinding will begin to accelerate.

However, it is worth noting that crucial changes were occurring prior to the banking crisis. First, large, highly profitable firms with outstanding credit ratings already depended on bonds and equities for their external financing. This eroded the simultaneous ownership of both debt and equity claims by Japanese banks. Second, foreign investors increased their stakes in these firms in the early 1990s. Subsequently, the share held by domestic institutional investors also rose. Institutional investors encouraged top managers to consider ROE and returns on investment. Third, it became evident that bank ownership was associated with low performance. This is possibly because higher bank ownership was associated with relaxed financial constraints, allowing firms to undertake more marginally acceptable investment opportunities.

These facts are extremely important because they explain the unevenness of the unwinding of cross-shareholding …

Managers of profitable firms with easy access to capital markets and high foreign ownership prior to the banking crisis found little need to maintain financial relationships with banks. This made the unwinding of cross-shareholdings a rational way to earn a high market valuation … [F]irms that actively reformed their boards of directors maintained high performance through capital market discipline. For low-profit firms with difficulty accessing capital markets and low foreign ownership in the early 1990s, cross-shareholding, in particular between banks and firms, was maintained since managers needed strong relationships with banks for both financing and to stabilize ownership. As a result, management discipline was sacrificed and this led to poor performance. These are the firms that are both reluctant to reform their boards of directors and still maintain main-bank relationships … They have fallen into a vicious circle of cross-shareholding and lax governance.

Notes and Questions

1. One distinguishing feature of Japan's corporate governance system has been cross-shareholding. Few controlling shareholders or even large block shareholders exist, and shares are, relatively speaking, widely dispersed. Nevertheless, company shares held for long periods in the hands of a substantial number of stable, "friendly" shareholders has led generally to Japan being classified together with Germany as a stakeholder system with influential "block" shareholders. Such a description may have been somewhat more accurate in the 1990s when "main banks" held substantial shares in their corporate customers. However, as noted above the shares of companies held by commercial banks has plummeted and they have largely been replaced by foreign shareholders.
2. Foreign activist investors still complain that the remaining management-friendly cross-shareholdings in Japan by industrial companies rather than banks, together with passive domestic institutional investors, continue to pose an obstacle not only to hostile takeovers but to all activist efforts to pressure management to adopt more shareholder-friendly policies. If that is true, does it mean that the unwinding of cross-shareholdings is unimportant?
3. Japan's corporate governance code (discussed at the end of this chapter) recommends that all companies with cross-shareholdings explain their policies behind such holdings, and this may put pressure, particularly on three megabanks, to reduce cross-shareholdings.

10.4.2 General Shareholder Meetings

Masanobu Iwatani and Toshio Taki, 'Evolution of General Shareholders' Meetings in Japan' (2010) 1 *Nomura Journal of Capital Markets*, http://ssrn.com/abstract=1423723

I. Introduction

Annual general meetings of shareholders (AGMs) in Japan have undergone a transformation over the past ten years. In the past, most of these meetings were rubber-stamp affairs with almost no opportunity for attendees to ask questions, and general shareholders did not give the AGM much thought. With shareholding racketeers (called *sōkaiya* in Japan) having become less active, however, meetings more open to the shareholders themselves have already become the norm. This trend toward more open AGMs has stoked greater interest in shareholder voting, and AGMs have begun to function as effective decision-making bodies …

II. From rubber-stamp meetings to meetings that are open to shareholders

1. AGMs open to shareholders

We define an AGM open to shareholders as a meeting that it is easy for regular shareholders to participate in. In the past, many companies held their AGMs on the last Thursday in June to make it harder for the *sōkaiya* to attend multiple AGMs, but meeting schedules have gradually become less concentrated ... it is now easier than it was before for shareholders to participate.

Secondly, the annual meeting has become a platform for investor relations (IR). At many companies, management now uses visual aids, such as PowerPoint presentations and videos, when explaining earnings and other details to shareholders, and executives have become more receptive to fielding questions. A growing number of companies are now encouraging individual investors to attend their shareholder meetings ...

Third, the AGMs are now designed so as to make it easier for nonresident shareholders to vote. Nonresident investors have long pointed out that, in addition to most AGMs being scheduled in late June, the short period between the time the notices are sent out and the day of the meeting does not leave enough time to closely review the proposals. A growing number of companies have responded to this complaint by sending meeting notices out early. After the commercial code was revised in 2001, there was an increase, albeit gradual, in the number of companies sending out notices and conducting shareholder votes electronically, and this is making it easier for nonresident shareholders to vote.

The opening of AGMs to regular shareholders resulted in an increase in both meeting attendance and the number of shareholder statements or questions, particularly from individual investors, and annual meetings are now taking longer to complete.

Bruce Aronson [writing anonymously], 'The Role of General Shareholder Meetings: Have Differences in Practice between the United States and Japan Disappeared?' (November 2012) *Shōji Hōmu Shiryōban*, at 32 [English translation of Japanese original]

Over the last few years I attended a number of general shareholder meetings of Japanese companies. My purpose was to compare current practice with what I observed decades ago. My Japanese friends who are legal professionals were surprised at my interest. "You will be bored," they said. In a sense they were right. But that is exactly what I found to be interesting.

Literature in the United States on general shareholder meetings in Japan was written some time ago and consistently focuses on the unusual role of *sōkaiya* in Japan ... There are no *sōkaiya* at general shareholder meetings, companies do not focus on the length of the meetings, and companies expect, and even welcome, questions from shareholders.

Today general shareholder meetings in Japan closely resemble those in the United States. The formal portion of the meeting to elect directors, etc., is only about 10 minutes. Most of the time is used by the chairman of the meeting (the president of the company) to explain the past year's business performance and the company's future business plans, aided by power point or video presentations. The information distributed to shareholders is extensive and roughly equivalent to that in the United States.

However, if general shareholder meetings are now "boring," largely because the main purpose – the election of directors and auditors – is decided far in advance due to proxy voting, then what is the purpose of holding general shareholder meetings? One often-stated reason is to increase communication with shareholders and provide them with an opportunity to question management. This is certainly true to some extent and can be valuable for shareholders in a company that has major problems. But it is less important in a typical general shareholders meeting.

The real purpose of ordinary general shareholders meetings today is the same in both the United States and Japan: it is an exercise in investor relations. Most of the time is spent by the president emphasizing the company's bright future prospects …

Although this investor relations function for general shareholder meetings may have originated in the United States, Japanese companies may now have surpassed U.S. companies in this regard. In Japan shareholders may appear at the place of a meeting just to receive presents and never attend the meeting. In addition, efforts by Japanese companies to attract individual shareholders now go well beyond the general shareholder meeting: the use of shareholder discount vouchers is at an all-time high. I was told, for example, that 70% of the shareholders of Keio railway live on the Keio line, since they are in a position to take full advantage of the discount coupons provided to shareholders.

The significant changes in Japanese practices related to general shareholder meetings are not generally known overseas, despite frequent criticisms of Japanese corporate governance …

Notes and Questions

1. Why were *sōkaiya* closely involved with general shareholders meetings in Japan? Is it a question of culture, institutions, or what?
2. Today there is no real involvement of *sōkaiya* in general shareholders meetings in Japan. What changed?
3. Today are general shareholder meetings in Japan very different from those in the United States. What is their main purpose?

10.5 Law and Enforcement

10.5.1 Shareholder Derivative Suits

Shiro Kawashima and Susumu Sakurai, 'Shareholder Derivative Litigation in Japan: Law, Practice, and Suggested Reforms' (1997) 33 *Stanford Journal of International Law* 9–60, at 10–11

In Japan, the shareholder derivative suit mechanism has recently attracted considerable attention. The reform of this mechanism, which was at the heart of the 1993 Japanese Commercial Code amendments, rejuvenated a forty-three year-old provision. With growing frequency, shareholders have been derivatively suing corporate directors for amounts unheard of in the past. The Daiwa shareholder suit is a perfect example of this form of recent shareholder activism in Japan. Increased use of the derivative suit has attracted the interest of business people, lawyers, and legal scholars …

While the increased use of the derivative suit mechanism represents renewed efforts to monitor the behavior of corporate management in Japan, it has also prompted some concern about the negative consequences of these suits. Some who have studied the history of the mechanism in the United States fear that derivative suits may have harmful effects. Some scholars claim that derivative actions have little impact on share prices and thus do not justify their costs. Moreover, recent research has found that any direct benefit to corporations appears very modest and may even be negative in some cases. Concern also exists that derivative suits offer greedy lawyers an opportunity to file frivolous lawsuits.

Japanese courts and commentators are concerned that recent reforms to the derivative suit mechanism will produce similar abuses in Japan. The 1993 Commercial Code amendments lowered and fixed the filing fees required to bring derivative actions, making the mechanism more accessible to shareholders. To dismiss meritless claims, Japanese courts have considered using the abuse of rights doctrine and the security for expenses provision in the Commercial Code. Courts are also trying to protect directors who have acted in good faith by importing the US business judgment rule, even though the Commercial Code does not explicitly authorize it …

With the dramatic increase in the number of derivative suits brought, Japanese courts are now struggling with procedural and substantive problems left unresolved in the statute, including plaintiff standing, access to information, res judicata, and settlement issues.

Bruce Aronson, 'Learning from Comparative Law in Teaching U.S. Corporate Law: Directors' Liability in Japan and the US' (2003) 22 *Penn State International Law Review* 213–42, at 222–7 [case study of the most significant shareholder derivative suit in Japan: *Daiwa Bank* case]

Factual Background to the Case

The tale begins with the 1976 hiring of Toshihide Iguchi as a local employee of the New York branch of the Daiwa Bank Limited ("Daiwa"). Presumably due to the miniscule size of the operation, Iguchi was later put in charge of both securities trading and custody as well as some related back office functions. He soon began to accumulate losses. He continued in unauthorized trades above the established limit in an attempt to recover the loss. Instead, losses steadily mounted, reaching $1.1 billion by the time the incident came to light in 1995. In order to conceal the growing losses, Iguchi began issuing unauthorized instructions to Bankers Trust (Daiwa's custodian) to sell customers' and the bank's securities. Iguchi's unauthorized trading (with some 30,000 trade confirmations) and sales of securities went undetected for eleven years; he ultimately sold some $377 million of customer securities.

Iguchi wrote a series of confession letters to Akira Fujita, the president of Daiwa, and other top officials in mid-July to early August of 1995. The very first of these letters to Daiwa's president dated July 17, Iguchi labeled his "honest confession." Up to that point Daiwa had been primarily a victim of unauthorized and unlawful actions by Iguchi. However, the actions of top management would shortly result in a new and legally more significant cover-up phase of the case.

Daiwa's president decided the bank's basic position, including maintaining secrecy, cooperating with Iguchi and reporting informally to the Japanese Ministry of Finance ("MOF"). There was reportedly no discussion of contacting U.S. authorities. On August 8, the president and other top executives of Daiwa met for dinner at the bank's guest house with the director general and the relevant section chief of MOF's Banking Bureau to report the matter. They described Iguchi's letter and the losses and asked about the timing of their write-off of the loss and public disclosure. The reported reply was that this was the worst time for such a financial scandal to be made public due to recent problems at a number of financial institutions and more general concerns about the state of the Japanese banking system. Daiwa's management believed that the government had agreed with its approach.

Once U.S. bank regulators and prosecutors learned of the loss, they levied the "death penalty" against Daiwa and Daiwa Trust, issuing consent orders requiring them to cease all U.S. banking business and surrender their banking licenses within 90 days …

Pressure on Daiwa gradually increased and it ultimately entered into a plea bargain on February 28, 1996 under which it pleaded guilty to 16 of the 24 counts in the indictment. The bank agreed to pay a criminal fine in the amount of $340 million, at that time the largest criminal fine levied on a financial institution in U.S. history … Although Daiwa and the branch general manager initially pleaded not guilty and claimed they were acting under the instructions of the Japanese government, they each entered into a plea bargain in order to resolve the matter …

Subsequently, shareholders of Daiwa filed two shareholder derivative suits with Japanese courts, to recover Iguchi's trading losses and the U.S. criminal fine (and legal fees) …

The Court's Decision

A. Summary

On September 20, 2000, the Osaka District Court, in a voluminous decision, ordered 11 of the defendants to pay a total of $775 million in damages in the two related cases. In Case A (the Trading Loss Case), the court found that the three directors who had been in charge of the New York branch during this time period and one Auditor were in breach of their duties. Proof of damages was found only for one defendant. He was found liable for the entire amount ($530 million) of the increase in Iguchi's trading losses which occurred during his tenure as director in charge of the New York branch. In Case B (the Violation of Law Case), the court found breaches of the duties of care and loyalty for 11 directors for specific illegal acts and failure to report, or cause the representative director to report, to U.S. authorities. Each of the 11 defendants was ordered to pay 20–70% of the total of $350 million (i.e., $70 million–$245 million).

Both sides appealed from the judgment of the district court; however, on December 20, 2001, a settlement was reached to end the dispute.

Dan Puchniak and Masafumi Nakahigashi, 'Japan's Love for Derivative Actions, Irrational Behavior and Non-Economic Motives as Rational Explanations for Shareholder Litigation' (2012) 45 *Vanderbilt Journal of Transnational Law* 1 (abstract)

Not long ago, there was a consensus in the legal academy that the Japanese were irrational litigants. As the theory went, Japanese people would forgo litigating for financial gain because of a cultural obsession with maintaining social harmony. Based on this theory, it made perfect (but economically irrational) sense that Japanese shareholders let their U.S.-transplanted derivative action lay moribund for almost four post-war decades …

The 1980s brought a wave of law and economics to the scholarship of Japanese law, which largely discredited the cultural explanation for Japan's (economically irrational) reluctant litigant. In this new academic era, reasonable minds could disagree as to whether the efficiency of settlement or high cost of litigation explained the dearth of litigation in Japan. However, the assumption that the Japanese litigant was economically motivated and rational (i.e., that they would litigate only when the financial benefit from doing so exceeded the cost) was virtually beyond reproach.

In the early 1990s, the number of derivative actions in Japan skyrocketed. Japanese shareholders suddenly found themselves as strange bedfellows with their American counterparts as the only shareholders of listed companies in the world that utilized the derivative action on a regular basis. This extraordinary change in the behavior of Japanese shareholders has largely been understood through the lens of the economically motivated and rational shareholder litigant.

This Article challenges the assumption ... Using original empirical and case study evidence, this Article demonstrates that in Japan, neither shareholders nor attorneys stand to gain significant financial benefits from derivative actions. To the contrary, this Article suggests that the non-economic motives (i.e., political and environmental motives and veiled extortion) and irrational behavior of Japanese shareholders (i.e., the use of inaccurate mental heuristics, self-serving bias, and herding behavior) are critical for providing an accurate explanation for one of the most dramatic increases in shareholder litigation in recent times. This revelation further suggests that the leading literature on shareholder litigation – which forms the basis for the current understanding of shareholder litigation in the United States – is flawed, as it overlooks the critically important role that noneconomic motives and irrational behavior play in driving shareholder lawsuits.

Notes and Questions

1. Who is the main beneficiary of shareholder derivative suits in Japan? Who has an incentive to bring such a suit, and what is that incentive? Is the situation in Japan different from that in the US, which is the source of Japanese law on shareholder derivative suits?
2. In the *Daiwa* case, the court found that a director's fiduciary duties include a duty of oversight within the basic duty of care, i.e. the board must construct appropriate policies and systems to ensure that mid-level and other employees do not violate the law. Should each director bear responsibility for oversight, or can some directors rely on the position and experience of other directors? How easy was it to find out Iguchi's unauthorized activities? What should the bank have done once the top management found out?

3. What about Daiwa's argument that the Japanese government informally authorized Daiwa to postpone disclosure of Iguchi's losses? What would you have made of that argument if you were the judge?
4. A substantial number of shareholder derivative suits in Japan have arisen over the last two decades – not nearly as many as the US, but significantly more than countries like Germany or other Asian countries. Do you suppose that this has a significant impact on corporate governance? Is it something to be considered by other countries in Asia? Note that in Australia (see Chapter 5) and Taiwan (see Chapter 12) government-related entities are involved in filing suits on behalf of shareholders unlike in Japan.

10.5.2 Hostile Takeovers and Defenses

Curtis Milhaupt, 'Takeover Law and Managerial Incentives in the United States and Japan,' in Zenichi Shishido (ed.), *Enterprise Law: Contracts, Markets, and Laws in the US and Japan* (Cheltenham, UK and Northampton, MA: Edward Elgar, 2014), pp. 182–7

The market for corporate control was not active during Japan's post-war high-growth period. In the post-war corporate governance regime, publicly traded firms were typically affiliated with a corporate group (keiretsu) with a major bank at the center. Group-affiliated firms cross-held shares of their affiliates, forming stable, friendly investor relationships involving significant percentages of the public float. Investor activism was rare and hostile takeover activity was condemned as antithetical to Japanese business norms, which conceptualizes the firm as a community of employees rather than an assemblage of financial assets to be bought and sold. But the situation began to change in the 2000s, as patterns of share ownership, the composition of corporate shareholders, and investor activism all began to change. Given the dearth of market activity, it is not surprising that until this period the legal regime for takeover regulation was minimalist. Indeed, Japan's relatively blank institutional slate as hostile takeovers began to occur in the early 2000s is loosely equivalent to the situation just described in the United States in the early 1980s …

In 2005, two simultaneous developments significantly altered this institutional landscape. In the spring of that year, a hostile bid involving two Japanese firms transfixed the public. The target company, Nippon Broadcasting, took defensive measures to defeat a hostile tender offer from Livedoor Corporation. Livedoor sued, and the courts ruled that the defensive measures were "grossly unfair" and thus invalid. In affirming the lower court's decision to enjoin the defenses, the Tokyo

High Court ruled that where a hostile bidder has an "abusive motive," defensive measures may be used to protect the interests of shareholders if they are necessary and proportionate …

A second development in Japanese takeover policy was culminating just as the Livedoor ruling was issued. In 2004, "in light of concerns about the steady rise of hostile bids," the Ministry of Economy, Trade, and Industry (METI) and the Ministry of Justice (MOJ) jointly established the Corporate Value Study Group (CVSG) composed of legal and policy experts to consider an appropriate policy response to hostile takeover activity. The CVSG conducted extensive research on Anglo-American takeover defenses and legal precedents and issued a report in March 2005, in the midst of the Livedoor bid …

Based on the report, non-binding Takeover Guidelines were jointly issued by METI and MOJ in May 2005. The Takeover Guidelines embrace three fundamental principles. First, adoption, activation, and removal of defensive measures should be undertaken to maintain or improve corporate value. Second, defensive measures should be adequately disclosed when adopted, and should be based upon the reasonable will of the shareholders. Third, defensive measures should be necessary and reasonable. The guidelines explicitly endorse the use of a shareholder rights plan as a defensive measure under Japanese corporate law. But, in a major departure from US law and practice, the Takeover Guidelines strongly recommend (but do not require) advance shareholder approval of defensive measures as a means of their ensuring fairness.

With the guidelines and the emergence of new judicial doctrine, Japan suddenly had a new, if still incomplete, institutional framework for hostile acquisitions …

As noted, a key element of the Takeover Guidelines is their endorsement of the shareholder rights plan, a distinctly American takeover defense. Promulgation of the guidelines sparked a small stampede by Japanese firms to adopt defensive measures. By 2011, 465 public companies, approximately 20 percent of companies traded on the Tokyo Stock Exchange (TSE), adopted a pill-like defense plan.

However, unlike the US shareholder rights plan, in Japan the overwhelming majority of defensive mechanisms are "pre-warning rights plans." This is not a legal instrument; it is a public statement in the form of a press release by the board setting forth the procedures to be followed should an acquirer contemplate a large-scale acquisition of the company's shares. The statement declares that if an acquirer starts an acquisition or takeover bid that would result in the acquirer holding a specified percentage (typically 20 percent) of the target company's outstanding shares, the target board will establish a special committee to evaluate the bid. If the committee determines that the bid would damage "corporate value of the company or the common interests of shareholders" (the typical formulation of the press release), it will recommend that the board issue warrants to shareholders other than the bidder so as to dilute the bidder's holdings.

Japanese defensive measures took on this distinctive, and highly uniform, cast due to the influence of another important actor in the takeover landscape: the Tokyo Stock Exchange. After the publication of the CVSG 2005 Report and Takeover Guidelines, the TSE published policy statements and listing standards formally incorporating the non-binding principles of the Takeover Guidelines. To ensure the effectiveness of the listing standards, the TSE requires that firms consult with it before adopting defensive measures. Firms that fail to do so, or whose defensive measures are deemed by the TSE to violate the listing standards, are subject to public criticism by the exchange, and ultimately to delisting if corrective action is not taken. Thus, the TSE's listing rules and policy statements have become the de facto mandatory rules governing takeover defenses for Japanese listed companies.

Importantly, promulgation of the Takeover Guidelines and the TSE's involvement in the adoption of takeover defenses did not eliminate the role of Japanese courts in takeover-related disputes. Because the pre-warning plan adopted by most Japanese firms lacks legal effect (as it is simply a press release issued before the appearance of any bidders), questions of legal validity may arise when the plan is actually triggered and warrants are actually issued in response to an unsolicited bid, as well as when a company without a pre-warning plan adopts a defensive measure in response to a particular unsolicited bid. The latter scenario generated an important, and highly controversial, set of judicial decisions: the Bull-Dog Sauce case.

In May 2007, US private equity fund Steel Partners launched a tender offer for a small, publicly listed Japanese condiment maker called Bull-Dog Sauce. The board of directors of Bull-Dog Sauce, with the support of employees, opposed the tender offer and sought to defeat it by issuing warrants to shareholders exercisable into additional common shares. Although as a shareholder Steel Partners would also receive warrants, they could be exercised only for cash, not shares. The proposal was approved by over 80 percent of the outstanding shares – virtually all shares other than those held by Steel Partners.

Steel Partners sued to enjoin the warrant issuance. The case made its way to the Supreme Court after the District Court's dismissal of the request for a preliminary injunction was affirmed on appeal. The Supreme Court also affirmed, concluding that the warrant issuance was necessary and reasonable. Like the District Court, the Supreme Court reasoned that it is for the shareholders to determine whether damage would arise upon acquisition of control by a particular shareholder. Accordingly, the court should respect the determination of shareholders unless there is a material defect in their decision-making process. Given the overwhelming shareholder approval, almost all shareholders other than Steel Partners had agreed that the defensive measure was necessary to prevent damage to corporate value. Thus, the allocation of warrants under the circumstances was not unreasonable or unfair under the corporate law. As a result, the Steel Partners bid was defeated, but it was entitled to a cash payment of just over ¥2.3 billion (about $19 million at then prevailing exchange rates).

This ruling was met with jeers by the foreign investment community, which viewed the decision as confirmation that corporate Japan remained insular and unwelcoming to foreign investment. Some domestic commentators, including the CVSG, also appeared to disapprove of at least the larger implications of the case … With an understated but unmistakable tone of concern that the Takeover Guidelines had been (mis)interpreted by management and even by the courts as approving any defensive step so long as shareholder approval were obtained, the 2008 report notes that "adopting defensive measures in accordance with the Guidelines does not mean that their implementation is permitted unconditionally." The 2008 report discourages payoffs to bidders by target management of the kind made in the Bull-Dog Sauce contest. More pointedly, the CVSG opines, "[t]akeover defensive measures that are … exploited for the purpose of managerial entrenchment should not be allowed."

Notes and Questions

1. Who should decide whether a company utilizes takeover defenses? The board of directors or the shareholders?
2. What is "corporate value?"
3. Should the Japanese government be issuing guidelines or regulations regarding takeover defenses or should such issues be left to courts?
4. Some foreign investors claim that it is not possible to accomplish a hostile takeover in Japan, and this harms the market. Why would hostile takeovers not be possible? Is it primarily a question of law or other norms and practices? Does a lack of hostile takeovers harm Japan?

10.6 Recent Developments: Abenomics and the New Role of Soft Law in Corporate Governance

During much of the postwar era in Japan, US business law, including corporate law and corporate governance, was the main model for reform. However, dominance of the US model arguably ended with the financial crisis of 2008. In recent years Japan has focused more on soft law approaches, more characteristic of the UK tradition.

Ongoing trends in the reform of Japanese corporate governance were accelerated beginning in December 2012 with the formation of the Abe cabinet and its well-known "Abenomics." Japan's growth strategy highlighted corporate governance reform as an important part of structural reform. The most significant changes were made under the new soft law approach, including the adoption of a Stewardship Code in February 2014, and the implementation of a Corporate Governance Code in June 2015.

The voluntary Stewardship Code recommends constructive dialogue between companies and shareholders. The biggest difference with the UK Stewardship Code was Japan's excusing institutional investors from disclosing individual votes in exercising proxy voting with respect to portfolio companies; however, a revision to the code in May 2017 states that institutional investors should disclose voting on an agenda item basis, and explain the reasons if they do not.

In the Corporate Governance Code, the clearest principle is that listed companies should have two independent directors. Japanese companies are also required to disclose their policies in a number of new and significant areas of corporate governance, including separation of management and monitoring function, advice on nomination and compensation from independent directors (e.g. via committees), succession planning for company president, cross-shareholding, and capital allocation.

Both codes have been widely implemented. Within two years nearly 80 percent of First Section listed companies have complied with the principle that listed companies have two independent directors as opposed to 22 percent in 2014 prior to the Corporate Governance Code. However, concerns remain about whether the "voluntary" codes may appear compulsory to prominent Japanese companies and whether Japanese companies will seriously reconsider important corporate governance issues or whether their code compliance is more a formality of "checking the box."

Other significant corporate governance developments would include the first amendment of the Companies Act in 2014 and the Tokyo Stock Exchange's creation of a new stock index in January 2014, the JPX-Nikkei 400, composed of large Japanese companies with good corporate governance, as determined by measures such as return on equity.

One reason for the new willingness of Japanese companies to respond to corporate governance reform is a business need: a number of large, complex, and increasingly global leading Japanese companies must refocus the board of directors toward strategic issues such as capital allocation among their various lines of business (and away from daily management decisions). One example of voluntary reforms to achieve more efficient decision-making is the substantial reduction in the average number of board members of listed companies to 7.50 members as of 2015, which is a reform that was not mandated by law or stock exchange rule.

Since the enactment of the Stewardship and Corporate Governance Codes, a popular anecdote is that there has been a "change in the conversation" regarding corporate governance, i.e. Japanese companies now engage with shareholders, particularly foreign shareholders, on issues such as dividends and capital allocation policy. This contrasts with the attitude of Japanese management five years ago, when companies may have dismissed the complaints of foreigners as concerns related to "short-term" investors rather than to long-term shareholders who consider the best interests of the company. Time will tell if such trend continues to develop.

Statutes and Regulators

Statutes

Companies Act (Law No. 86 of 2005, as amended)
Financial Instruments and Exchange Act (Law No. 25 of 1948, as amended; renamed the Financial Instruments and Exchange Act in 2006)

Soft Law

Corporate Governance Code
Stewardship Code

Regulators

Financial Services Agency (FSA)
Securities and Surveillance Commission (within the FSA)
Tokyo Stock Exchange
Ministry of Justice

11

KOREA

Joongi Kim

11.1 Introduction

Compared with other countries in the region, corporate governance in Korea consists of a complex mixture of unique features, challenges, and innovations. Historically, it hails from a government-led, stakeholder-oriented system with civil law origins. In the aftermath of the 1997 Asian financial crisis, its legal and regulatory framework received a massive transplantation of measures usually associated with shareholder-oriented, common law jurisdictions such as the US. Korean corporate governance significantly improved, given that during the time of the crisis an appropriate translation of the term "corporate governance" did not even exist. Legal and regulatory reforms have contributed to make Korean companies more transparent and their boards and managers more accountable.

Yet, in recent years, as reforms have stagnated, Korea's corporate governance has lagged behind other markets in the region. According to the Asian Corporate Governance Association's 2016 annual ranking, since 2012, out of eleven Asian countries surveyed, Korea still ranks eighth, not only below Hong Kong, Singapore, and Japan but also behind Thailand, Malaysia, Taiwan, and India. Other than its accounting and audit standards, it consistently ranks lower in terms of four core categories that are analyzed in the annual rankings: corporate governance rules practices, public and private enforcement, political and regulatory environment (such as government policy, regulators, the judiciary, and media), and governance culture in terms of voluntary efforts to improve. Despite economic success, poor corporate governance has led to a dreaded "Korean discount" under which Korean companies are undervalued and suffer from among the lowest price-to-earnings ratios in the region. In the eyes of investors, creditors, and analysts, corporate Korea does not instill governance-related confidence.

In principle, good corporate governance has become an essential goal for all companies. The degree that companies need to be "pushed" to this state of affairs or will be "pulled" to the attractions it offers, however, remains a key challenge. Many controlling shareholders and insiders still view corporate governance reforms as regulatory costs that chill business decisions instead of being considered as a means to enhance corporate value.

The biggest issue remains how to improve the corporate governance of Korea's largest companies that are part of family-controlled conglomerates called the chaebol. The ten largest conglomerates accounted for more than half of the market capitalization and the thirty largest conglomerates account for over 80 percent of operating profits among listed companies. Two companies in particular, Samsung Electronics and Hyundai Motors, together accounted for almost 40 percent of all operating profits of listed companies. The primary focus of corporate governance policy, therefore, will be large listed companies (LLCs), primarily from the chaebol, with over KRW 2 trillion (USD 1.7 billion) in assets.

From a regulatory standpoint, the Korean Commercial Act (CA), Financial Investment Services and Capital Markets Acts (CMA), Monopoly Regulation and Fair Trade Act (FTA), KRX listing regulations, the Korean Corporate Governance Code (CGC), and the newly established Stewardship Code are among the key laws, regulations, and codes. In the case of the CGC, however, it does not benefit from a comply-or-explain rule.

11.2 Purpose: from a State-Oriented to Shareholder-Oriented Model?

In Korea, the development of corporate governance can be best understood through a review of the rise of the chaebol, the large family-controlled conglomerates that dominate much of the traditional economy. From the 1960s and 1970s, Korean policymakers designed the chaebol to serve as the engine behind Korea's economic development, giving rise to a state-oriented model of corporate governance. With the decline of the role of the state, however, Korea has arguably transitioned to a shareholder-oriented model, given that the interests of other stakeholders are not explicitly considered.

Joongi Kim, 'A Forensic Study of Daewoo's Corporate Governance: Does Responsibility for the Meltdown Solely Lie with the Chaebol and Korea?' (2008) 28 *Northwestern Journal of International Law & Business* 273, 283–7

C. Chaebol Business Practice and Culture

The chaebols that dominated the South Korean economy shared many common features. Nurtured under the government's industrial-growth policy, they followed the same financing methods, business models, ownership structures, and operating practices. A state-oriented corporate governance modus operandi prevailed, as the country unified behind the chaebols according to the dictates of policymakers. Interested parties such as shareholders, employees, consumers, and managers received secondary priority given the nation's collective focus on economic development and employment during the 1960s and 1970s.

Under a state-oriented corporate governance system, the government operated in an intertwined, symbiotic relationship with the chaebols. Chaebols operated according to government policies, because following these policies allowed them to receive "preferential policy loans, tax credits, subsidies, protection and even bailouts when [they] got into financial trouble." The Korean government provided management friendly labor laws, condoned monopolies and oligopolies, gave out special licenses and permits, and set up trade and investment barriers to foreign competition. Chaebols received favorable treatment as long as they performed reasonably well. From one perspective, Korea's economic success evinces the merits of such industrial policies based upon close industrial and government cooperation. At its worst, however, such collusion led to illegal rent-seeking and predation. In the most egregious example, a dozen leading chaebol chairmen … contributed over 510 billion won ($638 million) in bribes during the 1980s and early 1990s to two Korean presidents during that period. These chairmen claimed they could not defy the presidents' solicitations for slush funds, yet the chaebols derived significant benefits in return. Policymakers also protected the control of chaebol families. Initially, like other Asian companies, families held a large, concentrated ownership in their companies. In the 1970s, however, the government browbeat chaebols into listing their major companies on the stock exchange. Listing by chaebols served two governmental purposes. First, compelling chaebol families to disperse their ownership to the public would lead to sharing of the benefits that chaebols received from the special preferences. Second, rights offering served to provide much-needed liquidity to the fledgling stock market. Families initially resisted listing their companies out of concerns that dispersion of their ownership could threaten their control. With generous indirect financing available from banks, the companies also had little need for equity financing. To convince them, the government decided to protect chaebols from the threats to ownership control by curbing shareholder and stakeholder rights for acquiring control and challenging board decisions …

During the period Korea was rapidly developing, chaebols routinely engaged in related-party transactions among affiliates. In fact, intraconglomerate assistance among affiliates without regard to corporate governance of individual companies was a common practice. Not only was such practice not punished, governmental administrative guidance often required affiliate support for risky but strategically important companies as a condition for receiving bank loans. Stronger companies helped start-ups and rescued troubled affiliates through equity infusions, debt guarantees, and transfer pricing, on non-market terms, according to the mandates of governmental policy. In the worst cases, controlling families or senior managers of the company used related-party deals to engage in self-dealing and to extract other private benefits of control …

Chaebols adhered to the "too-big-to-fail (*dae-ma-bul-sa*)" doctrine. Through their network of companies, they accounted for a predominant share of the country's employment, production, income, and exports. Their impact on the economy was multiplied considering downstream and upstream industries, suppliers, outsourcers, transporters, retailers, and distributors. Conventional belief under the doctrine held that bureaucrats did not have the nerve to endure the political costs and social dislocation generated by permitting the collapse of a chaebol, particularly one of the largest ones. Market participants therefore clung to this myth. Sophisticated investors, creditors, and reputational intermediaries, domestic and foreign alike, downplayed the importance of good corporate governance, because they believed chaebols had a sovereign guarantee from "Korea, Inc." Meanwhile, these beliefs nurtured a moral hazard that led chaebols to increase their sizes and assume undue risks because they believed that they could rely upon the government's safety net.

Notes and Questions

1. What are the unique challenges of corporate governance in Korea, particularly those related to large conglomerates called the chaebol that dominate the economy? What is the best way to reform the corporate governance of companies that are part of a chaebol conglomerate? Should there be special regulations just for the chaebol? Currently, the Korea Fair Trade Commission (KFTC) imposes special regulations on the largest conglomerates that include restrictions on circular ownership, related party transactions, and holding company structures.
2. How best can a country transition from a state-oriented form of corporate governance to another type of model?
3. Should Korea transition to a full-fledged shareholder-oriented model or adopt an enlightened shareholder value approach like the UK or go even further like India or some other type of model?

11.3 Board Function

11.3.1 Basics

In terms of corporate governance, the CA provides three important company organs to govern the corporation: the general shareholders' meeting, management (consisting of directors, the board of directors, and the representative directors), and internal statutory auditors. In theory, shareholders appoint and dismiss both directors who oversee management and internal auditors who audit management. In practice, the general shareholders' meeting has limited decision-making power and routinely approves the nominations and agenda items proposed by management.

Controlling shareholders instead dominate affairs, including the boards. Few listed companies have bona fide separation of ownership and control and are operated by professional managers. The controlling shareholder's disproportionate concentration of power stands as one of the key corporate governance challenges in Korea.

Although Korea's legal system originates from German civil law, Korea does not provide for co-determination through labor representatives. Nor does it require a separate supervisory board, but it does require an internal statutory auditor that derives from Japan's ***kansayaku***. Under a one-tier board system, directors and the statutory auditor are elected by shareholders. Over the years, the size of listed boards has decreased, and with an average of fewer than six directors per board.

Under the CA, to incorporate the interests of shareholders at large and as a means to provide a check and balance against controlling shareholders, companies must elect directors through cumulative voting. Companies, however, can opt out of the requirement through their articles of incorporation. As of April 2016, for instance, only eight companies out of the 165 listed companies that are associated with the largest twenty-five conglomerates have adopted cumulative voting.

Most Korean boards remain dominated by men. Legislative or regulatory initiatives to try to correct the gender imbalance have not survived. Among leading economies around the world, at 3 percent, Korea has the lowest proportion of women on listed companies. In 2016, among the ten largest chaebols, only 1.7 percent of the directors were women. The number of women who are chairs of boards or CEOs is even lower. The CGC only provides that companies should establish a board that is diverse in terms of knowledge, experience, and capability and does not specifically mention gender.

As of 2014, LLCs must disclose the compensation of registered and non-registered directors where it exceeds KRW 500 million a year (approximately US$ 440,000). Previously, only the combined amount was disclosed. Unlike in other countries, executive compensation has not been a major issue. According to a 2017 study, average compensation of directors was only seven times greater than the average employee.

11.3.2 Outside Directors and Committees

Securing the independence of outside directors remains an important step toward effective oversight and management. For LLCs, in particular, securing outside directors independent of controlling shareholders and their family members is considered critical. Outside directors first became mandatory after the Asian financial crisis of 1997–8. LLCs with total assets that are KRW 2 trillion (approximately US$ 1.7 billion) or more must have three or more outside directors and they must comprise more than half of the board. For smaller companies, only one-quarter have to be outside directors. A recent survey from CEO Score Daily found that 43.2 percent of outside directors were former government officials, 30.9 percent were academics, 13.7 percent were corporate professionals, 3.5 percent from the media, 2.4 from public entities, 2 percent from the accounting profession, 1.8 percent from the legal profession, and 0.3 percent were politicians.

LLCs must also establish audit committees and nominating committees with outside directors. LLC audit committees must have three or more outside directors and the outside directors must comprise more than two-thirds of the members. Banks, large insurance companies, and large investment business firms have the same requirements. Unlike in many countries, audit committees not only audit financial matters but also managerial decisions. Smaller listed companies may choose to establish an audit committee to replace the statutory auditor. For nomination committees, half of the members must be outside directors and nominees proposed by minority shareholders must be included. According to a 2015 report, out of 710 listed companies surveyed, 147 companies established nomination committees but only twenty-two companies voluntarily established them, whereas the rest were required to do so. Although not mandatory, approximately 30 percent of LLCs have established internal transaction and compensation committees.

Given that they rarely vote against management proposals, criticism persists that outside directors lack independence. One survey found that overall 79 percent of outside directors were ultimately recommended by controlling shareholders. According to a 2016 survey of the companies in the twenty-six largest conglomerates, for instance, only 0.4 percent of the board agenda items were not passed due to opposition from outside directors. Outside directors contend that this statistic underestimates their influence because many agendas will be changed or withdrawn due to their input before being tabled for a vote.

11.3.3 Legal Duties, Liabilities, and de facto Directors

Under the CA which also refers to the Korean Civil Act, directors have a duty of care under which each director also has a duty to oversee other directors and employees (CA, Art. 382(2) and Civil Act, Art. 681). Directors must do their utmost to observe the duties of prudence and faithfulness expected of a proper manager. They must perform their duties in the best interests of the company. The CGC recommends that directors perform their duties in the best interests of the company and its shareholders, while being impartial to all shareholders. Directors may also be liable for a breach of the duty of oversight when the company suffers damages due to other directors' acts. Directors also owe a duty of loyalty (CA Arts. 382–3).

Directors who have violated laws or the articles of incorporation or have neglected to perform their duties are jointly and severally liable for damages to the company. Unique when compared to many jurisdictions, directors in Korea who have neglected to perform their duties willfully or by gross negligence can be held jointly and severally liable for damages to third persons such as creditors (CA, Art. 410).

Korean courts have adopted principles similar to the business judgment rule. Managerial decisions made based on due diligence and rational judgments will not be subject to civil liability. The CA also allows companies to set a limit on director liability based on a certain multiple of annual compensation by amendments to their articles of incorporation depending on whether one is an insider or outside director. Directors who have willfully or by gross negligence neglected to perform their duties, or who have failed to comply with the duties of avoiding self-dealing, competition with the company, or corporate opportunity do not qualify for the limitation of liability.

Controlling shareholders are not subject to fiduciary duties such as the duty of care or loyalty. Controlling shareholders may not be formally appointed as directors, but still control an entire conglomerate. Technically, a controlling shareholder participating in the business of company by, for instance, instructing a director or holding a title of authority such as chair or president can be deemed a de facto director and held liable to the company and third persons, but this rarely occurs (CA, Arts. 401–2).

Notes and Questions

1. How should inside and outside directors be elected and how should boards be organized to provide better checks and balances against the controlling shareholder?
2. What can be done to strengthen board committees or the statutory auditor? What kind of incentives or disincentives could be considered?
3. Among major economies in the world, Korean companies have among the lowest percentage of women on their boards. Not only does Korea not have gender quotas, the country does not mention this as a goal even under its corporate governance codes or best practices. Should gender diversity and other forms of diversity on the board be considered and encouraged? If so, how? Should it be mandated like in India or at least promoted as best practice as in Australia?
4. Should the liability of directors be subject to limitations?
5. Related-party transactions are subject to disclosure requirements, but Korea is the only Asian market where shareholder approval is not needed and only a two-thirds board approval is required. Should this be changed?

11.4 Ownership Structure

11.4.1 Corporate and Conglomerate Ownership

As of 2013, foreign ownership accounts for approximately 32.9 percent of Korea's listed companies. Non-financial corporations then account for 24.1 percent; individuals, 23.6 percent; institutional investors, 16.1 percent; and, government and public institutions, 3.3 percent. Among institutional investors, banks represent 3.6 percent; pension funds, 3.99; collective investment vehicles, 4.96 percent, and insurance companies 2.75 percent. Overall, the decline in government and public institution ownership has been met with an increase in foreign ownership and non-financial corporate ownership. Foreign ownership is close to 50 percent for many of Korea's leading blue-chip companies. Overall, 95 percent of Korea's listed companies are family-controlled, but not necessarily family-owned, representing among the highest percentages not only in Asia but among OECD countries.

For the chaebols, a prominent feature was their unique ownership structure that was linked through cross-ownership among related companies and control by founding families with small personal stakes. The "owner" of the conglomerate, typically held a meager portion of shares but controlled the portions held by other affiliate companies within the group. No separation between ownership and control existed. Among the 1,519 affiliated companies associated with the forty-three largest family-controlled conglomerates, for instance, controlling shareholders did not own any shares in 85.9 percent of the same but still maintained control. This anomalous structure combined the controlling features of concentrated ownership found in continental European countries with quasi-dispersion based on the small stakes of "controlling" owners as associated with the US and UK. These "owners" with small stakes naturally developed incentives to pursue private benefits of control such as tunneling and improper related party transactions.

To try to contain the peculiar agency problems that arose out of this ownership structure, KFTC imposes special regulations on conglomerates with combined assets of at least KRW 5 trillion (US$ 4.25 billion). Cross-shareholding within these conglomerates is restricted and substantial internal transactions must be disclosed. KFTC releases information concerning the conglomerate's governance structures, shareholding structure, directors with family ties to the owner, and cases where minority shareholders exercised their rights. Guarantees of obligations and voting rights of financial or insurance companies are also restricted. The government also tried to tackle the ownership conundrum by encouraging conglomerates to transition to vertically holding company models. To qualify, the mother company of a conglomerate must own 20 percent of subsidiaries that are listed companies and 40 percent if they are unlisted. As of September 2017, a total of 183 holding companies have been established, consisting of 173 general holding companies and ten financial holding companies. Many believe that the holding company structures have helped curtail improper subsidization and tunneling of stronger companies to support weaker companies and abuse of private benefits of control.

As of 2017, the web of cross-ownership remains most pronounced at several of the largest LLCs such as the Samsung Group, Hyundai Motors Group, Hyundai Heavy Industries Group, and the Lotte Group, with significant decoupling occurring in the smaller conglomerates. Overall, only eight conglomerates out of fifty-two remain subject to special regulation arising out of the circular ownership. In contrast, smaller and medium-sized companies have simpler ownership structures with family ownership in the form of larger blockholders.

11.4.2 Bank Ownership

Over the past two decades, perhaps the most significant change in terms of corporate ownership has occurred in banks and non-bank financial institutions. First, after consolidations and mergers, the number of commercial banks declined from twenty-six in 1997 to nine financial holding companies or banks in 2015. Major banks, that were once state-owned and strongly state-influenced, are now largely dominated by portfolio and strategic foreign ownership. Excluding Woori Bank which is scheduled to be privatized and JB Financial Holdings, foreign ownership exceeds half of all banks or financial holding companies. Meanwhile, Korea maintains bank ownership restrictions such that a single shareholder can own only up to 10 percent unless special approval is obtained. For non-financial industry-linked companies, such as industrial companies, ownership is limited to 4 percent.

The ownership changes transformed governance in the banking sector and its repercussions have affected all corporations. Banks consistently receive the highest corporate governance ratings. Commercial banks outrank other non-bank financial institutions and listed firms in general in terms of shareholder rights, board performance, transparency, and auditing. Banks must have audit committees, outside director nominating committees, compliance officers, and are encouraged to have risk management committees. Sixty-nine percent of outside directors are considered to be independent from the bank's CEO or the controlling shareholder, and several financial holding companies and banks have even adopted cumulative voting. At the same time, banks have become more active monitors of the governance of corporate borrowers. They utilize their informational advantage as creditors, maintain early detection systems and take prompt corrective action against the governance risks of borrowers. Their demands have increasingly prompted companies to improve their governance.

11.4.3 Shareholder Rights

E. Han Kim and Woochan Kim, 'Changes in Korean Corporate Governance: A Response to Crisis' (2008) 20(1) *Journal of Applied Corporate Finance* 47–58

Korean shareholders have been traditionally passive as with other shareholders in Asian countries. In principle, they can legally exercise a variety of rights but, other than a limited number of instances, seldom have. Shareholder rights range from nominating outside directors to demanding cumulative voting and seeking injunctions against board decisions. Minority shareholders with at least 0.5 percent of shares, for instance, may recommend an outside director and such a person must be nominated to the shareholder's meeting by the outside director nominating committee as a potential candidate. Furthermore, when electing outside directors to serve on the audit committee the vote of large shareholders is capped at 3 percent of the total issued shares to guarantee their independence neutralize. Shareholders may also propose agenda items for consideration at a general shareholder meeting. Over the years, the requirements to exercise shareholder rights have been liberalized to facilitate their use. The levels were further reduced for LLCs with paid-in capital of at least 100 billion Won (USD 85 million). The minimum amount of stocks required to seek an injunction against directors, for example, has been reduced from 0.5 percent to [0.25] percent. To demand cumulative voting [for LLCs], the minimum requirement has been reduced from 3 percent to 1 percent.

Companies may provide in their articles of incorporation for the granting of stock options to directors, statutory auditors and employees. Stock options were hailed as a potential means to align incentives of managers and employees with shareholders at large. They could deter controlling shareholder abuses that would lower shareholder value. The board may grant stock options within an upper limit of 1 percent of the total issued shares for companies with paid-in capital of more than 300 billion Won or up to 3 percent for small companies. Executives of affiliates or subsidiaries who contribute to the concerned company's business may also be eligible for stock options as well. Despite criticism in many advanced markets surrounding the problems associated with options, Korean companies still prefer to grant stock options over stock for compensation. Over the past six years, a steady average of approximately 50 new companies per year have issued stock options. Employees of a company may easily acquire shares in their company at a lower cost through the Employee Stock Ownership Plan (ESOP). ESOP has unfortunately not served as a monitoring vehicle to advance shareholder rights due to its limited size and inability to resolve collective action problems.

Shareholders may also vote in writing in advance of a general meeting of shareholders without attending the meeting in person or by proxy … Companies may redeem their stocks with a special resolution at a general shareholders' meeting. KRX and KOSDAQ companies may redeem their stocks with surplus with board approval if provided for under the articles of incorporation. Korean companies have recently redeemed significant amounts of stock in order to raise share value and to help secure control.

11.4.4 National Pension Service and Shareholder Activism

With assets exceeding US$ 500 billion, Korea's National Pension Service (NPS) is the third largest pension fund in the world. They currently own more than 5 percent stakes in over 350 listed companies, making them the largest shareholder of a significant number of Korea's leading companies, particularly when compared to the controlling shareholders and families in the chaebols. As the largest institutional investor in the country that also has a public mandate, a central debate has focused on what role NPS should play in corporate governance.

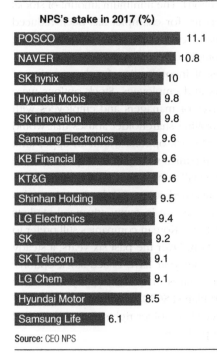

Figure 11.1 NPS's stake in 2017 (%)

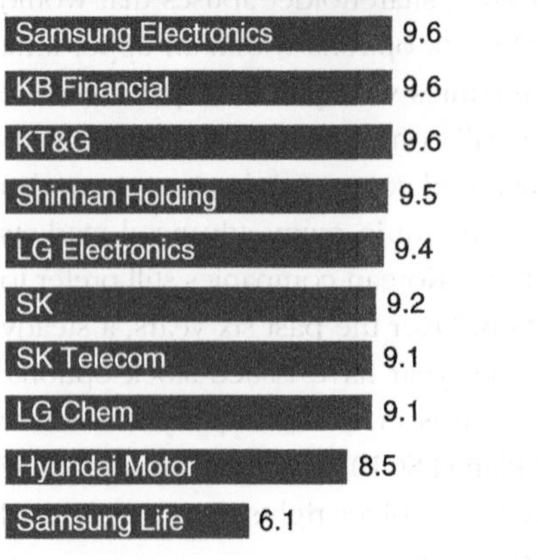

Source: CEO NPS

Yi Whan-Woo, 'Firms on Alert over NPS's Move: Pension Fund May Interfere with Boards' Decisions,' *Korea Times* (March 13, 2013)

The National Pension Service (NPS) is making major Korean companies sweat as the pension fund operator is expected to raise its voice at its upcoming shareholders' meeting. Market participants are paying attention to whether the NPS will exert its voting rights against key issues of affiliates of major conglomerates, such as the appointments of the companies' board of directors and compensation for executives. The operator of the public pension fund under the Ministry of Health and Welfare owns over a 5-percent share each in more than 200 firms, many of which are conglomerates or their affiliates.

For instance, the NPS has a 7.43-percent stake in Samsung Electronics, a 6.83-percent stake in Hyundai Motor, a 9.41-percent stake in SK Hynix, a 9-percent stake in LG Electronics, a 6.14-percent stake in POSCO and a 9.98-percent stake in KT, according to CEO Score, a website that provides information on corporate productivity. Samsung Electronics, LG Electronics and Hyundai Motor will hold a shareholders' meeting today, while SK, SK Hynix and Hyosung are scheduled to have their meetings on March 21.

Experts point out that the NPS' veto rarely affects the firms' board decisions because it is not the majority shareholder in many cases, but it is important that the pension fund has started raising a red flag against some decisions that may damage shareholders' values. Anxiety among these firms is particularly high as the NPS recently voted against some mid-size conglomerates' moves to select board members. Between January and February, the NPS voted against the board members selected by Sebang Group and Mando.

The NPS owns a 10.33-percent share in Sebang Group, a mid-sized conglomerate specializing in logistics services, and a 13.41-percent share in Mando, a leading auto parts manufacturer under Halla Group. The shareholders of Sebang Group and Mando approved the appointed board of directors despite the NPS' objection. However, a lobby group for local enterprises said the NPS' veto should be considered separately from those of other shareholders' when selecting the firms' board of directors.

"The NPS is a state-run organization that can be affected by the government and politicians," said Choo Kwan-ho, leader of the corporate policy team at the Federation of Korean Industries (FKI). "And its decisions as a shareholder of a firm can be very politically biased. Because a considerable part of the NPS' investments are financed by the taxpayers' money, it is crucial to make sure that the NPS exercises its shareholders' rights in a fair and objective way."

The NPS manages 424 trillion won ($399.35 billion) in investments as of November last year, according to the state-run organization. Some 19.7 percent, or

83.93 trillion won, of the investments was poured into the domestic stock market. The NPS, however, dismissed speculation about political bias in its decisions.

"We're responsible for yielding returns for the taxpayers in the long-term, and in order to do so, we have the right to make sure that the companies in which we own shares are being managed properly," said Lee Chul-hee, an NPS spokeswoman. She said the NPS disapproved of Mando's re-appointment of CEO Shin Sa-hyeon to the board because he "damaged the corporate value of the firm with unfair business practices." In a statement, the NPS said it decided to vote against Shin because he actively took a part in funding Halla Meister with 378.6 billion won. Halla Meister is a wholly owned subsidiary of Mando Corp. According to the NPS, Halla Meister spent the money to support the poorly performing construction affiliate, Halla Corp. The construction company is the largest shareholder of Mando Corp. with a 17.29-percent share. The NPS also claimed Shin was involved in a scheme to fund the builder through irregular business practices.

Kang Jeong-min, a researcher at civic watchdog Solidarity for Economic Reform, said the NPS should push to exercise its voting rights to correct the unfair business practices of enterprises. "Most of the board of directors are merely puppets of the firms for which they're appointed," he said. "That's why illegal business practices committed by CEOs are prevalent. For this reason, I'd say the NPS should be more active in persuading other shareholders to take action against incompetent board members." He also said the FKI's claim the NPS could be politically biased is wrong. "To prevent such politically biased decisions, the NPS runs a committee comprised of civil experts such as professors, so I don't understand where the FKI's argument comes from."

'Samsung C&T: Proposed Merger with Cheil Industries,' ISS Special Situations Research, Analysis (July 3, 2015)

Executive Summary

Since the hospitalization of Samsung group's patriarch, Kun-Hee Lee in May last year, many market observers have anticipated that Samsung would begin taking steps to unwind the group's cross-ownership structure, to facilitate handing down control from the ailing chairman to his three children and lower inheritance taxes.

A "merger" in Korea does not in general involve concepts like redundancies and facility closings, and the exchange ratio is set by law, based on historical trading prices, not through negotiations. For many investors, comparing some aspects of this merger with standard practices in other markets, such as the US, may be a comparison between apples and oranges … But 7.1 percent holder Elliott Advisors, which publicly opposes the transaction, questions why, of all the different alternatives to implement this proposed restructuring, the company chose one that implies a transfer of value from C&T shareholders to Cheil shareholders, among whom the Lee family is more prominently represented – and why C&T shareholders should permanently lock in what appears to be a material undervaluation of C&T shares, particularly by accepting what appears to be a materially overvalued Cheil currency.

Strategic Rationale

While management puts forward a list of revenue and synergy targets, the targets appear to be hugely optimistic and how such targets could be achieved remain unclear ... Shareholders wishing to have exposure to Cheil Industries' growth prospects could do so by simply investing directly in Cheil Industries. The argument that the merger will help offset Samsung C&T's deteriorating profitability while at the same time creating additional value for shareholders through synergies, remains vague and unconvincing, despite the board's assertion that the decision came after a prolonged review of alternative strategies, and an in-depth review of the merger proposal put forth by Cheil Industries ...

Deal Process and Governance

Given the legal requirement to let recent market prices dictate the exchange ratio, the timing of the board's decision to enter into a transaction is crucial, as the derived swap ratio and buyback price are the only safeguards available to minority shareholders. There seems to be little consideration in the merger rationale – which is more based on prospects for the construction business, which is only a piece of the puzzle – of the importance of this timing factor.

The most controversial board action, however, is one which occurred long after the transaction was approved and publicly announced: the surprise placement on June 11, 2015, the record date for this meeting, of all Samsung C&T's treasury shares – 5.8 percent of the company's issued shares – to KCC, the second largest shareholder of Cheil Industries. The board's decision to sell treasury shares to a buyer with a vested interest in making the deal happen on these terms has struck many investors as a blatant effort to overpower, rather than address, shareholder concerns over valuation. It also suggests the board's priority may simply be getting this transaction consummated, rather than the appropriateness of the economics for shareholders.

Conclusion

Although the terms of the transaction are fully compliant with Korean law, the combination of Samsung C&T's undervaluation and Cheil Industries' overvaluation significantly disadvantages Samsung C&T shareholders. Potential synergies the companies contend are available through the merger, even if credible, do little to compensate for the significant undervaluation implied by the exchange ratio. Instead of making a compelling case to demonstrate the benefits of the merger and address directly the concerns of unaffiliated shareholders, the board of Samsung C&T opted to make the second largest shareholder of the buyer a block shareholder of the company to secure the deal. The board argues the placement was agreed to for the benefit of all shareholders, but the decision itself suggests too facile a willingness to force through a transaction despite the concerns of unaffiliated shareholders, and perhaps even despite benefitting the buyer's shareholders at the expense of its own shareholders. A vote against the transaction may expose shareholders to some short-term downside market risk. However, shareholders also retain the possibility that a fairer valuation of the company – either in the public markets or in some future change-in-control transaction – will develop over time. Voting for this transaction on the current terms, by contrast, permanently locks in a valuation disparity which materially exceeds any short-term downside risk. A vote AGAINST the transaction, despite any short-term downside risk, is therefore warranted.

Elliott attempts to block the merger marked the most aggressive assertion of shareholders' rights, particularly by a foreign investor, involving a company controlled by a chaebol for years. Elliott complained that the terms over the merger were unfair and unlawful because Cheil's stock was overvalued and the deal was being pursued as a means to help with the succession to the heirs of the Samsung Group, particularly because they held more Cheil shares. Elliott cited the inflexible nature of the share valuation formula and challenged that it did not excuse the board from exercising their duty to act in the best interest of the company and its shareholders when deciding on whether to approve the merger itself. Samsung C&T argued the valuation was fair because it was based on statutory formula prescribed by law. Elliott also unsuccessfully tried to prevent KCC, the second largest shareholder of Cheil and a friendly subsidiary of another conglomerate, from acquiring all of Samsung C&T's common treasury shares. Sales of treasury shares to friendly white knights have been often used as a means to secure controversial board decisions. In the end, the merger barely met the required two-thirds vote, particularly after key institutional investors such as the NPS sided for the deal. The merger has been challenged in Korean courts.

Notes and Questions

1. Given the cross-ownership structure of large conglomerates, should Korea follow a traditional civil law-based model, or a model more commonly associated with leading common law countries? What can be done to mitigate the governance issues associated with the unique cross-ownership structure found in large conglomerates?
2. Should shareholders be further empowered? If so, how? Should cumulative voting become mandatory? If so, what downsides might exist?

3. What kind of role can banks play in corporate governance? What effect does foreign ownership of banks have on corporate governance?
4. Do stock options help align the incentives of directors with the shareholder at large?
5. Should the NPS play a more active role in the corporate governance of companies where it invests? Is aggression and activism, particularly by foreign investors, a concern or a blessing or a mixture of both?
6. What can be learned from the Samsung C&T and Cheil merger about the state of corporate governance in Korea? What would you have done if you were NPS or were on the board of Samsung C&T?

11.5 Law and Enforcement

As with many Asian countries, private enforcement and managerial discipline through the corporate control market have remained weak in Korea, although it has been more prominent than such leading jurisdictions as Hong Kong and Singapore. Traditionally, public enforcement has been also comparatively considered sluggish, yet signs of a shift continue to appear on the horizon.

11.5.1 Private Enforcement

Despite enforcement-related reforms, largely through transplants, private enforcement remains weak in Korea. Shareholders can technically remove directors and obtain injunctive relief barring directors from doing acts that are illegal or contravene the articles of incorporation, but this rarely occurs. Derivative suits, although infrequent, remain the most significant means of private enforcement. At present, a derivative claim can be brought by minority shareholders of listed companies who hold 0.01 percent of the shares against directors, auditors, and de facto directors. Multiple derivative suits where shareholders of a parent bring an action against the directors of a subsidiary company are not yet allowed.

Derivative suits were first introduced in 1962 when the CA was enacted but remained unused until 1997 when the minority shareholders led by non-governmental organizations such as the People's Solidarity for Participatory Democracy (PSPD) ushered in a new era of private enforcement. Private enforcement has been largely driven by PSPD and presently, its substantive successor, the Solidarity for Economic Reform. On behalf of shareholders, PSPD won a historic judgment against the directors of Korea First Bank (KFB). Shareholders have prevailed in a number of cases while many remain pending. Derivative suits have led to the imposition of director liability for the first time.

In 2005, Korea became one of the first countries in Asia to adopt a class action system for securities investors through the Securities-Related Class Action Act. Investors can bring claims for false disclosure, market manipulation and insider trading, and improper audits against directors or other related parties such as accounting auditors. The Act, however, has not yielded the type of private enforcement that was intended. As of 2017, only nine cases had been brought. While most cases remain pending, thus far only one group of shareholders has prevailed in a judgment. One of the biggest restrictions that was imposed out of concerns that it would lead to abusive entrepreneurial litigation was the requirement of court approval for the class action to commence. This approval process can be appealed all the way to the Supreme Court and has led to years in delays just to bring an action. Despite the existence of success fee structures in Korea that amount to contingency fee arrangements, the restrictions thwarted the development of class actions.

Bernard Black, Brian Cheffins, and Michael Klausner, 'Shareholder Suits and Outside Director Liability: The Case of Korea' (2011) 10 *Journal of Korean Law* 325, 326, 328–9, 344

One by-product of reform was that the previously moribund derivative action procedure became viable. While there were no derivative suits filed before 1997, at least 20 had been filed by early 2003, and 55 by the end of 2010, with some of the suits brought against directors of leading chaebol, including Samsung, LG, and Hyundai Motors. Commentators, echoing fears voiced in other countries, worried that legal risk would cause candidates not to serve, and "that Korean companies will be deprived of honest and competent directors precisely at a time when they are most needed" …

Moreover, the [CA] has just been amended to permit companies to amend their articles of incorporation to limit director liability to six times annual compensation for inside directors and three times annual compensation for outside directors, absent self-dealing. We expect, based on experience with similar provisions in the U.S., that many public companies will adopt these limits. This is precisely the kind of political reaction one finds in other countries when concerns about liability risk of outside directors arise. If most companies in fact do adopt a liability cap, this risk will be nearly negated. For outside directors, a liability cap of three times annual compensation is so low that it would make no sense to bring a suit motivated by financial recovery. Suits might be brought, perhaps by shareholder activists, to make an example of particular directors, so as to deter others. But the risk of giving back one's compensation hardly poses a serious financial risk to outside directors.

Is Korea's current resting place, including these limits on liability, a good policy outcome? Our assessment is that very low but non-zero risk for outside directors is a reasonable outcome. A substantially higher degree of risk is not readily achievable, and if achieved, might cause more harm than good by deterring good director candidates from serving and inducing risk aversion among those willing to serve.

At the same time, we believe that some exposure to liability is likely to be salutary. We worry that the new limits on monetary liability in suits under corporate law, coupled with the rarity of class action suits under securities law, and the likelihood that outside directors will not be named in these suits, might leave outside directors underexposed to the risk of liability. "Related-party transactions" – transactions between companies under common control, or between companies and their controlling shareholders – remain a problem for at least some Korean companies and chaebol groups. We would want outside directors to have good reason to police the fairness of those transactions, and believe a very low but non-zero risk of out-of-pocket liability helps to achieve this outcome.

Securities class actions may still pose a potential personal liability risk for outside directors. There has, however, been only one judicially sanctioned securities class action brought by shareholders under the Securities Class Action Act of 2004. This case was settled soon after it was approved by the court, with damages paid entirely by the company. The rarity of securities litigation is due partly to lawmakers including various provisions in the Securities Class Action Act designed to deter frivolous litigation, including the need for judicial approval before the suit can proceed and a ban on a particular shareholder or lawyer being involved in more than three other suits over the previous three years. The ban on lawyers being frequent players ensures that lawyers lack the incentive to develop the specialized knowledge that is needed to bring these suits effectively or efficiently. Moreover, the dynamics discussed above for other countries with a loser-pays rule for attorney fees, which ensure that outside directors are rarely named in securities suits, are in place in Korea as well.

... Derivative litigation creates, at least theoretically, liability risk for outside directors. Shareholding requirements for derivative suits are now low enough so that derivative suits are feasible, if a major institutional investor, or a shareholder group such as PSPD, is willing to bring them. Moreover, plaintiffs in derivative suits are exempt from Korea's usual loser-pays attorney fee rules unless the judge finds that the case was brought in bad faith. Also, for successful plaintiffs in derivative suits, the [CA] authorizes the plaintiff to obtain reasonable litigation costs, paid by the company.

The new era of private enforcement created a directors' liability insurance market. In the past, this market did not exist because there was no perceived risk of legal liability for directors. From 1997 this market has grown from approximately

Table 11.1 Directors' liability insurance annual total premiums

Year	1997	1998	1999	2000	2001	2009	2010	2011	2012
No. of companies	10	125	215	280	335	1,006	1,024	1,016	1,007
Insurance premium	2.5	24.5	39.2	48.5	58.0	68.0	59.4	57.3	57.2

(US$ million)

US$ 2.5 million in premiums for ten companies to US$ 57 million in premiums for 1,107 companies in 2012. Unlike in more advanced markets where more than 85 percent of listed companies acquire directors' liability insurance, in Korea only 21 percent have.

11.5.2 Public Enforcement

Joongi Kim, 'A Forensic Study of Daewoo's Corporate Governance: Does Responsibility for the Meltdown Solely Lie with the Chaebol and Korea?' (2008) 28 *Northwestern Journal of International Law & Business* 273, 333–7

Prosecutors, courts, and other public guardians such as the media remained passive in establishing an effective corporate governance framework. A tacit policy of soft enforcement prevailed in the treatment of white collar crime committed by corporate executives. Whether they were directors, executives, or controlling shareholders, corporate defendants faced criminal discipline or media scrutiny through prosecution, punishment, or public shaming only when companies collapsed. Furthermore, in the rare case of a conviction, Korean presidents have been notoriously generous in granting clemency. This created a lax compliance structure under which the failure to observe corporate governance duties, laws, and regulations became inconsequential events. Complacency toward legal discipline and public sanction for corporate wrongdoing developed from a variety of reasons, such as a socio-cultural legacy of leniency, emphasis on economic growth, lack of training, and improper influence. A dramatic shift toward serious enforcement against corporate defendants and their advisers took place after Daewoo executives received actual prison terms and some of the largest monetary penalties in history.

Overall, an unwritten custom existed that corporate defendants should be granted leniency due to their roles in developing the economy. Corporate executives of the largest companies received the most special status and benefits from soft enforcement. One theory propounds that those of privileged standing, such as chaebol executives, were bestowed preferential treatment as part of the Confucian tradition. Prosecutors and courts also expressed exaggerated concerns that punishing corporate defendants, especially from larger chaebols, would damage the reputation of the company and in turn cause serious economic damage to the country. Chaebol chairmen in particular received the most generous treatment compared to other corporate defendants. When being investigated for serious crimes, for example, prosecutors would accommodate requests to avoid media attention by questioning them in special locations away from the public view, under the rationale that negative media coverage would harm the economy. Similarly, for many years, prosecutors refrained from prosecuting the corporate bribe-givers and instead focused their efforts on the bribe-takers.

Courts acted similarly. Even when they found chaebol executives guilty, they routinely commuted their sentences based upon "enormous contributions to the economy." Actual imprisonment or civil liability hardly occurred ... [I]n the presidential slush fund trials ... a dozen leading chaebol chairmen were found guilty of contributing over 510 billion won ($638 million) in bribes during the 1980s and early 1990s to two presidents. All of them received suspended sentences due to their "contributions to the economy."

Korean presidents reconfirmed the environment of leniency in the enforcement process. The presidents routinely granted pardons to convicted controlling shareholders and executives of large companies ... Executive clemency could be viewed as part of a legacy from Korean history under which kings were expected to extend their benevolence upon those of privileged status ...

Likewise, the media did not fulfill their roles as the public guardians against corporate misbehavior. Investigative journalists rarely directed their attention toward governance issues. Domestic media scrutiny generally involved reporting events of wrongdoing after the fact. Critical reports analyzing Daewoo's state of affairs that could have foreshadowed its financial difficulties did not occur. Foreign media offered only marginally more critical reportage ... They too operated weakly as public guardians in shedding light on its problems ...

After the financial crisis, the overall environment of soft enforcement and public scrutiny dramatically changed. Public uproar led to piercing of the informal veil that had been shielding corporate executives ... Prosecutors then sought unprecedented, harsh sentences against Daewoo officials including Chairman Kim. The judiciary obliged and sentenced Kim, despite his age and poor health, to eight and a half years in prison and the former head of Daewoo Corp. and Daewoo Motor to five years, both without any commutation. Courts pronounced astronomical monetary penalties upon seven defendants. Matching the scale of the accounting frauds, disgorgement penalties of joint and several liability ranging from 21.25 trillion won ($17.7 billion) to 23.03 trillion won ($19.2 billion) were levied first against three junior directors and officers of Daewoo Corp. and then Chairman Kim. Four senior executives received smaller disgorgement penalties ranging between 1.47 trillion won ($1.75 billion) and 3.71 trillion won ($4.16 billion). The disgorgement penalties were the largest in Korean history, if not in the world.

The sentences and penalties sent a powerful message how executives and chaebols would be held accountable. A consensus emerged to levy actual prison sentences against senior executives of chaebols and to hold them responsible for the damages they caused.

11.5.3 Corporate Control

As with many Asian countries, Korea's corporate control market remains underdeveloped, given the sophistication of its capital markets and the size of its economy. Only a small number of contested takeovers have ever taken place, and practically none involving LLCs. In contrast, foreign competitors that operate in the international marketplace are able to expand through mergers and acquisitions, often financed by stock-for-stock swaps. Korean companies cannot undertake comparable transactions in advanced markets because they cannot persuade shareholders of their counterparts to accept an acquisition financed with Korean stock or obtain the necessary cash financing for a major acquisition. Companies with strong corporate governance benefit from the market discipline of an active corporate control market and enjoy cheaper access to capital, an enormous competitive advantage.

Many companies remain in the abnormal situation of being undervalued and poorly managed despite meager ownership by weak controlling shareholders. The development of a market for corporate control could facilitate the provision of much-needed managerial discipline. Yet, aggregate shareholdings in the chaebols through cross-ownership via affiliates, strong labor forces, political influence of controlling families and the lack of takeover-related financing have all combined to thwart even the threat of takeovers or any other type of corporate control market.

Various amendments were enacted to promote a more active corporate control market. Recent attempts at reforms to promote more corporate control-related discipline have focused on the establishment of homegrown private equity funds. One reason for these funds was to aggregate domestic funds for corporate governance purposes and to protect Korean companies in the process from takeovers by foreign companies. At the same time, limitations regarding public offerings have been lifted so that companies can now issue new equities during a tender offer period as a defense mechanism for corporate challenges.

Hwa-Jin Kim, 'The Case for Market for Corporate Control in Korea' (2009) 8 *Journal of Korean Law* 227–9, 276

Korea may be qualified as one of the "inefficient controlling shareholder systems" under the taxonomy proposed by Professor Ronald Gilson. Recent research shows that the average of controlling family ownership for public firms in Korea was 29.51 percent, compared with controlling families' cash-flow rights of 8.42 percent. In the case of Samsung Group, the largest Korean conglomerate, those numbers were 13.52 percent and 1.14 percent, respectively, for public firms in the group. The private benefit of control is also relatively high in Korea. The value of corporate control amounts to about 34 percent of firm market value in Korea, as compared to about 29 percent in Italy, 1 percent in Denmark, 9 percent in Germany, and 2 percent in the United States. The poor corporate governance practices of some large Korean firms are responsible for the still-continuing discussions on how to abolish the "Korea discount," i.e., how to eliminate or reduce agency costs in the inefficient controlling shareholder system. One of the solutions to the problem may be the increasing exposure of corporate control to the (global) market. This requires Korea to facilitate corporate takeovers and promote the market for corporate control. As a matter of fact, contested mergers and acquisitions emerged in the business world of Korea in the mid-1990's and have since served as a popular topic for the media.

Finally, in view of the foregoing discussions, we may quite safely conclude that Henry Manne was right after all. He was right also in an Asian civil law country under the Confucian culture such as Korea some forty years after he presented the thesis that the market for corporate control functions as a disciplinary mechanism for poor corporate governance. The cases described in this article show, even empirically in the SK case, that the validity of his thesis may transcend national jurisdictions and cultural differences. The Korean case, in particular the SK case, also shows that the increasing exposure of control to the market could eliminate the inefficient controlling shareholder system. Hostile takeovers cannot solve all corporate governance problems of large Korean companies with controlling shareholders. However, promoting contestable control is a way forward. The new [CA] should maintain a sophisticated balance between the active market for corporate control and effective takeover defensive tactics for the benefit of shareholders. Last, but not least, the usual emphasis on the role of judicial review in the controlling shareholder system should apply to the Korean case.

Notes and Questions

1. How important is public or private enforcement as a means to provide checks and balances given Korea's situation? Under the annual ACGA/CLSA rankings, Korea's enforcement has improved, but it still remains far below such countries as Singapore and Hong Kong. Or, could too much enforcement be counterproductive, have a chilling effect and deter corporate innovation, bold decision-making, and risk-taking? Are calls for stronger enforcement, another form of over-regulation?
2. Should public or private enforcement be further promoted? What is the ideal level of exposure to liability for directors? Should restrictions on class actions be lifted? Should Korea consider the enforcement models of Taiwan or Australia under which quasi-public entities hold directors accountable? Should the cap on director liability remain?
3. As in many civil law jurisdictions where judges are career judges and lack practical experience, some criticize Korean judges for being too generous in the application of the business judgment rule and abstaining from holding directors liable.
4. What role should the market for corporate control play? Given that many controlling shareholders wield far greater control than their cash flow rights, should corporate control market be promoted as "disciplinary mechanism for poor corporate governance"? Or, would this amount to another form of excessive interference into corporate affairs by short-term-oriented shareholders that could endanger the corporation's long-term health and welfare of its stakeholders at large?
5. Should corporate Korea be protected from challenges by foreign investors? Some suggest that the strongest and simplest defense for a Korean corporation would be to have stronger corporate governance since this would reduce any valuation discount and appease foreign investors into inaction.

11.6 Recent Developments

11.6.1 Stewardship Code

As of September 2017, over fifty institutional investors, including Korea's sovereign fund the Korean Investment Corporation and various leading asset managers, have adopted or declared their intention to adopt the Stewardship Code that was established in December 2016 by the KCGS. Pension funds, particularly the NPS, however, remain undecided. Given NPS's status as the largest investor in most of Korea's leading companies, much attention has been focused on whether they will adopt the Code. Overall, institutional investors on average own 15 percent of the stock market in terms of market capitalization and an ever-larger portion in LLCs.

Business interests are concerned that NPS is too susceptible to political pressure and would invite improper interference in managerial decision-making.

To advocates, widespread adoption of the Stewardship Code holds promise for institutions to be more actively involved as investors and to be better monitors of corporate governance in the interests of their beneficiaries. They believe this will benefit shareholders at large.

11.6.2 Electronic Voting

The adoption of more efficient, technology-based management systems can be an important area of reform. Despite its prowess in information technology, for example, Korea was slow to adopt advanced voting procedures such as electronic voting. Korea is uniquely situated to utilize its information technology infrastructure to make electronic voting, particularly through internet-based shareholder meetings a reality. This potentially creates effective shareholders' meetings that could solve collective action problems and contribute to the realization of shareholder democracy. Companies complain of the administrative burden and expense that they will incur and question whether it really benefits shareholders.

As of 2015, companies are no longer able to rely upon the shadow voting of non-voting shares to meet the voting quorum at shareholders' meetings. This has forced companies to rely on electronic voting. Electronic voting first became possible in 2010 but until 2014 few companies adopted it. As of 2015, however, over 450 listed companies have adopted procedures to allow electronic voting, including KEPCO, Korea's electric power company, which is the first company among the top ten in market capitalization. Among companies associated with the top forty conglomerates, only twenty-seven allow it. Electronic voting should help alleviate the difficulties for shareholders, particularly given that 70 percent of all listed companies hold their annual shareholder meetings on the fourth Friday of March, a practice that Korean companies most likely adopted from Japan. Policymakers are currently debating whether to make it mandatory.

11.6.3 Whistleblower Protections

Korea has also developed various protections for whistleblowers to allow them to report, detect, and deter accounting fraud. Insiders are inevitably best situated to prevent such fraud from happening and spreading to cause even wider damage. Those who report accounting fraud to the company's statutory auditors or external auditors or to the Securities and Futures Commission, for example, can be exempted from penalties or corrective measures. The company or its directors or officers cannot in any way retaliate against such whistleblowers. Companies that retaliate will be subject to fines of up to KRW 50 million (approximately US$ 44,000), whereas those in charge of the retaliation will be subject to up to two years' imprisonment or up to KRW 20 million (approximately US$ 18,000) in criminal fines. Furthermore, the company and the officers are jointly and severally liable in damages for "unfairly treating" whistleblowers of accounting fraud. In April 2017, the Financial Services Commission increased the rewards to accounting-related whistleblowers by ten-fold to KRW 1 billion (approximately US$ 877,000). Despite these protections, whistleblowing seldom occurs.

Notes and Questions

1. Are you persuaded by the merits of the Stewardship Code? Should NPS adopt it? Should it become mandatory?
2. Should electronic voting be mandated? Some suggest that electronic voting is overrated because shareholders can already submit their voting by proxy or in the case of over 200 companies that allow it by their articles of incorporation by written form in advance.
3. Should the practice of holding shareholders' meetings on the same day be regulated?
4. What are the merits and demerits of further promoting and protecting whistleblowers? Is this viable in an Asian jurisdiction which stresses collective culture based on mutual cooperation?

11.7 Conclusions

Korea has progressed in terms of corporate governance over the last forty years through a combination of legal and policy reforms, market forces, and various internal and external pressures. To establish a world-class corporate governance system commensurate with its status as an advanced economy, Korea needs to persevere to create the right combination of market forces supplemented by appropriate legal reform. The respective roles of lawmakers, regulators, and judiciary, together with investors, gatekeepers, creditors, and other stakeholders, are critical in creating the right ecosystem where investor protections are guaranteed and corporate value can be enhanced.

As with many countries in Asia, Korean companies need stronger and more independent boards of directors, greater transparency through fuller financial disclosure, and greater accountability of controlling shareholders, directors, and managers. Despite expanded regulatory monitoring, regulators, non-interested outside directors and internal and external auditors must be able to effectively monitor for improper related party transactions and other forms of insider trading and self-dealing transactions. An expansion of shareholder rights has resulted in a modest increase in shareholder activism. Overall private enforcement largely remains ineffective.

Business groups tend to be skeptical about legal reforms designed to increase accountability and transparency. They find it amounts to over-regulation that is costly and burdensome and leads to regulatory chill and stifles their competitiveness. They believe that corporate governance reform has gone too far, and market forces whether through the capital market, product market, or labor market can adequately address corporate governance problems. These concerns cannot be ignored and must be addressed.

Korea differs from most other Asian countries in the high degree of market concentration in its economy, the dynastic control by controlling families, and the high levels of intra-conglomerate transactions. As Korea considers further corporate governance reforms, some suggest that given the peculiar challenges that Korea faces innovative solutions are warranted even if they cannot be found in other jurisdictions.

Overall, many of Korea's premium companies continue to face skepticism about their transparency and accountability. Scandals and succession problems involving leading companies continue to shake confidence in Korean companies. The dreaded "Korean discount" undervalues Korean companies despite their earning potential because investors continue to harbor doubt about their integrity. Korea's corporate governance practice and standards continue to lag behind its level of economic development, contributing to the lowest corporate governance rankings in the region among developed economies. Korea must meet the challenge and establish a modern corporate governance system based on effective checks and balances that will instill confidence and enhance corporate value.

Notes and Questions

1. What kind of challenges makes corporate governance in Korea unique when compared with other Asian jurisdictions? Do unique factors call for unique solutions?
2. What can be done to improve Korea's corporate governance rankings? Is it necessary to be sensitive to such rankings? Is corporate governance overrated and should Korean companies focus more on their core competencies?

Laws and Regulations and Regulators for Public Companies

Law and Regulations Relating to Companies

Commercial Act (CA)

Financial Investment Services and Capital Markets Acts (CMA)

Monopoly Regulation and Fair Trade Act (MRFTA)

KRX listing regulations

Codes and Guidelines Relating to Public Companies

Korean Corporate Governance Code (CGC)

Stewardship Code

Regulators/Quasi Regulators

Securities and Futures Commission (SFC)

Korean Fair Trade Commission (KFTC)

Korea Exchange [KRX]

12

TAIWAN

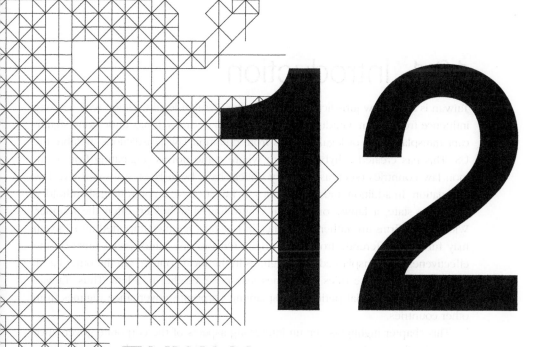

Christopher Chen

12.1 Introduction

Taiwan is a civil law jurisdiction following the German legal tradition with a strong influence from Japan. Gradually, in the past two decades, it has undergone significant transplantation of legal regimes from common law jurisdictions, notably the US. This has created a hybrid system where some norms originating from common law countries (such as fiduciary duties) have been layered upon a civil law foundation. In addition, most companies in Taiwan have a controlling shareholder, being the state, a family or a single controlling shareholder, often the founder. Widely held firms are rather rare. Thus, in practice, regimes imported into Taiwan may function differently from their origin. On the one hand, issues arise on the effectiveness of transplanted legal regimes in the local context. On the other hand, how to enforce those rules or regimes may pose another problem. Thus, Taiwan illustrates the potential peril of transplanting corporate governance regimes from other countries.

This chapter highlights certain interesting aspects of the corporate governance system in Taiwan. It starts by introducing the background to the transplantation of corporate governance rules from the Anglo-American system into a civil law jurisdiction. This paves the way for discussion of the basic internal governance structure of a company and the introduction of fiduciary duties, independent directors, and the audit committee. This includes discussions of the choice of corporate structures and changing regulations on mandatory cumulative voting. Finally, it evaluates Taiwan's unique invention of a hybrid of public and private enforcement by examining the derivative action regime and the quasi-governmental, nonprofit Investor Protection Center.

12.2 Legal Background and Ownership Structure

This section introduces excerpts from two articles that lay out the background of Taiwan's corporate governance framework and legal transplantation in the past two decades. It also briefly discusses ownership structure in corporations in Taiwan, paving the way for a further introduction to the internal governance system and enforcement of rules.

12.2.1 Overview

Andrew Jen-Guang Lin, 'Common Law Influences in Private Law – Taiwan's Experiences Related to Corporate Law' (2009) 4(2) *National Taiwan University Law Review* 107–38, at 110–11, 124–5

Taiwan is categorized as a civil law country. Most areas of private law are codified and so does the commercial law field. Many of Taiwan's statutes are patterned after or receptive from foreign laws ... Taiwan's Company Act was initially enacted in December 1929 comprising 233 articles and was heavily influenced by German, Japanese, and Swiss corporate law. However, the Anglo-American corporate law principles began to influence Taiwan's corporate law reforms after World War Two beginning from the 1946 Company Act Amendment. Taiwan's Securities and Exchange Act (TSEA) expressly indicates in the legislative material that the TSEA is patterned after the U.S. Federal Securities Act of 1933 (1933 Act) and the Securities and Exchange Act of 1934 (1934 Act). In order to have an overall picture of Taiwan's corporate law, it is necessary to look into the Company Act as well as the TSEA because the Company Act contains provisions governing the incorporation, corporate structure, the powers of internal corporate organs, corporate finance, business consolidation, and other relevant issues that can be found in the regular corporate law statute everywhere of the world, and a major portion of the TSEA contains provisions regulating the publicly held corporations ...

The concept of fiduciary duty did not exist in Taiwan until the amendment of the Company Act in November 2001 to introduce this term into this Act by adding the fiduciary duty into this Act. Article 23 Paragraph 1 provides that "[t]he responsible persons of a company shall have the duty of loyalty and duty of care as a good administrator in managing the corporate affairs, and shall be liable for damages incurred to the company as a result of his breach of those duties." However, because the concept of fiduciary, particularly the fiduciary duty of loyalty, is new to Taiwan's legal system and the provision does not provide any detailed elements or guidance for determining whether the responsible person has breached the fiduciary duties, there have only been a few judicial decisions holding defendants liable for breach of fiduciary duties under Article 23 Paragraph 1.

There are several possible reasons why there are not many judicial decisions applying this provision yet. First, the fiduciary duty arose from the law of trust and the law of trust is a new law in Taiwan too ... The concepts of fiduciary duty and trust have existed and developed in England and the United States for hundreds of years. It ... may not be an easy task for Taiwanese courts to determine a person's liability based on a concept that is new and developing in Taiwan's society. It is still in the transitional period for the courts to figure out how to make this concept into play. Second, more in-depth discussions and literatures on how the laws of fiduciary duty operate are needed and best of all if a guideline on how to determine whether the fiduciary duties are breached can be developed. Because there is no comparable concept in Taiwan, there have been different terms used to translate the fiduciary duty. People in Taiwan are still curious to know the answers of the following questions. What constitutes a fiduciary relation? Who can be treated as a fiduciary? What is the content of the fiduciary duty and how to determine whether it is breached? Whether the responsible person of a company owes fiduciary to the company only or to the shareholders also? Shall we completely recognize the law of fiduciary duties and widely applied, or incorporate only in selected statutes? All of these issues need more discussions to make the courts feel more comfortable to apply the law of fiduciary duty. Furthermore, in Paragraph 2 of Article 23, which provides that the responsible person shall be jointly and severally liable for the damages caused by the responsible persons during the course of business operations having violated any applicable law or regulation. Because this provision provides a relatively precise standard "in violation of the law or regulation during the course of business operation," it becomes easier for the court to apply Paragraph 2 rather than Paragraph 1 of Article 23 of the Company Act.

Notes and Questions

1. The transplant of legal regimes from the common law world into a civil law jurisdiction is a constant problem in East Asia and a recurring issue throughout this chapter.
   a. How far might the desire to climb various world rankings drive corporate governance reforms?
   b. Taiwan is ranked sixth in the CG Watch Ranking by the Asian Corporate Governance Association in both 2012 and 2014 and rose to fourth in the 2016 ranking, behind competitors such as Hong Kong and Singapore. In addition, pursuant to the 2016 World Bank's Ease of Doing Business Ranking, Taiwan ranks merely twenty-fifth regarding protecting minority investors, in contrast with an overall ranking of eleventh, falling behind regional competitors like Hong Kong, Singapore and Korea.
   c. Most countries deemed to have good corporate governance are from the common law family. Is it sustainable for a civil law jurisdiction like Taiwan to transplant legal doctrine from common law countries, given the differences in legal background, culture, and history?

2. How would you transplant a doctrine that is largely developed through case law by common law courts?
   a. How would you reconcile a new doctrine with existing ones?
   b. What would be the likely costs of such transplant?
   c. Compared with Japan and Korea, what could be the driving forces behind Taiwan's introduction of fiduciary duties or other corporate governance regimes?
3. Shareholder primacy:
   a. The Company Act does not clearly specify that the board must act to maximize shareholders' interest. However, the idea of "shareholder primacy" seems to be generally acceptable as a guiding principle.
   b. Interestingly, the old version of Article 5(1) of the Business Mergers and Acquisitions Act required the board of a company to "act for the best interests of shareholders" when conducting mergers and acquisitions. It was amended in 2015 to "act for the best interest of the company." What might the new amendment connote? Does it mean Taiwan has officially steered away from "shareholders' best interests" to "stakeholders' interests"?

12.2.2 Corporate Ownership and Governance Style

Yu-Hsin Lin, 'Do Social Ties Matter in Corporate Governance? The Missing Factor in Chinese Corporate Governance Reform' (2013) 5 *George Mason Journal of International Commercial Law* 39–73, at 60–2

The most important challenge in corporate governance in Taiwan is to constrain controlling shareholders' extraction of private benefits from minority shareholders. The corporate ownership of Taiwanese public companies is concentrated, family-owned, and divergent in its control rights and cash-flow rights. Yeh and Woidtke found that seventy-two percent of Taiwanese public firms had a controlling shareholder and that, among them, eighty-three percent were family controlled. The largest shareholders of Taiwan's nonfinancial firms controlled 62.69% of the board seats and 49.55% of the statutory-auditor positions. Hence, large shareholders in Taiwan not only own public firms but manage and control them as well …

The corporate-board structure of Taiwan generally follows the Japanese governance structure, which is a modified version of the German governance structure. In Germany, supervisory boards have the right to appoint or remove directors; however, in Japan and Taiwan, supervisors are nominated by boards and elected by shareholders. In addition, statutory supervisors or statutory auditors in Taiwan act individually, not collectively like their German and Japanese counterparts. According to the Corporation Law of Taiwan, a statutory auditor is an independent supervisory institution responsible for auditing the business conditions of companies and for evaluating the performance of companies' boards of directors and managers. However, a statutory auditor has the right only to attend board meetings, not the right to vote. In addition, the pre-reform law set no qualification for statutory auditors. In the past, many statutory auditors are relatives or friends of the given companies' founding families, controlling shareholder, directors, or top executives. Therefore, most statutory auditors of Taiwanese public companies are just "rubber stamps."

Notes and Questions

1. What is the effect of high concentration of ownership on the corporate governance system?
2. What are the pros and cons of mandatory public offerings? Taiwanese law no longer forces companies larger than a certain size to issue shares to the general public. Before 2001, a company with issued capital of more than NT$ 500 million (US$ 16. 6 million) was required to issue shares to the public subjecting it to regulation by the financial regulator.
3. Another feature of Taiwan's stock market is that over 60 percent of trading activities are conducted by individual investors. As a result, there are many small shareholders.
   a. How would this affect corporate governance?
   b. How would this impact the transplant of corporate governance doctrines from the West, in which institutional investors might play a larger role in monitoring management?
   c. It is not the case that there are no institutional investors in Taiwan. However, certain rules regarding some institutional investors may affect corporate governance of listed firms. For example, insurers cannot interfere with the management of a listed company in which they have investments. They do not actually exercise "voice" in general meetings. Should the law try to encourage those institutional investors to become more active?

12.3 Internal Governance: Board Function

This section introduces the internal governance system in Taiwan. It introduces the different models adopted in Taiwan from the traditional divide between the board of directors and supervisors to the modern adoption of independent directors and an audit committee. It further introduces some special features under Taiwanese law, including the cumulative voting regime and the judicial person director.

12.3.1 Different Models

Andrew Jen-Guang Lin, 'Common Law Influences in Private Law – Taiwan's Experiences Related to Corporate Law' (2009) 4(2) *National Taiwan University Law Review* 107–38, at 112–15

[Entering the twenty-first century,] how to enhance the monitoring function to watch the board of directors and management, at least to prevent self-dealing and fraudulent misconducts, has been the focus of the corporate governance reform in Taiwan. Regarding internal monitoring mechanisms, four major forces interactively monitor the performance of the board of directors and management: they are (1) exercising shareholders' rights and votes at shareholders' meeting; (2) corporate supervisors; (3) self-evaluation via internal control and internal audit system; (4) independent directors and/or audit committee.

With the influence of the Sarbanes–Oxley Act of 2002, [Taiwan's Securities and Exchange Act (TSEA)] was amended on January 11, 2006 to officially introduce independent directors and audit committee into the corporate structure of publicly held corporations to enhance the internal monitoring mechanism. The amendment sets forth that beginning from January 2007, publicly held corporations may be required by the competent authority to appoint independent directors into the board of directors and set up an audit committee to replace supervisors. Because not every publicly held corporation is required to appoint independent directors or set up an audit committee, there will be three major models of corporate structure for publicly held corporation in Taiwan after January 1, 2007. Generally speaking, a publicly held corporation has the option to decide the model of its internal corporate structure. However, the Financial Supervisory Commission (FSC) may designate certain types of corporations to appoint independent directors but maintain supervisors as the monitoring organ (Model Two), and designate certain types of corporations to establish an audit committee, composed of all independent directors, to replace supervisors (Model Three). Therefore, three different models will coexist after January 2007 …

1. *Model One – Two-Tier System*

The first model is the traditional and current corporate structure as required by the Company Act since its enaction in 1929. Under Model One, a company has a shareholders' meeting, a board of directors and supervisors. Shareholders elect both directors and supervisors. The board is composed of executives and some outside directors. Supervisors serve as the monitoring organ to monitor the performance of the board of directors and the management. Under this old fashioned two-tier corporate structure, supervisors are criticized for not being able to exercise the monitoring role because of the passivity and the close relationship with the controlling shareholders and directors.

After the amendment of the TSEA in 2006, non-publicly held corporations will maintain this two-tier corporate structure. As for publicly held corporations, if not designated by the FSC to appoint independent directors or to establish an audit committee, it may maintain the traditional two-tier board corporate structure.

2. *Model Two – Two-Tier System with Independent Directors*

As discussed in the earlier section, the FSC may order certain corporations to appoint independent directors into the board of directors but still maintain supervisors as the official monitoring organ. Under Model Two, supervisors serve as the monitoring organ. Although independent directors play some monitoring function, under this model, they are directors and do not have comparable supervisory powers held by supervisors according to the Company Act. Articles 14–2 to 14–3 and Independent Director Regulation promulgated by the FSC govern the appointment, qualifications, missions, and powers of the independent directors. The major function of the independent directors is to participate the board meeting and provide their professional and independent opinions regarding material corporate affairs as listed in Article 14–3 of the TSEA. It requires that the dissenting and reserved opinion of the independent directors be recorded in the minutes of the board meeting and published on the Market Observation Post System …

3. *Model Three – One-Tier System and Audit Committee*

The FSC may require certain publicly held corporation establish an audit committee. The TSEA does not clearly point out whether audit committee is a subcommittee of the board. However, if a company establishes an audit committee, it has to abolish supervisors. Therefore, audit committee is established to replace supervisors and serves as the supervisory organ. The TSEA explicitly delegate supervisory powers of supervisors to both the audit committee and its members. Therefore, unlike the independent directors of Model Two, independent directors under Model Three serve not only as a director but also enjoy the supervisory powers. In addition to the supervisory powers set forth under Article 14–4, important corporate affairs, as listed under Article 14–5, must obtain approval from the audit committee before it goes to the board meeting. However, the audit committee does not have the veto power. Although the audit committee disapproves the proposal, the board meeting still can approve it by approval of more than two thirds of all board members. It is necessary to note that the board is not required to be composed of majority independent directors. However, under such circumstances, the TSEA requires the minutes of the board meeting to record the disapproval of the audit committee and publish such information on the Market Observation Post System.

Notes and Questions

1. On supervisors:
    a. Under Taiwanese law, supervisors do not actually form a separate board. Thus, it is not exactly a "two-tier" system (compared with the "supervisory board" under German law). Instead, each supervisor can exercise power separately and independently. The function of supervisors and the board of directors are parallel rather than hierarchical in nature, and it thus is more like a dual board system.
    b. Supervisors are elected separately from the board of directors. This also means that the same controlling shareholder can vote twice, once for the board and again for the supervisors. How would this rule affect the function of supervisors?
    c. Taiwanese law grants supervisors some powers to monitor the board. For example, a supervisor has the power to bring a derivative action against a director or to inspect the company's books. A supervisor even has the power to call an extraordinary general meeting as he sees fit.
    d. Why have supervisors failed to exercise properly their function? One potential problem of supervisors is that they may not be independent of the management or controlling shareholder and they may not have sufficient expertise to monitor the management. For example, see the discussion around the Rebar scandal in section 12.5.
    e. Would the introduction of independent directors (see below) help to address the problem?
2. Why did Taiwan initially allow different models coexisting at the same time? What were the concerns?
3. Taiwan does not separate the role of the chairperson and the general manager, which is similar to the chief executive officer. It is common practice that the chairperson is also the controlling shareholder and has the ultimate management power in a company or business group. The chairperson is also usually an executive director. Should this common practice be changed?
4. According to a study, about 48.74 percent of listed companies in Taiwan did not have any independent directors (i.e. companies adopting Model 1 above) in 2005, but the figure dropped to 33.66 percent in 2014. Thus, there are more companies having independent directors on the board (i.e. adopting the Model 2 above) from 2005 to 2014. See Tsin-Ti Chang, Yu-Hsin Lin, and Ying-Hsin Tsai, 'From Double Board to Unitary Board System: The Corporate Governance Reform in Taiwan,' in Harald Baum, Luke Nottage, and Dan W. Puchniak (eds.), *Independent Directors in Asia: A Historical, Contextual and Comparative Approach* (Cambridge: Cambridge University Press, 2017). In addition, pursuant to data provided by the Taiwan Stock Exchange, about 19.91 percent of listed companies in Taiwan had established an audit committee (i.e. Model 3) by the end of 2014, and the

proportion rises to 36.66 percent by the end of 2016. See the website of Taiwan Stock Exchange: http://cgc.twse.com.tw/auditCommittee/chPage. In other words, as at 2014, about 46 percent of listed companies adopt Model 2 and nearly 20 percent adopting Model 3, with the rest still adopting Model 1.

12.3.2 Cumulative Voting and Juridical Person Director

Ching-Ping Shao, 'The Evolution of Company Law in Taiwan: A Focus on the Blockholder-Centric Model,' in Yun-chien Chang, Wei Shen, and Wen-yeu Wang (eds.), *Private Law in China and Taiwan: Legal and Economic Analyses* (Cambridge: Cambridge University Press, 2016), pp. 272–303, at 280–94

In the 1966 amendment … several changes were made pertaining to the directorship of juridical persons [in Art 27 of the Company Act]. First … it was mandated that directors be selected by corporate election. Second, governments and other juridical persons were allowed to be elected as directors. Legislative justifications for introducing this change at that time could not be found and remained unclear. A reasonable guess is that the designation rule was finally found to be unacceptable as the notion of corporate democracy and corporate election became widely well received. Second, governments and other juridical persons were allowed to be elected as directors. They could choose to send natural person representatives to participate in elections. By this means, such representatives were to be elected as directors in their own names rather than in the names of juridical person shareholders. Directors could no longer be unilaterally installed, but juridical person shareholders retained the right, as was allowed by the 1946 Company Law, to replace their original representatives with new representatives.

In the 1946 Company Law, election methods for directors were not specified explicitly. Corporations were left to autonomously decide which election method to use. The 1966 amendment constituted the first incorporation of cumulative voting and made it mandatory for all corporations …

In addition to the seeming justification of minority shareholders protection, two explanations can be offered for the adoption of mandatory cumulative voting in the 1966 Company Law. The first one is a legal transplant explanation. Cumulative voting acquired considerable traction in the late 1940s in the United States … The popularity of cumulative voting had declined since then, however. By the time Taiwan adopted cumulative voting in 1966, mandatory cumulative voting in the United States had largely abandoned. This anachronistic adaption is likely the result of the time lag in legal transplantation …

The second one is a path-dependence explanation ... To defuse the corporate governance crisis, policymakers decided to take the concentration strategy and adopt the mandatory cumulative voting rule. The function of cumulative voting is to allocate board membership appropriately in proportion to shareholding. Judicial-person shareholders could win broadly the same number of seats of directorship in the cumulative voting election as they could under the previous nonelection regime ...

Cumulative voting provides blockholders with the opportunity for representation on the board and possible access to corporate control ... Sitting on the board provides such raiders greater access to corporate information and allows them additional leverage to collaborate with others in the fight for corporate control. Thus, hostile takeovers may occur more frequently when cumulative voting is used ...

In the 1990s, the aforementioned scenario was particularly true in Taiwan. One of the most infamous cases involved the Kaohsiung Business Bank. As a local bank based in Southern Taiwan, it was long controlled by major shareholders from three families. In the 1995 annual shareholder meeting, insurgent shareholders, who had acquired only 0.03% of outstanding shares, purchased sufficient proxies and seized 5 out of the 15 director seats in the election. They also formed a coalition with three other directors. The coalition therefore constituted most of the board and replaced the management, meaning that they had majority control of the board and replaced the bank's management. Subsequently, loans of vast sums from the bank were offered to politicians and businessmen close to the coalition, and substantial losses were incurred. In 1996, the family blockholders, who retained ownership of 35 percent of the outstanding shares, finally called a special shareholder meeting and regained control of the bank. However, the bank was unable to recover from debts incurred under the previous management and finally went bankrupt ...

The rare incidence of opting out of cumulative voting in the wake of the 2001 amendment suggests that majority shareholders or blockholders consider it not cost-effective to initiate such an amendment. But the rationalist thinking also implies that majority shareholders will not hesitate to contend if conflicts among blockholders increase to such an intolerable level that the hope of maintaining an amicable relationship vanishes.

The Ta-I Inc. case is a case in point. During the 2007 director election season, Yageo Inc., the insurgent shareholder, secured more than 40% of Ta-I Inc.'s outstanding shares and expected to occupy nearly half of the seats on the board under the cumulative voting rule, whereas the Ta-I Inc. management group was expected to maintain a weak board majority. In the shareholder meeting notice sent to all of the shareholders, "charter amending" was listed on the agenda to be discussed in this meeting. However, no specific proposals on which of the articles of its charter would be revised were identified. When this motion of "charter amending" was in process, a shareholder abruptly proposed to amend the provision on the director election method in the charter. This extempore proposal was for eliminating the cumulative voting rule and adopting the straight voting rule. Yageo Inc. was caught off guard. Despite strong opposition from Yageo Inc., the amendment was passed. In the immediate ensuing election in which the straight voting rule was adopted, the Ta-I Inc. management group thus acquired all of the board seats, and Yageo Inc. left the meeting with none.

Be it fair or unfair for minority shareholders, judged from the perspective of legal technicalities, the manner in which the shareholder meeting of Ta-I Inc. was conducted complies with judicial and regulatory interpretations ...

... Regulators and lawmakers believed that only the revival of mandatory cumulative voting could prevent an inequitable outcome. Because cumulative voting remained the prevailing norm, the change from a permissive rule to a mandatory rule would influence only few corporations. Opposition to this revision proposal was rarely heard in the business community. By the end of 2011, the Legislative Yuan passed the revision of Article 198 and mandatory cumulative voting was reinstated in the Company Law.

Notes and Questions

1. On cumulative voting:
    a. What is cumulative voting under Art. 198 of the Company Act? What are the purposes of cumulative voting? Is it essential for enabling minority shareholders to obtain representation on the board?
    b. Cumulative voting was mandatory until 2001, when an amendment of the Company Act allowed a company to exclude it, largely in response to the Kaohsiung Business Bank scandal. However, only seven out of the top 1,000 Taiwanese corporations opted out of the cumulative voting regime.[1] Since December 2011, cumulative voting became compulsory again. What is wrong with allowing companies to opt out of cumulative voting?
2. Article 27 of the Company Act is a special feature under Taiwanese law.
    a. Under Art. 27 a juridical person shareholder (e.g. the government or a holding company) is entitled to appoint multiple representatives onto the board of directors on its behalf. It is widely used by companies in a variety of circumstances: state-owned enterprises (e.g. Chang Hwa Bank, see below), family-owned businesses (e.g. Fubon Financial Holdings), companies with a strong controller (e.g. Honhai/Foxconn), and even more widely held companies (e.g. Taiwan Semiconductor).

[1] See Ching-Ping Shao, 'Recent Reforms and Developments in the U.S. Corporate Director Election Regime – From a Comparative Law Perspective' (2009) 26 *National Chung Cheng University Law Journal* 1–62, at 35–6.

b. For example, in 2013, the board of Eva Air consisted of six directors in addition to three supervisors. All of them were representatives of other charities or affiliated companies owned by the controlling Chang family. In this situation, Art. 27 helped the controlling shareholder to monopolize both the management and supervisors.

c. For a battle of corporate control, it might then become a proxy fight for the number of representatives that a juridical person shareholder can appoint onto the board. For example, there has been an ongoing, controversial fight to control Chang Hwa Bank between a private investor and the state.

d. Art. 27 provides much flexibility for a major shareholder to control the board of directors and/or supervisors. However, the rule may confuse the role of a director and the person who actually exercises the function, when the director is itself a legal person, in terms of fiduciary duties, compensation and parties to shareholder derivative suits.

e. While Art. 27 seems to entrench majority control, it is not subject to any pressure to reform. Part of the reason might be that the state is a main beneficiary of the rules to control state-owned enterprises. Therefore, it has no incentive to revise the law and cut off a weapon to control companies.

12.3.3 Board Independence

Yu-Hsin Lin, 'Do Social Ties Matter in Corporate Governance? The Missing Factor in Chinese Corporate Governance Reform' (2013) 5 *George Mason Journal of International Commercial Law* 39–73, at 62

To equip a controlled board with checks-and-balances powers, the Taiwanese regulatory authority introduced the institution of the "independent director." In 2002, the TSE began taking a leading role in requiring all newly listed companies to have at least two independent directors and one independent statutory supervisor. In 2006, Taiwan's Congress revised the Securities and Exchange Law to introduce the institution of independent directors, essentially giving public companies the option to choose whether or not they would have independent directors. In the meantime, to speed up the pace of reform, the law authorized the Financial Supervisory Commission to implement the law in stages.

In March 2006, Taiwan's Financial Supervisory Commission ("FSC") mandated that all public financial firms and those non-financial listed firms with equity valued over NT$50 billion (US$1.6 billion) have at least two independent directors on their boards, and that the total number of independent directors should be no less than one-fifth the number of board members. On March 22, 2011, the FSC further expanded the mandate to firms with equity valued over NT$10 billion (US$345 million). As of August 2013, there were 425 out of 809 TSE-listed companies whose boards had at least one independent director. That is, 52.53% of the TSE-listed companies had at least one independent director on their board. Only 17% (137 out of 809) of TSE-listed companies adopted the United States-style board structure by establishing audit committees and abolishing statutory supervisors. Still, 47.47% of TSE-listed firms did not have any independent directors.

Notes and Questions

1. The requirement of independent directors and audit committee is provided in Arts. 14 to 14–6 of the Securities and Exchange Act rather than in a voluntary corporate governance code. What might be the sanction for failure to comply?
2. The Financial Supervisory Commission currently requires all public companies whose share capital is above NT$ 2 billion (about US$ 66 million) to have independent directors pursuant to the Securities and Exchange Act by 2017. In addition, public companies with share capital more than NT$ 10 billion must have an audit committee by 2017 and those with capital between NT$2 and 10 billion must have it by 2019 (there is no such requirement for companies under 2 billion). Thus, it is obvious that Taiwan's financial regulator wants public companies to adopt Model Three (see section 12.3.1).
   a. Would it be appropriate to require all public and listed companies to have independent directors and audit committees? Would it be better if companies had a choice of different models?
   b. Should we improve the function and independence of supervisors rather requiring a group of directors called "independent directors"?

12.3.4 Board Independence in Practice

Christopher Chen, 'Solving the Puzzle of Corporate Governance of State-Owned Enterprises: The Path of the Temasek Model in Singapore and Lessons for China' (2016) 36(2) *Northwestern Journal of International Law and Business* 303–70, at 353–8

[W]e now compare the data presented earlier with data collected from the component stocks of the Hang Seng Index (HSI) listed on the Hong Kong Exchange (HKEx) and the Taiwan 50 Index component stocks traded on the Taiwan Stock Exchange as of July 1, 2014. Each index contains fifty companies to allow comparison with the list of the top fifty companies on the SGX.

Table 12.1 Proportion of independent directors in top 50 companies in the three markets

Item (as in 2013 annual report)	Obs.	Mean (%)	Median (%)	Std. Dev.	High (%)	Low (%)
Overall						
Singapore: 50 largest companies by market capitalization (see Table 12.2)	46	57	57	16.55	90	33
Hong Kong: HSI component stocks	50	43	38	13.41	92	24
Taiwan: Taiwan 50 index component stocks	50	24	23	14.06	56	0
SOEs						
Singapore: companies in which Temasek holds a greater than 5% stake (out of the companies in Table 12.2)	17	65	64	13.57	91	38
Hong Kong: Chinese SOEs in the HSI	22	39	38	5.66	55	31
Taiwan: companies in the Taiwan 50 index in which the government owns 5% or more of the shares	11	22	22	18%	56	0

Yu-Hsin Lin, 'Overseeing Controlling Shareholders: Do Independent Directors Constrain Tunneling in Taiwan?' (2011) 12 *San Diego International Law Journal* 363–416, at 398–400

From where exactly do these independent directors come? This study classifies the occupation into ten categories ... The top three occupations for independent directors are: (1) corporate directors (29.03%) (2) professors (24.91%), and (3) managers (12.36%) (Table 12.2) ... In Taiwan, corporate directors and CEOs account for 41.2% of all independent directors, which is still a significant number. Together with managers, people from the corporate world make up over half (53.56%) of this population.

One remarkable observation about the population of independent directors in Taiwan is that "professors" is a significant group, accounting for 24.91%. No doubt,

Table 12.2 Occupations of independent directors

Occupations	Number	%
corporate directors	155	29.03
professors	133	24.91
managers	66	12.36
CEOs	65	12.17
accountants	39	7.30
others	30	5.62
lawyers	24	4.49
government officials	10	1.87
politicians	10	1.87
physicians	2	0.37
total	534	

Analyzed and categorized by the author. Source: Market Observation Post System, Taiwan Stock Exchange (October 2008)

the public image of professors fits perfectly well with the concept of "independent." Professors are generally thought as experts in their chosen field.

Yu-Hsin Lin, 'Do Social Ties Matter in Corporate Governance? The Missing Factor in Chinese Corporate Governance Reform' (2013) 5 *George Mason Journal of International Commercial Law* 39–73, at 63–5

Of the forty independent directors interviewed by this study, nineteen used the term "very close friend" to describe their relationship with controlling shareholders, other directors or CEOs within a given firm, and fourteen other independent directors stated that they were personally acquainted with controlling shareholders, other directors or CEOs within a given firm, but were not "very close friends" with these individuals. Only seven of the interviewees had not known the controlling shareholders, other directors or CEOs before being invited to join the board.

The interview results are stunning. Almost half of the independent directors described controlling shareholders, other directors or CEOs of the firms as "very close friends." While public companies are required to disclose the financial, familial, and business relations among independent directors, the companies and corporate insiders, almost no formal sources of information identify their close personal relationships. But such social ties might hinder the monitoring ability of independent directors. Although the interview results are hard to generalize because of the limited number of samples involved, most interviewees agreed that a majority of independent directors in Taiwan had some degree of *guanxi* with their controlling shareholders or other corporate insiders.

Independent directors have long been criticized as outsiders who rely on the firm and corporate insiders to provide information needed for carrying out directors' duties. There is an information asymmetry between independent directors and controlling shareholders, who are usually also managers in Taiwanese firms. It is hard for independent director candidates to decide whether to join a board if they were not first to obtain adequate information about the firm. Interestingly, to screen firms and decide whether to accept the offer, the key criterion used by independent directors in Taiwan is not the corporate governance of a company but the integrity of controlling shareholders or other corporate insiders.

The survey also shows that more than fifty-five percent of the interviewed independent directors in Taiwan had personally known their own firm's controlling shareholders, other directors or CEOs for more than ten years …

Except in a few large companies, most leaders of public companies in Taiwan seek independent directors with whom these leaders have personal relationships. As mentioned, controlling shareholders seek suitable independent directors. There also exists information asymmetry between candidates and controlling shareholders about the qualification and integrity of independent director candidates. *Guanxi* has been an important source of reliable information in Chinese society. It is no surprise that controlling shareholders seeking to fill a vacant board position would first invite someone with whom they have already established *guanxi*.

Notes and Questions

1. How do Taiwanese listed companies compare with listed companies in other markets in terms of board independence?
   a. Even if we discount companies that have not implemented independent directors as in 2014, the proportion of independent directors hovers around 30–40 percent. The data is similar to Hong Kong; but it is lower than Singapore. This also means that most companies only attempt to satisfy the minimum threshold of one-third of the board. Is that sufficient?
   b. The low average number of independent directors on the board of the largest fifty companies (as of July 2014) also means that in many companies all of the independent directors are also members of audit committees. Does this place too much burden on independent directors?

2. What could be the consequences of having many academics or professors on a board as independent directors, as opposed to professionals or other businessmen (as in the case of Singapore)?
3. While the idea of board independence might be compromised due to *guanxi* (relationship) or other connections (e.g. being classmates in the same MBA program or law school), should the idea be dropped? Would there be any way to examine or control such relationship?
4. Compared with supervisors, does the independent director regime represent an improvement?

12.4 Enforcement

This section first introduces the failure of Taiwan's derivative action regime and then proceeds to the creation of the Investor Protection Center, a unique invention.

12.4.1 Statutory Derivative Action

Wen-yeu Wang and Jhe-yu Su, 'The Best of Both Worlds? On Taiwan's Quasi-Public Enforcer of Corporate and Securities Law' (2015) 3(1) *Chinese Journal of Comparative Law* 1–27, at 10–11

Taiwan's law allows shareholders to act on behalf of the company in bringing a derivative suit against the company's directors or other responsible persons if such persons are in breach of their duty of care or loyalty to the company. In order to have the legal standing to bring the lawsuit, however, the shareholders must meet certain procedural requirements and hold at least 3 per cent of the company's outstanding shares for more than a year. This shareholding requirement is based on the assumption that 'the smaller a plaintiff shareholder's stake is in the company, the less likely it is that the plaintiff shareholder will internalize all of the economic impact that the derivative action has on the company.' In this respect, it functions as a safeguard against frivolous lawsuits. In reality, it blocks not only frivolous suits but also meritorious ones – especially since the 3 per cent shareholding requirement is an incredibly high threshold for a publicly listed company. This situation again effectively prevents derivative lawsuits.

In addition to a high threshold that prohibits most shareholders from bringing a lawsuit, the Company Law further discourages the initiation of derivative suits by way of raising the economic risks and burden on the plaintiff shareholders. First, if the court does not find in favour of the plaintiff in the derivative suit, the plaintiff shareholders must compensate the company for any damages incurred. A plaintiff shareholder thus takes on two kinds of major economic risk: not only does the shareholder risk bearing all of the costs of the proceedings, with the possibility of receiving only an indirect economic gain in the future if the company's share price rises as a result of the derivative action, the shareholder will also be punished if he or she loses. Second, upon the defendant's request, the court can order the plaintiff shareholders to post a security deposit. This rule imposes an additional heavy burden on the plaintiff. Finally, compounding these two problems, the Company Law is silent on whether a plaintiff shareholder may have his or her litigation costs reimbursed if the case is successful. The prospect of indemnification is unclear and requires the plaintiff to meet a number of onerous criteria under the general indemnification provisions of the Code of Civil Procedure.

Taken together, all of these stringent requirements and burdens imposed on a potential plaintiff shareholder, combined with the original lack of economic incentives, renders derivative lawsuits unattractive for minority shareholders to pursue and prevents lawyers from assuming the risk in their place. Against this seemingly built-in antagonism towards plaintiff shareholders, it is unsurprising that there were hardly any derivative suits in Taiwan before the modern IPC era.

Notes and Questions

1. Very few derivative actions have been brought in Taiwan. Pursuant to the author's own research, there were only twelve derivative actions (under Art. 214 of the Company Act) brought by shareholders between 2000 and 2013. Among the twelve lawsuits, eight were filed by supervisors on behalf of the company against its director(s). It should also be noted that none of these twelve lawsuits concerned listed companies. Thus, these lawsuits do not directly affect a large number of shareholders or investors, raising little public concern.
2. Compared with other countries, what are the key features of Taiwan's derivative action regime? What are the incentives and disincentives underlying the regime? How does it affect corporate governance?
3. Should Taiwan remove the threshold for bringing a derivative action under Art. 214? Would the abolition of the threshold lead to frivolous lawsuits? Have you seen other countries with similar thresholds?

12.4.2 Creation of the Securities and Futures Investor Protection Center

Yu-Hsin Lin, 'Modeling Securities Class Actions outside the United States: The Role of Nonprofits in the Case of Taiwan' (2007) 4 *NYU Journal of Law and Business* 143–98, at 167–70

2. *The Investor Services Center in 1998*

To cope with individual investors' need to claim damages and to establish sound investor-protection mechanisms, Taiwan's securities authority, the Securities and Futures Commission (SFC), established an Investor Services Center under the Securities and Futures Institute (SFI) in March 1998 to coordinate claims against public companies on behalf of individual investors. At the direction of the Taiwanese government, the SFI was founded as a nonprofit organization in 1984 and was funded by the Taiwan Stock Exchange and local securities and banking industries. Since its establishment, the purpose of the SFI has been to promote the globalization and liberalization of Taiwan's securities market. The SFI has supported the government's policy for national economic development.

Furthermore, the SFI has been a major force in promoting corporate governance in Taiwan and engages in both enforcement activities and non-enforcement activities. In bringing securities group litigation, the Investor Services Center of the SFI functions similarly to a public-interest law firm. The SFI not only overcame collective-action problems in coordinating investors to bring securities lawsuits but also, when necessary, budgeted the payment of court fees and lawyer fees. Some scholars even argue that the SFI, as a quasipublic organization, subsidizes the costs of private enforcement. As of 2002, before the SFI transferred investor services to the Investors Protection Center, the SFI had filed *de facto* securities class actions against 23 companies on behalf of 6,028 investors, seeking NT$3.56 billion (approximately US$108 million) in civil damages.

3. *Investors Protection Act in 2003 – Establishment of the Investors Protection Center*

Although the SFI has actively promoted the private enforcement of corporate governance in Taiwan, the legal environment is antagonistic to group litigation. To reduce the costs and the other risks associated with securities group litigation, in July 2002, the Legislative Yuan (Taiwan's congress) passed the Securities Investors and Futures Traders Protection Act (the Act), which took effect in January 2003. The Act created an Investor Protection Fund (the Fund) to compensate investors when securities or futures firms become insolvent and were unable to settle their transactions. The Act further established the Securities and Futures Investors Protection Center (IPC) to manage the Fund and provide mediation services for disputes arising from the trading of securities and futures.

Most important of all, the Act has opened a new phase of securities class action in Taiwan by granting the IPC a monopoly in bringing securities class actions on behalf of defrauded investors. According to the Investors Protection Act, the IPC may bring securities class actions or may undertake arbitration (doing so in its own name on behalf of investors) when the following conditions are met: (1) there should be a preoccupation with the public interest; (2) there should be a single event that causes damages to several investors; and (3) there should be more than 20 investors who delegate their litigation or arbitration rights to the IPC. The Fund is funded primarily by mandatory contributions from securities and futures firms and from self-regulatory organizations, such as stock exchanges, futures exchanges, and the OTC market. In addition to compensating the investors when securities or futures firms are insolvent, the Fund can help defray the expenses that accrue from the litigation or arbitration brought by the IPC.

90 As a non-government organisation with investor protection as its mission, the risk that it would put profit above the interests of investors is avoided. The seed fund for the SFIPC was provided by the major stakeholders in the Taiwanese securities and futures industry. At its inception, NT$1.031bn (approx US$31.8m) was raised. Continued funding for its operation comes from a levy on, first, contracts put through securities and futures firms, and second, transactions on the exchanges. From January 2003 to December 2005, the SFIPC received a total contribution of NT$1.54bn (approximately US$32.5m) from the industry. As the stakeholders have committed to providing a steady stream of funding for the SFIPC, the bottom line consequences of a suit are secondary. Indeed, the SFIPC is legally prohibited from seeking remuneration for its litigation services. Accordingly, there are not the same agency problems such as the lawyer's incentive to settle when he works on a contingency fee agreement. As a non-profit organisation enjoying public and private sector support, the law also makes special provision for waiving the security deposit normally required for a provision injunction, attachment or execution.

91 The two features of the Taiwanese model outlined above – expertise and funding – commend the use of the model in other jurisdictions. As a non-profit organisation whose adherence to its mission is policed by its diverse stakeholders, an institution like the SFIPC can perform its evaluative function and recommend

courses of action untainted by profitability considerations. While budgetary considerations will undeniably continue to apply, the insertion of a non-profit organisation removes the incentive to institute nuisance suits for economic gain, a nagging concern in for-profit litigation funding.

92 Accountability can be built into its governance structure. In the Taiwan SFIPC, assessment of cases is done by its staff but approval of the board must be obtained. The board of the SFIPC, two-thirds of which must comprise academics, thus exercises direct supervision over the litigation commenced by the SFIPC. A variety of alternative arrangements can, of course, be mooted to ensure that such an institution keeps true to its objectives and is not captured by those it seeks to regulate. The appointment of these representatives can be made directly by stakeholders subject to the approval of the securities regulator. Alternatively, appointments may be made by the executive branch after informal consultations with stakeholders. Public accountability can be brought about through annual reports to Parliament and the relevant government ministry, with additional oversight hearings before a parliamentary select committee if necessary.

93 The model is also attractive from a financing perspective. The aggrieved investor does not make a direct financial contribution in order for the SFIPC to litigate on his behalf. Its income is "taxed" out of the revenue stream of the securities and futures firms, as well as those of the exchanges. All investors contribute to it, if indirectly. The financing scheme is therefore akin to an insurance scheme, in which every investor makes an indirect contribution through a small portion of the transaction cost that is paid to the securities firms and exchanges. Indeed, it may be seen as a compulsory legal expenses insurance scheme to which each investor is enrolled once he transacts on the market. Such a scheme has the merit that it pools the market abuse risks of all transactions on the market, avoiding the moral hazard that typically plagues an after-the-event insurance scheme. From a public finance perspective, the budget does not come out of the public coffers; instead, it comes out of investors, securities firms and the securities exchange. This funding model is not novel …

Notes and Questions

1. What are the benefits of having a nonprofit organization (NPO) such as the Securities and Futures Investor Protection Center (IPC)?
2. What could be potential problems of the IPC regime? Is it appropriate to have one NPO to monopolize the market?
3. As of 2015, the IPC can bring a lawsuit in two ways. The traditional way is to file for a class action under Art. 28 of the Securities Investor and Futures Traders Protection Act (SIFTPA),

if the IPC is authorized by at least twenty investors. Since 2009, the IPC was given the standing to bring an action on its own under some conditions by the new Art. 10–1 of the SIFTPA. Why do you think this provision was added?

4. With the IPC's key management appointed and approved by the financial regulator, effectively the IPC is a quasi-public entity designated with the role of civil enforcement of corporate and securities law. How would this affect the role of IPC when pursuing civil actions or negotiating a settlement with a defendant?

12.4.3 Performance of the Investor Protection Center

Wen-yeu Wang and Jhe-yu Su, 'The Best of Both Worlds? On Taiwan's Quasi-Public Enforcer of Corporate and Securities Law' (2015) 3(1) *Chinese Journal of Comparative Law* 1–27, at 19

By the end of 2013, the IPC had brought 175 class action claims, seeking an aggregate amount of NT $42.9 billion in civil damages on behalf of approximately 108,000 total investors. The causes of the actions can be categorized into financial statement misrepresentation, prospectus disclosure misrepresentation, insider trading, and market manipulation. As of the end of 2013, there were 48 final judgments, among which 23 were found in favour of the IPC, and the remaining 25 went against it. The total amount of compensation claimed by the IPC in the 23 winning cases was NT $3.6 billion, out of which NT $2.84 billion, or 93.3 per cent of the total amount, was granted by the court. Out of this NT $2.84 billion, however, only NT $249.0 million has been collected, which amounts to a recovery rate of approximately 8 per cent. Thus, the compensation actually received by the investors compared to the losses claimed is low. This discrepancy shows that the IPC's compensatory function is less than satisfactory. It also suggests that the IPC has a low deterrence value …

Yu-Hsin Lin, 'Modeling Securities Class Actions outside the United States: The Role of Nonprofits in the Case of Taiwan' (2007) 4 *NYU Journal of Law and Business* 143–98, at 181

5. ***Reliance on Public Enforcement***

To solve information asymmetry problems, the IPC in Taiwan relies heavily on criminal prosecution to obtain information. When selecting cases for filing, the IPC will first consider the cases that are under either investigation or prosecution in which the government has already gathered evidence. Government enforcement actions are an integral part of IPC calculations when the IPC is deciding whether or not to bring a lawsuit. Among the 36 cases brought by the IPC, 34 have had parallel criminal proceedings: the criminal prosecutions of 30 cases preceded civil filings, and 10 civil claims "piggybacked" on criminal proceedings. A similar situation prevails in Japan. Of the 140 cases of shareholder litigation examined by West, 20 in which criminal penalties were imposed, 20 involving pending criminal cases, and another 13 were the subject of some sort of official investigation. In 50 of these 53 cases, criminal enforcement preceded civil enforcement.

Christopher Chen, 'Enforcement of the Duties of Directors by the Securities and Futures Investors Protection Center in Taiwan' (2014), SSRN, at http://papers.ssrn.com/sol3/papers.cfm?abstract_id=2588254

Through our survey of the LRRS system, we found 138 lawsuits involving the SFIPC that contain sufficient information for analysis [from 2000 to 2013] …

First, how successful the SFIPC was in those lawsuits? By analysing the final judgments available by the end of 2013, we find that the SFIPC has won (including a partial win) 45 lawsuits (32.61%) and lost 86 of them (62.32%), with 7 cases (5.07%) still pending after being remanded by the Supreme Court …

How successful is the SFIPC in ancillary civil actions? Among the 59 ancillary civil actions, the SFIPC won all but 6 cases (10.17%) with 3 cases still pending after being remanded by the Supreme Court. This is substantially lower than SFIPC's general winning rate. There is a statistically significant relationship between an ancillary civil action and the final result of lawsuit with a moderate negative correlation (i.e. SFIPC losing) ($chi2 = 24.23$, $p < 0.001$, correlation = −0.43). Thus, our data shows that there is no particular advantage if the SFIPC chooses to file an ancillary civil action instead of a direct civil action. Any saving from litigation expenses may not be justified by the very low winning rate for ancillary civil actions. It is also unclear how far the SFIPC could collect evidence from those criminal proceedings …

In contrast to ancillary civil action, the SFIPC did a much better job by filing a lawsuit directly to civil courts. Among the 79 civil lawsuits, the SFIPC eventually won 39 of them (49.37%) with 4 cases still pending after being remanded by the Supreme Court … [However,] so far the SFIPC does not have much success by filing an Art 10–1 action in its own capacity, winning only 1 case out of 8 lawsuits (12.50%) in our dataset.

Notes and Questions

1. While the IPC has been praised by some academics and has claimed compensation for investors, it is also subject to criticism.
   a. What problems might result from the IPC's heavy reliance on public prosecutors and criminal proceedings for evidence or to file civil actions?
   b. Research shows that on average it took nearly nineteen months between the occurrence of a scandal and the filing of a criminal charge and 36.5 months on average between a scandal and bringing a civil lawsuit. To acquire a final civil judgment, it might take another 3.5 years on average. Given this pattern, would you consider justice to be achieved if investors need to wait many years before receiving any compensation? How should we evaluate IPC's performance in this regard?
2. IPC has spent much effort in enforcing securities regulations, particularly for false disclosure or insider trading. However, it is questionable how far the IPC succeeded in bringing actions against delinquent directors.
   a. Do you think the new Art. 10–1 would help? Does it address problems from Taiwan's derivative action regime?
   b. Is it appropriate to expand the IPC's legal standing to bring a lawsuit without being authorized by victim-investors?
   c. Would it be possible for the IPC to bring a derivative action that is not in the interests of the company? Would it be in conflict with underlying company law principles when a nonprofit organization brings a derivative action on its own for the sake of the public interest?
3. Do you think other countries should import the IPC model?

12.5 Case Study: the Rebar Scandal in 2007

See the following for more details of the scandal and the problems surrounding it: Tai-Hui Chiu, 'Case Study of the Conglomerate Bankruptcy Scandal in Taiwan (the Rebar Group),' MIT, at http://dspace.mit.edu/bitstream/handle/1721.1/99010/921187517-MIT.pdf?sequence=1, 35–41

The Rebar scandal in 2007 was a huge corporate scandal that involved an industrial conglomerate and a bank. The scandal offered a classic example of corporate governance failure. During its heyday, the Rebar group covered a wide range of business activities from construction and cement to running hotels and shopping malls. The Rebar group also controlled a commercial bank called "The Chinese Bank." The controlling shareholder was You-theng Wang, a businessman well connected to top political figures in the 1980s and 1990s. The whole saga was triggered by a bank run of The Chinese Bank. It was revealed that Mr. Wang and his family committed a series of accounting fraud and financial crimes to hide bad loans of the group as well as to tunnel funds to the controlling family. Mr. Wang and his wife soon fled to the US and never returned to Taiwan. He died in a traffic accident in California in 2016. Many of his sons and daughters were serving jail sentences. There were also lawsuits brought by the Investor Protection Center to seek compensation for minority shareholders. The Chinese Bank eventually was sold to HSBC at a discount.

This scandal showed a total breakdown of corporate governance. On the one hand, the controlling Wang family used cross-ownership as a way to consolidate their grip over the group. This allowed them to have absolute control over the board of group companies without directly owning many shares. On the other hand, there was no proper check-and-balance in the firm. As the group did not adopt independent directors before it collapsed, supervisors and directors of Rebar group companies were often either Wang family members or employees of the group. Many of them served as multiple directors and/or supervisors within the group. In other words, there were no "outsiders" on the board. In addition, both the internal and external auditing function were compromised. The accountants and auditors inside the firm did nothing but follow the instructions of the boss. The external auditor of the group since 2002, as Chiu singled out, was a child of a former employee of the Rebar group. There was a strong suspicion of collusion. Therefore, there was no proper gatekeeper for investors on the frontline until the group could no longer hide the problems.

Moreover, as well discussed by Chiu in the paper, the Wang family also adopted a variety of financial techniques (e.g. creating a volume of short-term lending, investment or transfer of properties among group companies) to manipulate earnings. Some money eventually entered into the pocket of the Wang family at the expense of minority shareholders. Eventually, the bubble burst, resulting in probably the largest corporate scandal in the 21st century in Taiwan.

The paper by Tai-hui Chiu offered a good account of what happened to the Rebar group that contributed to its total collapse. It is worth a read and provides a good reflection on the evolution of corporate governance rules in Taiwan in previous parts.

Notes and Questions

1. You can find the cross-shareholding structure of the Rebar group at www.twse.com.tw/ch/about/press_room/doc/event_download_200703061132_03.pdf
2. The Wang family, which had strong political connections, controlled and owned Rebar. In 2006, Rebar's board had nine directors and two supervisors. All but two directors were members of the Wang family. The two directors not named Wang and the two supervisors all held executive positions in other companies in the same group. The scandal was not only a failure of internal governance but also of auditing services.
   a. Did the Rebar directors breach their fiduciary duties?
   b. Would more independent directors have helped avoid the scandal?
   c. Is Taiwan's corporate governance current regime sufficient to prevent the same scandal happening again?
   d. The strong political connections of the Wang family arguably might have helped the Rebar group to acquire funding or fend off legal threats until the bubble burst, thereby reducing the force of market surveillance. Interestingly, the scandal occurred when the political party in power was not the one to which the family was closely connected.
3. The Rebar scandal led to many criminal and civil law suits. The IPC did actively bring actions against delinquent directors on the ground of breaching securities regulation such as false disclosure, insider dealing, and fraudulent conduct. The IPC did have some success on grounds of false disclosure, however, several lawsuits regarding insider dealing were dismissed in the end.

Key Statutes and Regulators

Statutes and Rules

Company Act

Securities and Exchange Act

Business Mergers and Acquisitions Act

Securities Investor and Futures Trader Protection Act

Regulators

Ministry of Economic Affairs

Financial Supervisory Commission

Taiwan Stock Exchange

Taipei Exchange

Other Sources

Securities and Futures Investor Protection Center

Market Observation Post System

PART III

FUTURE/ CONCLUSION

13

STOCK EXCHANGE COMPETITION

BRUCE ARONSON AND JOONGI KIM

13.1 Introduction

In addition to the overall increase in the importance of securities law for corporate governance, companies listed on stock exchanges face an additional layer of regulation due to listing standards, public disclosure requirements, and related enforcement. Internationally, globalization has led to an increase in cross-listing of shares on foreign stock exchanges, with particular attention paid to multinational corporations from developing countries that cross-list on stock exchanges with stricter regulatory standards. This trend raises the question of the corporate governance implications of the wider choice available to multinational corporations and the reaction of stock exchanges to this changing environment.

Academics in the United States, a federal system of fifty states with their own corporate laws, have had a long fascination with the possibility of states using corporate law to engage in a regulatory competition to attract corporate charters. Opinions have been clearly divided as to whether any such competition would lead to corporate laws that are "stronger" (a "race to the top") or "weaker" (a "race to the bottom"). At the same time, it was thought that a company that listed its securities on a stock exchange did so to gain reputation and signal its trustworthiness by voluntarily "bonding" itself to the higher standards required of listed companies.

In the field of comparative corporate governance, these two trends combined in the late 1990s to produce a similarly popular theory of international competition among stock exchanges to attract listings from foreign companies, with a similar division of opinion as to whether any such competition acted to strengthen or weaken stock exchange regulation. The "race to the top" view focused on the possibility that cross-listing by multinational corporations from developing countries would lead to a form of functional convergence of corporate governance, with such companies "bonding" with the higher (increasingly "global") governance standards of leading stock exchanges. The "race to the bottom" view held that stock exchanges would lower regulatory standards in the face of competitive pressure to attract foreign listings.

At the same time, the business and organization of stock exchanges has undergone dramatic change in the 2000s due to globalization of both capital markets and businesses, technological development, and other factors. Whereas stock exchanges were formerly domestically oriented monopolies owned by their corporate members, there has been an increase in private competitors to stock exchanges for traditional securities trading activities (alternative trading systems), an explosion of new activities such as derivatives clearing, and structural changes in stock exchange organization, including demutualization and privatization, and attempts (both successful and unsuccessful) at consolidation of stock exchanges through both domestic and international mergers. Although competition among stock exchanges continues to be emphasized in academic debate, the importance of regulation in decisions by companies to cross-list securities remains unclear. In addition, globalization has also increased the need for cooperation among stock exchanges in enforcement and harmonization of standards.

This chapter explores the corporate governance implications of stock exchange competition (and cooperation) in a rapidly changing environment.

13.2 Competition among Regulatory Systems to Attract Corporate Charters: the US Experience

As the United States is a federal system, companies have a choice of fifty jurisdictions in which to incorporate. Debate revolves around which states might offer the "best" corporate law in order to attract company charters. But is the "best" corporate law one that has low regulatory standards and allows corporate managers to do as they please without regard to the interests of shareholders or other stakeholders? Or is the "best" corporate law one that, spurred by market forces and corporations' necessity to raise capital, provides legal rules that are attractive to investors for their protection? In addition, as a practical matter, how important are corporate law or other legal rules in a company's decision on where to incorporate?

William Cary, 'Federalism and Corporate Law: Reflections Upon Delaware' (1973–4) 83 *Yale Law Journal* 663–705, at 663

Delaware is both the sponsor and the victim of a system contributing to the deterioration of corporation standards. This unhappy state of affairs, stemming in great part from the movement toward the least common denominator, Delaware, seems to be developing on both the legislative and judicial fronts. In the management of corporate affairs, state statutory and case law has always been supreme, with federal intrusion limited to the field of securities regulation. Perhaps now is the time to reconsider the federal role.

Renee Jones, 'Rethinking Corporate Federalism in the Era of Corporate Reform' (2004) 29 *Journal of Corporation Law* 625–63, at 631

Defenders of the corporate federal system (referred to here as corporate federalists) argue that the very interstate competition that Cary so excoriated, has led instead to a "race-to-the-top" in corporate law. These theorists, led by Ralph Winter … argued [that] if Delaware law permitted managers to profit at the expense of shareholders, earnings of Delaware corporations would lag behind those of similar corporations chartered in other states. This would result in lower stock prices for Delaware corporations, increasing their capital costs and weakening their position in the product market, ultimately driving stock prices still lower and making such corporations attractive takeover targets. Race-to-the-top theorists thus conclude that market forces require corporate managers to seek out legal rules that are attractive to investors, which in turn encourages states to adopt legal rules that "optimize the shareholder–corporation relationship." Thus, in the view of race-to-the-top scholars, Delaware's laissez faire approach to corporate governance is superior to the interventionist model preferred by race-to-the-bottom theorists, simply because this laissez faire approach has "won" a vigorous competition among all states to attract the most corporate charters.

Lucian Bebchuk and Assaf Hamdani, 'Vigorous Race or Leisurely Walk: Reconsidering the Competition over Corporate Charters' (2002–3) 112 *Yale Law Journal* 553–615, at 553–8

Although Delaware is home to less than one-third of a percent of the U.S. population, it is the incorporation jurisdiction of half of the publicly traded companies in the United States and of an even greater fraction of the larger publicly traded companies. Delaware thus plays a central role in setting corporate governance rules for the nation's publicly traded companies …

The alleged vigorous race among states vying for incorporations, we argue, simply does not exist … [many] firms simply remain incorporated in the state where they are headquartered … Among firms that do "shop" for out-of-state incorporations, Delaware captures approximately 85% of all incorporations …

What explains Delaware's powerful and unchallenged dominance? … The "product" currently offered by Delaware should be viewed as including not only its rules but also its institutional infrastructure, including Delaware's specialized chancery court, and the network benefits currently enjoyed by Delaware corporations. As a result, a state that would offer the same rules, but charge lower incorporation taxes and fees, would not be able to attract many out-of-state incorporations …

Among other things … our account of state competition undermines the view that rules produced by state competition should be regarded as presumptively efficient … [O]ur account leads to the conclusion that states would tend to provide rules that, with respect to some issues, such as takeover protections, are more favorable to managers than would be optimal for shareholders.

Notes and Questions

1. Which argument do you find most persuasive: (1) a competition among US states for corporate charters produces the best corporate law rules that are efficient and value-enhancing; (2) the same competition produces the worst rules that favor management over shareholders; or (3) competition among states for corporate charters is either weak or non-existent? Why? Can the same arguments be raised at the international level in competition among countries?
2. Note that corporate law statutes do not differ very significantly among US states. "Corporate law," however, also includes court decisions and, more broadly, the institutions and infrastructure that support corporate law statutes. Such "institutional infrastructure" is thought to be particularly strong in Delaware, exemplified by its specialized business law court system.
3. What other factors might have an important impact on a company's decision on where to incorporate? What kind of lessons and insights can we draw in comparative corporate governance from the US experience?

13.3 Growth and Transformation of Major Stock Exchanges

Table 13.1 Ten largest stock markets by domestic market capitalization (1990–2008)

1990		(USD bn)	1999		(USD bn)
1	Tokyo SE	2,929	1	NYSE Euronext (US)	11,438
2	NYSE Euronext (US)	2,692	2	Nasdaq OMX	5,205
3	London SE	850	3	Tokyo SE	4,463
4	Deutsche Börse	355	4	London SE	2,855
5	Nasdaq OMX	311	5	NYSE Euronext (Europe)	2,444
6	TSX Group	242	6	Deutsche Börse	1,432
7	SIX Swiss EX	158	7	TSX Group	789
8	Borsa Italiana	149	8	Borsa Italiana	728
9	Johannesburg SE	137	9	SIX Swiss EX	693
10	BME Spanish EX	111	10	Hong Kong EX	609

2005		(USD bn)	2008		(USD bn)
1	NYSE Euronext (US)	13,632	1	NYSE Euronext (US)	9,209
2	Tokyo SE	4,573	2	Tokyo SE	3,116
3	Nasdaq OMX	3,604	3	Nasdaq OMX	2,396
4	London SE	3,058	4	NYSE Euronext (Europe)	2,102
5	NYSE Euronext (Europe)	2,707	5	London SE	1,868
6	TSX Group	1,482	6	Shanghai SE	1,425
7	Deutsche Börse	1,221	7	Hong Kong EX	1,329
8	Hong Kong EX	1,055	8	Deutsche Börse	1,111
9	BME Spanish EX	960	9	TSX Group	1,033
10	SIX Swiss EX	935	10	BME Spanish EX	948

Table 13.2 Twenty largest stock markets by domestic market capitalization (2016)

		(US$ bn)
1	NYSE Group	19,573
2	Nasdaq – US	7,779
3	Japan Exchange Group	4,955
4	Shanghai Stock Exchange	4,099
5	Euronext	3,460
6	Shenzhen Stock Exchange	3,213
7	Hong Kong Exchanges and Clearing	3,193
8	TMX Group	1,994
9	Deutsche Börse AG	1,716
10	BSE Limited	1,567
11	National Stock Exchange of India Limited	1,540
12	SIX Swiss Exchange	1,403
13	Australian Securities Exchange	1,268
14	Korea Exchange	1,255
15	Nasdaq Nordic Exchanges	1,248
16	Johannesburg Stock Exchange	951
17	Taiwan Stock Exchange	844
18	BM&FBOVESPA SA	759
19	BME Spanish Exchanges	705
20	Singapore Exchange	640

Source: World Federation of Exchanges

Notes and Questions

1. The rise of Asia. In 1990 the Tokyo Stock Exchange was the only Asian-based exchange among the top ten in the world. In fact, at the end of Japan's bubble era it was the world's largest stock exchange, although it faded shortly thereafter. By 2016, Asian stock exchanges comprised half of the top ten and also half of the top twenty of the world's leading exchanges. The most striking growth over the past decade has occurred in China. Considered together, the Shanghai and Shenzhen exchanges would rank as the world's third largest exchange, close behind the number two exchange (Nasdaq) in market capitalization.
2. What do you think are the causes of the growth of stock exchanges in Asia? What would you say is the significance of this trend?

13.4 International Stock Exchange Competition: Race to the Top, Race to the Bottom, or No Race at All?

13.4.1 The Bonding Hypothesis ("Race to the Top")

John Coffee, Jr. 'The Future as History: The Prospects for Global Convergence in Corporate Governance and Its Implications' (1999) 93 *Northwestern University Law Review* 641–707, at 673–9, 687–8, 699–701. (Reprinted by special permission of Northwestern University School of Law, *Northwestern University Law Review*)

E. Migration to Foreign Markets

The number of foreign listings on the principal U.S. exchanges … continues to grow rapidly …

The accelerating pace of this migration may seem surprising when one realizes that foreign issuers incur extensive regulatory costs when they enter the U.S. markets and that most have never thereafter made securities offerings in the United States. Why then do they list? Arguably, companies in smaller markets gain liquidity and possibly also some international recognition and prestige from a U.S. listing. But greater motivation probably lies in the finding, repeatedly observed by financial economists, that the announcement of a dual listing on a U.S. exchange by a foreign firm typically increases the firm's share value.

One explanation for the abnormal price movement on a U.S. listing is that such a listing represents a bonding mechanism: the foreign issuer is increasing the share value of its public shares by agreeing to comply with the generally higher disclosure standards that prevail in the United States.

F. The Need for Global Scale

Besides the desire to increase their stock price, other, more powerful reasons may explain the interest of foreign corporations in listing on a U.S. securities exchange. The decision by Daimler-Benz, A.G. ("Daimler") to list on the New York Stock Exchange in 1993 and to comply with very different accounting requirements that greatly reduced its reported earnings now comes into focus as a prelude to Daimler's 1998 acquisition of Chrysler Corporation in what was essentially a stock for stock exchange. Had Daimler been traded only in Germany in a much less liquid market and subject to less transparent disclosure requirements, the acquisition of Chrysler for Daimler stock would have likely been unattractive to Chrysler shareholders, and it is likely that the acquisition would have been infeasible as a cash transaction.

Yet the Chrysler transaction (or some alternative) may have been critical to Daimler if it believed that it needed to increase its scale in order to compete globally in the future ...

In a world of global competition, the fear of small and mid-sized firms (or at least their managements) is that they must "eat or be eaten" – that is, grow in size into one of the largest firms in their industry or expect to become acquisition targets ...

The implication, then, is that if a wave of global mergers occurs, the acquirors will tend to be either firms with high stock values – because their legal regimes protect minority rights – or firms with high reputational capital. Either way, the family-held firm is likely to be left in the wake, becoming either a target or a bystander ...

3. Corporate Governance. Although listing on a U.S. exchange or NASDAQ does not subject an issuer to U.S. corporate law, it is necessary for any issuer (foreign or domestic) to enter into a listing agreement with the New York Stock Exchange, the American Stock Exchange ("AMEX"), or NASDAQ in order to have its securities traded on such market. These listing agreements all contain corporate governance provisions, although those required by NASDAQ and AMEX are somewhat less demanding ... the NYSE does insist on some minimum governance standards for all issuers, including (i) an audit committee or similar body to monitor transactions between the company and its insiders (ii) an annual shareholders' meeting, and (iii) a requirement that any tender offer made by the company for its own shares or for those of another listed company give all holders of the target an equal opportunity to participate. Both the AMEX and NASDAQ follow substantially similar policies ...

E. The Centrality of Securities Regulation

This Article has said little about state corporate law, because it believes that the critical restraints that most limit agency costs are today contained in the federal securities laws ...

The immediate significance of this assessment that federal law has overshadowed state law variations lies principally in its implications for foreign issuers. Even if some foreign jurisdictions do grant controlling shareholders the discretionary power to take self-interested actions, this discretion may be significantly constrained by federal securities regulation. In short, the much discussed differences between the protections given by Anglo-American law versus Continental European law may be overshadowed by the legal protections implicit either in the U.S. securities law or in a "harmonized" international system of securities regulation. Although these disparities in the scope of securities regulations would be more significant than the variations among state law on corporate duties within the United States, these disparities may also be reduced or neutralized by the threat of both SEC and private enforcement in U.S. courts …

F. Markets Versus States: Does the Experience with State Charter Competition Have Relevance to the Prospect for Convergence?

… This Article has suggested that convergence at the level of securities regulation will outpace convergence at the level of corporate law. In essence, this is a prediction that international events will follow the de facto outcome of the U.S. charter competition experience. One reason for this prediction is that the forces that have produced a dominant supplier of corporate law at the state level, Delaware, have even greater impact in the international arena of securities regulation and thus make it even more likely that U.S. securities markets will become the dominant supplier of law for large publicly held corporations.

To understand this contention, it is useful to start with an obvious point that most commentators have largely ignored, namely, that virtually all publicly held corporations are regulated at two distinct levels: (1) their jurisdiction of incorporation, and (2) the various jurisdictions where their securities trade. This system of dual regulation applies not only to Delaware corporations trading on the New York Stock Exchange, but equally to Japanese corporations trading on the London Stock Exchange.

The nature of the competition at these various levels differs, however, dramatically. Proponents of a market for corporate charters have modeled charter competition as simply a contest among different jurisdictions offering their laws as a product that the issuer, as consumer, chooses from among many in a competitive marketplace … Thus, a small jurisdiction, such as Switzerland or Delaware, cannot as easily compete on equal terms with larger jurisdictions, such as the United States or New York, if the legal rules so offered do not carry with them access to securities markets. In short, Delaware or Switzerland could not become the predominant supplier of legal rules in the securities regulation context – unless the larger jurisdictions decided to relinquish their control by allowing access to their markets based simply on issuers complying with the law of some other jurisdiction.

Put differently, regulatory arbitrage works only to the extent that the party regulated can freely choose the law applicable to it, typically, by reincorporating in a less regulated jurisdiction. But, in securities regulation, it is not an attractive option for the issuer to flee a regulated jurisdiction if the issuer thereby also flees the principal market for its securities. For example, few issuers would willingly move from the New York Stock Exchange to the Milan Stock Exchange in the same manner that they might switch their jurisdiction of incorporation from New York to Delaware.

13.4.2 The Regulatory Arbitrage Hypothesis ("Race to the Bottom")

Amir Licht, 'Cross-Listing and Corporate Governance: Bonding or Avoiding?' (2003) 4 *Chicago Journal of International Law* 141–63, at 141–8, 162–3. (Reprinted with permission from the *Chicago Journal of International Law* and the University of Chicago Law School)

In their seminal survey of corporate governance, Shleifer and Vishny distill the issue into a blunt question: "How do [the suppliers of finance] make sure that managers do not steal the capital they supply or invest it in bad projects?" …

The American governance environment is out for rent. Foreign firms wishing to enjoy the benefits of being subject to the American regime can readily do so by cross-listing their securities on an American market-even without raising capital in the United States … In this view, cross-listing on a foreign stock market can serve as a bonding mechanism for corporate insiders to commit credibly to a better governance regime …

This article questions the bonding role of cross-listing … Indeed, the evidence supports an alternative theory, which may be called "the avoiding hypothesis." To the extent that corporate governance issues play a role in the cross-listing decision, it is a negative role. The dominant factors in the choice of cross-listing destination markets are access to cheaper finance and enhancing the issuer's visibility. Corporate governance is a second-order consideration whose effect is either to deter issuers from accessing better-regulated markets or to induce securities regulators to allow foreign issuers to avoid some of the more exacting domestic regulations …

A key weakness in some bonding-by-cross-listing theses – common among finance scholars – is that they are insensitive to crucial features of the US securities regulation regime … Generally speaking, the foreign issuer regime [in the US] "cuts corners" exactly on the issues of corporate governance relating to corporate insiders. The Securities and Exchange Commission ("SEC") has cut these corners on purpose. Evidence further suggests that the SEC complements this strategy with a "hands-off" informal policy of non-enforcement toward foreign issuers. The evidence surveyed in this article indicates that cross-listings in the US fail to reflect positive effects that could be attributed to corporate governance improvements.

II. BONDING 101

... In order to list on the New York Stock Exchange ("NYSE"), for instance, a non-US issuer must pay various fees that range in the hundreds of thousands of dollars. These are direct costs, to which one needs to add the expected costs of managerial time, underwriting, and professional fees (lawyers, accountants, printing), potential legal liability, and so forth. The reasons for bearing such considerable costs, therefore, should be quite compelling. This Part reviews the bonding paradigm against the general backdrop that surrounds it.

A. WHY CROSS-LIST?

Interest in cross-listing has been growing since the mid-1980s, in parallel with the growing number of foreign issuers listed on various American markets. Scholars advance several independent theories on the reasons that might motivate companies to cross-list their securities on foreign markets ...

Financial Gains. Cross-listings were originally thought of as a means for lowering firms' cost of capital – that is, for enabling firms to get more money from investors when they offer their stock to the public. This effect could stem from two related sources – diversification gains and segmentation gains. Segmentation occurs when similar assets in different markets have different prices, barring transaction costs ... Cross-listing brings foreign stocks closer to investors and offers several other straightforward advantages that stem from lower transaction costs.

Liquidity. Cross-listing may contribute to share value by increasing stock liquidity. Expected returns positively correlate with liquidity, measured in terms of the bid-ask spread. Narrower spreads following cross-listing generate improved liquidity, which increases share value ...

Increased Shareholder Base. By cross-listing its stocks, a firm could expand its potential investor base more easily than if it traded on a single market. As cross-listing brings foreign securities closer to potential investors, it increases investor awareness of the securities. This familiarity could lower expected returns. In business management terminology this aspect is called "firm visibility" – a broad notion encompassing frequent mentioning of the firm in the financial press and closer monitoring of its securities by securities analysts.

Visibility. The putative benefits of increased visibility in the host country go well beyond the expected increase in shareholder base. In addition to greater demand for its stock, listing abroad provides a firm with greater access to foreign money markets and makes it easier to sell debt there ...

Marketing Motivations. Using cross-listings for marketing reasons relates to the visibility rationale. According to this reasoning, foreign listing can boost corporate marketing efforts by broadening product identification among investors and consumers in the host country. The listing, it is claimed, creates greater market demand for the firm's products as well as its securities.

Technical Issues. Effecting a securities transaction abroad, even where feasible, is still more complicated and expensive than effecting it domestically. Cross-listing can improve a firm's ability to effect structural transactions abroad such as foreign mergers and acquisitions, stock swaps, and tender offers. Relatedly, cross-listing also facilitates and enhances the attractiveness of employee stock ownership plans ("ESOPs") for employees of large multinational corporations. Local listing in the foreign market provides foreign employees with an accessible exit mechanism for their stocks.

B. WHY BOND?

… Corporate governance mechanisms are supposed to minimize these risks, or, more technically, to minimize the adverse effects of the agency problem. The costs of such mechanisms are called "bonding costs" …

Any theoretical model that relies on choice of regulatory regimes immediately raises the problem of regulatory arbitrage – a process by which competition among regulators causes erosion in regulatory standards below a desirable, optimal level … The issue often boils down to whether the competition would lead to a "race for the top" or a "race for the bottom." The situation is more complex in my mind: By cross-listing, the issuer may opt into another securities regulation regime, but without severing its legal ties to its home country. The outcome is a rather complex legal regime in which some components might bring about an improvement in the composite regime governing the issuer but other components might erode its effectiveness.

Both Coffee and Rock are well aware of the race-for-the-bottom problem.

Rock argues that the SEC (as opposed to the NYSE) is the only entity that is able credibly to commit to enforcing its own regulations. This is due to its monopoly over criminal sanctions in the US and a history of enforcing high disclosure requirements. Coffee assumed that a race for the bottom is unlikely, because issuers will not delist from the NYSE to avoid the SEC's exacting regulatory regime and move to another stock exchange – say, Milan's – in a country with an inferior regime …

But if this were true, then the entire theory is turned on its head. Foreign issuers do not cross-list for the improved regulation but rather despite such regulation. "Foreign issuers will pay some price *in* increased regulation in order to obtain the advantages of the dominant market."

Recently, Coffee repeated his theory and revised it in light of developments in international stock markets and further empirical research. This version likewise envisions the possibility of a dual-equilibrium global environment. In this environment, "high disclosure" exchanges would serve as regional "supermarkets," providing bonding services to high-quality issuers, while firms less interested in attracting minority investors (but still desiring some degree of liquidity) might trade only on lower-disclosure exchanges …

VI. CONCLUSION

... Beyond this, preliminary evidence suggests that the overriding factors in this complicated setting are distance and cultural proximity. All the players in this game – from issuers to stock exchanges to regulators – understand this and make their moves accordingly. The upshot of the insights advanced in this article is not that cross-listing should be curbed. These transactions will continue to take place as long as they allow companies to expand their business and improve their financing. Improvements in issuers' corporate governance can be achieved primarily through sustained efforts by lawmakers and regulators in firms' home countries. Cross-listing is no quick fix.

Notes and Questions

1. How about competition among stock exchanges: is it a "race to the top," "race to the bottom," or no race at all?
2. Note that Coffee's theory of functional convergence through cross-listing of shares would be consistent with LLSV's "law matters" thesis discussed in Chapter 4: foreign companies cross-list on stock exchanges in countries with good protection of minority shareholders, as these are the only countries that can develop deep and liquid securities markets. But do we know if the development of deep and liquid securities markets is due primarily to legal protections afforded to minority shareholders?
3. Foreign companies that cross-list in the United States generally do so through the use of American depository receipts (ADRs), that are contracts entitling the holders to a fixed number of shares. The country with the most companies cross-listed on US exchanges is Canada. However, due to special arrangements Canadian companies can list without appending ADRs to their securities listings. Such Canadian securities are therefore indistinguishable from US securities and arguably cannot signal to the market an acceptance of higher governance standards. Does this phenomenon weaken the "bonding" theory?

13.4.3 Regulatory Standards and Stock Market Competitiveness: the US versus the UK

Cross-listing of foreign companies in New York boomed during the latter half of the 1990s, but London took the lead in the early 2000s. Was this due to tougher governance standards represented by the passage of the Sarbanes–Oxley Act in 2002 and changes to New York Stock Exchange listing standards in 2003? What, if anything, did the United States need to do to remain competitive with London as a global financial center?

Committee on Capital Markets Regulation, 'Interim Report of the Committee on Capital Markets Regulation, Executive Summary' (November 30, 2006), at http://capmktsreg.org/pdfs/11.30committee_Interim_ReportREV2.pdf

The United States has for many years been recognized as having the largest, most liquid, and most competitive public equity capital markets in the world. These well-functioning capital markets play a vital role in our economy … there is considerable evidence that countries with better financial markets, like the United States, enjoy more rapid economic growth, which creates more new jobs nationwide. The U.S. legal and regulatory regimes that promote accountability, disclosure, and transparency are an important element in the success of U.S. capital markets …

Few would argue that the level of regulatory intensity, in the form of new laws such as SOX, outcomes of shareholder and government litigation, and the behavior of securities regulators, has increased markedly in recent years. Many would say it was entirely merited by the (mis)behavior of companies and securities firms in the market bubble period of the 1990s. Regulatory intensity almost inevitably increases after periods of market euphoria and the subsequent market collapse. The question is: "Has the shift in intensity gone too far?"

It is the Committee's view that in the shift of regulatory intensity balance has been lost to the competitive disadvantage of U.S. financial markets. Yet, to make a reduction of regulatory intensity an end in itself would be self-defeating. Investors and companies raising capital participate in markets where they feel safe by virtue of effective laws and rules vigorously enforced by knowledgeable, transparent courts and even-handed, vigilant regulators.

In the Report that follows, the Committee examines four areas in which it believes adjustments need to be made to prevent a further erosion of the competitive position of U.S. capital markets. As an overall matter, the Committee concludes that the solution to the competitive problem of U.S. capital markets lies, on the one hand, in reducing the burden of litigation and regulation and, on the other hand, in increasing shareholder rights.

These areas, and the key recommendations in each, are:

1. Regulatory Process. We conclude that the SEC and self-regulatory organizations ("SROs") should engage in a more risk-based process, focused explicitly on the costs and benefits of regulation …
2. The Private and Public Enforcement System … while applauding the reforms enacted by the Sarbanes–Oxley Act of 2002, we conclude that the private litigation system needs modification in some dimensions and that the criminal enforcement system needs better balance.

3. Shareholder Rights. We conclude there is a danger that the United States, compared with other countries, is falling behind best practices in shareholder rights …
4. Implementation of Sarbanes–Oxley. We recommend no statutory changes in the Sarbanes–Oxley Act, including Section 404 … The same benefits can be produced at lower cost. We conclude that there need to be changes to SOX 404 implementation …

Craig Doidge, G. Andrew Karolyi, and Rene Stultz, 'Has New York Become Less Competitive than London in Global Markets? Evaluating Foreign Listing Choices Over Time' (2009) 91 *Journal of Financial Economics* 253–77, at 275–6.

The fact is that listing counts have been falling in London as well as in New York. This broader phenomenon makes it difficult to explain the decrease in New York alone using an argument that New York is becoming less competitive, perhaps because of SOX and other regulatory changes. It is true that the number of listings on AIM in London has been growing dramatically since 2001, but most firms that list on AIM are small firms that would have been unlikely candidates to crosslist on the U.S. exchanges …

Little evidence exists that firms have been making listing decisions differently in recent years from how they made them from 1990 to 2001 … With each approach, we find a listing premium for firms that list on US exchanges but no listing premium for firms that list in London. The listing premium is robust: It exists every year and it is permanent. We find no evidence that the listing premium falls after 2001, even for listed firms from countries with good investor protection ...

All of our evidence is consistent with the theory that there is a distinct governance benefit for firms that list on the US exchanges. This benefit is not shared by firms that list in the US outside the exchanges or in London. There is no evidence in our data that this benefit has weakened over time.

Notes and Questions

1. Is the US declining, is the rest of the world catching up, or are there fewer companies likely to cross-list on major stock exchanges?
2. Four factors for the US relative decline in IPO cross-listings are cited in the above report: (1) foreign public equity markets have better corporate governance; (2) US private markets

have better liquidity and availability for foreign investors (Rule 144A); (3) technology makes it easier for investors to invest directly in foreign markets; and (4) differences in legal rules – potential costs of litigation and SOX compliance in the US. Does corporate governance appear to be a key issue? If so, would it appear to be more a result of litigation risk in the US rather than regulation itself? As noted in Chapter 2, private enforcement in the United States is also considered a strength of the US corporate governance system.

13.4.4 Stock Listing in Asia: Do Chinese Companies Cross-Listing in Hong Kong (or Singapore) Represent the New Bonding Mechanism?

Jiangyu Wang, 'Regulatory Competition and Cooperation between Securities Markets in Hong Kong and Mainland China' (2009) 4 *Capital Markets Law Journal* 383–404, at 391–3

4. Cooperation and competition on listing of Mainland companies

Reasons for the listing of PRC companies in Hong Kong: financial, political and bonding

As noted previously, the listing of PRC companies in HKEx has been the largest driving force for Hong Kong's success as an international financial centre for over a decade. By the end of March 2009, 150 of the 1266 companies listed on HKEx (including both the Main Board and the GEM Board) are H-share companies that are incorporated in Mainland China ... The natural question is why, and how, did these companies list in Hong Kong?

This article argues that neither the business motivations nor the bonding hypothesis fully explain the listing of PRC firms in Hong Kong ... First, many, if not most, of the H-share companies were predominantly SOEs, at least when they applied for listing in Hong Kong. That is to say, they were hardly entities with independent interest and decision-making power. For H-share SOEs, the listing decisions, even at the firm level, were made by the relevant administrative official at some level of the Chinese government. Second, whether a PRC company can seek listing in Hong Kong is legally subject to state approval. Third, although it cannot be excluded that the government might have considered the respective firm's business interest, the decisions to send PRC enterprises to Hong Kong were based primarily on politically-oriented 'national considerations' rather than on firm-level business considerations ...

However, the desires of the individual companies cannot be ignored, as, in many cases, it was the firm that applied to the state for permission to offer and list shares in Hong Kong. The motivations of such firms are probably no different from those of private firms in matured market economies, namely financial gains, liquidity, visibility, employee incentives and global strategy. Not surprisingly, some of the firm-level considerations might converge with the Chinese government's national aims. It is, however, important to note that another key reason why many Chinese enterprises migrate to foreign stock exchanges is that they are not approved for listing in China, or they are frightened by the arbitrarily strict – sometimes unnecessarily draconian – regulatory rules controlling public offering of securities in the Mainland's own stock market.

Flora Xiao Huang and Horace Yeung, *Chinese Companies and the Hong Kong Stock Market* (London and New York: Routledge, 2014), p. 113

D. A summary of the differences between Chinese and Hong Kong listing rules

A comparison of China and Hong Kong listing frameworks shows that cross-listing serves as a mechanism for Chinese companies to tie themselves to a stronger market. The listing requirements in Hong Kong are, to a large extent, more stringent and comprehensive than those in China, mainly in post-listing obligations and prospectuses. Although China is moving toward a better disclosure system, its practice still has serious problems.

However, the comparison finds that cross-listing is also a means for Chinese companies to avoid an overly regulated market. But they are attempting to escape from a malfunctioning market rather than domestically higher standards, as the avoiding hypothesis suggests. This could be interpreted by the different roles of their market authorities. The two jurisdictions use differing offering systems. In Hong Kong, as long as the applicant satisfies all of the prescribed listing requirements of the HKSE, no further procedures are required. By contrast the CSRC can decide on major offering and listing matters, leaving the stock exchanges little control over them. This may create policy-driven markets. When domestic fundraising channels are restricted, companies find a way to list abroad. This idea can be supported by the CSRC decision to suspend all IPOs between September 2008 and June 2009 in order to stabilize the market and prevent investors from losing money in the economic downturn. Faced with this restriction, Chinese companies were forced to raise funds through alternative channels, including cross-listing. During this period ten Chinese companies went public in Hong Kong.

Neither a purely bonding nor a purely avoiding theory can explain the complexity of the Chinese case. The driving forces for a Chinese cross-listing may come from both a desire to bond themselves to a stronger market with higher standards, but also from a desire to avoid over-regulated Chinese markets.

Notes and Questions

1. Is the bonding theory the best explanation for the trend of Chinese companies cross-listing in Hong Kong?
2. What do you think of the view that Chinese companies list in Hong Kong to avoid over-regulation and political considerations in China? Does such a theory of "avoiding" China contradict the bonding theory, or might the two theories be compatible?

13.5 The New Era of Stock Exchange Competition and Cooperation

13.5.1 The Changing Organization and Activities of Stock Exchanges

Hans Christiansen and Alissa Koldertsova, 'The Role of Stock Exchanges in Corporate Governance' (2009) 1 *OECD Journal: Financial Market Trends* 209–38, at 212, 219, 222–3, 26, 231, 233–4

Part I. The traditional role of exchanges in corporate governance

The regulatory function of stock exchanges was in the past mostly limited to issuing rules and clarifying aspects of existing frameworks. The standard-setting role of stock exchanges was essentially exercised through the issuance of listing, ongoing disclosure, maintenance and de-listing requirements. On the enforcement side, stock exchanges have shared their regulatory function with capital market supervisory agencies. In addition to overseeing their own rules, stock exchanges were assigned the role of monitoring the compliance with legislation and subsidiary securities regulation. Since the promulgation of the OECD Principles of Corporate Governance, stock exchanges have often enlarged their regulatory role to embrace a wider palette of corporate governance concerns. They have contributed to the development of corporate governance recommendations and encouraged their application to listed companies …

Part II. Changing Landscape in the Stock Exchange Industry

Over the past 15 years, the exchange industry has been in a state of continued flux. Exchanges have demutualised and in most cases become listed, they have consolidated through mergers and acquisitions, and they have become subject to stiff competition from a host of new alternative trading venues. In other words, stock exchanges have become engaged in an intensified competition and are refashioning themselves to meet the challenge. This, in turn, is creating a new reality in exchanges' role in the capital markets regulatory framework, including with respect to corporate governance …

Increasing competition among stock exchanges … Implications for corporate governance

… The incentives faced by exchanges to establish and maintain high regulatory standards might weaken as they weigh the risk of deterring listings altogether or losing them to competing market places. This risk may be exacerbated by the pressures a demutualised exchange is subject to from its shareholders to give top priority to maximising profitability … Reflecting such concerns, the dichotomy between a listed exchange's regulatory function and its role as a for-profit entity has given rise to an active debate regarding their incentives to regulate … [P]otential conflicts of interest … include[e] risks to the maintenance of a proper balance between an exchange's public interest obligations and its commercial interests and the potential misuse of regulatory powers for commercial purposes …

Incentives faced by exchanges to maintain a high regulatory standard

Exchanges' investment in their regulatory capacity might be motivated by their unbundling of services in light of greater competition, whereby regulation has become one of their "core competences." The resultant competitive advantage would help explain why exchanges have rigorously defended their prerogative to maintain the regulatory function, introducing a variety of mechanisms to address the potential conflicts of interests that arise with respect to self- and issuer oversight …

Cross-border consolidation of stock exchanges … Implications for corporate governance

… The issue of cross-jurisdictional operation of stock exchanges has been addressed at different levels. Most basically, a number of OECD countries have introduced restrictions on the ownership and acquisition of stock exchanges including notification requirements, ownership caps and fit-and-proper requirements …

Emerging competitors: Alternative Trading Systems [ATSs] ... Implications for corporate governance

... [S]ince off-exchange trading is often less transparent and not regulated as rigorously as on-exchange trading, there could be repercussions for price discovery and other aspects of the markets for corporate control addressed by the OECD Principles. On the other hand ... listed companies have to comply with listing and disclosure rules of exchanges, and position themselves vis-à-vis their corporate governance codes ... [A] key corporate governance question is whether the timely disclosure of substantial acquisitions of shares as well as the communications of plans and financing of the transactions to shareholders suffer from the migration of trading volume from the regulated exchanges to ATSs ... A key distinction between ATSs and stock exchange regulation is that transactions via the former are based on private law contracts, not on stock exchange regulation. Furthermore, ATSs have no delegated authority to enforce companies or securities law, and have no power to de-list companies or adopt any other punitive measures against issuers ... Overall, understanding of the impact of trade fragmentation (in particular through less transparent platforms such as dark pools) is still at an early stage, and further exploration of this question may be useful.

John Gapper, 'The Death and Rebirth of the Stock Exchange,' *Financial Times* (March 10, 2016)

The clue as to why the London Stock Exchange has risen sevenfold in value in the past seven years is not contained in its name. The best days of being a stock exchange are in the past, when they were near-monopolies owned by market-making members and could easily make money. That was long ago.

But a funny thing happened on the way to their demise. The businesses formerly run as stock exchanges became more valuable despite a wave of disruption unleashed by regulation, technology and competition. They should be in trouble but the leading ones have instead been transformed.

This phenomenon is on show on both sides of the Atlantic. The IEX trading platform, made famous by Michael Lewis's book Flash Boys, has applied to become the 13th US stock exchange. The buttonwood tree under which 24 brokers agreed to form the New York Stock Exchange in 1792 has become a forest of competing bourses.

In Europe a battle looms for control of the LSE, which looked vulnerable after the 2008 financial crisis but is now highly prized. It is planning an agreed merger with Deutsche Börse and rivals such as Intercontinental Exchange (ICE), which owns the New York Stock Exchange, are considering counterbids.

The oddity of all this activity is that, as one equity trader puts it: "The core business of matching buyers and sellers is not very profitable and does not have great prospects." Being a stock exchange was fine while entry barriers were high and they could shield themselves from competition. As soon as that was undermined, particularly in the US, they became vulnerable.

The NYSE's share of US equity trading has fallen from 72 per cent to 24 per cent in the past decade amid competition from new exchanges and "dark pools" – platforms run by banks and others for institutions to trade privately. Exchange fees are razor-thin; some dark pools in effect pay to attract business.

IEX has provoked an uproar by seeking to impose an infinitesimal delay on outside orders routed through its exchange – 350 microseconds, or less than one-thousandth of the time needed to blink. The fact that regulators are wrestling over an interval of time that they would not even have noticed a decade ago shows how high-speed trading by computers has taken over.

Trading volumes are huge – the global number of trades rose by 55 per cent last year – and IEX says the delay is needed to stop equity markets being rigged in an arms race of rapid-fire trading. Exchanges were once strong enough to enforce discipline on brokers; they now accept fees to let high-speed traders locate servers in their buildings and gain a tiny time advantage.

If stock exchanges are so weak, why are the companies that own them so resilient? The answer is simple: the LSE is not really a stock exchange any more. Equity trading comprises about 10 per cent of its revenues (and 7 per cent of the revenues of ICE). The bulk of its business is based neither on shares nor on trading but on other securities and activities.

One of its biggest operations is clearing – taking care of the contracts after trades are done. Its SwapClear division now clears 95 per cent of the global market in over-the-counter interest rate swaps (private interest rate contracts reached by banks). This is less exciting or visible than equity trading but bigger and more profitable; SwapClear often clears $1tn of swaps daily …

Derivatives clearing has another advantage over share trading: it takes a long time. A clearing house holds cash to cover the moves in the value of a contract over weeks or months. It is a steady money-earner that is far less exposed to competition than a stock exchange. Fees such as these, from derivatives clearing, data and financial indices, are valuable.

The transformation of exchanges offers three lessons. First, regulation works. It does not always work as intended but it affects behaviour. US and European regulators encouraged stock exchange competition and, after the 2008 crisis, pushed banks to use clearing houses to curb risk. Exchanges altered course as their old business grew tougher and another one expanded.

Second, capitalism is highly adaptable. The world of stock exchanges was dominated for decades by entrenched institutions, particularly those in global financial centres such as London and New York. Changes in regulation and financial markets undermined that position so they adapted.

In some cases, such as the LSE's, stock exchanges remodelled themselves behind the scenes into clearing and data operators. In others, futures exchanges such as the Chicago Mercantile Exchange outstripped stock exchanges in value or acquired them, as ICE has done. Within a decade, stock exchanges were absorbed into exchange groups that mostly do other things.

Last, traditions endure. Exchanges are largely but not wholly unrecognisable from the days of the buttonwood tree. Networks remain powerful – exchanging contracts through a hub rather making a multitude of bilateral deals creates economies of scale. This applies as much to the central clearing of interest rate swaps as to exchange-based share trading.

Stock exchanges remain exchanges, despite all the fragmentation and upheaval. Unlikely as it once seemed, they are still in business.

13.5.2 Increasing Cooperation among Stock Exchanges

International Organization of Securities Commissions, 'IOSCO Approves the Enhanced Standard for Cross-Border Enforcement Cooperation,' media release (March 31, 2017)

The members of the International Organization of Securities Commissions (IOSCO) have approved the Enhanced Multilateral Memorandum of Understanding Concerning Consultation and Cooperation and the Exchange of Information (EMMoU), which offers securities regulators new enforcement powers for responding to the challenges arising from recent developments in global financial markets.

Since its launch in 2002, the Multilateral Memorandum of Understanding Concerning Consultation and Cooperation and the Exchange of Information (MMoU) has provided securities regulators around the world with key tools to fight cross-border financial fraud and misconduct that can weaken global markets and undermine investor confidence. For 15 years, regulators have used the MMoU to help ensure effective global cooperation and strengthen international securities markets.

Despite this vast success, securities markets have undergone sweeping changes in recent years, driven by things such as new technologies and regulation, and the growing role of market-based finance. These forces have spurred IOSCO to develop an enhanced standard on cross-border enforcement information exchange that goes beyond the MMoU and responds to recent market developments …

Both the MMOU and the EMMoU provide a mechanism for securities regulators to share essential investigative material, such as beneficial ownership information, and securities and derivatives transaction records, including banking and brokerage records. Both documents also set out specific requirements for the exchange of information, notably ensuring that no domestic banking secrecy laws or regulations prevent the sharing of enforcement information among securities regulators.

The EMMoU, however, provides for additional enforcement powers that IOSCO believes are necessary for continuing to safeguard the integrity and stability of markets, protect investors, and deter misconduct and fraud. The ACFIT powers, as they are known, will enable members to:

A: Obtain and share **Audit** work papers, communications and other information relating to the audit or review of financial statements;

C: **Compel** physical attendance for testimony (by being able to apply a sanction in the event of non-compliance);

F: **Freeze** assets if possible or, if not, advise and provide information on how to freeze assets, at the request of another signatory;

I: Obtain and share existing **Internet** service provider records (not including the content of communications), including with the assistance of a prosecutor, court or other authority, and to obtain the content of such communications from authorized entities; and

T: Obtain and share existing **Telephone** records (not including the content of communications), including with the assistance of a court, prosecutor, or other authority, and to obtain the content of such communications from authorized entities …

Securities regulators currently are required to sign the MMoU to become a member of IOSCO …

Of IOSCO's members that are securities regulators, 112 are signatories to the MMoU. In 2015, signatories made 3,203 requests for information, compared to only 56 requests in 2003 …

13.5.3 Case Study in Asia: Governance Standards and Attracting Stock Listings in Hong Kong and Singapore

The largest stock markets in Asia are Tokyo and Shanghai, largely due to the large domestic issuers located in those countries. However, Hong Kong and Singapore capture most of the attention in terms of cross-listing of foreign companies and deliberate policies to develop and maintain their status as important financial centers. Such financial centers must carefully weigh factors that make them attractive to foreign companies and the role of corporate governance. Hong Kong and Singapore have regularly finished first and second in the Asian ranking of corporate governance by the Asian Corporate Governance Association (see Figure 1.3). They also compete to become the "gateway" to China, i.e. a well-regulated and "safe" jurisdiction for investors who hesitate to invest directly in the PRC due to concerns about the rule of law and corporate governance.

13.5.3.1 Hong Kong and the Alibaba IPO

Hong Kong has been successful in attracting cross-listing from large Chinese SOEs and has an active IPO market. Hong Kong has listings of both "H" shares that are listed in China and "red chips" that are incorporated in other jurisdictions such as the Cayman Islands. Many of the PRC companies that cross-list in Hong Kong are traditional finance, property, and resource companies. Chinese internet companies generally go to New York for cross-listing. Competition arose for the cross-listing of Alibaba, which ended up listing in New York in 2014 with the biggest IPO to date. The controlling shareholder of Alibaba, Jack Ma, stated clearly that he preferred to cross-list in Hong Kong, which was its "natural" home, but was "rejected" by Hong Kong and therefore chose to list in New York.

The issue at stake was Alibaba's ownership structure, which permitted the founding partners (controlling shareholder) to nominate a majority of the board of directors even following the IPO, in violation of Hong Kong's "one-share, one-vote" rule. This is a sensitive issue in Hong Kong, which has numerous listed companies with controlling shareholders (both family-controlled local companies and cross-listed state-controlled companies from China) and where the "one-share, one-vote" rule is thought to be important to maintain investor confidence in the market.

US law and the stock exchanges in New York, where controlling shareholders are not common, permit company founders to maintain control following an IPO by the use of dual classes of shares (with the founders' shares typically having ten votes each, while the public shares have one vote). Such arrangements occur regularly in certain fields, particularly entertainment/media (e.g. Viacom) and tech (e.g. Google and Facebook).

Hong Kong considered changing or waiving its rules to accommodate Alibaba, but did not do so out of concern that such an action would have a negative impact on Hong Kong's image of following the rule of law and maintaining good corporate governance standards. Subsequently, in December 2017, Hong Kong announced a plan to list dual class shares. Singapore followed with its own similar plan a month later. In late March 2018, the Chinese government announced a plan to "lure back" large technology companies like Alibaba, by permitting them to list Chinese depository receipts (similar to ADRs in the US) in China. Hong Kong was second in the world (to New York) in the IPO market in 2013.

13.5.3.2 Singapore and S-Chip Companies

Singapore has a limited number of large domestic companies appropriate for listing on stock exchanges, and many of them are government-linked companies. In the late 1990s Singapore began a strategy of attracting smaller, private Chinese (PRC) companies to list in Singapore. Such companies, incorporated in offshore centers such as the Cayman Islands, are called "red chips," and the name for those who listed in Singapore became "S-chips." While their main business is in China and their controlling shareholder typically is Chinese, the S-chips are essentially offshore shell companies that are not directly subject to regulation in China. They also generally have no real business connection to Singapore.

Listing of S-chip companies in Singapore was initially successful in the 2000s. For example, there were some forty IPOs of S-chips in 2004, and their value increased by an average of 21 percent by January 2015. This enthusiasm continued, as S-chips led the market in Singapore from 2005 to 2007. However, beginning in 2007 a number of S-chips became embroiled in corporate governance scandals, typically triggered when external auditors could not confirm reported accounts receivable and cash balances. Such scandals dominated financial market news in 2008 and 2011.

Although similar issues had occurred with small Chinese companies listing in New York and Toronto, problems in Singapore highlighted weaknesses with the S-chip system. As the listed entities were shell companies incorporated in offshore tax havens and with no assets in Singapore, the owners were insulated from Singapore's regulators. Any enforcement action tended to harm primarily local minority shareholders. In addition, informal action or administrative guidance by Singapore's stock exchange and securities regulator, which was effective with regard to locally based companies, was generally ineffective with regard to the owners of S-chips. It was also not possible to obtain cooperation from regulators in China, as the S-chips had broken no laws there. By 2010 or so, the reputation of S-chips had declined, and their valuations and interest from investors also went down. It seemed that the system was no longer working properly.

In response, in 2012 the authorities in Singapore suspended listing by S-chip companies and also raised listing standards (quantitative admission criteria such as profits and market capitalization). The following year, Singapore reached an agreement with China's securities regulator (CSRC) to institute a new direct listing system for Chinese companies. Companies that were registered in China (e.g. rather than the Cayman Islands) and received approval by CSRC could list in Singapore if they also met the relevant standards there. This created a dual compliance system for Chinese companies in Singapore and simplified enforcement through cooperation with authorities in China. It also paved the way for increased listings in the future by SOEs, and not only by private companies.

Singapore has continued to have foreign companies as a substantial percentage of listed companies (some 40 percent) and remains known as a vibrant financial center in Asia. The S-chip experience illustrates the tension between the interest of for-profit stock exchanges in attracting listings by foreign companies and the interest in maintaining high regulatory standards and enforcement. "Good" corporate governance involves not only listing standards, but also, importantly, the effectiveness of enforcement measures. In addition, the new cooperative relationship with securities regulators in China demonstrates the increasingly complex relationship of both competition and cooperation among stock exchanges in Asia and in general.

Notes and Questions

1. Does increased enforcement and cooperation among stock exchanges make a difference? One study covering M&A transactions from 2009 to 2014 by the Cass Business School in London found a decrease in leaks concerning upcoming M&A transactions and attributed this decline to increased enforcement and higher fines for market abuse. The above IOSCO press release notes that requests for international cooperation increased from fifty-six in 2003 to 3,203 in 2015.
2. Competition among stock exchanges for large IPOs also continues. Plans announced by the world's largest oil producer, Saudi Arabian Oil Co., to go public and list on the Saudi stock exchange and at least one international market, have reportedly launched a fierce competition among stock exchanges in New York, London, Toronto, Tokyo, Hong Kong, and Singapore to attract a cross-listing. However, complex legal and regulatory issues related to separation of the company from the Saudi government have delayed the IPO and limited stock exchanges willing to list the shares to the small, local Saudi stock exchange (as of April 2018).
3. What do you conclude about corporate governance and the relationship among stock exchanges? Is it primarily a race to the bottom or a race to the top? Competition and cooperation among "frenemies?" Is corporate governance an important component of the relationship?

13.6 Recent Developments: Brexit

Piotr Skolimowski and Carolynn Look, 'London Will Be Weakened as Financial Center After Brexit, Warns Bundesbank Exec' (*Insurance Journal*, February 15, 2018)

Speaking in Frankfurt, he predicted Brexit would lead to higher costs for European companies by reducing the range of available financial services, weaken productivity and reduce market depth. There is also no guarantee that Britain's departure from the EU would spur an exodus of banks to the continent, he said.

"London will not, as some have suggested, maintain its current role as the financial center of the EU after Brexit," Wuermeling, who is responsible for financial-market operations at the German central bank, said in his speech. "Even with the best will in the world, there is no substitute outside the EU for the freedoms, rights and obligations that come with being part of the single market."

Determining the role of London in Europe's post-Brexit financial landscape is becoming increasingly important for policy makers and bank executives ahead of Britain's departure from the EU next year. Around 43 percent of all euro trades on the foreign-exchange market are handled in the U.K., and London accounts for 70 percent of trading in euro-denominated interest-rate derivatives.

Not Champions League

It is unlikely that any city in continental Europe could take over London's role after Brexit as they lack London's current heft to handle global transactions, said Wuermeling, adding that other financial centers of the world may emerge as real winners of Britain's divorce from the EU.

"Frankfurt, Paris and Amsterdam are by no means in the second division in this tournament, but neither are they candidates for the Champions League," he said in his speech at the Goethe University in Frankfurt. "New York, in particular, could well benefit from Brexit, as could other global financial hubs such as Singapore or Hong Kong."

In the case of Europe, Brexit could have a negative impact for already fragmented funding channels, and "from the point of view of financial-market efficiency, financial-market integration, financial stability, but also real economic development, a scenario such as this is clearly harmful," he said.

To counter that, Europe should seek to develop a digital infrastructure to better connect its financial centers and be able to match the "agglomeration effect" that London currently enjoys, according to Wuermeling. It should also further harmonize its legal frameworks to reduce costs of cross-border transactions.

Asked whether London's central role in European finance could result in post-Brexit market volatility, Wuermeling said "We don't see turbulence, we don't see crisis. What we do see is that the functionality in certain asset classes will to an extent be limited in the case of a hard Brexit."

European Commission, Mergers: Commission blocks proposed merger between Deutsche Börse and London Stock Exchange (press release, March 29, 2017)

The European Commission has prohibited the proposed merger between Deutsche Börse AG and London Stock Exchange Group under the EU Merger Regulation.

The Commission's investigation concluded the merger would have created a de facto monopoly in the markets for clearing fixed income instruments.

The proposed merger would have combined the activities of the two largest European stock exchange operators, Deutsche Börse AG (DBAG) and London Stock Exchange Group (LSEG). They own the stock exchanges of Germany, Italy and the United Kingdom, as well as several of the largest European clearing houses. Commissioner Margrethe Vestager, in charge of competition policy, said:

> The European economy depends on well-functioning financial markets. That is not just important for banks and other financial institutions. The whole economy benefits when businesses can raise money on competitive financial markets. The merger between Deutsche Börse and the London Stock Exchange would have significantly reduced competition by creating a de facto monopoly in the crucial area of clearing of fixed income instruments. As the parties failed to offer the remedies required to address our competition concerns, the Commission has decided to prohibit the merger.

Notes and Questions

1. There were a number of large international stock exchange acquisitions in the first half of the 2000s, culminating with two purchases in 2007: Nasdaq's acquisition of Nordic exchange operator OMX AB and the New York Stock Exchange's announcement of its plan to acquire Euronext. Since that time there continues to be a number of similarly large acquisition proposals, but none have been successful. Successful acquisitions have instead involved the purchase of more specialized exchanges, such as the Hong Kong exchange's purchase of the London Metal Exchange in 2012. In Asia, the Australian government rejected a proposed acquisition of the Australian stock exchange, ASX Ltd, by the Singapore Exchange Ltd in 2011. The failure of the proposed merger of the London Stock Exchange and Deutsche Börse is the latest example of this trend. Why do you think such proposed mergers are unsuccessful? What is the implication for global securities markets and stock exchange competition?
2. Many fear that Brexit will result in the loss of the UK's financial "passport" to access the EU single market, and that will lead to London's decline as a financial center as major financial firms relocate significant portions of their operations to other cities in Europe. On the other hand, Brexit proponents have argued that London could be in an even better position as a "super Singapore" with greater regulatory flexibility than the EU while still remaining in close proximity to the EU market. Which argument do you find more persuasive?

International Sources for Stock Exchange Competition/ Cooperation

International Organization of Securities Commissions (IOSCO) www.iosco.org
World Federation of Exchanges (WFE) www.world-exchanges.org/home

14

CONCLUSION

Bruce Aronson and Joongi Kim

14.1 Basic Issues

14.1.1 The Question of Asia

This book provides a new approach for understanding the important, but complex and controversial topic of corporate governance in Asia. One difficulty involves Asia itself. It is clearly important; Asia is arguably the most dynamic region in the world. Growing at an unparalleled pace and rapidly globalizing, Asian economies continue their reign as one of the most attractive places for foreign investment. At the same time, Asia is a diverse region and its countries could be divided according to a large number of criteria: geography, language, stage and form of economic development, political system/governmental structure, and legal origin/system, among others. As noted in Chapter 1, some even question the existence of "Asia."

At the same time, Asian countries exhibit a number of commonalities relevant to the study of corporate governance: the influence of a common economic model that originated in Japan, concentrated shareholder structures, general belief in a stakeholder system with a substantial public dimension to corporate governance rather than reliance on market mechanisms, a board function that focuses on managing more than monitoring, a general preference for public over private enforcement and, most importantly, a common challenge on how to deal with both domestic pressure from corporate governance scandals and international pressure from global institutional investors and others to implement corporate governance reform. The combined pressures include a greater role for "Western-style" governance, i.e. greater attention to general shareholder interests, monitoring of management, the use of independent directors, and more robust (particularly private) enforcement.

Against this backdrop, corporate governance has become an ever more important topic in the region. Asia may have succeeded *despite* its corporate governance challenges although some might suggest, as with the case of Singapore, that Asia's progress is partly *because* of its corporate governance. Others have attributed Japan's earlier economic success to a *lack* of concern with Western-style governance. Yet, policymakers, investors, employees, boards, creditors, and stock exchanges in Asia all compete to improve corporate governance. After the Asian financial crisis in 1997, Asian countries looked to the West, and particularly "Anglo-American" models for solutions.

The traditional "Anglo-American" model placed great faith in the efficiency and effectiveness of free markets, buttressed by the booming academic field of law and economics. More specifically, it emphasized shareholder rights, shareholder activism, a market for corporate control, and independent directors. As noted in Table 14.1 (reprised from Chapter 1), the US/UK system, including its

Table 14.1 Simplified classification of corporate governance systems

Type of system	Shareholder system (US/UK)	Stakeholder system (Japan/Germany)	Controlling shareholder system (family or government) (much of Asia)
Purpose	Maximization of shareholder wealth	Maximization of benefit for stakeholders and society	Maximization of benefit for controlling shareholder
Ownership structure	Widely dispersed	Relatively concentrated with block shareholder(s)	Highly concentrated
Monitoring	1950: shareholders generally today: independent directors/ institutional investors/market for corporate control	1950: replace corporate auditors with shareholders generally (Japan); supervisory board (Germany) Today: banks/financial institutions Institutional investors Employees	Controlling shareholder? Government control: separate monitoring organization (e.g. Temasek); family control: "trusted" independent directors as facilitators
Main problem	Agency costs – management will act in own self-interest, not in best interests of shareholders	Oppression of minority shareholders – management will act on behalf of block shareholder(s) and against interests of minority shareholders	Oppression of minority shareholders – controlling shareholder will obtain private benefits of control
Solution to main problem	Reduce agency costs (protect shareholders generally from management) through legal rules and economic incentives	Protect minority shareholders from block shareholder(s) through legal rules and economic incentives	Protect minority shareholders from controlling shareholder through legal rules and economic incentives

basic corporate governance problem, is fundamentally different from corporate governance systems in Asia. It is therefore unsurprising that solutions for US/UK problems, i.e. transplants in the form of independent directors, audit, nomination and compensation committees, and class actions, have not uniformly taken root across a region that has different underlying systems and does not share this confidence in reliance on markets. At the time, transplantations of these concepts were often pointed to as the "cure" for Asia's corporate governance ills. Many of these prescriptions were adopted, but over time were tailored to the local situation in each country. As Puchniak and Lan note in Chapter 8, for instance, traditional US independent directors had to be independent from managers, but in Asia this has focused more on independence from controlling shareholders. Turning the tables, Asia has even developed innovative solutions, such as public enforcement of shareholder claims against directors for breach of fiduciary duties, that the West should consider transplanting.

14.1.2 The Concept of Corporate Governance

Apart from the problem of "Asia," a second equally, if not more difficult, issue lies with the concept of corporate governance and the framework of analysis utilized in comparative corporate governance. Corporate governance remains a fascinating, but often frustrating, field. There is no agreed-upon definition of corporate governance or on the appropriate analytical framework for making comparisons among corporate governance systems. Corporate governance is a multidisciplinary field, which both enriches it and makes it more difficult to reach agreement on these basic issues. Ironically, economists such as LLSV emphasize legal protections for minority shareholders while lawyers often emphasize how the development of markets preceded (and created the demand for) the development of legal regulation (see Chapter 4). Views on corporate governance can also be muddied by changing perceptions of different countries' "success," often based on economic success that may not be directly related to governance issues. The implicit goal of studies in comparative corporate governance may, in fact, often be an attempt to emulate or capture the economic dynamism or success of whatever country appears to be doing well during a particular period of time.

Discussions in this book highlight the fact that definitions and theoretical frameworks matter. Like differing views on the role of a corporation, i.e. a legal entity (with a focus on state regulation) or a nexus of contracts (with a focus on markets), the definition used for corporate governance both acts to determine who is included within its scope and identifies both the problem and solution for any corporate governance system (see Table 14.1). The US shareholder-oriented system, with Berle–Means corporations and grounded in law and economics theory, tends to rely on a narrower set of interests and on market functioning, while stakeholder-oriented systems provide a greater role for a broader range of interests in society. These definitions are exaggerated stereotypes, as no real-world system is a pure shareholder or stakeholder system, but the accepted definition does wield considerable influence on the basic issue of the extent of the public dimension included in corporate activities and governance.

However, the above definitions and theoretical frameworks remain contested, and the purpose of corporate governance and its real-world impact remain unclear. A correlation between "good" corporate governance and improved economic performance, while intuitively appealing, has yet to be clearly demonstrated. Limitations remain on the "proof" provided by multi-factor regression analysis utilized by financial economists in the field. It is quite difficult to come up with a single number to represent "good" corporate governance (the number of independent directors is likely an inappropriate proxy). Improved economic performance can mean either improved profitability (which is rarely found) or improved stock price (which is, in fact, sometimes found, but an argument that centers on a lower cost of capital runs the risk of circularity in that it defines "good" corporate governance as being whatever investors believe it to be regardless of actual economic performance). Given the above, it is unsurprising that the impact of "good" corporate governance is difficult to measure and that corporate governance ratings can be oversimplifications that are potentially influenced by conflicts of interest.

14.2 Framework of Analysis

This book's contribution to the study of comparative corporate governance is two-fold. First, it uses the Asian experience to contribute to general theory by adding the column on controlling shareholder systems to Table 14.1. Controlling shareholders always existed, and they have been particularly prominent in a number of European countries as noted in Chapter 3. However, they have not been included explicitly as a type of system within a classification regime of corporate governance systems or in an overall comparative corporate governance framework. Including a controlling shareholder system is useful to highlight the basic corporate governance issue and possible solutions in controlling shareholder systems. It also serves as a starting point in questioning and evaluating the use of Western concepts such as independent directors in Asian systems.

The second contribution is the use of local context. This book is an example of the valuable "middle ground" of comparative research discussed in Chapter 1. It does not focus narrowly on a comparison between a specific country in Asia and one in the West, and it does not focus very broadly on matters like law the role of law in economic development. Rather, it emphasizes local context and in-depth evaluation of the corporate governance of each jurisdiction covered by an expert. At the same time, it provides its analysis through a uniform template that is applied to each country. This allows us to look at both similarities and differences, both among Asian jurisdictions and, more broadly, between Asian countries' implementation of "Western" ideas with how those ideas are incorporated into corporate governance systems in the West.

The traditional framework, which appears in the first two columns of Table 14.1, is crude but still useful as a starting point. It has a number of weaknesses: it emphasizes differences over similarities, focuses on large, listed companies and is rigid, both demanding unrealistic transformation to affect the classification regime and ignoring change, i.e. the normal, and significant, course of evolution that occurs in all corporate governance systems.

The traditional categories in Table 14.1 are extremely broad. Is there, in fact, an "Anglo-American" (or US/UK) model of corporate governance? Such a model exists only in the broadest sense of systems sharing fundamental characteristics such as a shareholder orientation, dispersed ownership, relative emphases on the board's monitoring of management and the role of markets in enforcement activities. The differences, as summarized in Table 2.1, are also quite substantial. Such differences include the purpose of the corporation itself, as the UK's enlightened shareholder value seems substantially broader than the US's shareholder-oriented system; the role of the board, as the UK emphasizes separation between the CEO and the board chair over a supermajority of independent directors; and enforcement, as the UK emphasizes soft law to spread best practices and permits hostile M&A through an administrative process involving a takeover panel, rather than through the US's emphasis on directors' fiduciary duties and private litigation. A similar comparison could be made concerning the broad similarities and substantial differences between the stakeholder systems of Germany and Japan.

The continuing evolution of all corporate government systems presents something of a moving target for analysts, but that is true for all comparative research. This issue is exacerbated, however, by the rigidity of the traditional framework which allows only for complete systemic transformation. This book explores evolutionary change and we have attempted to account for such change through our focus on local context. The significance of evolutionary change is evaluated within the context of the local corporate governance system of the jurisdiction in question through country-specific chapters. This conclusion chapter examines each of the elements of our template with a view toward teasing out broader trends across a number of Asian jurisdictions and the possible implications for best corporate governance practices in Asia.

Are trends in Asian corporate governance going in the same direction? Are they moving toward "Western" corporate governance practices? These are not easy questions. Debate has historically been very broad and crude, with one focus on the possibility of a common path of economic development for transitional economies based on the strength of their legal protections for minority shareholders. As noted in Chapter 4, this thesis is generally subject to strong criticism. And Chapter 8 directly contradicts this thesis by pointing to Singapore as arguably the world's most efficient economy despite doing everything "wrong" (including a strong governmental role as the country's largest shareholder, no truly independent directors or a market for corporate control, weak enforcement of shareholder rights, etc.).

A second broad focus of debate is whether there will be a "convergence" of corporate governance, presumably toward Western, and particularly US, standards and practices. This first assumes there is a strong global competition among countries to achieve "efficient" corporate law and governance systems. However, Chapter 13 demonstrates that the theory underlying this view – that in the US there is an important competition among states over "efficient" corporate law to attract corporate charters – is no longer dominant in the US, and that we may now view the relationship among stock exchanges as a complicated mixture of competition and cooperation that is not driven primarily by corporate law and governance standards.

On a more practical level, there is no evidence that as a whole Asian corporate governance is becoming like that of the West. However, there is also no denying the persistent influence of certain ideas and norms generally associated with Western practices, such as an emphasis on shareholder interests, the monitoring role of the board and independent directors. One focus of the country-specific chapters is to look precisely at how these ideas have been introduced and developed in the local context of each jurisdiction. Like the categories in Table 14.1, some broad similarities coexist with wide individual variation.

Undoubtedly, the influence of the US model has weakened following the global financial crisis of 2008. There is now increasingly widespread use of UK-style soft law (the spread of best practices through a "comply or explain" approach) throughout Asia, including in Japan which was arguably the biggest holdout against the use of independent directors. This new (if ill-defined) multipolar model makes the "convergence" debate both less focused and less relevant; however, the wider range of choices and flexibility under this new multipolar model does aid in the continuing evolution and ongoing reform of corporate governance in Asia.

Since there is no explicit comparison between Asian countries and the US (or the UK), this book does not evaluate Asian jurisdictions based on the level of adherence to formal institutions in Western countries. Reform in Asia is not judged by a transformation to a shareholder-oriented system, but rather is compared primarily to other Asian systems, particularly with respect to the introduction and implementation of Western ideas in a manner that "fits" local context and practice.

14.3 Purpose

The use of purpose as one of the three criteria in the classification of corporate governance systems is useful, but can also be misleading. Purpose generally complements other criteria in a corporate governance system and aids our understanding of such systems. At the same time, however, any description of purpose is necessarily broad and general to an even greater extent than the other elements of such a classification framework.

In fact, every corporate governance system has multiple, competing visions of the purpose of corporate governance and, as noted above, in reality there is no "pure" shareholder-oriented or other corporate governance system. Even in the US, for example, which is well known as the clearest shareholder-oriented system that emphasizes the important role of shareholders as residual owners of the corporation, an alternative view, represented by Dodd, has always existed that emphasized the social role of corporations. As a result, even the US has "exceptions" to the primacy of shareholder interests such as state constituency statutes that permit directors to consider non-shareholder interests. Although Berle–Means analysis dominated discussion during the heyday of the law and economics approach to corporate law from the 1980s through the 2000s, that has not always been the case. The influence of Berle–Means and the efficient market hypothesis may also be in decline in the aftermath of the 2008 financial crisis.

Complications concerning the purpose of a corporate governance system are even more pronounced from a comparative perspective. As noted above and in Chapter 2, there is a real question as to whether the US and the UK are sufficiently similar to constitute an "Anglo-Saxon" model of corporate governance as implied by the first column of Table 14.1. The UK approach of "enlightened shareholder value," embodied in the UK Company Act, emphasizes paying attention to non-shareholder interests. Even if shareholder interests remain favored, this approach arguably represents a substantial difference from the overall US emphasis on shareholder value.

Although US influence in Asian corporate governance systems has been, and remains, significant, the UK approach has substantially influenced Asian countries in recent years, particularly British Commonwealth jurisdictions. Australia has clearly adopted its own enlightened shareholder value purpose, although it takes the form of recommendations in its Governance Code rather than in its Corporations Act. Singapore allows directors to adopt enlightened shareholder value through its Companies Act and through court interpretation. India now arguably represents the strongest example of enlightened shareholder value in Asia. India's Companies Act 2013 both requires the creation of a CSR board committee with one independent director and a CSR policy, and provides that companies spend 2 percent of profits on CSR measures or disclose the reasons for failure to comply with this provision.

In light of the above, Chapter 7 notes that with the enactment of the Companies Act 2013, India's black-letter law goes beyond the UK's approach of favoring shareholder interests while permitting consideration of broader stakeholder interests. Instead, India has chosen a new "pluralistic" or "neutral" approach that treats shareholder and stakeholder interests equally. Accordingly, India might be considered to have evolved from a (controlling) shareholder-oriented system to a stakeholder-oriented system. Even acknowledging that controlling shareholders retain strong influence in practice, this rather startling conclusion again illustrates the rigidity of the categories within the traditional classification of corporate governance systems, and suggests that the purpose of corporate governance may represent a continuum of theories and practices.

Stakeholder-oriented systems have their own issues that show both complexity and evolutionary change. Germany is often considered the "classic" stakeholder-oriented system, with an emphasis on long-term, sustainable results and a priority given to workers' interests. Japan is generally regarded as the Asian equivalent. However, virtually all of the Asian corporate governance systems covered in this book began with a corporate law and governance framework derived from either Germany (i.e. Japan, Korea, Taiwan) or the UK (i.e. Australia, Hong Kong, Singapore, India), and have been pressured by global institutional investors and others to reform based on US ideas, such as the importance of shareholder interests and independent directors. While specific examples are discussed below, has there been any impact on the purpose of corporate governance in Asian corporate governance systems?

Japan provides a good illustration of a classic stakeholder-oriented system that has changed from one that strongly resisted US ideas to one that talks constantly about the goal of improving corporate value. A cynic might say that "corporate value" is not very meaningful since it is vague and could be used to emphasize the interests of either shareholders or stakeholders and that, in fact, the popularity of the phrase derives precisely from its vagueness. Nevertheless, as noted in Chapter 10, enactment of UK-style stewardship and corporate governance codes and other changes have reportedly led to a "change in the conversation" between management and shareholders in which shareholder interests are given substantially greater priority than in the past.

The new category of controlling shareholder corporate governance systems, as represented in the third column in Table 14.1, also proves useful but raises its own difficult questions. As with many issues concerning controlling shareholders, much may depend on the identity of the controlling shareholder, particularly whether it is a family or government entity. Although the main discussion on controlling shareholders follows below in section 14.5 on ownership structure, we note here one important concern related to the purpose of corporate governance systems: the stated purpose of a controlling shareholder system (see Table 14.1), i.e. maximization of benefits for the controlling shareholder, may not be as widely accepted as are the purposes in shareholder-oriented and stakeholder-oriented systems, particularly with respect to private controlling shareholders.

14.4 Board Function

Asian countries are generally known as having managing boards, in which the board of directors plays an active role in day-to-day management, as opposed to monitoring boards in the US and UK. However, throughout Asia there has been significant domestic and international pressure for greater monitoring and transparency. The monitoring board model in the US developed over many decades and boards in Asia are evolving as well. Many jurisdictions in Asia that have controlling shareholder systems also face the broader question of defining the public dimension of corporate activities in systems built around benefits for controlling shareholders.

The increase in independent directors throughout Asia is perhaps the most significant indication of the evolution of board function. By now all of the jurisdictions covered in this book have some requirement or recommendation (in the form of comply or explain) for a minimum number or percentage of independent directors for listed companies. Board committees are also frequently required or recommended. The specific requirements, which vary broadly, include a supermajority of independent directors and an independent chair of the board in Australia, independent directors comprising one-third of the board in Hong Kong and China, two independent directors in Japan and Taiwan, and more stringent requirements for large companies in Korea (independent directors for one-half of the board as opposed to one-quarter for smaller companies).

The difficult question is the true "independence" of independent directors, particularly in controlling shareholder systems. Australia and Singapore clearly state that independent directors must be independent from controlling shareholders, but that is not generally true throughout Asia. The chapters on China and Korea emphasize that so-called independent directors are not, in fact, independent from controlling shareholders, since it is often the controlling shareholders who have the power to nominate such "independent" directors.

Taken as a whole, the main strategies for reducing agency costs in controlling shareholder systems, as discussed in the Singapore chapter, are strengthening rights for minority shareholders ("participative strategy") and constraining the power of controlling shareholders ("controlling strategy," discussed in section 14.5 on ownership structure). Most of the effort has focused on strengthening shareholder rights, and indeed they are typically more numerous in Asian countries than in the US (which emphasizes the fiduciary duties of directors to protect shareholder interests rather than shareholder rights). Generally, it appears that enhancement of shareholder rights has not had a significant impact on the ability of controlling shareholders to control their companies.

One often-touted solution is to require cumulative voting so that minority shareholders would be able to elect directors to represent their interests. However, the examples in the book are not promising. In Korea, most companies have taken advantage of an opt-out provision to avoid cumulative voting. The most striking example is Taiwan, which has gone from mandatory cumulative voting (1966) to an opt-out system (2001) and back to mandatory cumulative voting (2011). Somewhat surprisingly, however, it appears that the law on cumulative voting has had little overall impact on Taiwanese corporate governance practices.

Corporate supervisors or auditors in several Asian jurisdictions constitute another institution that could monitor management. Japan and other East Asian countries (Taiwan, Korea, China) have looked to Germany's two-tier board system, in which the supervisory board (elected by the shareholders) appoints the management board. The Asian variation is a "dual board" system in which both the board of directors and corporate supervisors or auditors are elected by shareholders.

There is an ongoing debate, often with little or no empirical evidence, about the role and effectiveness of corporate supervisors. In Japan, they audit for "illegality" and possibly a broader range of issues related to the best interests of the company. The role of corporate auditors (*kansayaku* in Japanese) was strengthened several times in the hope that they could serve as both adequate monitors of management and as a practical substitute for independent directors. They have some legal powers that are unavailable to directors, but are often criticized as being ineffective, particularly compared to independent directors. To date, however, no jurisdiction in Asia has abolished the role of corporate supervisor or auditor. Instead, Japan and Taiwan have offered companies a choice of corporate structures, with options including a traditional structure that relies on corporate supervisors and a "Western-style" system that focuses instead on independent directors. Except for the largest listed companies, Korea offers a similar choice between electing a statutory internal auditor or establishing an audit committee.

The trend, however, is a movement toward a greater role for independent directors. All of the four countries that continue to have corporate supervisors or auditors now also have additional requirements for independent directors that apply even to the traditional corporate structures that feature corporate supervisors. And in lieu of the full "Western-style" system of three board committees (audit, nomination, and compensation committees) with independent directors, Japan and Taiwan now provide a simpler "one-committee" system in which the corporate supervisors are replaced by an audit committee of the board. Debate continues as to whether this trend represents a "watering down" of Western monitoring institutions or a clever broadening of monitors through new structures that provide a good "fit" for Asian countries.

Executive compensation, a hot topic in Western countries, is generally not emphasized in Asia. One practical reason may be the rather modest compensation of executives in Asian countries, particularly when compared to the US (although controlling shareholders may have other means to extract benefits from companies they control). Other than Australia and India, most countries do not have a "say on pay system" in terms of executive compensation. Australia is unique to the region as it buttresses this with a "two strikes rule" under which the entire board, except the managing director, may have to stand for re-election if more than 25 percent of shareholders disapprove of the compensation plan two consecutive years. India requires the establishment of a remuneration committee and compensation of directors must be approved on an individual basis through a binding vote by shareholders.

One of Asia's greatest weaknesses is the lack of diversity on its boards. In particular, gender diversity remains among the lowest in the regions of the world. India is the only country covered in the book that mandates the appointment of at least one female director. Although not covered in the book, Malaysia also has a hard quota. Australia promotes gender diversity through a best practices regime, but most Asian countries have not even established targets through best practices or codes. Unsurprisingly, the proportion of women among board directors remains paltry with the number of senior executives and CEOs even lower. Japan and Korea rank among the lowest in the world in both categories. In many Asian countries, even the women that are elected to boards tend to be family members.

14.5 Ownership Structure

Traditional corporate governance theory has focused primarily on dispersed share ownership systems and secondarily on block shareholder systems. Controlling shareholder systems are relatively new to corporate governance theory and are an important focus of this book. More generally, concentration of ownership is increasing globally, as noted in Chapter 1. In that sense, this book represents a discussion not only of share ownership trends in Asia, but also in the "rest of the world" outside the US/UK. The rise of Asia which contains many concentrated ownership systems, combined with the increasing reconcentration of share ownership even in dispersed shareholder systems (due to increased holdings by institutional investors on behalf of beneficiaries, now sometimes referred to as "agency capitalism"), may mean that concentrated ownership constitutes the "new norm" and must be considered whenever discussing issues of comparative corporate governance.

The Asian countries covered in this book constitute a broad spectrum of share ownership structures ranging from "somewhat concentrated" to "extremely concentrated." On the relatively dispersed end of the spectrum, Australia is generally classified as a dispersed shareholder system, although as Chapter 5 points out it is nevertheless more concentrated than the US/UK and concentration is increasing. At the other extreme, most companies in India, Korea, and Taiwan are family owned and controlled, constituting much of the stock market. Large Korean conglomerates, however, generally have an anomalous structure whereby they are family controlled but not family owned.

Between these two extremes, Japan is generally classified as a (somewhat dispersed) blockholder system that does not feature controlling shareholders. Beyond that are a number of controlling shareholder systems that have family-controlled and government-controlled companies. Family-controlled companies are prominent in India and Taiwan, while Hong Kong, Singapore, and China have both types of controlling shareholder companies, with government-controlled companies being more influential. The general trend appears to be toward greater concentration rather than dispersion. Another strong trend is increasing foreign ownership, both as portfolio investment and as foreign-controlled companies. The clearest example of the latter is Hong Kong, where the stock market is dominated by companies incorporated outside of Hong Kong, particularly from China.

As noted above, family-controlled companies and government-controlled companies represent different corporate governance challenges. For example, the role of independent directors in both family-controlled and government-controlled companies is discussed at some length in Chapter 8 through the example of Singapore. It suggests that even if independent directors are not free to directly oppose or contradict controlling shareholders in family-run corporations, they can nevertheless serve a highly useful role by maintaining the trust of the controlling shareholder and acting as a mediator between the increasing demands of society and the controlling shareholder. Although such a role may not be consistent with Western-inspired theory concerning the corporate governance role of independent directors, it may represent a useful adaption to local conditions. As discussed above, there is an increasing emphasis on the public dimension of corporate activity in controlling shareholder systems, as also illustrated by the prior discussion of the case of India in section 14.3 (on purpose) of this chapter. The domination of family control across Asia has also created succession problems with the aging of founders and the prospect of transferring control to second or third generation heirs.

The nature of the public dimension of corporate activity is also the main topic with respect to state ownership, however with a different twist as the state theoretically already represents the public. The contrast between China and Singapore is instructive. In China, political control of SOEs remains firmly entrenched, even as efforts to make such entities more efficient and to encourage the private sector proceed on course. Whether state ownership is a "helping hand" or "grabbing hand" is a constant subject of debate. By way of contrast, in Singapore the underlying assumption is nearly the opposite, as economic efficiency comes first, and government control is limited to the "normal" shareholder role of monitoring management for economic performance that is prevalent in other types of corporate governance systems. To a lesser degree, Taiwan is another jurisdiction that is a mix of family and state ownership.

As noted above, the difficult question of accountability has led to an expansion of general shareholder rights. Although it has inconsequential private enforcement, Singapore is considered to have the strongest shareholder rights among Commonwealth countries. Less effort has generally been made to directly constrain the power of controlling shareholders. In addition to the increase in independent directors, the most notable effort to constrain the power of controlling shareholders has been made in the regulation of related party transactions, which is the most typical method used by controlling shareholders to reap private benefits of control and is thus a highly significant issue in controlling shareholder systems.

The problem of related party transactions has received close attention throughout Asia. Laws and regulations typically require (in addition to board approval) disclosure and disinterested shareholder approval (a "majority of the minority") for large transactions. China may be the outlier, as it continues to rely primarily on (board approval and) information disclosure to combat the serious problem of related party transactions. Japan and Korea are among the few jurisdictions in Asia that have no provisions for disinterested shareholder approval; Korea instead relies on a two-thirds majority vote of the board and prohibits other types of transactions. Overall, disclosure and disinterested shareholder approval measures are likely very helpful in certain circumstances such as for large and conspicuous transactions, but it appears that related party transactions remain a serious problem.

The creation of a general fiduciary duty owed by the controlling shareholder to the company is one potentially effective method of constraining controlling shareholder power that has not been implemented in Asian countries to date. Ironically, in the US, where there is generally not a controlling shareholder problem, we can find cases where a controlling shareholder is found to owe a fiduciary duty to the corporation (and sometimes minority shareholders), particularly in cases of self-dealing where decisions are not made by independent directors. The lack of such a duty in Asia is discussed in the chapters on Singapore and Korea.

14.6 Law and Enforcement

Much of the impetus for corporate governance reform in the 2000s originated from the US with its reliance on mandatory requirements under the Sarbanes–Oxley Act and its substantial group of global institutional investors who advocated for similar changes in countries throughout Asia. However, UK-inspired soft law, i.e. voluntary codes of best practices buttressed by mandatory disclosure requirements (comply or explain) has played an increasingly significant role in Asia. This is especially true since the 2008 financial crisis, which saw a weakening of the idea of US practices representing a global standard and a partial replacement of the US model with a multipolar model that placed a greater emphasis on corporate governance codes.

In a number of Asian countries, particularly British Commonwealth jurisdictions, soft law has arguably become the main engine for corporate governance reforms such as increasing the number of independent directors. The main outlier to this trend is India, which in its Company Act 2013 re-emphasized mandatory requirements under corporate law to improve corporate governance practices. East Asian jurisdictions, with their German law influence, have tended to focus more on hard law, but even here soft law is assuming an increasing role. The main recent example is Japan, which enacted stewardship and corporate governance codes within the past few years. Japan has seen a significant increase in the number of independent directors after resisting this trend for many years. In comparison, Korea also has a corporate governance code and recently established a stewardship code, but they have not been as influential.

Enforcement remains a difficult issue everywhere, and particularly in a region that is dominated by controlling shareholder systems. Western practices do not provide particularly robust models. Private enforcement through shareholder derivative suits is rare in the UK and even rarer in Germany, while in the US directors are effectively insulated from any obligation to pay monetary damages. It is therefore unsurprising that shareholder derivative suits have not become popular in Asia, although they nevertheless remain the primary means of private enforcement in most jurisdictions.

The reasons for the paucity of shareholder derivative suits are well known. They include the shareholders collective action problem, recovery going to the corporation rather than to the shareholders, lack of funding and contingency fees, and other restrictive requirements such as prior demand on the corporation (see Chapter 9 on China), a "loser pays" rule in most jurisdictions, a security for expenses provision, etc. Japan, and to a lesser degree Korea, are partial outliers in this regard, with the shareholder derivative suit system achieving at least partial success in producing a substantial number of lawsuits and creating a modest level of risk for directors who violate their fiduciary duties. One important reason may be the existence of lawyers (and plaintiffs) who are willing to pursue litigation for non-economic reasons. Singapore lies on the low end of the spectrum since it has yet to see a single shareholder derivative action.

Class actions are arguably a more effective means of enforcement in the US, but are also more controversial. Australia may be the only jurisdiction in Asia with a functioning private class action system. Korea enacted legislation in 2005, but fears of abuse resulted in stringent restrictions and very few cases (and only one case with a finding of liability; see Chapter 11). To overcome the backlog in its judiciary, India has recently established a National Company Law Tribunal that will hear class action cases. As discussed below, a special type of class actions are regularly undertaken in Taiwan as part of its quasi-public enforcement system.

The most interesting developments in enforcement in Asia may well be in public enforcement, as both Australia and Taiwan have developed models for the public enforcement of shareholder rights for the breach of fiduciary duties by directors. In Australia, enforcement is carried out directly by the government's securities regulator (ASIC). The government assesses civil penalties against directors for breaches of fiduciary duties, which are not astronomical amounts for individual directors to pay. As a result, there is a substantial body of cases and a real possibility that directors can be liable for a breach of the duty of care.

Taiwan's system of quasi-public enforcement may be of special interest to and a model for other countries in Asia. The Investor Protection Center (IPC) is a government-established nonprofit organization which is financed by mandatory contributions from stakeholders in the securities industry and a securities transaction tax. In addition to filing shareholder derivative suits, the IPC has a monopoly on class actions and can also arbitrate investor claims. Enforcement actions proposed by the IPC staff must be approved by its board, two-thirds of which are academics, as being in the public interest. IPC lawsuits often "piggyback" on criminal investigations. Recovery rates in the form of compensation for shareholder claims are low, but the IPC arguably achieves its purpose of providing some deterrent effect against the breach of fiduciary duties by company directors.

Traditional means of public enforcement, especially criminal and regulatory enforcement, are not covered extensively in this book. One reason is a trend in which the main thrust of enforcement efforts has been changing from public to private enforcement in some countries such as China (which created a statutory derivative action in 2005). Singapore and Hong Kong are known for their strong public enforcement but weak private enforcement. However, in many Asian countries traditional public enforcement, particularly involving white collar crime, has generally been weak. There historically was a view in Asian countries that was accepting of soft enforcement against business executives due to their substantial contributions to economic development. This view may now have changed in some countries, as evidenced by recent events in Korea. Formerly, prosecutors, judges, and the media had been generally accommodating with respect to violations of law by executives of chaebol conglomerates, who even if arrested and convicted regularly received presidential pardons. However, criminal sentences and penalties are now harsh and even top executives now serve jail time.

Corporate governance theory has long emphasized the market for corporate control as the most effective external force in providing incentives to management to operate efficiently and create corporate value. Australia is the only jurisdiction in Asia that has a market for corporate control, although successful hostile takeovers are substantially fewer than in the US or UK. To encourage market efficiency, Australia has adopted a version of the UK's Takeover Panel. As in the UK, the Takeover Panel focuses on preventing actions that restrict offers to shareholders rather than on judging the purpose of the actors' conduct. Unlike the UK, the Takeover Panel in Australia is not proactive and only decides applications brought before it.

Elsewhere in Asia there is no real market for corporate control. As a typical example, mergers and acquisitions in Hong Kong are virtually always friendly: generally occurring within family-controlled groups or utilized by companies from China to facilitate outbound investment. In both Korea (2003–4) and Japan (2005–7) a few attempts at hostile takeovers briefly generated great controversy and came close to success, but ultimately failed. Japan is left with an unwieldly legal doctrine that combines elements of Delaware law focusing on the purpose and reasonableness of defensive actions by the target's directors and UK law which provides that shareholders should make decisions about hostile bids. Fear of hostile acquisitions remains, and many companies still have shareholder rights plans that are used as poison pills. There has been no real hostile takeover activity across most of Asia for a decade, and foreign investors remain convinced that hostile takeovers are not practicable in many Asian jurisdictions.

If this potential source of management discipline is missing, what is the impact on corporate governance? Management may act inefficiently by, for example, hoarding cash. As a theoretical matter, it may mean that controlling shareholders in such countries are "inefficient controlling shareholders" as described by Gilson in Chapter 1. As a practical matter, there is speculation that global institutional investors who value the market discipline of a market for corporate control are more reluctant to invest in such countries, thus resulting in a "discount" in the stock market.

Shareholder activism also appears to be generally weak in Asia, although activists may be starting to play a greater role. India may represent one of the few countries in Asia which is seeing a significant rise in shareholder activism despite the overall dominance of controlling shareholders. The cited causes range from the changing views of investors, nudges from the regulators and the emergence of a number of local proxy advisory firms. But in India as well, shareholder activists are generally not as successful as those in Western markets and evidence is mixed concerning whether the benefits of such activism justify the costs. Other countries with notable but weaker levels of shareholder activism include Hong Kong, Japan, and Korea. In Singapore, the minimal presence of proxy advisory firms is a factor that hampers shareholder activism.

Hong Kong may represent a typical case, in which dissatisfied shareholders generally follow the "Wall Street rule" and sell their holdings. However, even here shareholder activists are reportedly evolving from short-term corporate raiders to long-term investors acting for the good of the company. The ultimate question throughout Asia may be whether activists can obtain the support of traditional institutional investors (particularly domestic institutional investors) in Asian countries, as has notably occurred in the US over the past few years.

14.7 Epilogue

Whether in the East or West, the quest for each country to find the right form of corporate governance remains a perennial, almost Sisyphean, challenge. The discussion remains heated because the stakes are high given that successful corporations are the cornerstone of a successful economy. Challenges continue as corporations and the environment in which they compete continue to evolve. What was once considered a distinct advantage soon faces scrutiny as being anachronous in a globalizing world. Critics suggest that companies from advanced and emerging economies can no longer remain competitive unless they learn to adapt to modern trends of corporate governance. At the same time, corporate governance is not a panacea that will guarantee that a corporation will generate more profits or better performance. Wherever the location, better corporate governance should, however, help improve corporate valuation, productivity, investor protection, and corporate decisions, and curb wrongdoing and such ills as self-dealing. A key focus is employing the right policy mix of regulation and market forces to create the optimum playing field for corporations to thrive. Through an Asian perspective, this book provides a new approach for understanding the important, but complex and controversial topic of corporate governance. One of its central goals is learning through comparative insight obtained from the study of corporate governance systems which have both similarities and unique local context.

This book treats Asia as comprising "normal" countries, i.e. jurisdictions that can be analyzed and compared through standard academic theory and methodologies without resort to broad cultural stereotypes. This is accomplished by expanding the traditional classification of corporate governance systems into shareholder and stakeholder systems to a broader classification that accounts for the prevalence of controlling shareholder systems in Asia and comparing these systems by means of both a common template and an in-depth evaluation of local context. Application of this framework to Asian jurisdictions produces interesting observations concerning each element of our template, as Asian countries struggle to address corporate governance problems associated with controlling shareholder systems and adapt "Western" ideas concerning reform. Just as corporate governance in Europe or the Americas is not uniform, countries across Asia have unique and different histories, legal backgrounds, social priorities, and levels of economic development. While much can be learned from other jurisdictions, awkward transplants that are not attuned to local context have shown to be short-lived and even ill-advised at times.

The purpose of corporate governance systems continues to evolve and may be better represented as a continuum than as rigid categories. Each type of corporate governance system is presumably "successful" in protecting the interests of its favored group (general shareholders, stakeholders, or controlling shareholders), but in Asian countries there is continuing domestic and international pressure to reduce agency costs and place a greater emphasis on the public dimension of corporate governance systems (particularly in the case of controlling shareholder systems).

For board function, the question of transparency and monitoring looms large for controlling shareholder systems. The various strategies that have evolved in Asian countries, including adaptation of the role of independent shareholders, has begun to emphasize function over formal structure. Asian countries generally have concentrated ownership structures and are tilting the global standard regarding share ownership toward that direction. Concentrated ownership may be becoming the new norm, and concentrated ownership structures, particularly from Asia, may no longer be ignored or dismissed as exceptions. Instead, they must now be integrated into general corporate governance theory and comparative analysis.

In terms of law and enforcement, the increasing influence of soft law has had a substantial impact on corporate governance practices in Asia. Enforcement remains a problematic issue, particularly in controlling shareholder systems. It is difficult to measure the costs and benefits of enforcement measures, and robust US-style private enforcement may appear to be costly and disruptive. Countries in Asia are trying different approaches, with some of them, such as Taiwan and Australia's public enforcement of private shareholder rights, being among the most innovative.

The perhaps unsurprising result of the application of the book's framework to corporate governance systems in Asia is that Asian countries, as they do in other regions, exhibit both similarities and differences. As noted at the beginning of this chapter, however, the similarities among Asian countries differ from those among countries in other regions such as Europe, consisting instead of an amalgamation of the influence of a common economic model, concentrated shareholder structures, general collectivist belief in a stakeholder system, boards' focus on managing more than monitoring, general preference for public over private enforcement and domestic pressure from corporate scandals and international pressure from global investors and others to implement governance reform.

The commonly asked question to date concerns the extent of Western influence on Asian corporate governance systems and practices. However, many Asian countries are now economically developed, with some of them demonstrating greater economic success than their Western counterparts. Experimentation and innovation in Asia in law and corporate governance practices, not just in economic development and business practices, has reached the point where Asian countries must be accounted for in, and can contribute to, general theory concerning corporate governance. At a time when a re-evaluation of the well-known monitoring model is beginning to be undertaken in the US, with a new emphasis on the competence and experience of outside directors and not just their independence, and when scandals at high-profile companies from advanced economies continue unabated, we must strive to develop and implement neutral frameworks for comparative analysis so that we can better learn from each other. We hope that this book represents a step in that direction. Countries from the East such as those in Asia have demonstrated their willingness to consider comparative lessons from the West. Perhaps, it is time that the West should be more disposed to contemplate the same.

INDEX